# Photography

AFTER

# Photography

# Photography

AFTER

# Photography

GENDER, GENRE, HISTORY

---

Abigail Solomon-Godeau

*Edited by Sarah Parsons*

DUKE UNIVERSITY PRESS *Durham and London* 2017

Designed by Amy Ruth Buchanan
Typeset in Arno Pro by Copperline

Library of Congress Cataloging-in-Publication Data
Names: Solomon-Godeau, Abigail, author. | Parsons, Sarah (Sarah Caitlin), [date] editor.
Title: Photography after photography : gender, genre, history / Abigail Solomon-Godeau ; edited by Sarah Parsons.
Description: Durham : Duke University Press, 2017. | Includes bibliographical references and index.
Identifiers: lccn 2016037598 (print) |
LCCN 2016039356 (ebook)
ISBN 9780822362517 (hardcover : alk. paper)
ISBN 9780822362661 (pbk. : alk. paper)
ISBN 9780822373629 (e-book)
Subjects: LCSH: Photography, Artistic. | Photography—Philosophy. | Feminism and art.
Classification: LCC TR642 .S64 2017 (print) |
LCC TR642 (ebook) | DDC 770—dc23
LC record available at https://lccn.loc.gov/2016037598

Cover art: Cindy Sherman, *Untitled #304*, 1994. Chromogenic color print, 61 × 41 inches. Courtesy of the artist and Metro Pictures, New York.

## CONTENTS

# ILLUSTRATIONS

PREFACE

# May the Bridges We Burn Light the Way

*Sarah Parsons*

Like many other readers, my introduction to Abigail Solomon-Godeau's work was her article "Going Native: Paul Gauguin and the Invention of Primitivist Modernism" published in the July 1989 issue of *Art in America*. Taking the 1988 blockbuster exhibition on Gauguin at the Grand Palais in Paris as her subject, she produced a withering critique of art historical mythologies relative to the heroic, misunderstood genius-artist, French colonialism, exoticism and eroticism, and, hardly least, the ways in which "femininity is conventionally linked, when not altogether conflated, with the primitive."[1] In so doing, she carefully delineated the curatorial and scholarly strategies that conceptually naturalized these formations that produce and reproduce fantasies about cultural production.

That issue of *Art in America* was passed to me as an undergraduate by an older student with a "psst, check this out" excitement normally reserved for the exchange of purloined erotica among adolescents. It helped that one of our more conservative professors was among the two scholars Solomon-Godeau chose to represent the essentialist, ahistorical, sexist, and, frankly, inane analyses regularly imposed on Gauguin and his artistic output. But the extensive degree to which this essay has been anthologized and cited since its original publication suggests that its devastating institutional and discursive critique resonated widely.

The writing is not easy ("adumbrate" is not a word commonly found in *Art in America* and certainly sent me to the dictionary) nor does Solomon-Godeau go to great lengths to simplify the French deconstructionist theoretical frame from which she drew her lines of argument. Yet the analysis is so specific in its details and so pointed in its targets that it read as a call to arms, at least among my ragtag group of young feminists, frustrated and alienated by much of what we were being taught. Reading it felt remarkably like having the curtain pulled back on the Wizard of Oz. Rereading it now, I am reminded of a recent essay by Rebecca Solnit, in which she introduces the term "mansplaining," which, as Solnit is careful to point out, is not a universal flaw of masculinity (although the hubris of white male scholars pontificating on gender and race was/is not rare) but is "just the intersection between overconfidence and cluelessness where some portion of that gender gets stuck."[2] In this regard, Solomon-Godeau's summary of the literature on Gauguin (most of it the work of male scholars) might justly be described as a dissection of "mansplaining" in the field of art history.

Throughout the 1980s, Solomon-Godeau curated and published extensively, both as a critic and as an art historian. These roles informed one another in productive ways. As "Going Native" demonstrates, her criticism is historically and philosophically grounded (largely in feminism, critical theory, psychoanalysis, and deconstruction), and her scholarly essays have an urgency and directness of argument that is more rare than one might expect in academe. Those arguments she presented in "Going Native" derived from her doctoral research with the renowned feminist art historian Linda Nochlin at CUNY on gender and representation in nineteenth-century French visual culture. Looking back on it now, the decision of a graduate student, even one highly accomplished and already published, to identify *by name* specific scholars in such a public forum was audacious at best. Academic fields are surprisingly small worlds. In fact, the second scholar identified for his unconvincing views on Gauguin was a senior faculty member at the University of California at Santa Barbara, where Solomon-Godeau was hired shortly after the publication of "Going Native." Then again, if you want to reframe the core questions in the discipline, a little awkwardness is bound to ensue.

Solomon-Godeau's driving concern has always been how the history of visual culture—elite and mass—is discursively constructed, what these constructions put in place, ideologically speaking, and why that matters. A modern master such as Gauguin thereby served as a sensational hook, but Solomon-Godeau had previously developed a similar line of critique within photography criticism and history, then a less visible but burgeoning outpost of the art world. One of her first contributions to the topic appeared in a special 1981 issue of *October* journal consecrated to "Art World Follies" that also featured contributions from Rosalind Krauss, Douglas Crimp, and Benjamin Buchloh. As a group, these essays examined the overinvestment in the idea of the singular artist while probing the relationship between the art market and discourses of art. Solomon-Godeau and *Village Voice* photo critic Ben Lifson contributed a conversation about the contemporary photography scene titled "Photophilia." Even at this early moment, Solomon-Godeau's assessment of the danger of framing photography in terms similar to those that art history had used in constructing its own discipline was clearly prescient: "Photography," she observed, "is an art form only some of the time but an art-critical vocabulary is being used almost all the time" (102). This, she continued, was problematic because with respect to her own approach to the medium, which was profoundly influenced by Walter Benjamin, it seemed evident "that there is a *fundamental* difference between photography and earlier forms, and I think the rejection of [Benjamin's] insight—no, the suppression of it—is the single greatest fallacy in the discourse of photography today" (118). Adopting an art historical approach or applying art critical terms to the medium, she claimed, is not without consequences: it literally changes what we see when we look at photographs: "The first thing that happens with such an approach is that the subjects of the photographs are jettisoned in favor of the artist," which in turn is further reinforced by the mechanisms of the contemporary art market: "You need artists, so you look for artists" (104). Discussing Mapplethorpe and other celebrity photographers, she observed, "How their photographs are seen is predetermined by whom they photograph, where they show, and who will see them" (110).

The culmination of Solomon-Godeau's early work on historical and contemporary photography was the book *Photography at the Dock: Essays on Photographic History, Institutions, and Practices*, published in 1991, still in print and regularly cited. In her introduction, Solomon-Godeau argued, "The history of photography is not the history of remarkable men, much less a succession of remarkable pictures, but the history of photographic uses" (xxiv). She carefully charted how a relatively new but seemingly insatiable market shapes the discourse through which we understand photography, what kinds of photographs we consider important, and what sort of questions we ask of them. As in her reference to the marketing of Mapplethorpe, she described the players in this new field, shaped by an intertwined and fluid group of collectors, artists, patrons, dealers, curators, auction houses, critics, and scholars.

In the same introduction, Solomon-Godeau remarked that she had begun writing about photography in the early 1980s, "at what now appears to have been the crest of the photography boom." In retrospect, Solomon-Godeau was surfing a rising wave. In 1991, Andreas Gursky and the production of vast numbers of supersized art photographs was just an emerging trend. Vancouver-based conceptualist Jeff Wall had only a modest bibliography and several exhibition catalogues, as opposed to the massive scholarly/curatorial industry he has since generated (and quite deftly influenced). From the standpoint of 1991, it would have seemed highly unlikely that the blue-chip modernist art historian, Michael Fried, would turn from Manet and Courbet to spend years writing a book titled *Why Photography Matters as Art as Never Before* (2008), itself largely a love letter to Wall's genius (and the object of Geoff Dyer's comical critique of self-referential academic writing.)[3]

Photography was established in the academy, as Solomon-Godeau has pointed out, through dedicated art history faculty appointments that began in the 1980s. Nevertheless, art history's claims to preside over the study of photography have rested on a somewhat shaky foundation. For the many years before academic institutions assimilated photography as a serious object of study, important work on the medium was produced in other fields. After all, Roland Barthes, the patron saint of postmodern photographic studies, was a literary scholar by training and primary practice. From the mid-twentieth century on, a number of museums were collecting, exhibiting, and conducting research on photographs as art objects. But with respect to the development of photography theory, much of it was produced outside the academy and the museum. Important contributions to 1970s criticism was produced by writers such as Susan Sontag and John Berger, who, among others, constituted a body of fundamental texts still drawn upon by contemporary scholars and critics. That nonacademic tradition continues today in the work of Geoff Dyer (who has academic appointments but has chosen not to work from within the academy), Luc Sante, and Rebecca Solnit, whose 2003 book on Eadweard Muybridge is a widely cited contribution to the field.

For the first decade or so after photography became a bona fide field of study in the United States and Canada, art historians dominated the scholarly study of photography, but after the peak, marked somewhat by *Photography at the Dock*, art history lost control of the discussion. This is not to suggest that art historians are failing to produce important work on photography. On the contrary; but efforts to limit its study to art history/visual culture, as suggested by Douglas Nickel's "State of the Research" essay in *Art Bulletin* (2001) or Blake Stimson and Robin Kelsey's *The Meaning of Photography* (2008), seem limited by their preoccupation with aesthetic questions and artistic lineages. The field of photographic studies has now become a broadly interdisciplinary undertaking, with some of the most significant and influential texts produced by scholars working in areas such as geography, history, cultural and literary studies, sociology, education, anthropology, performance studies, political science, communication studies, and film studies. As Solomon-Godeau argued in her contribution to James Elkins's anthology *Photography Theory* (2006), the problem is largely with art history and visual culture's focus on the medium as such and its putative specificity, itself disconnected from social, material, and viewing relations. There, she argued that "conceptualizing photography as a unitary or autonomous entity is doomed to fail, just as would the case with any other technology that has become braided into all aspects of modernity, and now postmodernity."[4] In that text, she responded to many of the contributors' preoccupation with "indexicality," remarking how this fixation (now increasingly hallucinatory and irrelevant in the digital age) distracted attention from more significant issues. More pressing, she remarked, are questions around discourse, ideology, commodity culture, subjectivity, and gender and the necessity of critical approaches—all foreclosed if we approach the subject as an isolated, autonomous, or specific medium. As scholars in various fields tackle increasingly global histories, practices, and cultural production, many have been directly influenced by Solomon-Godeau's pioneering research. Accordingly, for scholars in diverse fields, *Photography at the Dock* has been a cornerstone of any (now almost de facto) understanding that photographs cannot adequately be analyzed as fragments of reality outside of their place in history, politics, and ideology. As Henry Giroux argues in his essay on education after Abu Ghraib, acknowledging Solomon-Godeau's work, "This is not to suggest that photographs do not record some element of reality as much as to insist that what they capture can only be understood as part of a broader engagement over cultural politics and its intersection with various dynamics of power, all of which informs the conditions for reading photographs as both a pedagogical intervention and a form of cultural production."[5] In a similar vein, for cultural historian Jonathan Long, Solomon-Godeau's work helps explain how photographs were able to play such an important role as a tool of power in colonial, anthropological, medical, and forensic discourses. Wendy Hersford uses Solomon-Godeau's essays to unpack the reality effect of photographs in human rights discourse.[6] Criminologist Eamonn Carrabine employs Solomon-Godeau's critical perspective on photographic truth to explore the role of the medium in criminology.[7] In his historical study of Indian boarding schools, Eric Margolis outlines a methodology for studying photography as social practice, drawing on Solomon-Godeau's essay "Who Is Speaking Thus?": "In her perceptive chapter on documentary. . . . [She] set forth a project for those who would use photographs in social and cultural research: '. . . individual documentary projects, themselves the product of distinct historical circumstances and milieus, 'speak' of agendas both open and covert, personal and institutional, that inform their contents and, to a greater or lesser extent, mediate our reading of them. It is properly the work of historians and critics to attempt to excavate these coded and buried meanings, to bring to light these rhetorical and formal strategies that determined the work's production, meaning, reception, and use.'"[8] Similar interest in the historical construction of social identities has helped make Solomon-Godeau's essay "The Legs of the Countess" (1986) a key text for performance studies, women's art production, and fashion history, as well as feminist cultural studies.[9] Sociologist David Andrews drew on this essay in his 2006 essay on representations of basketball superstar Michael Jordan, writing, "My intention is to engage the type of critical pedagogy of representation vaunted by Solomon-Godeau by 'contextualizing specific practices of representation within particular historical and cultural circuits of power.'"[10]

This current volume brings together essays written between 1995 and 2014 in which Solomon-Godeau returns squarely to this question of historical and cultural circuits of power as they shape and inform the practice, criticism, and historiography of photography. Just as feminist analysis provided one of the key critical tools Solomon-Godeau used in *Photography at the Dock*, so too is this new collection informed by her emphasis on gender as a useful category for historical analysis, as Joan Scott famously claimed.[11] But equally, Solomon-Godeau considers the intersections of gender with genre, for genre, as Jacques Derrida argued in an influential essay, operates as a form of law.[12] In tandem with other critical methods, such analyses enable us to remap, refigure, and revise the disciplinary object of "photography," to probe its circuits of power, and to rethink photographic practices previously categorized and dismissed as marginal.

In the last section of her earlier book, Solomon-Godeau described her grouping of essays on Connie Hatch, Francesca Woodman, and erotic photography as somewhat provisional efforts to map a way forward and to "reflect on the possibility of other aesthetics, other histories, other kinds of questions to be asked" (*Photography at the Dock*, xxxi). As the citations above demonstrate, the results of Solomon-Godeau's efforts at remapping photographic studies and seeking new directions of inquiry have proven to be fertile, especially as they have been taken up by scholars in the social sciences. However, this influence seems not to have extended as much to Solomon-Godeau's stress on feminism or to questions of sexual difference as to her other, related concerns.

On one hand, the elision of feminism is never surprising. As Peggy Phelan cautions, the "influence of feminist theory should not be underestimated but it almost always is."[13] On the other hand, this elision is somewhat surprising given that popular discussions of photography often acknowledge the place of photographic representation in figuring sexual difference and reproducing hierarchies of gender. For instance, fashion photography is frequently held to account for its role in constructing an impossible and unhealthy vision of femininity. A fleeting consideration of issues such as celebrity photo hacking, photo sexting, and revenge porn indicates the continued relevance of Solomon-Godeau's insight in *Photography at the Dock* that "photography has been—and remains—an especially potent purveyor (and producer) of sexual ideologies."[14] Even writing about photography is gendered. After all, Rebecca Solnit's essay "Men Explain Things to Me" revolves around the story of her conversation with a successful older man who simply could not hear (or recognize)—despite being told multiple times—that it was the young woman he was talking to (or at) who was the author of the brilliant new book on Eadweard Muybridge that he was extolling.

As it seems to fade from academic favor, feminism is increasingly relevant, if by no means univocal as a form of broad cultural analysis. In the realm of popular entertainment it is worth remarking that superstar Beyoncé performed in front of a twenty-foot projection of the word "FEMINIST" after succinctly identifying the term as a nexus of desire and economics: "You know, equality is a myth, and for some reason, everyone accepts the fact that women don't make as much money as men do. . . . And let's face it: money gives men the power to run the show. It gives men the power to define value. They define what's sexy. And men define what's feminine. It's ridiculous."[15] True as that may be (and disingenuous as it may be for Beyoncé to point this out), most public invocations of feminism become highly visible because of the anxieties, even vitriol, that feminism (still) engenders. A very different set of power relations were at play when cultural critic Anita Sarkeesian announced a Kickstarter campaign in 2012 for a video series called "Tropes vs. Women" that would explore the representation of women in video games. In doing so, she triggered a wave of violent misogyny that is still raging years later, including death and rape threats, weaponized pornography, and even a video game in which players may punch her in the head. Smart and well-researched, Sarkeesian's analysis in nevertheless a fairly rudimentary feminist cultural analysis of "women is distress" and "women as background decoration." Sarkeesian reworks critiques originally developed through film studies, literature, and art and applies them to the medium of video games, thereby daring to instate gender issues within the still male-dominated world of video games. As I write this, the multibillion-dollar gaming industry has not responded by offering her much public support, nor does it seem likely that changes are imminent in the marketing of their products. Like armaments and militarism, culture wars are here to stay. In light of the seemingly never-ending backlash against feminism, Solomon-Godeau's query of 1991 is still perfectly and depressingly relevant: "Whose culture and whose aesthetics are threatened by the tiger at the gate?" (*Photography at the Dock*, xxxi).

The essays collected in this book argue that there is still much to be gained from asking questions about culture, gender, and power, including interrogations of the ever-changing relationship between photography and the art world, photography as an academic "object," and photography as it is being historicized. Art history has shaped and often occluded our understanding of photography, but the relationship is also reciprocal in that the reproducibility and omnipresence of photography have also shaped the direction of art history. In *Photography at the Dock*, Solomon-Godeau chronicled how the languages and discourses of art and art history "reframe" or reposition the multiplicity of photographic practices to produce newly minted artistic entities. In *Photography after Photography*, Solomon-Godeau continues this investigation into how the twentieth-century establishment of discrete photographic genres operates to "discipline" the diversity of actual photographic practice. To illustrate this argument, Solomon-Godeau takes as her examples so-called landscape and so-called street photography to examine how the imposition of genres (what she calls "genre-fication") "function to obscure those historical, sociological, and indeed psychological formations that shape if not determine forms of cultural production, and do their own ideological work in transforming problems into givens" (chapter 5). Given these fundamental concerns, it is not surprising that the essays in this volume focus primarily on photographic work that has gained cultural currency in the art world by being drawn into a constantly expanding market and entrenched within various legitimizing aesthetic discourses. The essays are organized in chronological rather than thematic order. However, Solomon-Godeau's overarching argument, flowing in different ways through each of the essays, is that we must never lose sight of photography's embeddedness in social practice, material relations, and ideological formations even (or especially) when it is it produced, repurposed, or circulated as art.

Throughout this collection, Solomon-Godeau continues to wrestle with the legacy and usefulness of the term "documentary" as a way of thinking about the relationships between photographers, subjects, and viewers. The question as to whether the relation (or nonrelation) of the photographer to his or her subject determines the effect or affect of the work produced with respect to the viewer is thus one of the recurring themes and frames of "Inside/Out," originally published as a catalogue essay for a San Francisco Museum of Modern Art exhibition titled *Public Information: Desire, Disaster, Document.* Solomon-Godeau begins with Susan Sontag's indictment of Diane Arbus as a predatory photographer, outsider, and voyeur, inevitably exploiting the people she photographed. Solomon-Godeau argues that this distinction between insider and outsider is by no means a simple division between the presumed empathy of the former and the presumed objectification of the latter. The ethical and political distinction between insider and outsider photography may obscure a slippage between viewing relationships, those that operate between photographed subject and actual viewer. Nan Goldin and Larry Clark stake their claim for authenticity (and "non-objectification") on their belonging to the milieus they have photographed. In Goldin's case, she appears sometimes in her photographs along with her friends, and thus exposes herself as she does her other subjects. However, this presumed intimacy among the subjects does not necessarily alter the nature of the viewing relationship between the viewers of the *Ballad of Sexual Dependency* and the subjects depicted. Rejecting this notion that being "inside'" a particular milieu automatically exculpates the photographer from a voyeuristic and objectifying role, Solomon-Godeau asks whether it is not possible to consider the photographer's utter exteriority as no more (or less) capable of rendering a certain truth within the limits of what is given to be seen. "If we are then to consider the possibility that a photographic practice ostensibly premised on insiderness ultimately reveals the very impossibility of such a position in the realm of the visual, might it conversely be the case that a photographic practice that affirms its own implacable exteriority yields a certain truth of its own?"

"Written on the Body" also probes the structure of visual analysis, in this case, turning to the "discursive eclipse of beauty by desire." Solomon-Godeau begins with a consideration of beauty as employed in art criticism, psychoanalysis, and photography, taking as one of her examples the photographs made by the Baron Wilhelm von Gloeden in Taormina, many of nude male adolescents. Solomon-Godeau investigates how the depiction of bodies requires coding and inscription in ways that signal not just the difference between various representations of the human body, but difference itself and its inherent erotic significance. However, this coding, this writing on the body is always somewhat occluded by the powerful naturalism and presumed indexicality of the photographic image itself: " . . . by virtue of its indexicality, its potent illusion of a reality produced by the camera, photography has been an indispensable purveyor of dominant ideologies (of gender, race, class, nation and their subcategories)." As Solomon-Godeau argues, the circuits of desire are shaped not only by aesthetic contemplation and individual sexual desire but also by wider systems of power such as colonialism, and that such representations require forms of "supplemental coding if they are to be intelligible." Following from this acknowledgment, Solomon-Godeau examines these codes as they function to mark bodies and subjects according to their status as objects of desire, abjection, subjection, or as specimens or fetishes.

In "*The Family of Man*: Refurbishing Humanism for a Postmodern Age" Solomon-Godeau examines what is coded by absence in one of the most famous projects in post–World War II photography, the extraordinarily successful American Cold War exhibition that toured globally. Solomon-Godeau here examines the recent permanent restaging of the exhibition in Luxembourg (birthplace of curator Edward Steichen) and its prior history. For Solomon-Godeau, drawing on the arguments of Viktoria Schmitt-Linsonoff, this Cold War blockbuster is better viewed not so much as a token of American triumphalism but as a covert symptom of American trauma. The nature of this trauma is complex, occasioned by the war itself, as well as the revelation of genocide, the new threat of nuclear destruction, and the effects of demobilization on notions of manhood. But where should this symptomization of trauma be located? Should it be located in those who produced the curatorial project itself (Steichen and his assistants)? In the American picture press from which most of the images were drawn? Or somewhere in the general Cold War psyche? Solomon-Godeau asks who is really the "author" of this exhibition? As she argues, "Although it is unquestionably the 'work' of Steichen—his concept, his orchestration of the project, his final say on the selection of pictures, texts, lighting, and design—by its very nature, both exhibition and catalogue are root and branch collective entities. In other words, as cultural artifacts, both exhibition and catalogue require a kind of analysis associated more with critical readings of film or theater than with individual productions, be they visual or textual." Solomon-Godeau therefore seeks to identify the structuring absences of the exhibition and its catalogue through a methodical analysis of the sources and subjects of the 503 photographs and their suturing into a naturalized whole. Gender too is at stake in this compilation of images, for as Solomon-Godeau remarks, in agreement with Allen Sekula, "It would thus seem justified to look at the exhibition's Edenic representation of the patriarch and the patriarchal family as compensatory strategy, warding off the anxieties of demobilized and variously traumatized masculinity."

In contrast to the masked trauma of the *Family of Man*, there is no escaping the tangible violence and active force played by relatively poor-quality digital photographs in the more contemporary Abu Ghraib scandal. As Solomon-Godeau suggests, these carefully staged photographs function not so much as document (outside of their actual status as evidence in law) but rather as spectacle. And yet, despite their digital production, they carry the weight of truth, of capturing something horrible that not even President Bush disputed as occurring at the time the pictures were made. "Torture at Abu Ghraib: In and Out of the Media" explores the various ways race, class, gender, religion, and nationality all shaped the creation and circulation of these images. Solomon-Godeau, as others have done, recognizes the visual tropes of amateur pornography as they inform the "carnivalesque atmosphere, its eroticism, and its S/M trappings and staging," within which the participants function as both actors and directors. She then turns to the circulation of these images to "consider the implications of the visual archive itself; not only in terms of what shaped the forms of 'abuse' it depicts, but also, how that archive then functions once its contents are made public and become accessible for various uses, especially critical ones." Solomon-Godeau argues that the art historical references invoked by Stephen Eisenmann or W. J. T. Mitchell, among others, are inadequate analogies because the photographic record, even if digital, is fundamentally different from graphic or painting representations, whether or not those accounts are based on observation. As a whole, this archive (still only partially revealed) points to a terrifying dark side of the role of representation in building community and collective identity. In this respect, the Abu Ghraib archive might be considered the infernal double of so-called worker photography of the 1920s and 1930s, producing not an emancipatory and collective self-representation but a lethal bond of murderous fraternity. For at Abu Ghraib, community was in part constructed through torture performed for the camera, based, as Solomon-Godeau remarks, "on fantasies of imaginary possession and appropriation."

From these grainy images of spectacle and trauma, the next essay turns to consider a form of documentary photography solidly embraced by art photography, namely "street photography," a recently (ca. 1970s) institutionalized genre unique to the medium of photography. (There exists, as Solomon-Godeau remarks, "no category of 'street painting'"). Starting with a close examination of the work and reputation of a canonized modernist, Harry Callahan, Solomon-Godeau presents a critical and alternative history of street photography that rejects the notion of "genre." She explores how and why this practice of photographing people unawares on the street became both legitimized and elaborated precisely *as* a genre. Using Callahan's photographs made in Chicago and a few other cities as her examples, she suggests that there are other meanings within such work that exceed their nominal subject matter, conscious authorial intention, or, indeed, modernist aesthetics. Among these are the gendered attributes of public space and the psychosexual dynamics at work in male photographers' clandestine looks at the (unaware) female pedestrian. Critiques of street photography are fairly common in discussions of the work of less abstract and more confrontational photographers such as Garry Winogrand and Diane Arbus. However, Solomon-Godeau seeks to understand the logic of inclusion and exclusion that generates a genre and thus suggests that no matter how "abstract" Callahan's work, it remains always and already embedded in social and political circuits of mastery, desire, fear, and control, especially in the context of postwar US politics and culture.

Magnum photographer Susan Meiselas has always self-consciously foregrounded the politics in her documentary projects. In her essay on Meiselas's *Carnival Strippers* (1973–78), Solomon-Godeau reflects on if and how a work that foregrounds voyeurism can complicate its mechanisms. Meiselas spent four summers working on this project, photographing the performers at work and in their private lives, along with their boyfriends, managers, and customers. Over these months and years, Meiselas got to know her subjects and included their voices (audio and written) in addition to their images in the original project and in its subsequent exhibitions and publications. Ultimately, Meiselas created a work that disturbs the familiar objectification of the female body, especially when on display, and, as Solomon-Godeau remarks, "raises issues about the activity of looking itself and the forms by which looking is bound up with gender, with sex, by mechanisms of objectification, fetishism, and projection, especially when the depicted subject is that of the female body." But Solomon-Godeau also cautions that, irrespective of efforts to critically intervene within the gendered regimes of looking and being looked at, these relations are ultimately overdetermined by preexisting conditions of class and gender and their predetermined relations of domination and submission. In any case, we cannot talk about the meaning of *Carnival Strippers* without addressing "its discursive framing, the context of viewing, a host of cultural assumptions and beliefs, and our own subjectivity, conscious and unconscious. And it goes without saying that the meanings of any cultural object are more dependent on these determinations than they are on the photographer's intentions."

"Framing Landscape Photography" (like her earlier essays on Eugène Atget, Auguste Salzmann, and calotype photography in France) traces how a category called "landscape" was imposed on a quite different and by no means "aesthetically" motivated production.[16] As Solomon-Godeau argues, by the mid-nineteenth century, landscape had become one of the most popular genres in French painting, from the most official forms to the more innovative versions exemplified by the Barbizon school and, later, Impressionism. However, although many photographers directed their cameras at "nature," few of the results, she maintains, can be categorized as "landscape" or, much less, "nature." That is to say that such imagery belonged more often to a nineteenth-century category of the "view," or to categories of topographic documentation or, somewhat later, touristic souvenirs. Solomon-Godeau here traces the technological developments and social shifts that enabled these various forms to be gradually unified under the titular genre of landscape, observing at the outset that "many standard photography histories seamlessly write these heterogeneous photographic practices into discussions of landscape photography, thereby obscuring not only the specificity of many nineteenth-century photographic practices, but superimposing upon the extant record what is essentially a modernist conception of photography, oblivious to the historical contingencies of vision, viewing, and visual production." This retrospective construction of a presumptive genre shapes the way we view such photographs. As products of modernity, the imagery of forest, park, or indeed "nature" itself comes to serve, paradoxically, as a respite from modernity (expressed through the subjectivity and "authenticity" that only an artist can deliver), as well as collapsing difference into a unitary category. This notion of a genre of photographic landscape historically parallels the commodification of nature itself in the form of national parks such as Fontainebleau, which in fact served as the site of many of these nineteenth-century photographs. As the depiction of an aestheticized, mythologized nature, this "repurposing" of topographic document and view also obscures conflict over natural resources and their exploitation, both of which invisibly underpin images of rural spaces. In light of the current scale of environmental destruction across the globe, exhibitionary practices and art historical writing that uncritically frame work within the genre of landscape continue this process of mystification by providing for almost a century and a half the prepackaged "spectacle of nature."[17]

In "The Ghosts of Documentary," Solomon-Godeau continues her investigation of the problem of documentary (a problem that she considers as epistemological, ethical, and political). She examines how changing technologies have affected truth claims in various manifestations of "documentary" photography. Such an inquiry requires distinguishing particular practices from a rather inchoate range of representations stretching from journalism to social documentary, all anchored by the presumed evidentiary and indexical nature of photography, which, needless to say, has been put in question by the now general use of digital technologies. As for the subset of the vague category of "social documentary," the unifying logic is generally attributed to the goals of progressive politics and reformist intentions. In one sense, it seems that the category of "documentary" as it has traditionally been defined is a historical artifact that contemporary photographers who identify with its goals can only mourn, and Solomon-Godeau examines the nature of this mourning process. But if we step away from the notion of documentary as a genre implying political intent and consider it as a style, as many scholars have argued, Solomon-Godeau observes that it remains alive and well (which is by no means to say that she endorses it). These recent manifestations of documentary, some of which are assimilated into artistic networks and markets, are haunted by the eclipse of evidentiary certainty but simultaneously entranced by the artistic prospects that digital tools offer. But here, too, as Solomon-Godeau remarks, "what is at stake . . . is the phenomenon of documentary (or photojournalistic) subjects repurposed as art objects, where subject matter once perceived as the purview of documentation—are now resignified (after various formal and contextual transformations) as images for aesthetic contemplation."

Ghosts also haunt the extraordinary case history of Vivian Maier, a Chicago nanny unknown until after her death in 2009. Like Callahan, Maier made many of her images on the street, although she also created self-portraits and candid images of her young charges. Maier's is a story of how an enormous corpus of photographs, made by an unknown photographer, and never intended to be seen by anyone, can now be reconstituted and reframed as an organic "oeuvre," her identity refigured as artist, and a market created from zero, complete with catalogues, films, and exhibitions. In stark contrast to the more gradual recognition of Francesca Woodman as a major artist over a forty-year period, Maier's legend has been almost instantly manufactured by the owners of her work through social media, thereby sidelining the mechanisms of museum, scholarship, and criticism, and delivering her work directly to the market primarily through digital networks of reproduction and dissemination. Drawing again on Rosalind Krauss's discussion in "Landscape/View," and on her own earlier discussion of canon formation in the case of Atget, Solomon-Godeau traces the role of Maier's collectors and of the media in shaping the production of Maier the artist photographer. While Maier's photographs made on the street (as opposed to her much more idiosyncratic self-portraiture) are not especially different from those of other photographers working in black and white and depicting urban life, their familiar quality, and their immediate recognition as "street photography," combined with Maier's "outsider" identity, elusive biography, and staggering production, combine to forge an instant legend. And photography discourse and markets are ever in search of them.

In "Robert Mapplethorpe: Whitewashed and Polished," Solomon-Godeau returns to the Grand Palais in Paris, and a satellite exhibition at the Musée Rodin, which presented Robert Mapplethorpe's work simultaneously in 2014. Apparently, not a great deal has changed in the quarter century since its Gauguin exhibition that inspired "Going Native." In the Musée Rodin exhibition, Mapplethorpe's pictures and objects, assembled in the museum's "Chapel" space, were counterpoised with Rodin's small sculptural studies. Reflecting on the critical reception of the exhibitions in the French press, Solomon-Godeau draws attention to the conspicuous lack of any commentary about race, insofar as Mapplethorpe's nudes are exclusively of black men, often on pedestals, and often with large or erect genitalia. Insofar as both exhibitions were supported by the Mapplethorpe Foundation, Solomon-Godeau points out that "it is [now] the combined force of investment—in all its senses—from the ideology of the great artist to the monetary value of the work, from the increasing dependence of institutional art spaces such as the Grand Palais on corporate financial support and blockbuster attendance, which determine exhibitions." However, she insists, no one can will away the problematic aspects of the work or its racial and sexual politics by containing it within the space of the museum, even (or especially) if certain works are exhibited in a separate space, veiled with a curtain, and accompanied by a warning message. Whatever the transgressive or subversive capacities that one might identify in these photographs, their highly aestheticized presentation and museological placement deprive their presentation of any critical potential, congealing each photograph in its own fetishistic universe in which the black male body and the luxury object are seamlessly united. Solomon-Godeau concludes, "If feminism teaches us anything in terms of the politics of corporeal representation, especially photographic representation, it is that relations of domination and subordination, and ideologies of gender, voyeurism, objectification—and, preeminently, affirmations of fetishistic desire—are inevitably sustained if they are not subverted, desublimated, or otherwise 'ruined.'"

Along with Rosalind Krauss, Solomon-Godeau was one of the first scholars to study Francesca Woodman's work after her suicide at twenty-two, and, with Krauss, was the first to write about Woodman's work in the 1986 exhibition catalogue that launched her remarkable posthumous career. In "Body Double," Solomon-Godeau seeks to understand the way Woodman's work and legacy have been subsequently framed. As she did with Gauguin, Solomon-Godeau surveys the existing literature, much of it characterized by mechanisms of projection and identification that shape the writers' interpretations. Even considering the most rigorous work on Woodman, Solomon-Godeau argues that Woodman's ascension to the pantheon of modern or contemporary art has been accomplished by effacing the political issue of gender and the psychological problem of sexual difference. Solomon-Godeau thus maps the way in which Woodman's positioning has been variously interpreted by connecting her work to that of various important male artists or, alternatively, inserting her into a lineage of female photographers without attention to historical context. Further, with respect to debates as to how or if one might use the designation "feminist" to modify "artist," Solomon-Godeau makes the point that whether or not Woodman defined herself personally as a feminist or was making "feminist" art is less important than acknowledging the existence of a "cultural and political environment in which she came of age and where many of her own preoccupations were writ large." Solomon-Godeau thus asks what we might learn by thinking about the wider context and determinations within which such production was possible, and the various positions available to female spectators in relation to Woodman's work.

In the final essay in the book, "The Coming of Age: Cindy Sherman, Feminism, and Art History," Solomon-Godeau tracks the gradual diminishing of feminist approaches to understanding or situating art production. Addressing Cindy Sherman's production since the late 1990s, she focuses on three aspects of aging as it relates to a major artist whose work has been centrally concerned with the imagery of femininity, fetishism, and the problem of sexual difference. Thus she considers the aging of feminism, the aging of the artist herself, and the image of aging women in two different series that Sherman produced, as well as the commentary it provokes, or fails to provoke. In an earlier essay on Sherman, Solomon-Godeau described how Sherman's well-deserved elevation to the first rank of major artists *necessitated* her transformation from "woman artist" to universal artist, and, concomitantly, the downplaying of the political, that is, the feminist, aspects of her work. In this later essay, however, Solomon-Godeau focuses on the later work to argue that the "problem" of the (white, middle-class) woman's aging can either be treated as a political issue for art making (as in the theoretically informed work of Mary Kelly) or, alternatively (in the case of a brilliantly intuitive artist such as Sherman), risks the reduction of the subject to parody or social satire. In contrast, therefore, to the polemical tenor of many of the essays in this volume, this essay strikes a somewhat somber note. Although Solomon-Godeau remains critical of left-wing nostalgia or melancholy, her commitment to feminist thought and politics makes her especially attentive to the consequences of the backlash to feminism, to antifeminism (a.k.a. postfeminism), and to feminist theory's marginalization in art criticism and theory. In contrast to her unapologetic characterization of her critical work in photography as "raining on the parade," in her reading of the discourse around even the most celebrated women artists (living or dead), she reminds us that feminism is not only the longest revolution (per Juliet Mitchell) but one that retains, however precariously, a transformatory potential, a promise far from being realized, especially at a time of its massive repudiation.

# INTRODUCTION

The earliest essays in this volume were written at a time when photography was generally, but not universally, considered to be a discrete artistic medium. However, the most recent essays, including this introduction, were completed at a time when the boundaries that separate photography from other forms of artistic production are anything but clear. These essays span about twenty years of photography criticism, and all were written after the publication of my previous book on photography (*Photography at the Dock,* 1991). As originally conceived, this volume, like the previous one, was to be "about photography," but many of my essays written in the 1990s and after (particularly those dealing with contemporary art or women artists), are not medium specific, even if the artists discussed often used photography as one of their mediums (e.g., Ana Mendieta, Birgit Jürgenssen, Walid Raad, and Alfredo Jaar). Necessarily, then, these were excluded from consideration, but in keeping with larger changes in the art and photography world, it is clear that medium specificity is no longer an adequate organizing principle in contemporary visual culture. For these and other reasons, compiling a collection of essays that respects the category "photography" as the object of criticism seems itself anachronistic, even if the essays seek to engage with larger questions that arise in a given body of work.

Clearly, there are those who deplore the eclipse of medium specificity as the foundation of artistic practice, but whatever the nature of the various arguments, there can be little dispute about current "facts on the ground." As abundantly demonstrated in current practice, "medium" has become variously hybridized, problematized, or even dematerialized. Which is not to deny the enduring presence of those whose work remains rooted in formalist paradigms or other modernist forms of art photography. Such work does not seem to be at any immediate risk of extinction and has validation and support from numerous quarters.[1]

In terms of the book's organization, I had first thought to duplicate the structure of my previous book within which the essays were grouped under thematic categories (i.e., "histories," "institutions," and "practices"), but this turned out to be intractable. As my editor Sarah Parsons and one of the early readers for the press justly observed, almost any of the essays could fit into any of the categories I proposed. Whether for good or ill, this has to do with certain of my critical preoccupations that regularly recur with respect to entirely different kinds of photography and their related discourses. Likewise, the mechanisms of fetishism (commodity and psychic), voyeurism, and objectification that are frequently invoked in these essays, as they were in my earlier work, remain relevant to feminist analyses of photographic practices of all types. These terms, employed in photographic theory and criticism since the late 1970s, far from being démodé, provide important critical tools to investigate the ethics and politics of representation.

Among other recurring issues are those relating to "genre-fication," by which I inelegantly refer to those processes providing the institutionally necessary illusion that photography can be "disciplined," as is evident in the discursive construction of "landscape photography," "street photography" or "documentary."[2] "Museo-fication," another clunking neologism, functions similarly. And while the use of categories is necessary to organize a given field, genre-fication and museo-fication function generally, then as now, to produce questionable art histories of photography provided with requisite ancestries, pedigrees, and (needless to say) canonized masters. Two recent examples of these formations are the newly minted categories of "aftermath" photography and the rebranding of large color work, often digitally produced, as "tableau" photography.[3] The former has functioned to foster the integration of images (variously repurposed and reformatted), often first produced as photojournalism, into the vastly more prestigious and remunerative circuits of contemporary art.[4] The latter has not only served to better align photographs with the history of painting (including history painting itself) but has also functioned to refurbish aspects of both formalist and modernist art theory (including its auteurist bias) so as to embrace forms of art photography intended specifically for museum, gallery, and other spaces for artistic display—exhibition value thus fully replacing discursive value and communicative function.[5]

Although the increasing importance of photography in art production was already perceptible in conceptual art and feminist-influenced art of the

1970s, within the contemporary globalized art world and its various venues and institutions, the place of camera-made imagery, digital or analogue, is now fully taken for granted. Nevertheless, there is some irony in the fact that it was only in the 1980s that the medium was more or less securely integrated into university departments and curricula, museum collections, art criticism and its journals, galleries, and, not least, an expanding marketplace. And then, in a temporal blink of an eye, photography was everywhere and everything within contemporary art, no longer largely dependent on consecrated spaces or publications, and decoupled from traditional notions of "realism" based on its analogical technologies.[6]

Consequently, those spaces or institutions once exclusively dedicated to the medium must now reinvent themselves, orienting themselves to the more inclusive domain of *the* image and its various technologies, including video, hybridized media installations, and even film. In tandem with this development, at least since the 1990s, if not before, there developed a conceptual reorientation of theoretical discourses addressing the nature, terms, and problematics of *the* image—although, considered in its broadest sense, this has been a recurring preoccupation in Western philosophy (as well as religion) going back to Plato. But in its more contemporary incarnations in the United States and elsewhere, whether associated with the emergence of visual studies as a disciplinary entity or with such formulations as W. J. T. Mitchell's "pictorial turn" (or in yet another related concept, "picture theory"), such a programmatically inclusive and ecumenical domain poses its own set of problems.[7] For just as the theoretical object dubbed *the* image risks an ahistorical essentializing of what is actually a boundless heterogeneity, so too does current thinking about *the* photograph elide the no less boundless field of photography's plurality.

Considering the material as well as discursive changes that have marked the photographic field since the 1990s, there are a number of other significant developments that need to be taken on board. Certainly, the most obvious one has to do with the epistemological upheaval provoked by the advent and subsequent triumph of digital technologies of imaging. In this respect, the question of the identity of an entity once simply labeled "photography" is fractured not only by digital technologies (subject of endless discussion), but also by current practices themselves, whether professional, amateur, or artistic. Notwithstanding these debates on the implications of digitally produced photographs, for those whose investments in photography pivot on its status as an art form, digital technologies that sever photography's umbilical link to what it represents merely expand the medium's artistic purview, enabling bigger, more complex, more striking, more "pictorial" representations, celebrated in the concept of the "tableau." It is not for nothing that Andreas Gursky's supersized digital pictures command the highest prices of any photographer at auction.

Be that as it may, the dominance of digital technologies provides yet another reason to dispense with traditional notions of the "photographic" as such, and to come to terms with the transformed terms of photography in all its uses. As a now "residual" form, analogue photography did in fact attain its modernist respectability under the sign of medium specificity. But the eclipse of both this particular technology and its associated aesthetics is not reason for celebration, mourning, or nostalgia. All of the problems posed by image culture, spectacle, and simulation in the globalized networks of late capitalism and the complex articulations between them are as proper to one technology as to the other. Similarly, questions related to reception, spectatorship, regimes of viewing, subject formation, and processes of signification remain important areas of investigation, no matter what technology is at stake. Accordingly, such phenomena as the explosion of "selfie" pictures, the billionfold circulation of images in social media, and the speed by which digital images are produced and disseminated does not by that token herald a "post-photographic" condition.[8] Rather, it might be better considered as an intensification and proliferation of what was already implicit in the nineteenth-century industrialization of photography.

This helps explain why many of the medium's foundational essays of the twentieth century (such as those by Siegfried Kracauer, Walter Benjamin, André Bazin, Roland Barthes, etc.) remain productive touchstones for contemporary theorists. Indeed, much of what counts in contemporary theory still takes many of its cues or engages directly with Benjamin and Barthes, especially Barthes's last book, *Camera Lucida*, although far less so in relation to the work of Pierre Bourdieu, Jean Baudrillard, and Paul Virilio.[9] None of these latter theorists was especially concerned with ontological formulations, and all have been in a certain sense "channelled" into subcategories of photography discourse variously assimilated to cultural studies, sociological inquiry, and technological analyses.

Also less influential for current theorists (or so it appears in the English- and French-language photographic literature) has been the work of Vilém Flusser, a Jewish Prague-born philosopher who fled Czechoslovakia in 1939 and spent most of his life in Brazil, the last decade in France. Written in mostly in German and Portuguese, and in a defiantly antiacademic and stylistically idiosyncratic manner (no footnotes, no citations, no references to others' work), many of Flusser's works were not translated into English until after his death in 1991; thereafter, his writings were almost immediately recognized as being of major significance by media historians, media theorists, and philosophers.[10] Among the French theorists cited, his work is perhaps closer to that of Virilio's, as can be seen in the short book originally published in German, *Für eine Philosophie der Fotografie* (1983), published in English in 2000 as *Toward a Theory of the Photograph.* Overall, his work is hard to categorize, although many of his commentators associate it with figures such as Marshall McLuhan or Thomas Kubler rather than Benjamin or Barthes. Which is only to remark that when, how, and why particular theorists are taken up in photographic discourse depends as much on the vagaries of translation as to how photographic discourse defines its objects.

This in turn depends on the nature and terms by which the medium is constructed as precisely a "theoretical object," as opposed to an aesthetic, material, or historical one.[11] But to broadly, if not crudely, overstate the issue, photographic theory as such tends to be largely couched in the most general of terms, insofar as the inquiry is oriented toward ontological, epistemological, or phenomenological questions. Consequently, actual practices, past or present, or individual photographers and technological accounts occupy a somewhat different discursive terrain. In this respect, the territorial division between what is defined as photography theory (or philosophy) and what as photographic history or institutional analysis might be analogized with respect to the disciplinary divide between aesthetic philosophy and art history. Histories of photography, be they technological, artistic or generic, may refer to theoretical paradigms but rarely produce them; conversely, photographic theory is rarely concerned with the nuts and bolts of specific forms of production, except incidentally, or with reference to artistic usages vis-à-vis individual artists or photographers.

It must be also recognized that the foundational texts in photography theory, including post-1970s intellectual formations—those drawing on post-structuralism, semiotics, and psychoanalysis—did not emerge from either photographic *or* art historical discourse, but were variously assimilated by those working on photography *après coup*. Moreover, inasmuch as film studies was far more responsive to continental theory in the 1970s, it was often the case that photography criticism, including my own, took this body of work as a model, and sought to adapt it to the critical analyses of the still photographic image. But it nonetheless remains the case that art historians and photography historians quote theorists, but theorists rarely quote art or photography historians.[12]

My own writing on photography has been generally concerned with particular bodies of work, or with particular photographers, and exists in a difficult-to-define space between journalistic, academic, and polemical modes of description and analysis. I do not consider my work to be particularly theoretical, although my writings on photography, like those on art history or contemporary art, are informed by the theorists, past and present, who have shaped my thinking overall. Perhaps my essays are best characterized as a form of practical criticism insofar as they engage with specific bodies of work, historical contexts, social relations, and institutional structures, rather than with the more philosophical questions manifested in the new field of the philosophy of photography. This philosophical approach has become far more prevalent in academic discourse since the 1990s, at least in the United States, Canada, and the United Kingdom. Notwithstanding the diversity of this literature, generally speaking, it seems relatively unconcerned with the diversity of individual practices or with their instrumentalities, but when it does address particular practices, it is art photography—again, Jeff Wall is the ubiquitous figure—that is most often taken as the exemplary practice supporting or illustrating the theory.

My own primary intellectual debt and commitment is to feminist theory and criticism, and, of course, politics—praxis. I am hopeful that the reader will perceive how this intellectual/conceptual/political framework underlies the critical analysis I bring to bear on nominally unrelated issues. Feminist criticism is for me not about the subject as such—even when the subject addressed is the work of women photographers or women artists. Feminist criticism is grounded in the ways one reads cultural production, what questions are asked of it by the critic, and, in turn, what questions and issues are raised by the work itself. But considering the field of photography in terms of its scholarly production overall, feminist approaches to theory or practice in the past decade or so seem to have diminished rather than expanded. It is notable that in many recent anthologies of photography criticism, or special issues of academic journals, feminist (and women's) contributions are notably rare.

Consequently, the apparent marginalization of feminist investigations of the image world of photography thus subtly shapes what kinds of questions can be posed, what kinds of research can be supported or legitimized, what new interpretive or analytic languages can be developed. We should not confuse the growing amount of monographic studies or exhibitions devoted to women photographers, past or present, with feminist work *on* photography in any of its diverse manifestations, although, it goes without saying, both are necessary. A feminist orientation necessarily addresses the complex relations between the individual viewer and image, and the coding of photographic images (conscious or not) through which the multiform components of individual and collective gendered identities are produced, confirmed, or contested. This diminished presence of feminist analyses, whether oriented to gender or to sexual difference (they are not the same), therefore functions in photographic discourse as a structuring absence, evident, to take one example, in the presumption of a universal male photographer and a universal male spectator.

Whether the "critical object" of inquiry is vernacular photography, photographic histories and contexts, specific photographic practices, or photography as a particular element (or medium) in artistic production, we remain always, in some sense, subject to its very ubiquity, its interpellative powers, and its collective shaping of our conscious (or preconscious) existences. The close-up view, so to speak, of *any* photographic practice may tell us something about the power of the image, so various in its effects and affects, so contingent on the subjectivity of the viewer, so mutable in its meanings according to its framing contexts. Despite the illusory autonomy a photograph may have as it hangs on a museum or gallery wall, no image ever stands alone. Even as we consider the ways that photographs, however generated, produce their effects, it is also the case that this imagery is harnessed to and embedded within larger configurations far more politically, socially, and culturally determining than the imagery itself. Similarly, it should also be acknowledged that while photography as a museum art implicitly or explicitly prompts most photographic theory, criticism, and art journalism, this tends to overshadow more important considerations of the specific and heterogeneous instrumentalities of photographic production. Collectively, these participate in and contribute to our life world shaped by the powerful forces of capitalism, consumerism, globalism, and the naturalization (or occlusion) of relations of domination and subordination. Nevertheless, and notwithstanding the conspicuous pluralism of current production, including atavistic returns to older technologies (e.g., view cameras, analogue film, Lubitel cameras, and darkroom legerdemain), there are reasons to identify alternative, more critical initiatives. By this is meant a diverse array of practices that seek to invent new forms and artistic languages that speak to and of contemporary circumstances, conditions, and social relations, as opposed to those that revamp, repurpose, or reiterate familiar and already-institutionalized types of production. Consequently, while the artistic uses of the medium, especially those that emerged from various historical avant-gardes (e.g., Dada and Surrealism, and Russian Constructivism and Productivism) or other formations, may have once functioned as counter-discursive critical interventions, photography in its vernacular usages is an essentially affirmative medium. That is to say, it functions affirmatively by virtue of its (mythical) transparency, its solipsistic ratification of the way things are, its illusory affirmation of the truth of appearances, and its identification (however contested) with the veridical notion of the index. Even in the digital era, we still use photographs for drivers' licenses and passports, and now, alarmingly, for access to voting rights. In any case, and specifically in the case of artistic production, there is reason to conclude that work that does not contest, destabilize, subvert, or otherwise "ruin" dominant regimes of representation can only represent the ways things are and therefore forecloses even the imaginative or utopian possibility that things might be otherwise.

The process of selecting the essays for this compilation was harder than I had anticipated, and this collection was long—very long—in the making. Some of the essays chosen for inclusion in this volume were never published in English. Others are not readily accessible, and both this introductory essay and the one on documentary photography were written expressly for this volume.

For anyone assembling an anthology of essays, some published long before the selection process, the immediate question is whether to revise or not to revise. There are, of course, all manner of revisions possible, from the correction of factual errors in dates or misspelled names to the editing of the texts themselves (which can be major or minor) to the incorporation of new material to and the updating of the terminology, notes, and bibliography. With respect to this collection, at least one of the essays included, "Torture at Abu Ghraib: In and Out of the Media," posed particular questions inherent to its subject—a reflection on the images from Abu Ghraib prison (renamed Baghdad Central Prison in 2009). Since the essay was written in 2005 and published in French in 2006, there has been a succession of lawsuits, trials, Freedom of Information requests by ACLU attorneys and various journalists, and many kinds of fallout (although no senior military personnel have ever been charged, much less convicted). Furthermore, there is now a massive bibliography on all aspects of the events that fall under the shorthand designation "torture at Abu Ghraib." Thus, my choice was whether to try and incorporate new information, to describe subsequent developments and significant scholarship, or whether to let the essay stand as written. In this particular case, I decided to append a short update, as this seemed the most efficient expedient for addressing an event whose consequences continue to unfold.[13] In every instance, however, I considered it necessary to provide the original date of the essay, and the occasion or type of publication for which it was written. Where subsequent critics and scholars have amplified or enlarged upon my particular subject in significant ways, I have sometimes added footnotes to the text.

# 1

## Inside/Out

(1995)

In her withering critique of the work of Diane Arbus—itself part of a larger thesis about the baleful effects of photography's colonization of the world and its objects—Susan Sontag argued that certain forms of photographic depiction were complicit with processes of objectification that precluded either empathy or identification with their subjects. In producing a photographic oeuvre featuring subjects who were physically deviant (e.g., giants, dwarfs) or those deemed socially deviant (e.g., transvestites, nudists) or even those who through Arbus's singular lens merely looked deviant (e.g., crying babies), and by photographing them in ways that defiantly renounced either compassion or sympathetic engagement, Arbus was indicted as a voyeuristic and deeply morbid connoisseur of the horrible:

> The camera is a kind of passport that annihilates moral boundaries and social inhibitions, freeing the photographer from any responsibility toward the people photographed. The whole point of photographing people is that you are not intervening in their lives, only visiting them. The photographer is a supertourist, an extension of the anthropologist, visiting natives and bringing back news of their exotic doings and strange gear. The photographer is always trying to colonize new experiences or find new ways to look at familiar subjects—to fight against boredom. For boredom is just the reverse side of fascination: both depend on being outside rather than inside a situation, and one leads to the other.[1]

Sontag's critique of the touristic and anomic sensibility informing the work of Arbus (a critique that was clearly meant to encompass many other comparable practices) turns, among other things, on the binary couple inside/outside. In fact, Sontag closes the paragraph cited above by remarking of Arbus that "her view is always from the outside." This binarism, which is but one of a series that underpins much photography theory and criticism, characterizes—in a manner that appears virtually self-evident—two possible positions for the photographer. The insider position—in this particular context, the "good" or "virtuous" position—is understood to imply a position of engagement, participation, and privileged knowledge. Whereas the second, the outsider's position, is taken to produce an alienated and voyeuristic relationship that heightens the distance between subject and object. Along the lines of this binarism hinges much of the debate concerned with either the ethics or the politics of various forms of photographic practice. In this respect, Sontag's critique is best characterized as an investigation of the ethics of photographic seeing. This might be contrasted with Martha Rosler's no less uncompromising critique of traditional documentary practice—I refer here to her 1981 essay "In, Around, and Afterthoughts (On Documentary Photography)"—structured around an explicitly politicized analysis of how such photography actually functions. "Imperialism," she wrote, "breeds an imperialist sensibility in all phases of cultural life," a comment that might be paired interestingly with Sontag's "Like sexual voyeurism, [taking photographs] is a way of at least tacitly, often explicitly, encouraging whatever is going on to keep on happening."[2] Accordingly, where Rosler sees the issue of photographic voyeurism and objectification as a synecdoche of a larger political and cultural totality, Sontag tends to locate the problem in the photographic act itself. Nevertheless, and despite the important difference between the terms of an ethical or a political critique, both Sontag and Rosler are equally aware of the problematic nature of the photographic representation of the other, whether that other is incarnated by the handicapped, the freak, the wino, the poor, the racial or ethnic other—the list is obviously endless. And although the inside/outside dichotomy for Sontag pivots on the possibility (or lack) of empathy and identification, and where for Rosler it devolves on issues of power and powerlessness, it is nonetheless significant that from either a liberal or a left perspective, the inside/outside couplet is a central theme. Among other things, such a distinction operates to differentiate the kind of practice Rosler calls "victim photography" and at least one possible alternative—the putative empowerment of self-representation. In other words, where the inside/outside pairing is mobilized with respect to the representation of the other, the operative assumption is that the vantage point of the photographer who comes from outside (the quintessential documentarian, the ethnographer or anthropologist, the camera-wielding tourist) is not only itself an act of violence and appropriation but is by definition a partial if not distorted view of the subject to be represented.

Without necessarily disagreeing with this characterization, I would suggest, however, that the terms of this binarism are in fact more complicated, indeed far more ambiguous than they might initially appear. One of the lessons of deconstruction is to look closely at the structure of binary oppositions, not merely to reveal the hierarchy masked by their juxtaposition but also to identify those areas of undecidability and equivocation that subvert the supposed stability of the opposition, uncovering suppressions, destabilizing the very terms of the binary. And while there is a perfectly commonsensical way in which we all grasp what is meant by Sontag's description of a photographer being "outside rather than inside a situation,"[3] and the implications thereof, there is yet a stubborn resistance in photography, even a logical incompatibility with these terms. We frequently assume authenticity and truth to be located on the inside (the truth of the subject), and, at the same time, we routinely—culturally—locate and define objectivity (as in reportorial, journalistic, or juridical objectivity) in conditions of exteriority, detachment, of nonimplication.

It is in this context suggestive, therefore, that one of the recurring tropes of photography criticism is an acknowledgment of the medium's brute exteriority, its depthless-ness, perceived as a kind of ontological limitation rendering it incapable of registering anything more than the momentary accident of appearances. "Less than ever does a simple reproduction of reality express something about reality," wrote Walter Benjamin (citing Brecht) on a photograph of a Krupp munitions factory.[4] "Only that which narrates can make us understand," cautions Sontag nearly forty years after Benjamin's essay. "The knowledge gained through still photographs will always be some kind of sentimentalism, whether cynical or humanist."[5]

But if the medium is itself understood in this quasi-ontological sense as inescapably limited to the superficiality of surface appearance, how then does one gauge the difference between the photographic image made with an insider's knowledge or investment from one made from a position of total exteriority? If the inside or outside position is taken to constitute a difference, we need to determine where that defining difference lies. In other words, is the implication (from the Latin, *implicare*—to be folded within) of the photographer in the world he or she represents visually manifest in the pictures that are taken, and if so, how? Are the terms of reception, or, for that matter, presentation, in any way determined by the position—inside or out—of the photographer making the exposure? Does the personal involvement of the photographer in a milieu, a place, a culture, and a situation dislodge the subject/object distinction that is thought to foster a flaneur-like sensibility? And what exactly is meant by the notion of "inside" in relation to an activity that is by definition about the capture—with greater or lesser fidelity—of a momentary appearance?

This dialectic of inside/outside, considered in relation to the artists exhibited in *Public Information: Desire, Disaster, Document,* has multiple resonances.[6] Insofar as the work of most of the artists represented, including the painter Gerhard Richter, reflects on the various modalities or instrumentalities of photographic representation (including video and film), it is possible to chart the paradoxes and ambiguities of the inside/outside binarism in much of the featured work. In this respect, Ed Ruscha's photographic book works, such as *Every Building on the Sunset Strip* (1966), or Dan Graham's *Homes for America* (1965–70) might be considered the degree zero of photographic exteriority, for not only are the photographs themselves exterior views, they model themselves directly on the impersonality, anonymity, and banality of the purely instrumental image. Insofar as the former work is structured as an arbitrary inventory, providing nothing other than the external signs of its own given parameters, it can be said to thematize the perfect solipsism of the instrumental photograph. In fact, it is precisely this evacuation of subjectivity, the refusal of personality, authorial style—in short, the rejection of all the hallmarks of photographic authorship, no less than the nature of the subject matter itself—that would seem to situate such work logically as the "outside" pole of photographic practice. It was, furthermore, these very qualities of vernacular photograph (its lack of complexity, its humdrum ordinariness, and, of course, its mechanical reproducibility) that fostered its widespread use by artists like Ruscha in the first place, as well as by so many of the artistic generation that succeeded abstract expressionism, including Warhol and Richter.

At the other pole of photographic representation is the "confessional" mode represented by Larry Clark and Nan Goldin, who deploy a photographic rhetoric of lived experience and privileged knowledge, and who declare their personal stake in the substance of their representations. Such work is one of the historical legacies of art photography to the degree that it affirms the medium's capacity to render subjectivity, whether that of the photographer or that of his or her subjects. Putting aside for the moment discussion of the viability of this claim, it is nevertheless the case that the work of Clark and Goldin raises some of the same issues posed by the work of Diane Arbus, for the subjects of these works are variously outlaws, hustlers, drug addicts, marginals, transvestites,

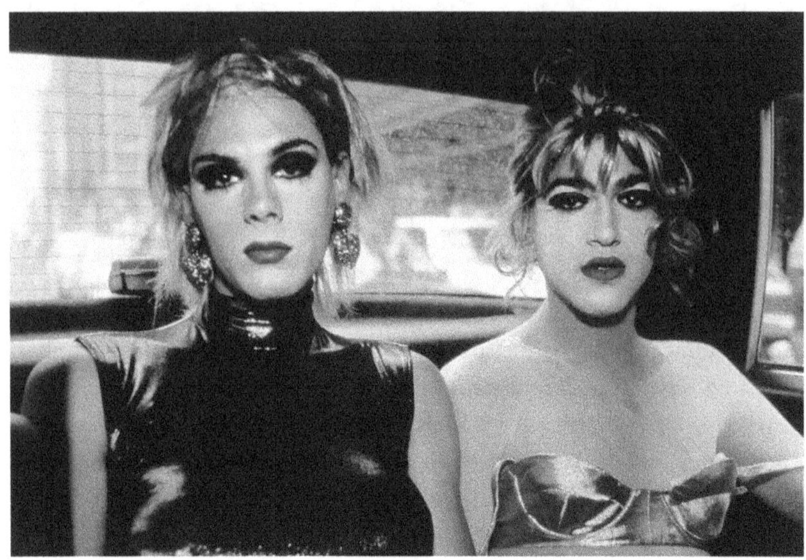

1.1 Nan Goldin, *Misty and Jimmy Paulette in a taxi, NYC,* 1991. Cibachrome, 30 × 40 in. © Nan Goldin. COURTESY OF MATTHEW MARKS GALLERY.

and so forth. Notwithstanding how their photographic representations were originally intended or used, they exist now in a nether zone between art and spectacle, on view for the gallery- and museumgoer or the purchaser of photography books. In contrast, however, to Arbus's manifestly different class and social position vis-à-vis many, if not most, of her chosen subjects, Nan Goldin's *Ballad of Sexual Dependency* (1986) or, more recently, *The Other Side* (1992) are the products of an insider's position:

> People in the pictures say my camera is as much a part of being with me as any other aspect of knowing me. It's as if my hand were a camera. If it were possible, I'd want no mechanism between me and the moment of photographing. The camera is as much a part of my everyday life as talking or eating or sex. The instance of photographing, instead of creating distance, is a moment of clarity and emotional connection for me. There is a popular notion that the photographer is by nature a voyeur, the last one to be invited to the party. But I'm not crashing; this is my party. This is my family, my history.[7]

In both of Goldin's photographic projects, we are therefore presented with the residents of her own social and sexual world, and, in *The Ballad of Sexual*

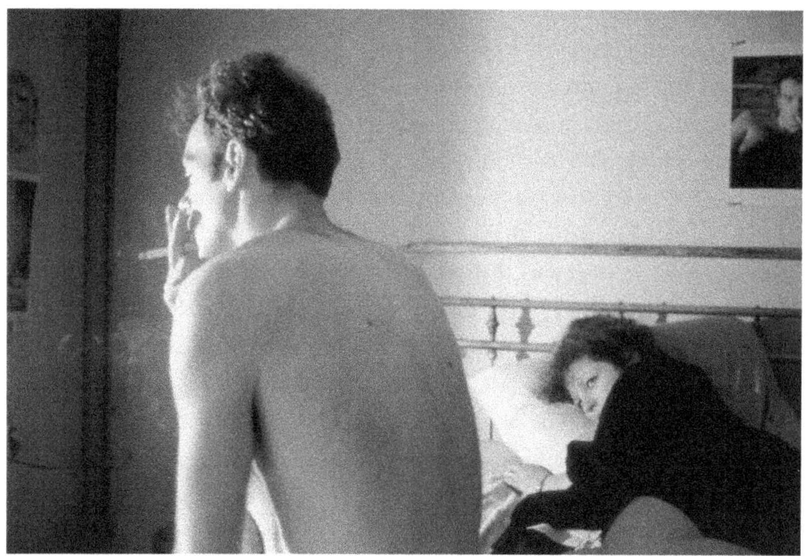

1.2 Nan Goldin, *Nan and Brian in Bed, NYC,* 1983. Cibachrome, 20 × 24 in. © Nan Goldin. COURTESY OF MATTHEW MARKS GALLERY.

*Dependency,* with several images of Goldin herself. She appears, for example, in the jacket photograph, lying in bed and looking at her boyfriend, who is smoking and seen from the back (fig. 1.2). She appears in another picture with battered face and blackened eye, after having been beaten by her boyfriend, and in two other instances, is photographed in explicitly sexual situations. Although she is not represented in the photographs that constitute *The Other Side,* in her introductory essay she acknowledges her emotional, and indeed romantic, involvement with the drag queens, transsexuals, and transvestites who are the subject of the work. For all these reasons, both *The Ballad of Sexual Dependency* and *The Other Side* can be considered as exemplary of the insider position, a position further established by what I have termed the "confessional mode"—*le coeur mis à nu* ("the heart laid bare"; Charles Baudelaire).

In the case of the latter project, and by way of examining the terms by which insiderness comes into play, the viewer can readily assume from the content of the images that the photographer is in a position of intimate proximity with her subjects. This is suggested by the depiction of the conventionally private activities of dressing and undressing, bathing, and putting on makeup; the apparent physical closeness of the camera's lens to its subjects in many of the pictures; and, lastly, toward the end of the book, three images of one of the transvestites and his lover in bed together.

But having said this, how does the insider position—in this instance, that of someone who has lived with the subjects (i.e., the pictures from the 1970s taken in Boston), who loves and admires them and who shares their world—determine the reception of these images or even the nature of the content? The dressing/undressing images, for example, which could be said to signify effectively the intimacy of the relation between photographer and subject, have a specific valiancy with respect to cross-dressing and transvestism. In other words, whether or not one considers these to be indicative of identities, roles, masquerades, or "third genders," the very nature of the entity "drag queen" or "transvestite" is predicated on the transforming act of dressing up, on gender identity as a form of performance. To photograph different moments in that transformation from biological male into an extravagant fantasy of made-in-Hollywood femininity and glamour is to document a ritual that is itself about exteriority, appearance, and performance. For it is, after all, on the level of appearance that drag queens stage their subversive theater of gender.

In the first grouping of photographs that opens *The Other Side*, the intention seems to be to produce—actually to reproduce—the desired personae of the subjects. In this sense, Goldin's insider relationship facilitates her ability to produce the image of the subject's desire—but this is not structurally different from any other photographic collaboration between photographer and model. In fact, certain of the Boston pictures (which are all in black and white) resemble nothing so much as arty fashion photographs, very much in the style of the period. One would not necessarily think that certain of the portraits—particularly those of the person called "roommate"—represented anything other than a fragile-looking, fine-boned woman. But this too subverts the privilege and authority of the insider position, insofar as one confronts what is itself a perfection of simulation. Later in the book (and later chronologically) the style changes; the photographs are now in color, more informal, more spontaneous looking. It seems as though the stylistic referent shifts from art photography to cinema verité, and, analogously, the images of the subjects become more revealing, pictured often in various in-between states of physical transformation. Still later in the book, after New York, Paris, and Berlin, the action moves to Manila and Bangkok, where the drag queens, transvestites, and transsexuals are portrayed in the bars they work at, at the revues they perform in, or, in a few instances, in the midst of their families. Insiderness here, as elsewhere, can thus be seen to be about access and proximity, but whether one can argue for a nonvoyeuristic relationship in consequence of the photographer's position is another matter entirely.

As with Arbus's photographs of freaks and deviants, the risk is that the subject, irrespective of the photographer's intention, becomes object and spectacle for the viewer, if not for the photographer who made the exposure. Where the subjects are in reality so often victimized, marginalized, discriminated against, or even physically assaulted, as is often the case with drag queens, the political and ethical terms of their representation are inseparable. Goldin may well claim her devotion and emotional closeness to her subjects, but does this mitigate the prurience, or indeed the phobic distaste, so often manifested toward her subjects by the straight world? Does a photographic representation, however sympathetic, of drag queens and transsexuals constitute an effective intervention against the political and ethical problem of homophobia? In any event, it would be naive to disclaim the nature of most people's interest in photographs of drag queens, and surely part of the fascination of these photographs lies in the uncanniness of gender masquerade itself. Thus, there are the drag queens who so astonishingly simulate female beauty as to destabilize the very nature of the divide, and then there are those who retain—disturbingly—the signs of both sexes, both genders. To the degree, therefore, that the photographer produces a seamless illusion of the subject's successful performance of "femininity," we are not so far from the photo studio of the fashion photographer. To the degree that the masquerade is revealed as such, we are in the province of the exposé. In neither case does the camera transcend the exteriority of appearance, nor, for that matter, does it provide an interiorized truth of the subject.

Moreover, to the extent that the very concept of voyeurism entails a sexual stake (in Freud's original clinical meaning it refers to sexual pleasure derived from looking), the privileged "look" at subjects who are in a sense defined by their sexuality is doubly charged. Although Goldin's lived relationships with her subjects are based on emotional closeness and personal knowledge, the very presence of a camera as they dress or undress, make love or bathe, instates a third term, even as the photographer wishes to disavow it. ("If it were possible, I'd want no mechanism between me and the moment of photographing. The camera is as much a part of my everyday life as talking or eating or sex.") The desire for transparency and immediacy, and the wish that the viewer might see the other with the photographer's own eyes, is inevitably frustrated by the very mechanisms of the camera, which, despite the best intentions of the photographer, cannot penetrate beyond that which is simply, stupidly there at the moment of exposure.

Larry Clark's photographs, which at least in respect to certain projects, notably *Tulsa,* can also be considered the product of an inside position, raise many of these same issues. However, in an almost stereotypical gender division, whereas Goldin's works are meant as affectionate homages, the rhetoric with which Clark frames his works is aggressively macho, a combination of hipster-speak and jive. Clark's first book, *Tulsa* (1971), which almost immediately established his reputation, consists of fifty deceptively artless black-and-white photographs, depicting his own milieu at that period of his life. These white, apparently working-class young men and women are caught by his camera variously shooting speed, shooting (or brandishing) guns, getting shot ("accidental gunshot wound"), having sex, having babies, burying babies, beating up informers, and generally incarnating lumpen life, American suburban style. Like Goldin's confessional rhetoric, *Tulsa* opens with an equivalent certificate of authenticity: "I was born in Tulsa Oklahoma in 1943. When I was sixteen I started shooting amphetamine. I shot up with my friends every day for three years and then left town but I've gone back through the years. Once the needle goes in it never comes out."[8]

From the outset, much was made by critics of Clark's having been in all senses "on the inside." Only from such a position, it was assumed, could one generate such gritty, not to say brutal, close-ups of shooting up, getting high, and making out. There is, undeniably, an outlaw glamour in such pictures, a funky lower-depths appeal, that is very much a part of American culture and readily romanticized. My own favorite of the series is a luminous sunlit photo of a hugely pregnant young woman, seated in profile, calmly shooting up (fig. 1.3). Such imagery, it must be said, functions as a tonic antidote to the sentimentalism of mainstream representations of pregnancy. Although not narrativized in the strict sense of the term, *Tulsa* is structured in such a way that several of Clark's (named) subjects take on the role of leading characters, notably David Roper and Billy Mann (under one of whose portraits Clark curtly appended the legend "dead"). As with Goldin's work, however, the manifest insiderness of Clark's position begs the question of the nature of such works' reception and the nature of the viewing relationship between subject and subsequent viewer, occurring in gallery or museum, or in the pages of his book.

Following the success of *Tulsa* came *Teenage Lust,* a book of photographs Clark introduced in the following terms:

> Since i became a photographer i always wanted to turn back the years. always wished i had a camera when i was a boy. fucking in the back seat. gang-

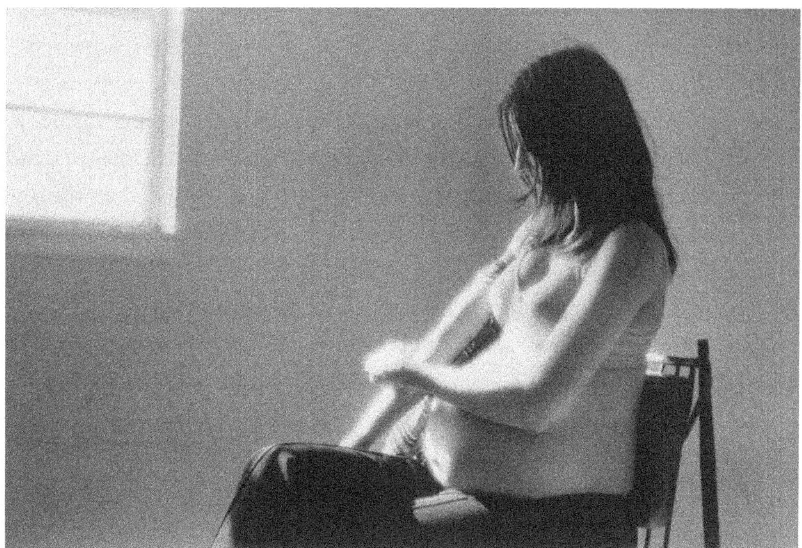

1.3 Larry Clark, *Untitled*, 1971. From *Tulsa*. Black-and-white photograph, 11 × 14 in. © 1971, Larry Clark. COURTESY OF THE ARTIST AND LUHRING AUGUSTINE, NEW YORK.

> bangs with the pretty girl all the girls in the neighborhood hated. the fat girl next door who gave me blow jobs after school and i treated her mean and told all my pals, we kept count up to about three hundred times we fucked her in the eighth grade. i got the crabs from Babs. Albert who said "no i'm first, she's my sister." once when i fucked after bobby hood (ol' horse dick) i was fucking hair and air. a little rape. in 1972 and 1973 the kid brothers in the neighborhood took me with them in their teen lust scene. it took me back.[9]

Like the lowercase usage and lack of punctuation, the substance of the text is as much a warranty of style as of content. As one might expect from such a prefatory note, much of *Teenage Lust* depicts adolescents having sex, although, as in *Tulsa*, there are other sorts of images—portraits, collages, pictures of hanging out, and also random texts. Consistent with much of Clark's work, the emphasis is on masculinity, specifically adolescent masculine sexuality; women and girls for the most part play supporting roles. Although male arousal is visual—available to the camera—in a way female arousal is not, the relative ubiquity of hard-ons and fellatio in Clark's photographs, as well as the sheer numbers of portraits of more or less seductive youths in postures of display, suggests an intense identification with and investment in the male adolescent (fig. 1.4). In the case of *Tulsa,* the nature of Clark's participation is fairly obvious. There, being "inside" operates on the level of the performative; Clark was an active participant. But what is the meaning of being "inside" in *Teenage Lust*? In glossing the series with the information that "in 1972 and 1973 the kid brothers in the neighborhood took me with them in their teenage lust scene. it took me back," Clark acknowledges not merely that his teenage years are far behind him but also that rather than "being somewhere," he is in fact "being taken somewhere." What is the "inside" position in relation to the boy hustlers of 42nd Street who both pose and expose themselves for Clark's camera? If the nature of this investment seems oblique to the viewer—if it does not unambiguously announce itself as erotic, sociological, or personal in nature—how should we here understand the dynamics of inside/outside? Like the invisible and unacknowledged camera that accompanies intrepid explorers in *National Geographic* specials as they comb ocean floors and climb impossible mountains, so too does Clark provide the heady illusion of the viewer's unmediated access to his subjects. For example, an extended sequence in *The Perfect Childhood* recording the course of a blow job, performed on a naked adolescent boy by a fully clothed older woman (a prostitute? a friend? a client?), inescapably elides the presence of both Clark and his camera.[10] But the presence of Clark and his camera is by no means a supplemental detail; it is, in every sense, a part of the action, acknowledged or not. But does this privileged vantage point—this quite literally voyeuristic position—provide the analogously privileged knowledge to which the insider is supposed to have access?

In retrospect, *Teenage Lust,* even more than *Tulsa*, seems to have established Clark's terrain; namely, the fraught depiction of adolescent sexuality in contemporary America. Accordingly, his portraits of boy hustlers in midtown Manhattan or, more recently, those in *The Perfect Childhood* or the collage installations in *Public Information* draw directly on social and sexual contradictions including those attached to pedophilia as well as gay sexuality. Knowingly, they allude to the commodification of adolescent sexuality as purveyed by advertising and the mass media. And Clark's own preoccupations are themselves paralleled by the cultural fascination with adolescent pathology (e.g., the teenage rapist, the feral youth) and an equal fascination with adolescent vulnerability (e.g., the adolescent as victim, as sexual prey).

In considering the ambiguities and contradictions attendant on the insider position as exemplified in the work of Goldin and Clark, we need acknowledge the fact that to the extent that such work is "about" sexual lives or sexual

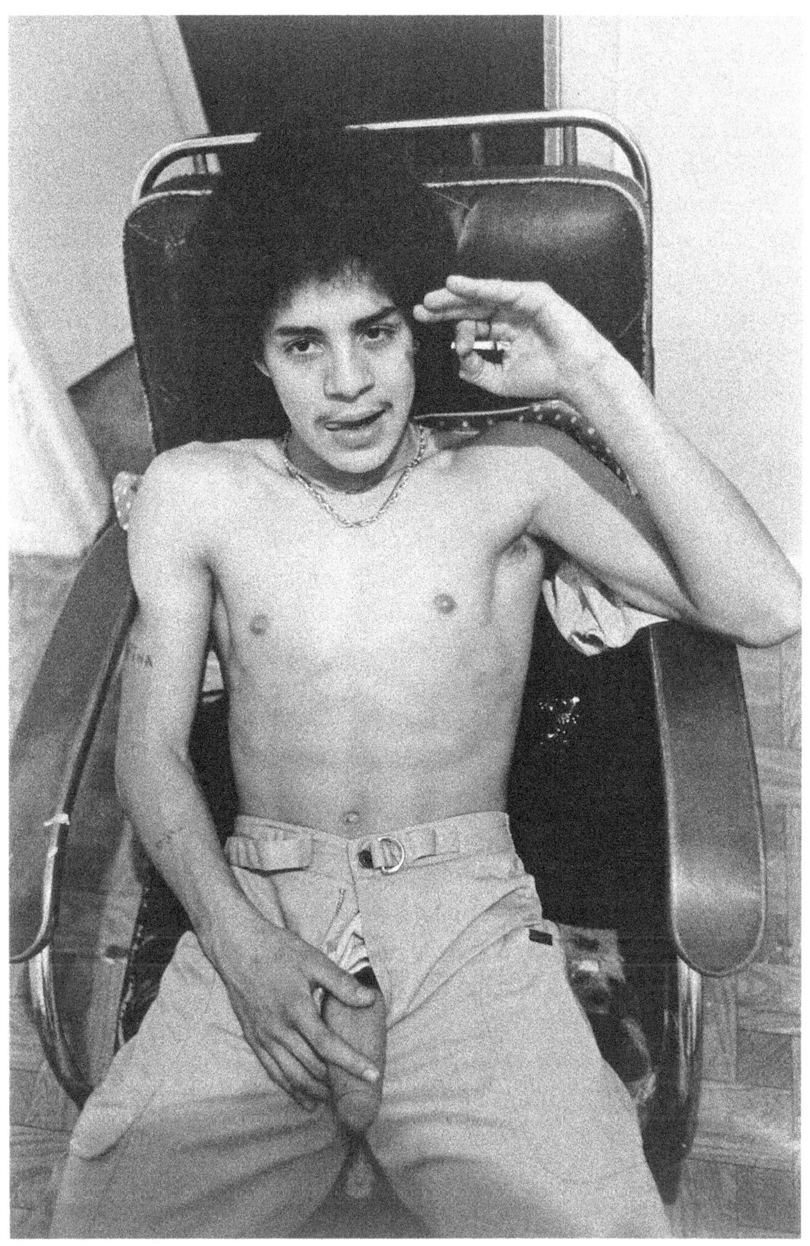

1.4 Larry Clark, *Booby (from the 42nd Street Series)*, 1978. From *Teenage Lust*. Black-and-white photograph, 14 × 11 in. © 1978, Larry Clark. COURTESY OF THE ARTIST AND LUHRING AUGUSTINE, NEW YORK.

activities, it necessarily intersects with the sexuality of the individual viewer. Indeed, it may well be the case that all photography that deals with sexuality or eroticism, of whatever stripe, engages with the workings of the inside, insofar as there is, in psychic terms, no outside of sexuality, no Archimedean point from which photographer, subject, or viewer is neutrally positioned. Alternatively, one could as well argue that it is inevitably the case with photography, especially photography that attempts to make visible the operations of subjectivity and sexuality, that the resulting image is both fixed and fixated on the outside; it cannot tell what the photographer knows, it cannot reveal a truth of the subject.

Inside or out, one remains confronted with the ethical and political issues posed by Sontag and Rosler, which foreground the question of the representation of the other where the analysis depends on notions of voyeurism and objectification, tourism or imperialism. Certain alternative strategies have in fact emerged within photographic practice, albeit these are found for the most part in galleries and art spaces. One strategy might be described as a form of radical iconoclasm that Rosler herself pioneered in her photo-text work *The Bowery in Two Inadequate Descriptive Systems*. There, the crucial intervention consisted in precisely not representing the men of the Bowery, substituting instead the textual—the verbal lexicon of drunkenness—and limiting the photographs to the vacant storefronts and doorways of the Bowery pointedly evacuated of their resident winos. In refusing to spectacularize the more-than-familiar image of the skid row drunk, Rosler could be said to have displaced this particular "social problem" from the register of the visual, the register of appearance (within which it is mindlessly consumed), to that of the politics of representation. Jeff Wall's use of illuminated Cibachrome light-box installations constitutes another practice that takes serious cognizance of the inside/outside problematic. For all their deceptive visual realism, Wall's tableaux are entirely theatrical: calculated stagings that use actors, locations, and directorial strategies.

But where simulation or iconoclasm function more or less to counter or obviate the problematics of inside/outside, it is perhaps more to the point to question the validity of the binarism itself. For what is really at issue is the fundamentally unanswerable question of how reality is in fact to be known, and in this respect, the truth claims of photography—always disputed—are increasingly rejected. In any case, the nature of the debate that turns on the capacity of photography to represent truth or reality obviously depends on the notion that truth or reality, as opposed to appearance, are in fact visually representable. While photographic representation retains its evidentiary or juridical status for purposes of individual identification, police procedure, the courtroom, and the racetrack, the truth status of photography has not fared well in the epoch of postmodernity. Thus, if *pace* Althusser, no less than Baudrillard, we are given to understand that reality is always mediated through representational systems, is always in the final instance a question of representation itself, on what basis is photography found more or less capable of rendering, however imperfectly, the real?

The debate that turns on the adequacy of photographic representation to the demands of the real therefore has several modalities, depending on whether the discursive object is "photography"—itself an abstraction—or a particular subset or practice within it. But the binarism of inside/outside has meaning only within the context of particular practices, not as an ontological given. If we are then to consider the possibility that a photographic practice ostensibly premised on insiderness ultimately reveals the very impossibility of such a position in the realm of the visual, might it conversely be the case that a photographic practice that affirms its own implacable exteriority yields a certain truth of its own?

By way of example, consider the now legendary photographs taken in 1955–56 and assembled in Robert Frank's *The Americans*, first published in 1958. At least since romanticism, there has existed a tradition of considering the artist as an outsider within his culture (I use the masculine pronoun intentionally). Estrangement, alienation, if not outright rebellion, are in this tradition considered to be the sine qua non by which the artist is empowered to apprehend his own culture, to criticize it, or even to imagine a different one. Thus, whether the stakes are the representation of one's own culture, its time and place (the photographic analogue of the painter of modern life), the critical reflection on social relations, or the imagining of utopian alternatives, the outsider status of the artist is taken as the evidence of his integrity and the acuity of his artistic vision. Exteriority and detachment are here conceived as the necessary condition of comprehension as well as critical reflection. In the case of Frank, an outsider by birth and language (Swiss émigré), as well as by temperament, it was precisely his vantage point as outsider that produced what many consider to be one of the definitive, evocative, and, indeed, authentic portraits of fifties America. For me, Frank's America is as much a construction as the America purveyed by *Life* magazine. But Frank's brooding vision is predicated on wholly different referents and codes: among them, film noir and the various racial and cultural identifications generated in white male hipster culture. Still, to say that *The Americans* is not *the* truth of America in the 1950s is not to say that it doesn't possess *a* truth; certainly there is truth in its evocation of the lonely crowd, the class and racial divisions in evidence throughout the United States, the anomie, in short, the underside of the official representations of America purveyed by the media or by corporate advertising.

Similarly, and most recently, Chantal Akerman's film *D'Est* (*From the East*) is a filmic journey that makes of outsiderness its very structuring principle (fig. 1.5). Traveling through Eastern Europe in 1991, without linguistic access or, for that matter, any specialized knowledge, Akerman made a film constructed as a series of long looks, including panning shots, at people (mostly women) in their interior spaces, of peasants in the fields, of people in a railroad waiting room, but mostly seemingly endless tracking shots of people on the street, in queues, at bus stops, in the midst of a snowy Moscow winter. The camera observes, mutely; there is no text, no narration, no explanation, and no commentary. There is no sound other than what is heard in the ambient environment. Nothing other than this apparently nonselective and passive outsider's look, scanning landscapes, faces, bodies, postures, and gestures. Like Ed Ruscha's laconic photo books, or Dan Graham's *Homes for America, From the East* seems to occupy the degree zero of exteriority, but as with *The Americans*, there is produced, nonetheless, a kind of knowledge, a certain kind of truth. It is a truth that is perhaps best characterized as a truth of appearance, which, accompanied with a sort of principled modesty and discretion, refuses "interpretation" altogether. Akerman's notes, written before and during the making of the film, evidence the same combination of obliqueness and neutrality as does the film itself:

> The film would begin in the flowering of summer, in East Germany, then in Poland. Just the look of someone who passes by, someone who does not have total access to this reality.
>
> Little by little, as one presses forward into the country, the summer fades to give way to autumn. An autumn muffled and white overcast by fog.
>
> In the countryside, men and women nearly lying on the black earth of Ukraine, merging with it, picking the beets.
>
> Not far from them, the road rutted by the continuous passage of ramshackle trucks from which escape black fumes.
>
> It is winter and in Moscow, where the film constricts its focus. It will hopefully allow one to perceive something of this directionless world with its postwar atmosphere, where each day gotten through resembles a victory.

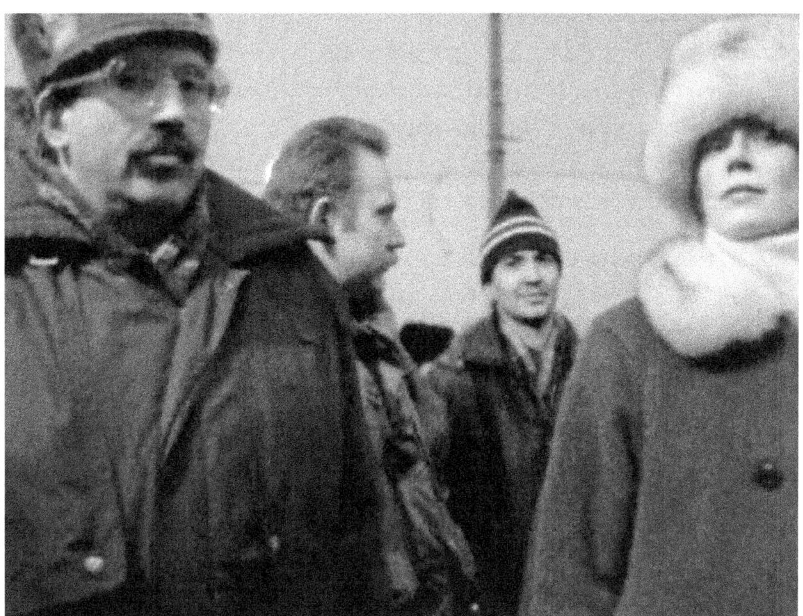

1.5 Still from *D'Est*. DVD. Directed by Chantal Akerman. Icarus Films, Brooklyn, 1993.

> This may seem terrible and insubstantial, but in the middle of all this, I will show faces, which when they are isolated from the mass, express something yet untouched and often the opposite of this uniformity which sometimes strikes us in the movement of crowds, the opposite of our own uniformity.
>
> Without being too sentimental, I would say that these are unspoiled faces which offer themselves; they present themselves as they are, and sometimes erase the sentiment of loss, the world at the edge of the abyss which sometimes seizes us when we cross the East, as I have just done.[11]

This cinematic looking cannot logically be distinguished from the more negative concept of cinematic tourism, and yet, for all that, one does not particularly have the sensation of intrusion or visual mastery, the imperialism of representation. What Akerman's film suggests, as do the somber photographs of Frank, the bleak suburban-scapes of Dan Graham, the neutral inventories of Ed Ruscha, is a way to think about a truth of appearance that without prodding reveals itself to the camera, escaping the absolute binary of inside/outside. This runs counter to a cultural bias that maintains the existence of a truth behind appearance, a truth always veiled, reflecting the philosophical divide between seeming and being. But, as Walter Benjamin observed, "It is a different nature that speaks to the camera than speaks to the eye." It may well be that the nature that speaks to our eyes can be plotted neither on the inside nor the outside but in some liminal and as yet unplotted space between perception and cognition, projection and identification.

# 2

## Written on the Body

(1997)

Just as simulacra seem to be poised to take over the world,
it is all the more important to attempt to decipher them.
—LAURA MULVEY

In the past ten years or so, there has emerged a scholarly discourse concerned with investigating the unstable couplet vision/visuality. Somewhat divorced from earlier inquiries premised on perceptualist, existentialist, or phenomenological models, recent work examines the ways in which vision and visuality are variously shaped by psychic, social, cultural, and historical determinations. Such an inquiry is wholly at odds with older beliefs in an innocent or uncultured eye; to quote André Breton, "The eye exists in its savage state."[1] On the contrary, the gist of contemporary thinking on the subject proposes that there is no state of visual innocence, much less a savage state of grace. To a greater or lesser extent, the gaze, the look, the visual field are now conceived as inscribed within a semiotic web of signs, language, and socialization. Hal Foster's cogent differentiation between vision and visuality and the stakes in their respective investigation is useful here: "Although vision suggests sight as a physical operation, and visuality sight as a social fact, the two are not opposed as nature to culture; vision is social and historical too, and visuality involves the body and the psyche. Yet neither are they identical: here, the difference between the terms signals a difference within the visual—between the mechanism of sight and its historical techniques, between the datum of vision and its discursive determinations—a difference, many differences, among how we see, how we are able, allowed or made to see, and how we see this seeing or the unseen therein."[2]

Prompted in part by the centrality of vision in the work of Jacques Lacan, and the no less influential work of Michel Foucault, but equally encouraged by the (often unacknowledged) influence of feminist thought and its critique of ocularcentrism (such as Sarah Kofman and Luce Irigaray, to name two of the best-known philosophers of the patriarchal structuring of the visual field), much of this critical work attempts to map the mechanisms of desire as they form and inform this field. It is therefore significant that even when reflecting on the psychic and cultural determinations of picture viewing, few of these recent works on the visual field traffic much with the notion of beauty. What might be called a discursive cleavage has occurred, such that discourses of beauty have become detached from their historical locations in philosophy, aesthetics, and art making. Obviously, the cultural site that now generates the most powerful and explicit discourses of beauty and desire is that of women's fashion magazines, but Hollywood films, as well as other kinds of mass media, have been equally important sites of such production. Nevertheless, if beauty is now largely the redoubt of cultural conservatives, or is perceived as belonging more appropriately to the realm of "commodity aesthetics,"[3] the theorization or analysis of desire (in its distinctly modern libidinalized sense) has become a central preoccupation throughout a wide range of disciplines and practices, within both the humanities and the social sciences. Desire of the subject, powers of desire, female desires, forms of desire, desire in language, desire in looking, policing desire, tradition and desire, the obscure object of desire—desire is a discursive field with an ever more extensive purview.[4] Beauty, however, once the fetish of aesthetic philosophy, and even art history, has largely been eclipsed by other concerns.

The discursive eclipse of beauty by desire in contemporary philosophical and aesthetic thought is, however, like any other tidal shift in *mentalités*, very much overdetermined. In the case of art production, the replacement of beauty—*le beau*—as an aesthetic standard by other criteria was the task and the legacy of modernist avant-gardes. By challenging or jettisoning classical notions of beauty as an objective, unchanging, and atemporal order or canon, from romanticism on, modern art practices did much to delegitimize beauty as a quasi-juridical entity. When not dismissing beauty as an outmoded concept, modernist movements alternatively expanded, revised, relativized, or subjectivized its terms. Outside of aesthetic discourse, where concepts of beauty and desire have conventionally been understood to be implicated in each other's terms, "beauty" has usually been lodged within the context of a discourse on "Woman." Similarly, it has figured within discourses of femininity, or in relation to the visual imagery of ideal femininity. Overwhelmingly, for the past two centuries femininity has been directly aligned, if not coterminus with, the concepts of beauty, eroticism, and desire. This is not only a staple topos in nineteenth-century writing on "Woman" (for example, Jules Michelet's *La Femme*) but is also a recurring association in art criticism. Nowhere is this more apparent than when writers describe the act of painting female nudes. "When Titian arranges a purely carnal Venus, softly stretched out . . . in all the fullness of her perfection as goddess and as subject for paint, it is obvious that, for him, to paint meant to caress, a conjunction of two voluptuous sensations in one supreme act in which self-mastery and mastery of his medium were identified with a masterful possession of the beauty herself, in every sense."[5]

An exception to this discursive cleavage is Francette Pacteau's *The Symptom of Beauty*. It is her deceptively simple thesis that the attribution of beauty is as much shaped by unconscious mechanisms and drives as by cultural conventions. Which is to say that those acts of visual production and reception that mobilize concepts of beauty and desire have their wellsprings in both the imaginary and the symbolic order. Citing Freud's observation that "the love of beauty seems a perfect example of an impulse inhibited in its aim," thus, a psychic formation forged in the unconscious, she reflects on the various tropes and figures for feminine beauty and reads them symptomatically. "I am interested," she writes, "in the psychical apparatus to which the beholder's eye is attached: that is to say, I am interested less in the contingent object of desire than the fantasy which frames it."[6] Unsurprisingly, her reading of a range of cultural artefacts—Renaissance love poetry, nineteenth-century novels, and contemporary photographs—reveals that where feminine beauty (clearly, a highly mutable entity throughout the centuries) is defined or described, what is actually at stake are the desires and anxieties of masculine subjectivity. Thus, although beauty is inarguably a socially and culturally defined set of conventions, there is nonetheless a fantasmatic component to the ways in which beauty is both imagined and articulated. And because discourses of beauty are historically patriarchal constructions, it is male subjectivity, itself historically contingent, that determines its expressions.

Studies such as Pacteau's build on a legacy of feminist work on representation inaugurated initially in psychoanalytic film theory and subsequently elaborated on or revised by a quarter century of feminist scholarship and theory. Because these have sought to understand the relations between representation and the historical real, and given the ways in which concepts of beauty affect women's lives, the constellation beauty, desire, femininity, and representation has been an important area of investigation. When these investigations are further integrated with analyses of the gaze, or the politics of looking, it is clear that such inquiries are anything but academic. In this regard, Pacteau assumes that the subject's negotiation of sexual difference and the unconscious fantasies that attend it are necessarily and inescapably involved in all aspects of visual perception and reception. These have real (and differing) consequences for male and female subjects. Moreover, as Jacqueline Rose has observed, the field of vision is traversed and disturbed by the vicissitudes of the instinct, the diversions of the aim, the contingency of desire.[7] If, for example, classical conceptions of female beauty, from fifth-century Greece to the end of the nineteenth century, required the suppression of both body hair and sex organs on female bodies, it is difficult to account for this durable convention outside of the psychoanalytic model of fetishism. Made to the measure of masculine desire, the female body is consequently understood to function as an unconscious locus of castration fears, a figure for the collective unconscious of patriarchy. Taking into account these social, psychic, and historical determinations, a critical consideration of beauty and desire as they are produced, mobilized, and celebrated within [visual] regimes of representation might well begin with the questions "Whose beauty?" and "Whose desire?"

These questions are, to be sure, political rather than aesthetic, contradicting the assumption of universality and universal judgment that Western concepts of beauty have historically implied. When considered, however, in relation to photographic representation, there arise issues specific to the medium, beginning with the fact that the figures depicted in any photograph are or were actual human beings, not artistic inventions. While all types of figuration, especially those loosely categorized as realist or naturalist—operate ideologically, and are variously instrumental in sustaining, or (rarely) transgressing norms of gender, the photograph's transcriptive capabilities make it especially powerful because it is especially convincing. The common perception of the photograph as an unmediated representation has both underpinned and intensified its ideological potency. In this respect, photographic depictions intended as instances of human (but usually female) beauty must be examined in terms of their sexual as well as representational politics.

Addressing these issues with reference to the staged tableaux of Wilhelm von Gloeden and his cousin Wilhelm Pluschow, to E. J. Bellocq's enigmatic photographs of prostitutes in New Orleans, or to the far less artful fare of anonymous pornographers makes clear, however, the difficulties attending the task of "thinking" overfreighted concepts such as beauty and desire in relation to photography. Whether it is a question of specific images, specific procedures, specific photographers, or photography sui generis, the medium stubbornly resists painting's clear division of signifier and signified insofar as most viewers perceive a given photograph as a unitary sign.

The vast production of Wilhelm von Gloeden and his cousin Wilhelm Pluschow, produced in Taormina circa 1890–1910, is unusual however because much of it is devoted to male subjects, mainly adolescents (figs. 2.1 and 2.2). These, however, reveal the same contradictions as do the photographs of female nudes. Consider, for example, von Gloeden's own orchestration of beauty and desire in a study of three young boys (ca. 1900; fig. 2.3). Here, in semiotic collision, are the clashing codes of iconicity and indexicality, the latter term complicating, if not subverting, those concepts of desire and beauty that depend on idealist (and idealizing) aesthetics. On the side of iconicity is the photograph's status as picture and as aesthetic artefact/object. Also on the side of iconicity are the picture's literal components—what can be identified and named within the pictorial field and its formal organization. These include its denotative elements (for example, naked boys, the Mediterranean setting, and stagy classical props such as the embroidered fabric and the Greek *oinochoe*). Connotative meanings are also on the side of iconicity: "Greek love," as well as various high-toned artistic and literary allusions—academic poses and Arcadian themes. This particular iconography was long a staple of academic painting, and, like so many art photographers before and after him, von Gloeden strove assiduously to appropriate literary and pictorial motifs for photography.[8]

Nevertheless, and despite von Gloeden's stage managing (or, for that matter, his entrepreneurial success), the medium destabilizes the fantasies it illustrates. In a short, uncharacteristically arch essay he wrote for a catalogue of von Gloeden's photographs, Roland Barthes remarks on these features: "The contradictions are 'heterologies,' friction from diverse and opposing languages. . . . These little Greek gods (already a contradiction because of their dark color) have peasants' hands, somewhat dirty, with large, misshapen nails; hardened feet, not very clean; and swollen, clearly visible prepuces which are unstylized, that is, not slender and tapered: our attention is drawn to the fact that they are clearly uncircumcised: the Baron's photographs are at the same time sublime and anatomical."[9]

Few observers, however, either in von Gloeden's epoch or our own, would necessarily find the youths in his pictures to be objectively beautiful. On the other hand, there are many reasons to suppose that for von Gloeden himself, and for part of his substantial clientele, such youths were objects of desire.

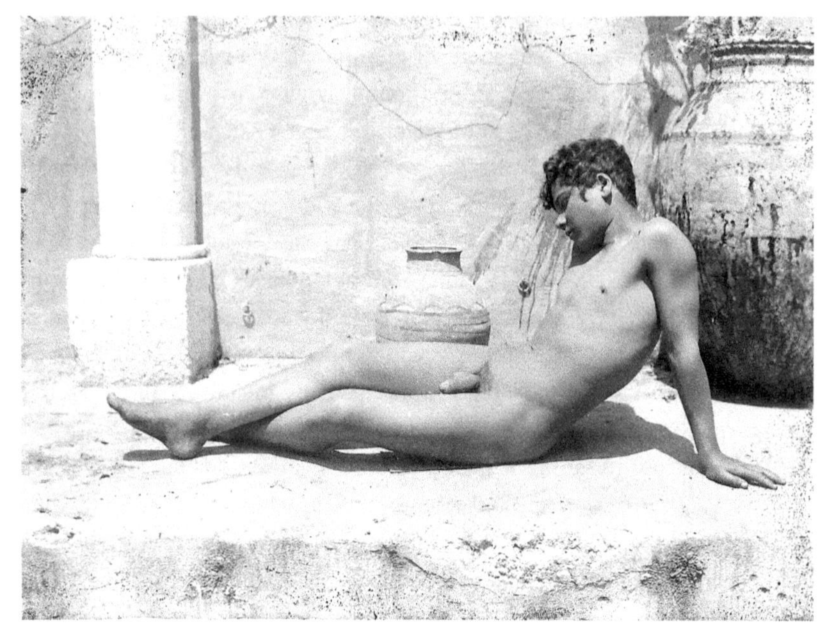

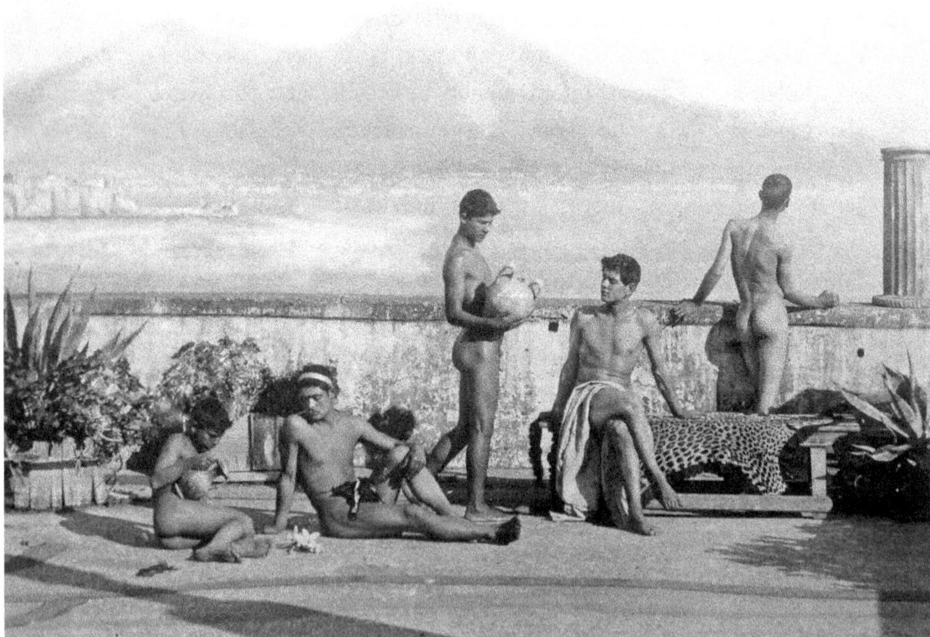

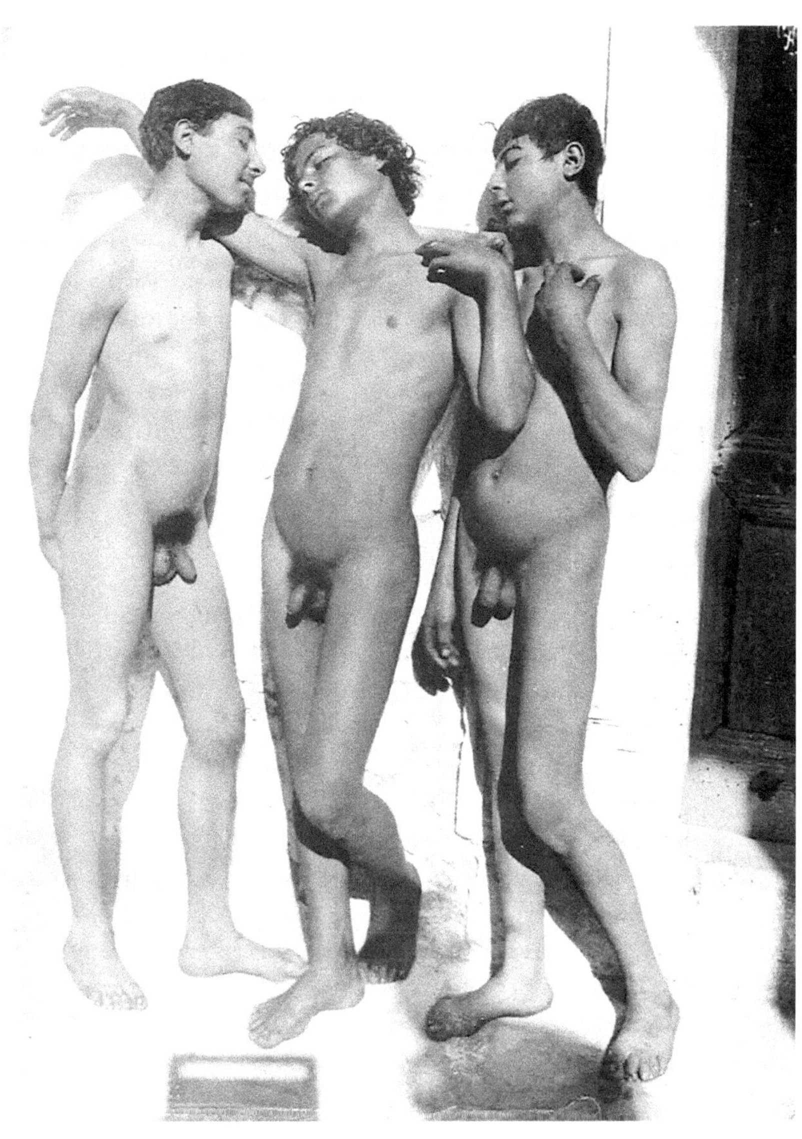

2.1 (*opposite, top*) Wilhelm von Gloeden, *Ragazzo disteso / Reclining Nude Boy*, Taormina, Sicily, Italy, ca. 1890. Albumen silver print, 16.4 × 23.2 cm.

2.2 (*opposite, bottom*) Wilhelm von Gloeden, *Terra del Fuoco / Land of Fire*, Naples, Italy, before 1895. Albumen silver print, 30 × 40 cm.

2.3 (*above*) Wilhelm von Gloeden, *Le tre grazie / The Three Graces*, Taormina, Sicily, Italy, ca. 1900. Albumen silver print.

In this respect, one might note that where the perception of beauty may well provoke the spectator's desire; conversely, desire has no intrinsic need of beauty, conventional or otherwise, as is perfectly evident in the case of most industrially produced pornography.

That said, a connoisseur of art photography might consider the photograph itself to be beautiful, in keeping with that aspect of modern aesthetics that detaches the beauty or ugliness of a work's nominal subject from the quality of a work *qua* work. A vintage print made by von Gloeden before 1910 may exhibit those sensual qualities of the photographic print (e.g., the hues that black-and-white prints may acquire, a kind of patina according to the picture's age, the paper used for printing, the printing process itself, or the kind of film stock used). Other formal qualities such as composition, lighting, and resolution are elements of the picture's aesthetic qualities. There exists, then, the possibility that the picture itself, as material object, on shiny or matte paper, in sepia or monochromatic tones, might be as much the object of desire as the youths who occupy its pictorial field. In this respect, and as Victor Burgin observed, "identification need not be with any overt depicted 'content' whatsoever: if we bear in mind the *gestalt* orientation of the mirror-phase—its emphasis on surface and boundary—we can admit that a narcissistic investment may be made in respect of the very specular brilliance of the tightly-delineated photographic surface itself. . . . Such fascination with the 'glossy' may recall the celebrated *glanz* fetishized by one of Freud's patients, and indeed the photographic look is ineluctably implicated in the structure of fetishism."[10]

Insofar as a photograph reveals no external marking, no touch of the hand (darkroom manipulations notwithstanding) that would connect the image to its material manufacture, it creates the illusion that "the world appears to speak itself."[11] The world, of course, does not speak itself, and this is one of the ways by which the indexical subverts the iconic. In other words, that aspect of photographic function that registers the trace of the real, and, accordingly, material and historical reality, lies on the side of indexicality. These include actual lived social relations, as impoverished Sicilian youths undressed and modelled for a titled German photographer resident in Taormina, as well as the issue of who has access to the means of representation. To recall Marx's comment of the plight of the peasantry: "They do not represent themselves; they are represented"—the Sicilians had no camera.[12] But also on the side of indexicality are those elements of the photograph that contradict or violate the protocols of painting that treat similar subjects. Instead of the wax museum perfection of, say, Lawrence Alma-Tadema's or Hans von Marées's ephebes, von

Gloeden, as a photographer, necessarily worked with what he had on hand. Most of his models violate the canons of ephebic beauty: the contrast between tanned hands and faces and white bodies gives the lie to heroic nudity; the clumsy limbs and the black shocks of pubic hair affirm the brute materiality of the living subjects.[13] Significantly, it was precisely around this aspect of photographic indexicality that mid-nineteenth-century debates about the propriety of the photographic nude revolved. If the nude was, by definition, an aesthetic abstraction, a sublimatory ideal only nominally connected to the naked body, how could a photograph of an actual naked person pass muster? Unlike many other contemporary art photographers who, by various means, elided the "problem" of their models' genitals, von Gloeden appears to have reveled in them; many of his male models, even prepubescent ones, seem particularly well-endowed. Given that one of the distinguishing features of the classical male nude was the diminutive size of the genitals, von Gloeden's choice of models disobeys another venerable aesthetic precept, suggesting that where it is a question of a commodity that traffics in eroticism, desire can readily trump beauty.[14]

But even if one argues that what has been lost in beauty is recuperated for desire, the critical question of whose desire nevertheless remains. Contrary to the wish-fulfilling speculations of von Gloeden's modern partisans, it is unlikely that the hundreds, if not thousands, of photographs von Gloeden (and later, his cousin and business partner, Pluschow) produced of naked boys, girls, and even children have anything to do with their models' desire. On the contrary, many of the models appear bored, stupefied, or merely impassive, obediently enacting their prescribed roles and poses. While this is hardly evidence of coercion, it gives little support to the hypothesis that his models were active, much less enthusiastic, participants in von Gloeden's Teutonic Arcadia.[15] We should therefore reckon with another issue of the photographer's deployment of beauty and desire, and that is power—less in the biographical/empirical sense of von Gloeden's wealth and privilege and his models' poverty (although this should not be minimized either) than in the discursive power of inscription. Thus, the power to "textualize" bodies, to make of the body of the Sicilian peasant a possessable, consumable object that provisionally confirms the photographer's or viewers' mastery, is what links the work of von Gloeden to explicitly pornographic pictures such those made of Arab men fondling each others' genitals (fig. 2.4), or, for that matter, the examples of mid-nineteenth-century pornographic stereocartes. In the former, the staging of the models suggests an allegory of colonialism itself; the men "feminized" in terms of their posing, their submission to the camera, their identity as colonial subjects, and their flaccid penises. The colonial subject is revealed as reassuringly passive and impotent, but the power of inscription derives not merely from the photographer who hired and posed the models but also from a larger geopolitical context. Thus, just as the encompassing terms of the patriarchal imaginary can be said to ultimately "author" the presiding conventions of heterosexual pornography and its fetishistic libidinal economy, so too is the representation of the colonial "other" a cultural product that overarches the intentions of the individual photographer.

Considered in these terms, nineteenth-century illicit photographs of women or couples are as much testimonial to the workings of power as to the working of desire and the commodities it engenders. Again, it is not merely the historical reality or the sociological fact of poor or working-class people making their lives as sex workers that raises these issues but, more profoundly, the ways in which the production of these kinds of imagery is effectively conjured, summoned up, incited by power. Michel Foucault's influential description of this complex circuitry is worth quoting:

> A proliferation of sexualities through the extension of power; an optimization of the power to which each of these sexualities gave a surface of intervention: this concatenation, particularly since the nineteenth century, has been ensured and relayed by the countless economic interests which, with the help of medicine, psychiatry, prostitution, and pornography, have tapped into both this analytic multiplication of pleasure and the optimisation of the power that controls it. Pleasure and power do not cancel or turn back against one another; they seek out, overlap, and reinforce one another. They are linked together by complex mechanisms and devices of excitation and incitement.[16]

Nowhere, however, are the processes of inscription more apparent than in the representation of the female body, and it is here that Burgin's observations on the implication of the photographic look in the structure of fetishism is most apparent. In this respect, a consideration of erotic and pornographic representation has much to tell us about more mainstream representations, and the conditions and terms of their articulation. Consequently, it is this form of image production within a continuum of representation that makes it an instructive object for feminist analysis. As Annette Kuhn has remarked, "A deconstruction of pornography makes it possible to handle the specificity and complexity of its different forms: its cultural variability, its diverse technologies and modes of production and consumption, its status as at once commodity, industry and representation. Such an approach also insists that pornography is, after all, not that special, it is not a privileged order of representation; that it shares many of its modes of address, many of its codes and conventions, with representations which are not looked upon as a 'problem' in the way pornography is."[17]

Nineteenth-century pornographic stereocartes and other photographic formats, unlike their deluxe daguerreotype ancestors, were hastily and of course clandestinely manufactured and sold.[18] Where the first generation of daguerreotype pornography (ca. 1848–55)—especially in stereographic forms—was artisanally produced, often carefully tinted or hand-colored, and elaborately framed, the mass-produced forms were usually crudely made and relatively cheap. Their mass production was enabled by the invention of the wet plate positive/negative process, which, in contrast to daguerreotype technology, was a technology of multiples. Historically such photographic imagery represents the democratization of erotica, insofar as its lower cost and infinite reproducibility made it affordable to those of modest means and, ultimately, to working-class consumers. These were not necessarily all male, but certainly men made up the majority of purchasers. Where the daguerreotypes might be eligible for the category of "beauty" by virtue of their lapidary qualities, a function of the particular technologies, the majority of the mass-produced ones are decidedly not. Here, too, desire trumps beauty, as the working-class models, who risked fines, even imprisonment, for their activity, were rarely attractive, and, as one would expect, are often ravaged and unhealthy-looking, or sometimes well past their youth. As with the von Gloeden photographs, power is manifest in the social relations producing the illicit subculture of the nineteenth-century pornographic industry itself, with its lumpen models, and its more affluent photographic entrepreneurs, distributors, and consumers.[19] For the most part, these photographs represent what have become commonplaces of modern pornography: scenes of coitus, "beaver shots" (which can themselves be seen as a further corroboration of Foucault's arguments), scenes of "lesbian" sex, and, beginning in the later part of the century, homosexual tableaux as well as various sadomasochist or otherwise perverse activities (von Gloeden and Pluschow's business included a profitable traffic of erotica sold clandestinely and pitched to a gay clientele). The only motif that seems to have been relatively common in the nineteenth century and to have become (apparently) less frequent in the twentieth is the image of a woman on a chamber pot. Based on what can be only anecdotal evidence, it seems that

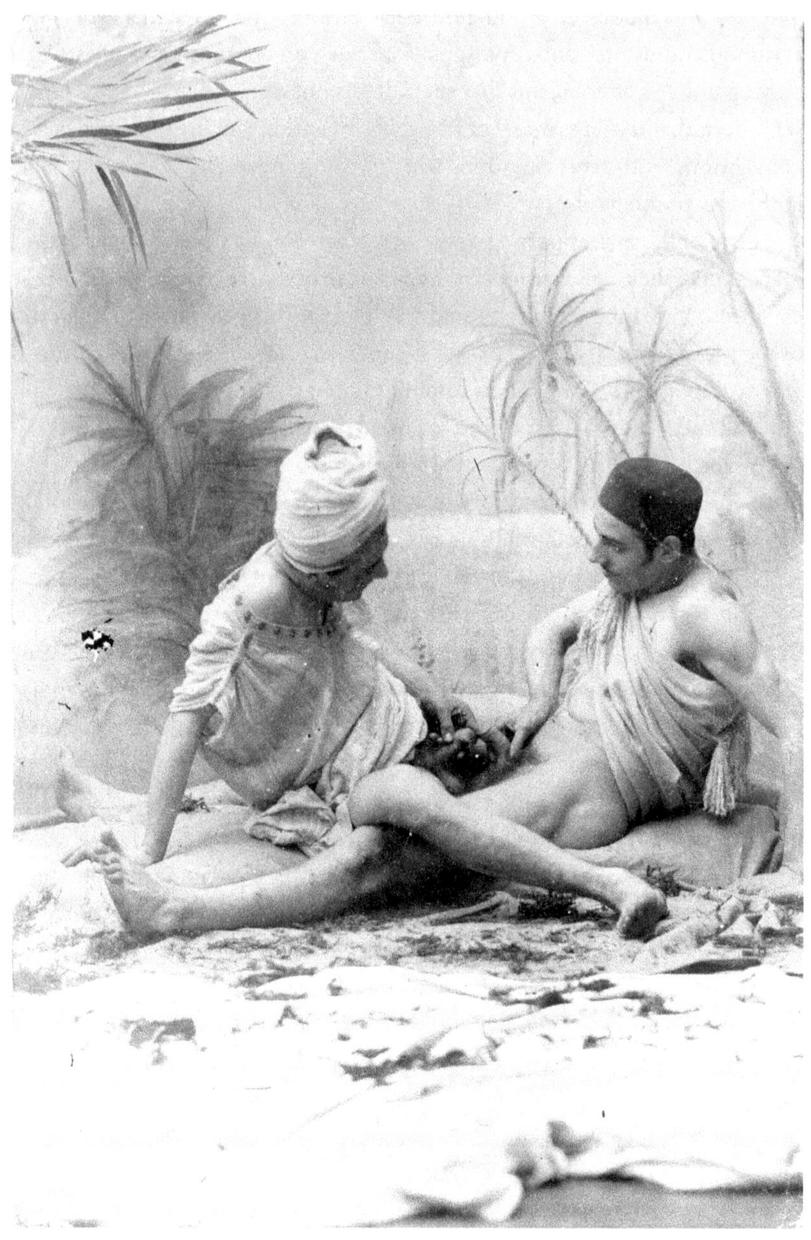

2.4 Unknown photographer, *Homosexual Male,* late nineteenth century. Albumen print. COURTESY OF THE KINSEY INSTITUTE FOR RESEARCH IN SEX, GENDER, AND REPRODUCTION (KI-HI: 44073).

the proliferation of "beaver shots" and the decline of those featuring simulated urination demonstrates the historicity of sexual practice, but so too does it affirm the persistence and durability of the aims and objects of fetishistic desire. Where the imagery of idealized, beautiful, and aestheticized femininity represents the disavowal of castration by transforming the feminine image into a fetish itself (a formation that Freud designated as "fetishistic scopophilia"), the imagery of "pornographized" femininity is characterized by a voyeuristic gaze that seeks to investigate, demystify, or degrade. Whence then the pleasure derived from viewing evidence of its fantasized castration? For Freud, the genitalia were not beautiful, they were frightening: "Probably no male human being is spared the fright of castration at the sight of a female genital."[20] In an interesting discussion of the paradox of this viewing contradiction, Paul Willemen proposed the coexistence of another kind of look: "Porn also often plays on a second, more reassuring type of looking which can quite easily coexist with the fetishistic look, although it is in some sense its inverse. It is less a disavowal of 'her' castration than a confirmation of the viewer's phallic power. This specular relation is dependent on the emphatic direct address interpellating the viewer as possessor and donor of the phallus, the one who is required to complete the picture, as it were."[21] But, as Willemen also points out, "In porn . . . it is the loss generated by the friction between the fantasy looked for and the fantasy displayed which sustains the desire for ever-promised and never-found gratification."[22] Similarly, and as Annette Kuhn remarks, "Whatever it does, pornography is, of course, exactly a commodity: it is produced and bought and sold. To the extent that porn participates in the disruptive potential of sexual passion, it is indeed dangerous merchandise. But in its attempt to articulate sexual fantasy through particular regimes of representation, pornography seeks, at the same time to contain those very qualities of fascination and disruption—in the process becoming literal, earnest, clinical. Porn is often, in consequence, profoundly disappointing to its consumers . . . there is always the hope, after all, that it can be assuaged by trying (and buying) again."[23]

But if the pornographic representation, despite itself, risks becoming clinical, even putatively scientific, ostensibly objective images of the female body are prone to erotic inscription, a consequence of the discursive associative train linking woman/sexual difference/body/eroticism. As Linda Williams has shown, Eadweard Muybridge's representations of the female body from his *Human Figure in Motion*, like von Gloeden's boys, need supplemental coding if they are to be intelligible. In her compelling discussion of these images, Williams frames her argument with Foucault's formulations about the relation of power

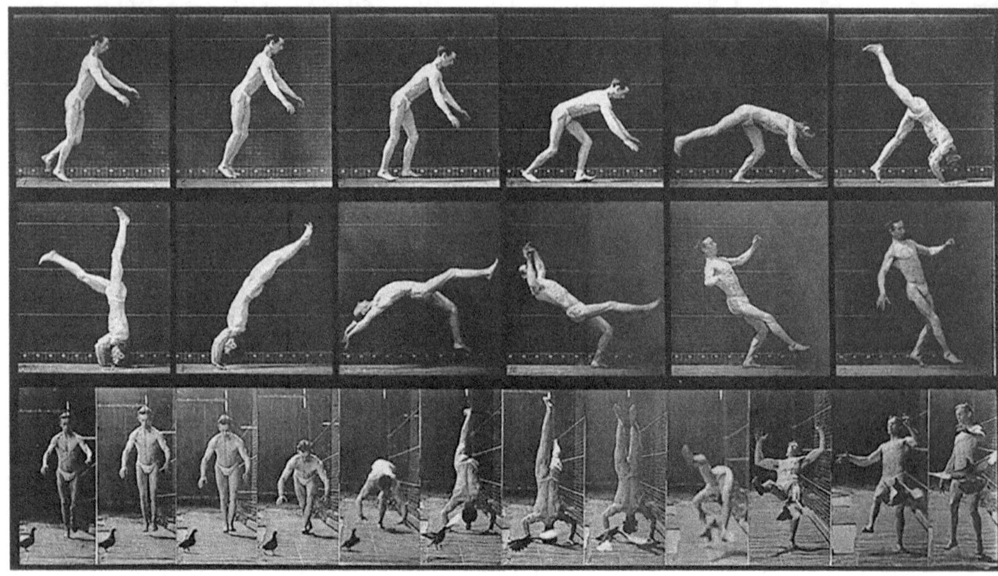

2.5 Eadweard Muybridge, *Head-Spring, a Flying Pigeon Interfering.* From *Animal Locomotion: An Electro-Photographic Investigation of Consecutive Phases of Animal Movements, 1872–1885*, vol. 9 (Philadelphia: University of Pennsylvania, 1887), plate 365. Collotype. 

to sexuality.[24] But equally important to her argument is the hypothesis that the female body "poses a problem of sexual difference which it then becomes the work of the incipient forms of narrative and *mise-en-scène* to overcome."[25]

Muybridge's *Human Figure* is divided into three categories: men, women, and children, photographed in a gridded progression of movement from simple to more complex motor activity (as many as forty-eight cameras were employed to register this movement; figs. 2.5 and 2.6). But it is specifically in the representation of the female nude that what Williams terms a "gratuitous fantasization and iconization of the women" occurs, securing, it would seem, what could be termed the "feminization" of the female body: "Some of the movements and gestures in the women's section—walking, running, jumping—parallel those of the men. Yet even here, there is a tendency to add a superfluous detail to the women's movements—details which tend to mark her as more embedded within a socially prescribed system of objects and gestures than her male counterparts."[26]

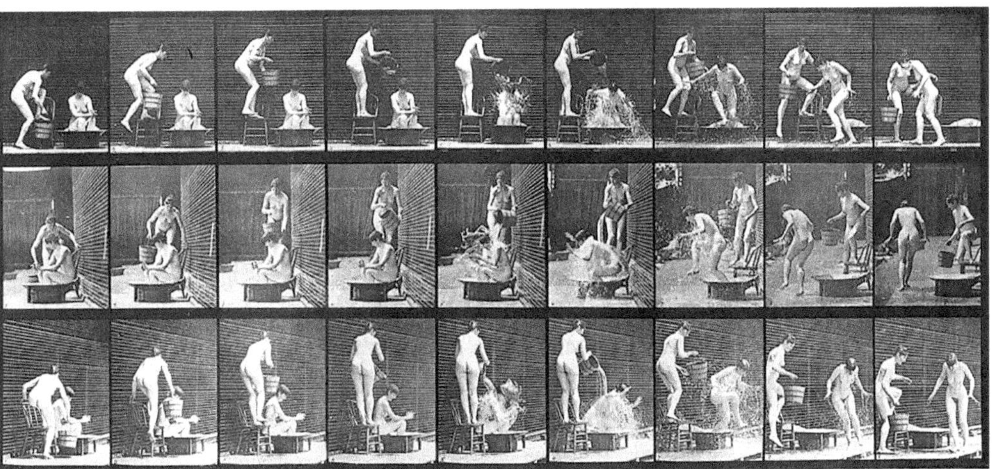

2.6 Eadweard Muybridge, *Animal Locomotion* (plate 408). From Muybridge, *Animal Locomotion: An Electro-Photographic Investigation of Consecutive Phases of Animal Movements, 1872–1885*, vol. 4 (Philadelphia: University of Pennsylvania, 1887), plate 408. Collotype. 

As the sequences unfold, the women are further inscribed within a narrativized framework. For example, when the female model lies down (as does the male model), she lies down in a hammock or in a bed; the woman is adorned with transparent wisps of fabric that accentuate her nudity; she dresses or undresses; in sequences that feature two women, they are engaged in enigmatic and subtly eroticized interactions altogether different from the hearty shared activity of two men. In some of the studies, one woman throws a bucket of water over another; in another, water is poured into a woman's mouth; in yet another, two women dance together. In another sequence, the movement of a running woman, hand over groin, arm shielding her face, suggests nothing so much as a woman unwillingly exposed, caught out in her vulnerable nakedness, fleeing the gaze that pursues her, a scenario that both intensifies the voyeurism of the look and underscores the sadism that may accompany voyeuristic scopophilia.

As Williams demonstrates, even when the ostensible purpose of the representation is a scientific and objective demonstration of the motor mechanisms of the body, the female body will be variously coded and inscribed in ways that signal not just its difference but its inherent erotic significance. This tendency is observable in anatomical texts going back to the sixteenth century, in wax museum models, even in the display of dermatological maladies made in the early twentieth century for the Hôpital Saint-Louis in Paris.[27] Moreover, this writing on the body, these processes of textualization and narrativization, should not be exclusively attributed to Muybridge-as-author but should be understood as culturally authored, as well as authorized. In both individual and collective manifestations, sexual difference is registered within all forms of cultural production and is one of the sites in which is it is socially and culturally produced. By virtue of its indexicality, its potent illusion of a reality produced by the camera, photography has been an indispensable purveyor of dominant ideologies (of gender, race, class, nation, and their subcategories). Notwithstanding the possibility of transformative readings, the mobility of spectatorial desire, the nonfixity of subject positions, the bisexuality of human subjectivity, and other salient factors, it is primarily within the arena of critical art practices—for example, Cindy Sherman's extraordinary work—that concepts of beauty and desire can be made objects of conscious and deliberate political analysis. Such practices are important not merely because they transform beauty from a given attribute or quality to a problem but because they understand desire to be no less problematic. To acknowledge the obdurate bedrock of the psyche, the unconscious, the dark continent of human subjectivity (not femininity) does not, by that token, absolve us of the political and ethical tasks of decipherment, demystification, and, ultimately, transformation.

# 3

## *The Family of Man*

### REFURBISHING HUMANISM FOR A POSTMODERN AGE

(2004)

By any practical reckoning, the 1955 exhibition *The Family of Man* organized by the then head of the photography department at the Museum of Modern Art, Edward Steichen, should be considered one of the most popular museum blockbusters ever mounted. Between its 1955 opening at MoMA and 1963, when the exhibition was "retired," it toured thirty-eight countries, within which it made ninety-one stops and was seen by nine million viewers. Initially bankrolled by the Rockefeller family to the tune of $100,000, and with corporate sponsors such as Coca-Cola, it then toured the world in four different versions under the aegis of the US Information Agency. A paradigm of Cold War "cultural diplomacy," it graced Guatemala City a bare four months after the US overthrow of the democratically elected Árbenz government, and memorably featured in Moscow in 1959 as part of the American National Exhibition, the site of the "kitchen debate" between Khrushchev and Nixon. As for the exhibition's accompanying catalogue, which reproduced almost all the photographs in the original exhibition,[1] it has never been out of print. Although the exhibition has been subject to devastating critiques—as photography exhibitions go, it is perhaps the ultimate "bad object" for progressives or critical theorists—its phenomenal success requires consideration for several reasons. Among them is the fact that since 1996, the exhibition has been reassembled as a permanent installation at the Château de Clervaux, a renovated castle just outside the city of Luxembourg, and has since become a major tourist attraction.[2] But if we are able retrospectively to account for its first success in terms of Cold War liberalism or the needs of American propaganda, or its reassuring humanist pieties, what explanatory framework should we look to now, post–Cold War, in the age of global corporate capitalism, when by all accounts the exhibition still exerts the same attraction for a great number of spectators? In this essay, therefore, I want to ask if nearly half a century since its inception, we might now approach this exhibition symptomatically, not simply on the level of the conscious intentions of the organizers and their institutions, but rather in terms of the unconscious of the exhibition and the cultural imaginary in which it was formed. Such a reconsideration of this monumental cultural production might consider the exhibition's structuring absences, for such an investigation may help to account for its success with its audience, at least in the United States. Second, albeit to a lesser extent, I want to consider the exhibition as a subsequent point of departure for other—that is to say, critical—art practices. For if *The Family of Man* is to be taken as a textbook example of hegemonic culture, or an example of Theodor W. Adorno's culture industry in action, then the other side of this characterization should include acknowledgment of those counter-practices that it subsequently provoked. To overlook the various contestations of this redoubtable humanist behemoth is to ignore the possibilities of opposition and critique, of parody or *détournement*, and while these may seem fragile and ephemeral, it is the fact of their existence that needs to be registered. In keeping, therefore, with this two-part agenda, I begin the first section of this essay with a question.

## American Triumph or American Trauma? How Should We Now Read *The Family of Man*?

I never saw the actual *The Family of Man* exhibition in its original installation in the Museum of Modern Art; like millions of others, I first encountered the exhibition through the catalogue. My second encounter with the exhibition was perhaps at least twenty years later, when I first read the essays by Roland Barthes assembled in the collection *Mythologies* in 1972. The essay in that collection, "La grande famille des hommes," originally published in 1956 after the exhibition had traveled to Paris, remains, forty years later, a small masterpiece of what might be called discursive deflation. With characteristic brevity and wit, Barthes gracefully dispatched the pious humanism exemplified by the exhibition, its catalogue, and its heuristic agenda. Among other things, his essay remarked on the religiosity that underpinned the show's conception:

> This myth functions in two stages: first the difference between human morphologies is asserted, exoticism is insistently stressed, the infinite vari-

> ations of the species, the diversity in skins, skulls and customs are made manifest, the image of Babel is complacently projected over that of the world. Then, from this pluralism, a type of unity is magically produced: man is born, works, laughs, and dies everywhere in the same way; and if there still remains in these actions some ethnic peculiarity, at least one hints that there is underlying each one an identical "nature," that their diversity is only formal and does not belie the existence of a common mold. Of course this means postulating a human essence, and here is God re-introduced into our Exhibition: the diversity of men proclaims his power, his richness; the unity of their gestures demonstrates his will.[3]

For those of us who intellectually came of age as postmodernists, poststructuralists, feminists, Marxists, antihumanists, or, for that matter, atheists, this little essay of Barthes's efficiently demonstrated the problem—indeed the bad faith—of sentimental humanism, and all that the exhibition represented ideologically, no less than photographically, could be consigned to the same media dustbin as *Life* magazines from the 1950s, or Norman Rockwell's *Saturday Evening Post* covers. Mutatis mutandis, however, on the cusp of the new millennium, we have now had a major touring show organized by the Guggenheim Museum (no less) of the art of Norman Rockwell and, since 1993, and the permanent reinstallation of *The Family of Man* in the Château de Clervaux. Which suggests that there is no such thing as a media dustbin but rather an ever-resurrected or refurbished repertoire of tropes of American mass culture, one of the few major export items of the American imperium.

In all candor, I was not initially convinced that there was much left to say about the exhibition that had not been brilliantly said by Barthes, or by scholars and critics such as Eric Sandeen and Allen Sekula, until I read Viktoria Schmidt-Linsenhoff's fine essay "Die Banalität des Guten," which demonstrates that there is indeed much more to be said if one asks different questions and hazards different kinds of analytic stratagems.[4] For Schmidt-Linsenhoff, the repressions of the exhibition are its most significant feature. Insofar as she takes the Shoah—and her use of the Hebrew term is implicitly part of her argument—as the defining event of the twentieth century, *The Family of Man*'s avoidance of the subject is, she remarks, a kind of apotropaic and indeed defining gesture. As she further asserts, to acknowledge not just the magnitude of the genocide in World War II but also its fundamentally modern, bureaucratized, and industrialized character would be to give the lie precisely to those reassuring pieties about the essential goodness of man that the exhibition tendentiously labors to produce. To re-present and thus acknowledge charnel heaps of anonymous and desecrated bodies would have raised questions about death being a universal fact of life, consecrated with ritual, and dignified in its acknowledgment of the worth of an individual life. To Schmidt-Lisenhoff's inventory of the exhibition's repressed, I would add much else of recent world history. Hiroshima and Nagasaki are represented emblematically by the photograph of the atomic mushroom cloud (excluded from the catalogue), a photograph Schmidt-Linsenhoff characterizes as having become something of a naturalized icon of the sublime. Here we might note that the second of the two pictures dealing with the subject—the little Japanese boy from Nagasaki—like so many of the photographs in the exhibition, was cropped from a larger one. The original, one of a suite of pictures taken by Yoshito Matsushige, who survived the blast, actually depicts the boy's mother, splattered with blood, holding the hand of the boy. Both mother and child hold rice balls, the emergency rations distributed by the authorities. In fact, as is the case with most captionless pictures, and given the grainy and often murky quality of the original catalogue's halftone reproductions, there is no way to grasp that this is a postatomic bombing document, an ambiguity that was clearly intentional. (Lesson one of *The Family of Man*, therefore, is yet another demonstration of the infinite pliability of photographic meaning, a pliability that Steichen expertly orchestrated to produce the exhibition's upbeat message).

Schmidt-Linsenhoff's arguments are especially interesting because, critically speaking, the exhibition has long been considered a statement of American postwar triumphalism rather than a symptom of its repressed anxieties. To revisit Cold War cultural spectacles through the lens, as it were, of trauma theory, is an interesting and timely endeavor. We must consider, however, *where* to locate the signs of trauma, which in turn raises the question of the authorship of the exhibition. Where is the "origin" of *The Family of Man*'s repressed? Is it to be situated in the sociocultural imaginary of Steichen himself, of the picture press, or of Cold War America?

As a number of commentators have pointed out, *The Family of Man* is in all its parts quintessentially an American production. Not merely because Steichen was himself a naturalized American; not because the vast majority of the exhibited photographs were taken by Americans and had already been reproduced in American magazines in great numbers; not merely because it was the Museum of Modern Art that furnished its initial venue; and not even because the show was underwritten by Nelson Rockefeller and swiftly purchased by the US Information Agency—a sibling of the CIA—in four identical versions for global circulation.[5] While all of these are certainly elements of the exhibition's unmistakable "Americaness," and indicate the exhibition's manifest utility in Cold War cultural politics, the aspects of the show that most forcefully demonstrate its national character are its religiosity (although of an ecumenical variety), its paternalism (not to say patriarchalism), and its conception of the (more or less) nuclear family as a foundational, universal, and benevolent institution. To these bedrock American convictions—still very much part of American official culture—we should also consider as part of its characteristic "Americaness" its blithe elisions of the political, the economic, and the ideological (which is not to say, *pace* Barthes, that it isn't all the more ideologically invested for that). In keeping with this triumphalist characterization, one might further observe that the United States, as World War II's global winner par excellence, had the money and the resources to mount such an extravaganza in the first place, as few other countries were in a position to do. And insofar as the exhibition posited a basically harmonious worldview unriven by any essential difference, its universalist agenda has been likened to Henry Luce's conception of the American Century, which, like the Pax Romana, intended to enfold the world's peoples in its civilizing arms. If one accepts the triumphalist thesis, we are able to make some sense of the exhibition's resurrection in Luxembourg in the early 1990s. In this respect, the definitive collapse of the Soviet Union and the near-global victory of corporate capitalism is an apposite moment to once again celebrate a model of universality that reinforces Western bourgeois values and ideologies. And what more appropriate site than Luxembourg, a world banking center with a small, well-to-do population of half a million, almost homogeneously white, 97 percent Catholic, whose "others" consist principally of Portuguese and Italians? Which is to say that one might suggest that humanism refurbished for a postmodern age has more in common with a Benetton advertisement than with, for example, the earnest if naive beliefs of Magnum photographers in the 1940s.

Contrary, however, to this triumphalist reading, Schmidt-Lisenhoff's perception that the exhibition is an anxiety-management machine is extremely suggestive. Antipositivist in her methodology, and informed by her sense of what she calls the "fractures of modernity," Schmidt-Lisenhoff, like the attentive psychoanalyst, is concerned with tracking the symptom of the trauma via the signs of its repression.[6] In this respect, we might recall the arguments of Guy Debord, who, in his still-indispensable study *The Society of the Spectacle,* argued that in modern times, an excess of display has the effect of concealing the truth of the society that produces it, providing the viewer with an unending stream of images detached from any mooring in material or historical reality. Moreover, and as Peter Wollen observed, such an image display "condemn[s] the viewer to a world in which we can see everything, but understand nothing. . . . The world of the spectacle is an imaginary world, offering transient and illusory satisfactions, while thereby denying access through the signifier to cure or truth."[7] But, as Wollen continues,

> Display, however, when its flow is arrested, can still have a revelatory power, provided it is seen, not in terms of the image, but in terms of the symptom. In fact, it is only through display that the truth is revealed—not, of course, directly, but obliquely and *en travesti.* It is through modes of display that regimes of all sorts reveal the truths they mean to conceal. Above all, it is necessary to place the myriad contemporary forms of display in a historical context. The main effect of the interminable transience of modern spectacle, as Debord noted, is to efface history and historical understanding. Each historic period has its own rhetorical mode of display, because each has different truths to conceal.[8]

So what might be some of the hidden truths of *The Family of Man,* besides, as Schmidt-Linsenhoff argues, the traumatic fact of the Holocaust and the need to deny its implications? As I have indicated, part of the difficulty of such an interrogatory enterprise is the question of where and how to locate the sites of agency and meaning, including repressed meaning, if these are not to be identified with the nominal "author" and his or her ostensible intentions, psychology, and biases. Which is to say that in the case of an exhibition and catalogue such as *The Family of Man,* although it is unquestionably the "work" of Steichen—his concept, his orchestration of the project, his final say on the selection of pictures, texts, lighting, and design—by its very nature, both exhibition and catalogue are root and branch collective entities. In other words, as cultural artifacts, both exhibition and catalogue, require a kind of analysis associated more with critical readings of film or theater than with individual productions, be they visual or textual. In searching, therefore, for the latent as well as the manifest meanings of *The Family of Man,* I wish to both "arrest the flow" as Wollen suggests, and consider, as Schmidt-Lisenhoff has done, the implications of what has been repressed—the structuring absences that shape the exhibition.

To begin with, we should at once dispense with any illusion that the 503 photographs from sixty-eight countries represent some sort of wide-ranging sample of world photography, as Steichen claimed and as many later commentators have reiterated. By my count, of the 503 photographs, the vast majority were culled either from photo agencies or from the files of the American illustrated press. Thus, of the established photo agencies, Magnum overwhelmingly leads the list, with forty-three photographs, followed by four other agencies.[9] From the American picture press, no less than seventy-three pictures came from the *Life* magazine files. No other magazine remotely approached the same number; and combined with the agencies, this is approximately 35 percent of *The Family of Man*. Of the remaining 65 percent, seven came from the Farm Security Administration (FSA) files, and nine from other governmental, corporate, or United Nations sources. There were only two anonymous photographs in the entire exhibition; one depicting Jews marched out of the Warsaw ghetto (the only image of the Holocaust, but neither place nor date given) and a photograph of a man throwing stones at a tank, also without identification. Still another important source was those photographs made by well-known photographers not represented by photo agencies and whose selected pictures had not been previously reproduced. Steichen himself was modestly represented by five photos, but the photographer who had the greatest number of pictures in the exhibition—thirteen—was Wayne Miller, Steichen's principle assistant for the project. All other photographers—a fifth of the show—were represented by a single picture.

In compiling this numerical breakdown—an extremely boring task, I might add—I found only two surprises. One surprise was the large number of women photographers selected for the show—forty by my count, which is probably more than one finds nowadays in most large group exhibitions. While this might be thought to reflect Steichen's openness to women photographers, it might also be because the exhibition features large numbers of photographs of children, and, in fact, certain women photographers, Suzanne Szsaz, for example, specialized in this subject. The other surprise was the great preponderance of already-reproduced photographs and pictures from agency files—far more than one would have expected given the "open call" process Steichen initially used to acquire his images. This is significant because in the descriptions of the planning and the picture research that preceded the actual exhibition by three years, all the published accounts emphasize Steichen's desire to have all kinds of photographs represented (including those by amateurs), as well as the absolutely staggering number of photographs that passed through Steichen's and Miller's hands. According to Miller, for example, of the two million photographs officially logged in, the first culling left 10,000, which over the course of the following two years was ultimately winnowed to the final 503.[10]

Returning to my proportional breakdown of the picture sources, the question then becomes, why did Steichen and his assistants need to trawl through two million pictures when, in the final exhibition, more than a third could have been gotten with a subway ride from Steichen's office to the offices of *Time/Life*, Magnum, and the other magazines and agencies? Cronyism aside (and it would be naive to discount this as a factor; think here of Wayne Miller's thirteen pictures), my point here is not to do with bad faith in the selection process. Rather, what I want to suggest is that if Steichen and his colleagues ended up with so many photographs that had already been, so to speak, processed for the American mass media, it was because in a very profound sense, Steichen found there what he was really looking for.

What was Steichen looking for? One way to approach this question is by enumerating what subjects he was certainly not looking for. These include any pictures that might be read at the time as having a *parti pris*. Strikes, protest actions, Ban-the-Bomb demonstrations, civil strife itself (as opposed to warfare) was scrupulously avoided. In this respect, much of the subject matter of photojournalism from the daily press was ruled out of court, as opposed to other kinds of imagery. To the extent that the "political" is in any way explicitly denoted in *The Family of Man*, it is limited to a couple of pictures of the United Nations, or the act of voting. Insofar as this sequence of images depicting people of various nationalities putting ballots in boxes (including Communist China), we may recall that it is a deeply entrenched article of belief in American culture that the act of putting a ballot in a box is equivalent to democratic process. With respect to racial issues, there is not a single interracial couple (or group) in evidence. Indeed, the only picture of black and white subjects together are in both senses of the word "innocented," as Barthes might say, by virtue of their youth. American people of color are for the most part represented in relation to what passes in the exhibition for the erotic or, even more predictable in terms of racial stereotyping, engaged in dancing or playing jazz. Significantly too, with the exception of a troubled-looking South African man, presumably meant to symbolize racial oppression there, pictures of African subjects invariably represent them as primitives—naked or scantily clothed, outside of civilization and modernity, akin, it would appear, to nature itself.

Excluded as well were works by photographers whose "vision" was presumably considered too personal, too quirky, too arty, or too downbeat to pass muster. Thus, photographers like Diane Arbus are represented by one entirely uncharacteristic picture, or, in the case of Robert Frank, by pictures that did not overtly declare themselves either stylistically or affectively as representative of his dystopic vision of 1950s America.

Returning again to my question about Steichen's search and its successful resolution, I want to suggest that what constitutes the explicitly ideological co-ordinates of *The Family of Man* involves, just as Louis Althusser so mordantly described, an overdetermined act of recognition: "That's obvious! That's right! That's true!"[11] This is reality speaking itself. Thus, as Edward Steichen and his assistant Wayne Miller burrowed through the accumulated hundreds of thousands of agency and magazine photographs, what did they find? They found, for example, that men do men's work and women do women's work. Men's work is heroic, physical, about building and making. Women's work, needless to say, is about washing up and childcare. Exceptions, when they occur, are blandly "negative": the dowdy woman typist, the mindless labor of assembly line production (as schematically rendered in Gjon Mili's motion studies). These are pointedly opposed to the presumed dignity of manual labor. Overwhelmingly, however, Steichen and Miller found, or rather, as they intended to find, a world based on the unit of the heterosexual couple.[12] Moreover, it also turns out that, with a single exception, the man is always positioned to appear taller than the woman (doubtless a subliminal preference). Steichen and Miller selected photographs that with respect to American life, confirmed the old-time virtues, exemplified in the folkloric community of the rural general store. They found, in short, what the American consciousness industry had been assiduously purveying as the very fodder of America's mythic self-representation. In other words, their task exemplified what Walter Benjamin, quoting Bertolt Brecht, observed about German cultural production in 1936: "The lack of clarity about their situation that prevails among musicians, writers and critics," he wrote, "has immense consequences that are far too little considered. For, thinking that they are in possession of an apparatus that in reality possesses them, they defend an apparatus over which they no longer have any control and that is no longer, as they still believe, a means for the producers, but has become a means against the producers."[13]

In fact, "thinking that they are in possession of an apparatus that in reality possesses them" might well be taken as the definitive description of the situation of those photographers, both professional photojournalists and photographers tout court who felt that the exhibition misrepresented them, irresponsibly decontextualized their work, or, in the case of the various croppings or collage-like organization, subordinated their respective "statements" to the overweening requirements of the exhibition's message. But even more broadly, the ways in which mass media photography is routinely employed, in Steichen's time or our own, makes nonsense of the aspirations of commercially employed photographers to control the meaning of their own work. In this respect, it is worth remarking that some of the negative criticism of *The Family of Man* can be characterized as aesthetically conservative (photographically speaking) insofar as it reflects an ultimately idealist conception of photographic usages based on authorial intention, integrity, and the primacy of personal "vision." What appears therefore superficially to be Steichen's (or his team's) choice of image to purvey his message is, as I am suggesting, an entirely overdetermined encounter.

## People Are People (the World Over)

Defending *The Family of Man* from its present-day critics, numerous commentators have remarked that the exhibition needs to be understood in the context of its own time. Such a rationalization effectively dismantles the exhibition's own claims to universality and its positing of eternal verities and values. That said, I want to examine a bit more closely what might be at stake in the exhibition's own time, as well as in ours, insofar as I am concerned here with the reasons for its current rehabilitation and resurrection. If we take "its own time" to mean the period of its practical initiation, planning, organization, and completion, then we are looking at the United States in the years 1953–55. However, as we know from various memoirs and documentation, many of the concepts shaping the exhibition, both formal and practical, as well as its ideological starting points, must be located earlier and, furthermore, must be considered in relation to its governing institutions. For example, as Christopher Phillips has documented, the Museum of Modern Art was concerned to develop greater support for its relatively new photography department, and, concomitantly, to respond to the hostile criticism of the photographic press that claimed to represent the millions of American amateur photographers.[14] As Phillips describes it, under the modernist aesthetic regime of Beaumont Newhall, Steichen's predecessor, "the department was called 'snobbish,' 'pontifical,' and accused of being shrouded in 'esoteric fogs.'"[15]

In this sense, the populist orientation of Steichen's shows, from the beginning of his tenure as the department's director in 1947, was itself institutionally determined. Newhall, after all, had been fired for his indifference to populist and popular requirements. From the start of his directorship, Steichen was variously allied to the former Bauhaus artist/designer Herbert Bayer, for Bayer's influence on the mechanisms of display is very much in evidence in the design of *The Family of Man*. Bayer's importance in the design of Steichen's exhibitions in turn leads backward to the landmark exhibitions of El Lissitzky (for example, the Soviet Pavilion in Dresden in 1930) as well as to various Bauhaus exhibition designs. Writing in 1939, Bayer described his idea of the modern exhibition in the following terms: "[it] should not retain its distance from the spectator, it should be brought close to him, penetrate and leave an impression on him, should explain, demonstrate, and even persuade and lead him to a planned and direct reaction. Therefore, we may say that the exhibition design runs parallel with the psychology of advertising."[16]

This insight informed Bayer's first collaboration with Steichen, the 1942 MoMA show *The Road to Victory*, and reached its culmination with *The Family of Man*. As designed by Bayer, *The Road to Victory* departed in every way from the previous photography exhibitions organized by Newhall: "Spectators were guided along a twisting path of enormous, freestanding enlargements of documentary photographs—some as large as ten by forty feet."[17] With its dramatic enlargements, texts, narrative chains, abutments, theatrical lighting, and so forth, *The Road to Victory* was a crucial precedent for *The Family of Man*, and given Bayer's role in the design, connects both shows genealogically to those innovative and avant-gardist design practices that had emerged in the 1920s.

A more recent influence, but one with important resemblances to American propaganda of the war years was a series of picture essays that appeared in *The Ladies Home Journal* in the 1940s. Titled "People are People the World Over," under the direction of the picture editor John Morris, these picture stories debuted in 1948. Professing to illustrate the shared humanity of people from fifteen different countries (including the USSR), these were undoubtedly an influence on Steichen's later conception of *The Family of Man*, as were the structure and narrative tactics of the illustrated magazine picture essay itself. Finally, much of the copious imagery of women, children, and babies was either literally from, or prompted by, a projected book by Wayne Miller on the family that he had been commissioned to produce.

Allan Sekula has written of the primacy of the figure of the father in the exhibition, and its ideological work within the exhibition as a whole. As Marc-Emmanuel Melon has glossed Sekula's analysis, these photographs of fathers teaching their sons to hunt, do gymnastics, play the clarinet, and so forth, occupy a highly significant role for several reasons: "What can a father teach if not the flower of his country's culture? . . . The place of the father in the photos of the family at the heart of the exhibition is not innocent: "Always in the background, standing, the head subtly higher than those of the wives, mothers or children. The Father, he is the summit of the pyramid, the source of life, the existential heart of the family nucleus, of society, of nation, of the great family of men."[18]

Sekula's and Melon's acknowledgment of the centrality of the patriarch marks an element that provides a point of entry into the issue of the unconscious of the exhibition, that aspect of Wollen's "rhetorical mode of display that has a truth to conceal." In this respect, it has often been the case that critics of the exhibition, particularly in Europe, have had a tendency to assume that the ideologies expressed therein—be they familial, political, or sexual—are to be understood as reflections, however idealized, of the American reality of the 1950s. Thus, the gender ideology, so relentlessly deployed in the pictures is often read as "reflecting" the suburban nuclear family, crowned, as Melon remarks, with the patriarch at the apex of the pyramid. As it happens, however, the postwar period in America has been characterized, alternatively, as a chapter in the recurrent saga of afflicted manhood, signaling what various theorists have identified as a crisis of masculinity.[19] For what was at stake in this period was not merely the practical tasks of demobilization—tasks at once economic, social and cultural—but a form of domestication of postwar manhood by which the martial values of the war were transformed into the far more passive ones of wage-earning, sexually monogamous, family-oriented, mortgage-paying and dutifully consumer goods–purchasing "responsible" husbandhood and fatherhood. Such a restructuration of the definition of ideal manhood was not without its costs, and certainly not without its contradictions. The manifestations of this crisis in masculinity are everywhere to be seen in 1950s America. Whether symptomatized in Hollywood scenarios of castration from *The Best Years of our Lives* to *The Incredible Shrinking Man*, or variously diagnosed in the spate of bestsellers such as Philip Wylie's *A Generation of Vipers* (which coined the term "Momism" to define a world in which voracious wives and mothers devoured their husbands and sons), or William Whyte's *The Organization Man*, or David Riesman's *The Lonely Crowd*—these and many others articulated a pervasive dis-ease about what it meant to be manly in the world of postwar America.[20] It would thus seem justified to look at the exhibition's Edenic representation of the patriarch and the patriarchal family as compensatory, warding off the anxieties of demobilized and variously traumatized masculinity. In all these respects, *The Family of Man* represents precisely what is meant by a collective production, meaning that it is the American mass media in general, as much as the dictates of MoMA or the personal preferences of Steichen and his team, that determined the contents, both manifest and latent, of the exhibition and its catalogue. The question remains how one is to get at the structuring repressions, the truth that is to be grasped, as Wollen says, *en travesti*. It is here I would suggest that we might consider not only the nature of what the exhibition does not show, but consider as well several of its strange and anomalous inclusions as indices of anxieties that are both unspoken or otherwise acknowledged.

Consider, for example the oddness of the inclusion among the dozens of photos of children, of Lewis Carroll's 1863 photograph of a flower-crowned adolescent girl. There are in fact relatively few pictures of adolescents in the exhibition as a whole, although children and babies abound. This lacuna is noteworthy because it was in the United States, and especially in the postwar period, that the "teenager" was definitively invented. The teenager, moreover, was a conception of a particular stage in life that appears to have been accompanied by considerable ambivalence and anxiety, especially with regard to its threat of precocious, unlicensed sexuality. The decade that generated powerful anxieties about the "bad girl," the girl "in trouble," not to mention the social danger of the juvenile delinquent, might be said, therefore, to find its antithesis in the image of virginal Victorian girlhood innocence. Why else include one of the only two nineteenth-century pictures in the exhibition? In other words, this archaic "renegade" photograph fulfills the function, presumably unconsciously, of establishing a mythic innocence of female adolescence, a counterpoint to the "primitive" adolescent boys learning to hunt with their fathers. Similarly, the single other nineteenth-century photo, that of the dead Civil War soldier, photographed by one of Mathew Brady's team (probably Timothy O'Sullivan), operates to assuage another kind of anxiety, as does the pendant photo of a dead Korean war soldier. Both bodies are intact, both facing down, neither is especially violent or disturbing. In this respect, and like most of the imagery of warfare in *The Family of Man*, the Civil War soldier helps construct an individualistic and effectively "timeless" conception of war in which, to use the insistently androcentric language of the show, Man is pitted against Man. In fact, and as Steichen was extremely well placed to know, modern warfare had become mechanized, increasingly impersonal, and needless to say, increasingly waged against civilian populations, as the bombings of Dresden, Hamburg, Tokyo, Hiroshima, and Nagasaki so clearly demonstrated. Again, I would suggest that what is being kept at bay, like the memory of the Holocaust itself, is an uncongenial reality that subverts the humanist perspective that the exhibition sought to impose even upon war itself. The intactness of the body, the absence of blood or visible wounds, creates an effect that is elegiac, melancholy, but neither horrific nor traumatic. As such, war itself can be enfolded within a reassuring category of "humanity,"—even in its conflicts, an aggregate of individual human beings. In this respect, Schmidt-Linsenhoff's perception that the exhibition's unconscious raison d'être is its denial of the Holocaust might be broadened to include the new reality of global war, and war waged against civilian populaces.

What about the presence of the Farm Security Photographs, US government–commissioned pictures taken during the Great Depression for propaganda purposes? Exemplified by Dorothea Lange's *Migrant Mother* (already iconic in 1956), or her *Damaged Child*, the FSA pictures are among the only ones to depict American poverty. It is as though poverty itself was a timeless category, or perhaps an outmoded historical one, as though both rural and urban poverty in contemporary America did not exist in the present and the imagery of want, hunger, or desolation could be presented only in a way that denied its contemporary rural or urban presence. This representational "pastness" of American poverty is thus another form of travesty, repressing its well-documented existence in the historical present.

If *The Family of Man* operated in 1950s America as a way to elide or manage traumas and crises ranging from the Holocaust to the dislocations of postwar masculinity, what accounts for its extravagant refurbishment in the midst of Luxembourg? In this context, and flash forwarding to the 1990s, one might consider the ways that "humanity," in its diversity, is now figured in the contemporary image world, and it should come as no surprise to observe that this representational work is now performed almost exclusively by advertising. It is, after all, not such a great leap from the humanist pieties of *The Family of Man* to Benetton's, Nike's, or IBM's vision of a multicultural and harmonious family of consumers. Notwithstanding the specifics of how *The Family of Man* ended up in Luxembourg (Steichen was not only a native son, but evidently one of the few Luxembourgers who became famous) it would appear that the exhibition can now stand for a kind of advertisement of "diversity" itself, a diversity largely absent from the principality Luxembourg, haven for international banking. The exhibition must thus be understood as performing a very different kind of work in the present than it did in the 1950s. For what is now at stake is a kind of Benetton ad—an image—of Luxembourg which thereby advertises its liberalism and ecumenicism, just as Toscani's photographs for Benetton bespeaks the ecstatic multiculturalism of pullovers and chinos, a world united under the all-embracing sign of the commodity fetish.

It should, however, be evident that the history of this exhibition includes not just the original version, its successors, and its most recent avatar in Luxembourg. On the contrary, the history of the exhibition should also include the history of its critiques and its contestations, and should take cognizance of the critical practices or the interventions of artists and curators. In this respect, it is worth mentioning at least a few of these, insofar as they produce forms of critique that in some cases produce their own commentaries on the nature of such exhibition practices themselves.

In 1985, for example, Marvin Heifferman, a freelance photography curator, designed for PS1 in New York (an alternative space for exhibitions, now an outpost of MoMA) a "sequel" exhibition titled *The Family of Man 1955–1984*. As a counter-exhibition, Heifferman's project operated on several registers, all making reference to the formal and ideological elements constituting the original show. Steichen's exhibition had been elaborately designed and organized to secure a certain narrative progression, to foster a particular trajectory for the spectator, and by way of dramatic discrepancies in scale and viewing position, to enfold the spectator in a quasi-cinematic environment. Heifferman's organization was itself a comment on the structure of the spectacle. Here, the viewer was confronted with a Baudrillardian delirium, an explosive and multicolored riot of hundreds upon hundreds of tear sheets clipped from magazines, advertisements, and newspapers, punctuated by the occasional photograph made by an artist or art photographer. These pictures and advertisements, pinned to the walls from floor to ceiling, rejected all notions of exhibition "design" and the narrative structure that the original exhibition's design entailed. Professing to re-examine the "great themes" of the previous show—children, love, marriage, war, old age, and death—these were illustrated by a grab bag of imagery and publicity ranging from baby food and sanitary napkin boxes to hard-core pornography, from detergent boxes to fashion photography, a cornucopia of consumer culture much of which, in one way or another, could be seen to engage the same themes purveyed in *The Family of Man*. In a certain sense, Heifferman's riposte to Steichen's show made the useful connection between the spectacle of the exhibition and the spectacle of the commodity, suggesting that both must be understood within the framing context of late capitalism. In its indiscriminate if ironic paean to consumption, in its glut and excess, in its "ecstasy of communication," Heifferman's revisionary exhibition operated as a kind of homeopathic antidote to all that the original *The Family of Man* exhibition sought to celebrate.

In 1988, Mark Lewis, a Canadian artist, produced a work that took its cue not only from *The Family of Man* but from the ongoing Benetton ad campaign as well. Alluding to the architectural structure of a bus kiosk, the three-paneled multimedia work, titled *We Are the World/White Noise*, bore the legend "We Are the World/You Are the Third World" on the middle panel, with a Parsi translation on the left, and a Korean one on the right. Each panel, framed respectively in red, white, and blue, used the format of *The Family of Man*'s original catalogue cover as its formal matrix, the central part of each panel consisting of a collage of male models from men's fashion ads on both the left and right panels, and, in the center, Benetton-type pictures of "exotic" women. In the gallery installation, a pump behind each panel exuded an industrial imitation of an expensive perfume ("Giorgio"); the air itself thereby permeated with the commodity form. Like "White Noise" itself, the perfume is at once perceptible and part of the larger environment, analogous to commodity culture itself—the air we breathe. The work's legend, no less than the formal references to the original exhibition, makes very clear who is the "we" and who is the "you," who is the "one," and who is the "other."

Although Lewis's *We Are the World/White Noise* is more specifically concerned with the power of the commodity sign, the work resonates directly with parallel critiques of *The Family of Man* by other commentators. As Allan Sekula succinctly observed in 1986, "The peaceful world envisioned by *The Family of Man* is merely a smoothly functioning market economy, in which economic bonds have been translated into spurious sentimental ties, and in which the overt racism appropriate to earlier forms of colonial enterprise has been supplanted into the humanization of the other so central to the discourse of neocolonialism."[21]

Thus, Lewis's legend on each of the panels, "We Are the World/You Are the Third World" (a reference to the Coca-Cola ad, "We are the world"), makes clear that in reality, it is the West that continues to be epistemologically as well as economically and culturally dominant. Moreover, and as Irit Rogoff observed in relation to *The Family of Man*, "A representation of a system of knowledge underpinned by nationalism, sustained by the regulating bureaucracies of the international agencies of the U.N., viewed through the tropes of ethnographic, documentary photography. All of which had been made possible through a traditional assumption which to quote [J. M.] Blaut's 'Colonizer's Version of the World' is grounded in 'the unique historical advantage of the West—the West makes history, it advances, progresses, the rest of the world keeps up or it stagnates.'"[22]

Rogoff's essay is reproduced in the catalogue of an exhibition organized in Berlin in 1996 titled *Family Nation Tribe Community* under the aegis of the collective SHIFT. Here too was a counter-exhibition that took its cue from *The Family of Man,* and many of the artists who produced work for the show, or the critics and curators who contributed essays to the catalogue, were at pains to expose, via their own critical practices, the mystifications, elisions, and ideology of the latter. Thus, Christian Philipp Müller, to take one example, reproduced an ensemble of seven black-and-white photographs of Austrian subjects, some blown up to billboard size, and including as well a number of glass display cases containing traditional Austrian costumes and other artifacts, collectively titled *The Family of the Austrians.*[23] The shift from universal to particular is given an added edge by Müller's choice of nationality, but it must also be said that the invocation of "family" as a nationalist or ethnic designation reminds us of its exclusive or exclusionist mechanisms.

In a rather different vein (but, like Müller, responding to the provocation of the original show) was Loring McAlpin's *Family of Mine.* Using family snaps of his ancestral relations, including John D. and Nelson Rockefeller, and his father David McAlpin, and citing some of the gnomic wisdom of the exhibition's epigraphic *pensées,* McAlpin contrived a kind of gloss on Barthes's observation in his 1956 essay that the greatest mystification of *The Family of Man* was its collapse of history into nature: "Tout ici, contenu et photogénie des images, discours qui les justifie, vise à supprimer le poids déterminant de l'Histoire: nous sommes retenus à la surface d'une identité, empêchés par la sentimentalité même de pénétrer dans cette zone ultérieure des conduits humaines, là où l'aliénation historique introduit de ces 'différences' que nous appellerons tout simplement ici des 'injustices.'"[24]

These are necessarily a cursory, if not a random retrospective view of some of the counter-practices that have found in the original 1955 exhibition an object that is, to borrow Clifford Geertz's formulation, "good to think with." In so doing, and in taking the exhibition as their point of departure, these artists have attempted to make visible the ethical and political problems that inhere in its very conception.

If we speak today of the significance in refurbishing and resurrecting *The Family of Man* and the sentimental humanism it exemplifies, we are ethically compelled to examine and investigate what it masks. Does not the celebration of a specious universalism of "Man" deny those real differences that even as we speak are shaping the world, be it for the better (as in de-colonization, or emancipatory movements like feminism, which is itself about the politics of difference) or, in most other cases, for the worse? Have we not by now learned that the universalist notion of "Man" is a figure of exclusion and repression? Does not a specious universalism, as implied in the Benetton ads, mask the challenge, indeed the perceived threat, of multicultural societies (whichever one we live in) that confront us all with the heterodox, the heterogeneous, the complex, and the contradictory? Finally, does not the nostalgia that is an inevitable component of sentimental humanism actively function to imply that there is, after all, a "natural" place for women, for people of color, for children? All of which is to say that the decryption of *The Family of Man* operates in a double sense: in the literal sense of its emergence from the crypt—physically removed from storage, restored, and placed in elaborate museological display—but also decrypted in the sense of decoded, indeed actively deconstructed. Even if in the face of the platitudes and the "family values" of the exhibition, one feels that from our own contemporary reality something has been lost (and any real sense of the past must be about loss), there are other losses about which one can only say they are well worth losing.

# 4

## Torture at Abu Ghraib

IN AND OUT OF THE MEDIA

(2007)

### Abu Ghraib: The Movie

When the histories of the ongoing catastrophic and illegal war in Iraq are written, one blip in its general unfolding will be remembered, and that will be the widespread dissemination of pictures of torture made by the torturers themselves.[1] Although previous wars, beginning with the American Civil War, have generated their own photographic archives, the US war in Iraq has produced a quite singular one. I refer to the photographs and videos made in Abu Ghraib prison and released by the media on April 27, 2004.

Torture is not new, but its detailed photographic representation is shockingly, stunningly new. A sixteenth-century woodcut illustrating the practice of what is now called waterboarding is one such example, taken from a legal codex (fig. 4.1).

But few would have imagined that when pictures were released of American soldiers torturing their prisoners, many of these would resemble nothing so much as homemade pornography.[2] For the eroticization of domination and submission that is a staple feature of the pornographic (while in no way limited to it) has rarely if ever been so explicitly demonstrated. Among other things, the Abu Ghraib visual archive is a collective portrait of a group of American reservists, MPs, enlisted soldiers, CIA personnel, and civilian contractors who, almost overnight, become jailors of Iraqis. In the span of a few months, one group of (mostly) white and (mostly) working-class men and women were given life-and-death power over dark, mostly male foreigners, the majority of whom, needless to say, did not speak English and whose culture was altogether alien to the occupying Americans.[3] The unprecedented aspect of this

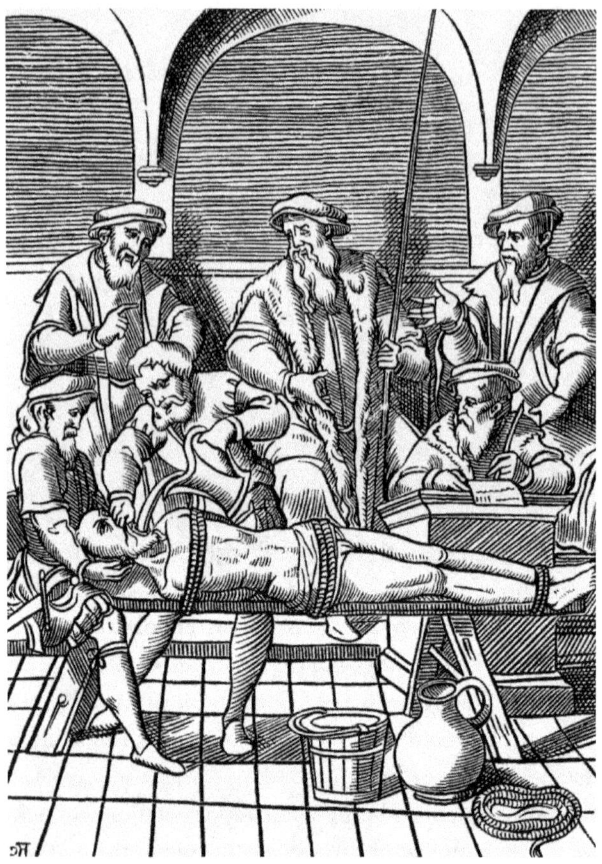

4.1 "Water torture" woodcut, sixteenth century. Facsimile of a woodcut in J. Damhoudère, *Praxis rerum criminalium* (Antwerp, 1556).

phenomenon—I refer to the participants' act of collective self-representation as they tortured their prisoners—should not be underemphasized.[4]

Certainly it is of some significance that despite the ready availability of the camera, routinely practiced tortures such as waterboarding, beating, or electrical shock have rarely if ever been photographically documented as part of the torture process itself. Whether officially sanctioned, as in the dirty wars in Chile, Argentina, Guatemala, and El Salvador, or, further back, the Algerian War of Independence, as far as is known, neither the torturers nor the observers thought to visually record, circulate, or, indeed, publicize their activities.

Apologists for torture object that the horrific and often lethal forms associated with nations other than our own should be distinguished from the so-called abuse routinely practiced at Abu Ghraib, as well as in Guantanamo prison.[5] Definitions of torture however, whether from international agreements, human rights organizations, or even American military rules of conduct, do not distinguish between torture that leads to death or incapacity and other forms, such as electric shock, exposure to loud noise, and isolation, that may leave no physical traces on the victim. Nevertheless, it has been one of the goals of the Bush administration to redefine torture in ways that make nonsense of existing covenants and less partisan definitions.[6]

Despite President George Bush's insistence that "Americans do not torture," or the various disavowals of right-wing commentators, it is clear that Americans, both civilian and military, *do* torture.[7] Thus, the photographic record provided by the release and dissemination of the Abu Ghraib photographs and videos are of enormous political as well as ethical significance.[8] Although human rights groups have cited data to the effect that six hundred American service members or intelligence officers have been accused of having been involved in the torture or murder of detainees, only ten, the lowest in the military hierarchy, have thus far received prison terms of a year or more.[9] In this essay, however, I want to consider the implications of the visual archive itself, not only in terms of what shaped the forms of "abuse" it depicts but also how that archive then functions once its contents are made public and become accessible for various uses, especially critical ones.

As I have indicated, and with respect to those features of the Abu Ghraib archive that seem unprecedented, certainly the most striking one is the desire of the participants to visually record their activities. Where some writers have made reference to photographic precedents (e.g., the lynching photographs recently published and exhibited in New York City at the New-York Historical Society in 2004[10]) or to the concentration camp photographs that are for many the benchmark for atrocity imagery, others have looked back historically to the representation of torture in the visual arts, as represented in the prints of Jacques Callot and Francisco Goya, as well as certain paintings by Leon Golub.[11]

But this evocation of an art historical genealogy, if that is what it is, misses one of the central features of the Abu Ghraib archive; namely, its carnivalesque atmosphere, its eroticism, and its S/M trappings and staging. In this sense, the photographic record is less a "documentary" than an "entertainment," a spectacle, a kind of aggregate movie, comprising both still and moving pictures (i.e., videos) whose participants function as both directors and actors who perform their roles for one another as well as for an implied spectator. These feature particular forms of torture, imply certain forms of viewing, and involve circuits of transmission and reception that distinguish much of the imagery from Abu Ghraib from, say, the nightmarish depictions of rape, mutilation, and carnage that Goya depicted in his *Disasters of War*. But the central problem with the reference to examples taken from the visual arts is the elision of the distinction between the imaginative rendering of torture in graphic or painterly forms and the indexical properties of the photographic—even if digital—record. Which is merely to say that a photographic record is categorically different from a graphic one, even if the torture represented in graphic form "really" happened, or was "really" observed by the artist.[12]

In stressing the singularity of the Abu Ghraib photographs, it is an open question as to whether such activities might not be practiced elsewhere, or might have been recorded in other prisons. But what is paramount in the Abu Ghraib photographic record is the fact that the activities were in many instances clearly orchestrated and staged for the camera. The pyramid of naked bodies, buttocks facing the lens, was set up deliberately to be photographed, as was much else in Tier 1 of Abu Ghraib prison. This is why the "roles" of the smiling, joking reservists, MPs, and intelligence officers who posed for their photographs, and the ways in which the torture of detainees was elaborately staged, makes the visual record much closer to the conventions of pornography than to straightforward photographic documentation, just as other kinds of pictures made by Americans in Iraq belong to other recognizable genres in photography, such as the tourist snapshot (fig. 4.2).[13]

It would seem reasonable to assume that one of the factors inciting the particular types of torture at Abu Ghraib was the presence of women, mostly young women, as jailors, military police, and soldiers. Reportedly, among the huge number of photographs and even videos recorded in the prison are images of the reservists and other military personnel having sex with one another, although these have not been released. Reportedly, there are unreleased images of rape and sodomy. There is a complex form of psychosexual circuitry at work here, for as feminist and queer theorists have long recognized, the women "between" men may function as the circuits (or circuit breakers) of desire that circulates between men, *especially* when homosexual desire is proscribed, and the psychosocial environment is homophobic.[14] In this respect, that a considerable amount of the staged torture in the prison involved "homosexual" tableaux (e.g., collective masturbation and fellatio, anal penetration) cannot but suggest something about the disavowed desires of

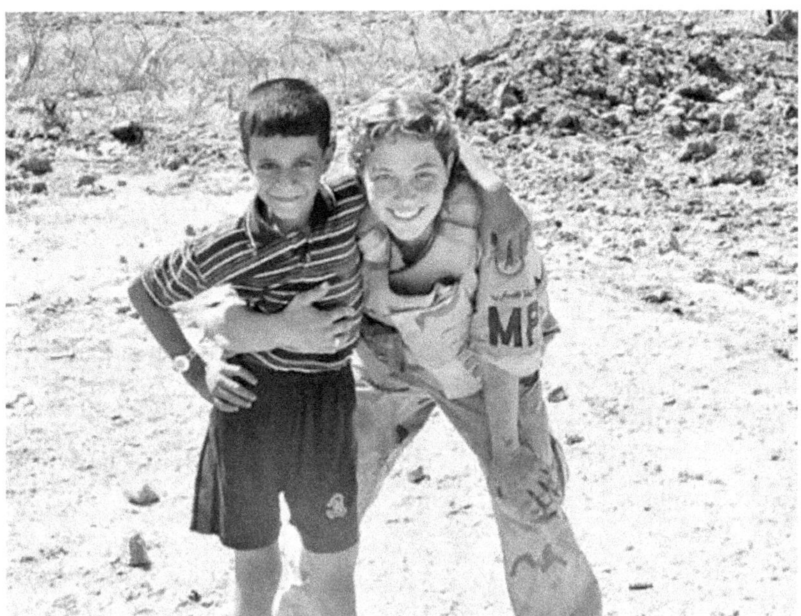


4.2 US Army specialist Sabrina Harman smiling with child, Al Hillah, Iraq, n.d.

the torturers themselves. If sexual violence, exemplified in rape, is crucially an act of power and domination, then the presence of women in the theater of torture obviously added its own determinations, contributed its own frissons and shocks, and functioned as a narrative element in what I am calling Abu Ghraib, the movie.[15]

Private first class Lynndie R. England, for example, who posed with a dog-leashed detainee made to crawl on the floor, becomes, in the theatre of torture, transformed into the stock figure of the dominatrix—lewd, powerful, dangerous. But this power is exercised only in relation to the detainees, not necessarily in relation to her male cohort, with whom this spectacle was jointly orchestrated (her relationship with her then lover, Charles Garner, who was sentenced to ten years in prison but released in 2011 after serving six, does not sound like that of a dominatrix). That torture, as in this notorious set of images, should be explicitly sexualized does not make it *not* torture, nor does it make it *not* sexual; it is both, as in any act of forcible rape.

It is this that gives the Sadean charge to so many of the images. It is also why the pictures that were made for the cameras in Abu Ghraib can be generically differentiated from the other horrors photographed there: the barking, biting dogs assaulting prisoners; the traces of blood on the floors; the bound and immobilized bodies; the hooded figures connected to wires; and so forth. It should not be forgotten, however, that many of the other forms of sanctioned "abuse" are not necessarily visually, that is, photographically, representable (e.g., the use of blaring, constant sound; isolation; sleep deprivation; and other "stress-inducing" techniques).

When the pictures from Abu Ghraib were first disseminated in 2004, many commentators sought to exhume examples from other photographic archives. Dora Apel, Hazel Carby, and Susan Sontag, among others, made particular reference to the photographs of lynchings in small-town America, most of them representing festive crowds of white folk milling beneath the dangling bodies of lynched men and boys.[16] Lit by magnesium flare (because generally shot at night), these photographs too function as a form of collective self-representation of a particular community. Many of these photographs were made into postcards by the enterprising photographers who recorded the event; these were passed from hand to hand or mailed to relatives and friends. It is thus the *self-representative* aspect of these images, as well as their distribution, that manifests the closest structural resemblance to the visual archive of Abu Ghraib. The exchange of the images is a form by which participants and witnesses constitute and affirm themselves as a collectivity, a community. That these particular communities (white Christians at a lynching, young reservists in a military prison) bond through the torture and murder of their victims tells us frightening things about the Janus face of collective identification. Be that as it may, the Abu Ghraib pictures are nonetheless very different in their affect from these excruciating lynching photographs; they are novel and disturbing in unfamiliar ways. There is, first of all, the ways in which many of the pictures, no matter how horrific the plight of the victim, affirm the perception that the activities on Tier 1 at Abu Ghraib were an occasion for "fun" ("Animal House on the night shift," as described in one of the official reports by James R. Schlesinger[17]). Second, insofar as so many of the images depict specifically sexual acts—real or simulated—and the omnipresence of naked male bodies, the pictures summon responses in the viewer that are inevitably voyeuristic and thus especially charged. Because they so insistently provoke the "pornographic" gaze (nudity, sexual acts, penetration of bodies, etc.), the viewer's look, notwithstanding her own perspective, values, or principles, carries its own inescapable complicity, for the viewer is structurally positioned as the receiver of the torturers' pleasures as well as the detainees' abjection and suffering. "Point of view" in this instance, as with photographic imagery in general, is predetermined by the photographer; the viewer *as* viewer takes the place of the photographer and looks with his or her eyes.

As Sontag and others have observed, such pictures reflect the mainlining of the pornographic imaginary, as well as the disclosure of the sexual dynamics operative in relations of domination and submission, whether they occur in prisons, fraternities, or theaters of war. This, however, is not to say that the forms of sexual abuse revealed are not part of the continuum of torture itself.[18] But the evident emphasis on the sexual in the abuse of prisoners at Abu Ghraib—the enforced nudity, compelled acts of fellatio and masturbation, and so forth—were, it appears, both programmatic *and* improvisational. In other words, while we have since learned that hooding, waterboarding, depriving prisoners of clothing and sleep, and "acting on their fears" were all practices approved at the highest levels of government and practiced on the prisoners at Guantanamo in Cuba and in Bagram prison in Afghanistan, there is no evidence that those who formulated these techniques specifically included, intended, or envisaged activities that would fall under the rubric of sexual violation or any of the other manifestly sexual acts prisoners were compelled to perform.

Nevertheless, the architects of the interrogation procedures employed at Abu Ghraib were well aware of the physical modesty prescribed by Islamic religious precepts, and were surely aware of the religious injunctions relating to defilement.[19] Defilement is not so much a violence inflicted on the body as it is a violence inflicted on identity, self-respect, and personhood, typically in forms that will be experienced precisely *as* defilement. Actions such as putting women's underpants over the heads of prisoners, forcing a detainee to insert a banana in his rectum, smearing at least one prisoner with feces, putting fluids said to be menstrual blood on prisoners' bodies—are no less instrumental as techniques of torture than waterboarding or making detainees think they were about to be electrocuted.

Accordingly, if the stripping of prisoners was desirable because it induced shame in the victim, it was a logical conclusion to photograph those who were thus variously shamed, thereby intensifying the indignities. If, on the one hand, those who tortured prisoners at Abu Ghraib were inspired by their own imaginative resources (e.g., the human pyramids, the dog-leashing of prisoners, the menstrual blood—real or not—splashed on prisoners, etc.), these were, on the other hand, merely improvised elaborations based on the tacit understanding that the induction of shame was a valid part of interrogation procedure.

Abu Ghraib, the collective movie, or, perhaps better, the collective home movie, reveals, therefore, a sort of general plotting of respective roles, although there is, of course, no chronological narrative. There are three sets of protagonists: American servicemen, MPs, and other civilian male personnel; American servicewomen, reservists, and MPs; and the Iraqi detainees. Within the film's own given terms, the Americans, if not necessarily cast as heroes, are cast as the human beings, the individuals, the agents, the subjects. The Iraqis are cast as the subhumans, the abjected, the craven objects of their masters' will. They are not simply the designated enemies, as acknowledged in the official (and internationally recognized) status of POWs, but a species of being that exists outside of the formal rules of engagement, interrogation, or incarceration.[20] Since they are a priori identified as belonging to a demonized collectivity (e.g., "terrorists," "insurgents," "unlawful combatants," jihadis, etc.), with little attention having been given in the period 2002–4 to distinguish among common criminals, combatants, or hapless civilians caught up in mass arrests, they fall outside of all legal protection. Moreover, the presence of the women as jailors, as I have indicated, serves to foster the conventions of this particular "movie," mobilizing the eroticism between themselves and their male colleagues as well as eroticizing the kinds of torture exercised on the bodies of the victims. At the same time as the complicity of the torturers serves to reinforce male homosocial bonding, it simultaneously works to affirm the putative heterosexuality of both the men and women in contrast to the imputed—albeit compelled—"deviancy" of their prisoners. As Alessandro Camon has observed, "Torture, despite its need for secrecy, also needs its own representation. It's usually meant not only to inflict pain but also to instill terror. It's sometimes meant to please the torturer. Therefore, the ritualistic, fetishistic, 'spectacular' aspects of torture are an integral part of the practice. As a spectacle, torture is akin to porn—S/M being the obvious shared territory. It elicits voyeurism and a morbid fascination."[21]

The infernal home movie of Abu Ghraib is thus like any home movie insofar as it serves the purpose of collective self-representation; affirms the reciprocal ties of family, friends, or community; and positions the protagonists as the intentional agents of their own life experience. As such, Abu Ghraib, the movie, tells us nothing about the victims who are the ostensible subjects of the movie, but tells us a great deal about the psychosexual components of torture, of military occupation, of the sadism mobilized in carceral environments, and, hardly least, the sordid and vicious underside of the American values that the war in Iraq is intended to affirm and propagate.

## The Archive

The photographs and videos made in Abu Ghraib, from the moment of their recording, became an archive, an image repertoire. As an archive, the collective representation of the torture at Abu Ghraib circulates in the world with newly acquired meanings and significance. In the ether of cyberspace, the pictures were initially exchanged and circulated between a few dozen of the Americans posted in Iraq, and now, since 2004, they have spread internationally. Interestingly, although these images were made with digital media, they prompted no challenge to their authenticity (they have, however, remained censored; much of the image archive has never been released). But as a digital archive now available to anyone with access to the web, the archive is located nowhere in particular and everywhere that it comes into use. It is, moreover, a constantly expanding archive, enlarged not only by the release in March 2006 of hundreds of previously censored images and videos but also expanded daily via all the applications, appropriations, and usages to which the images lend themselves. These include but are not limited to the use of the photographs in the international media; the conscription of the imagery for political posters, artworks, street theater, political cartoons, and demonstrations; and other various oppositional uses.

One of the uses of the archive in the United States that sparked controversy was the exhibition of certain of the images, downloaded from various websites, in art venues. I refer specifically to exhibitions held at the International Center of Photography in New York City and the Andy Warhol Museum in Pittsburgh in 2004.[22] In this regard, the presentation of manifestly nonartistic pictures whose significance lay only in *what* they depicted (as well as the form of digital media itself and its modes of dissemination) sparked comment on the risks of the "aestheticization" of the imagery, or, alternatively, the argument that a museum (a priori defined as a space for aesthetic contemplation) had no business trafficking in such pictures in the first place. These were arguments that were made previously around the exhibition of the James Allen archive of lynching photographs, although in that instance, the first venue was the New-York Historical Society, not an art museum. Putting aside the merit of either argument, the more important point here is how archives—especially digital archives—lend themselves to these plural applications, addressing different audiences, becoming variously re-signified in the process, and, in turn, generating new discourses; for example, the debates that were sparked about what material is or is not appropriate for museum exhibition, and the conflict between the government's withholding of part of the archive versus the public's right to know.

Another element in the discursively generative capacity of an archive is the phenomenon of "iconization." By this term, I refer to the process by which certain images, for a variety of reasons, become generally symbolic not only of the particular event depicted but also of a larger entity or situation. In other words, the "iconic" image, such as that of the hooded detainee, precariously poised on a box, wires dangling from his limbs, became for many a synecdoche of the evil of the war itself as well as an evidentiary rebuttal to President Bush's claim that "the US does not torture." For certain commentators, such as W. J. T. Mitchell, the symbolic as well as the discursive power of this single image lay in its evocation of the crucifixion.[23] Whether such an association is what made this particular picture *the* iconic representation of torture at Abu Ghraib is less important than the scale of its diffusion. "As famous as advertising logos and brand icons like the Nike Swoosh or the Golden Arches, the image rapidly mutated into a global icon, that 'had legs,' to use the Madison Avenue expression," Mitchell writes.[24] In this particular respect, almost as soon as the Abu Ghraib pictures were released to the American media, this harrowing picture became just such an icon.[25] In fact, the hooded man was reproduced on political posters in Baghdad and Teheran within days of its release, and has since become ubiquitous as an indictment of the war and the policies that accompany it.

In its various appropriations, the original meaning of the hooded detainee thus became re-signified, transformed from the American jailors' orchestration of one man's terrorization to a signifier of defiance, a call for revenge, a rallying point for opposition. And because the images, however abstracted (as in many of the antiwar posters and other graphic media), were drawn originally from the photographic archive, the hooded man retains the shock of the indexical—a living, terrorized body, precariously tottering forever on its box. Nowhere is this "indexical shock" better illustrated than in the picture's conscription to antiwar cultural practices. In this regard, especially noteworthy are the posters designed and distributed by an anonymous group of artist-activists based in Los Angeles who produce their work under the collective name Forkscrew.

Among Forkscrew's graphic works is a set of posters mimicking the Apple iPod advertisements one routinely sees on billboards and in other public spaces. The "iRaq" posters, which are available as free downloads on the group's website, circulate both virtually and materially, and can be possessed by anyone.

In public space, the iRaq images seamlessly blend into the urban landscape and, if not really looked at, can pass undetected. But when they are noticed, it is in the split second between the viewer's automatic—i.e., distracted—perception of the poster *as* poster, and the shocked recognition of the identity of the silhouetted figures, that enables the possibility of reflection rather than visual consumption. The mobilization of shock effects was and remains a tactic of oppositional or dissident cultural production, but what is important here is the *kind* of shock the iRaq posters mobilize. There is first of all the shock of recognition; the instant when one recognizes the hooded detainee from Abu Ghraib, or any of the poster's other icons of resistance, as the sources of the silhouettes. Then there is the shock of dissonance—the desirable commodity transformed into confrontational emblems of warfare or torture. In this respect, the use of the iPod—a technology not only of solitary entertainment and distraction but also a globalized commodity that "everyone" recognizes—is significant. Sequestering the user in his or her hermetic aural world, the iPod is thus likened to the indifference or disregard that has, among other things, prevented any serious consequences for those in the Bush administration who sanctioned and indeed prescribed the use of torture. However, one reason for the visceral impact of the spectral silhouettes in the iRaq poster made by the Forkscrew collective is the shock of recognition following hard upon the routine act of visual consumption of an advertisement in public space. Thus, in the act of recognition, the viewer is reminded of the ongoing issue of torture as part of the US "war on terror," and perhaps even perceives a grisly reality that underlies the phantasmagoria of the commodity fetish.

That artists have also made use of the Abu Ghraib archive is another example of the unforeseen applications of the digital archive as it spawns new avatars. These range from the works of the well-known Colombian painter Fernando Botero (who as of 2006 had produced eighty-eight large-scale paintings and drawings) to Hans Haacke's *Stargazing* to the restaging or simulation of the events at Abu Ghraib by photographers such as Andres Serrano and Clifford Fein to large-scale installation works by Jenny Holzer. But the imagery of Abu Ghraib is by no means limited to antiwar, anti-torture cultural production, nor in the Arab world is it limited to indictments of American policies and practices. In 2006, an issue of Italian *Vogue* featured a fashion spread titled "State of Emergency" by Steven Meisel that clearly took its visual cues from the Abu Ghraib archive.

The history of the public exposure of this archive is a story in itself. At first, there were no images, but there were rumors of images that began to surface after October 2003, the most intense period of abuse by military personnel at Abu Ghraib. These reports triggered the American Civil Liberties Union and the Center for Constitutional Rights to initiate ultimately successful lawsuits forcing the government to release documents and images.[26] However, the first images entered the government archive in January 2004 when a single soldier based at Abu Ghraib forwarded some of the pictures to army investigators. In the following months, selections from the archive were leaked to CNN and to Seymour Hirsch, whose *New Yorker* article published April 30, 2004, included some of the images. And in March of 2006, several hundred more previously censored images and videos were leaked to the Australian television news program *Dateline* and almost immediately after were acquired and reproduced by Salon.com.[27] As of today, the ACLU, the Center for Constitutional Rights, and other organizations are still seeking release of hundreds of other images and videotapes under the Freedom of Information Act.

The pictures from Abu Ghraib will never go away, even long after this war is over. While it is possible to destroy "original" physical pictures, electronic media are forever. Like other visual evidence of American atrocities (for example, the massacre at My Lai), the proof of what goes on in this war is having its effects, metastasizing globally, functioning to rally opposition, to foment hatred of the United States and its policies, and to give the lie to America's stories about itself and of its moral and ethical exceptionalism. Although what the Abu Ghraib archive depicts is hateful, shameful, and sadistic, insofar as it documents one vicious aspect of a conflict that has been subject to unprecedented visual censorship, it is finally better—necessary—to have these records of the horrors than not.

The central question raised by the Abu Ghraib visual archive has been raised before. Has the capacity for shock or outrage that might be conceivably provoked by the photographic imagery of torture been irrevocably diminished as a consequence of repetition and familiarity? Has the almost quotidian exposure to the photographic record of carnage, cruelty, and victimization operated to numb the affective capacities of viewers? Has the mass media's exploitation of simulated violence in TV, or especially film, neutralized the perception of real violence? These are among the central questions raised by Susan Sontag and several other writers addressing the meaning and significance of the Abu Ghraib archive.

In her 1977 book *On Photography,* Sontag argued that one of the consequences of our immersion in the image world of photographic representation is that we become inoculated to the horrors that photographs enable us to see.[28] In certain essays, Sontag continually referred to the deadening attributes of photographic imagery, at least in its collective manifestations.[29] "To suffer is one thing," she wrote; "another thing is living with the photographed images of suffering, which does not necessarily strengthen conscience and the ability to be compassionate. It can corrupt them. Once one has seen such images, one has started down the road of seeing more—and more. Images transfix. Images anesthetize."[30]

In her last book, *Regarding the Pain of Others* (2003), Sontag returned to the problem of photographic imagery in relation to war. The problem as she then saw it was that the photographic revelation of carnage, destruction, and death, brought daily into the domestic space of readers and viewers, could only be descriptive, like any other photographic document.[31] The photographic evidence of any war's destruction and human suffering could not analyze, explain, narrate, or contextualize. It could not, in and of itself, prompt action, affect political beliefs, or shift perceptions. "To an Israeli Jew," Sontag said, "a photograph of a child torn apart in the attack on the Sbarro pizzeria in downtown Jerusalem is first of all a photograph of a Jewish child killed by Palestinian suicide-bomber. To a Palestinian, a photograph of a child torn apart by a tank round in Gaza is first of all a photograph of a Palestinian child killed by Israeli ordnance."[32] But even more pointedly, Sontag observed that a century of unbearable, previously unrepresentable photographic pictures of the casualties of war, increasingly civilian, has done nothing to make warfare less frequent.

Sontag's last published essay, "Regarding the Torture of Others," remains unsurpassed in its scenographic analysis of what happened at Abu Ghraib prison. As a canny anatomist of camera culture, Sontag was especially attentive to the staging of these photographs, the modes of staging particular kinds of torture. The essay, whose tag line in the original *New York Times Magazine* format was "The Photos Are Us," stressed the generic categories to which Abu Ghraib belonged: tourist snapshot and homemade pornography. In the former instance, the perpetuators' desire to document their activities were likened to vacation snapshots, recording the subject's temporary occupancy of a foreign place, sometimes with the natives, sometimes in picturesque or recognizable settings. As such, the torture photo, like the touristic souvenir snapshot, is a kind of visual trophy. In this respect, those Abu Ghraib pictures depicting the perpetrator posed, often smiling, with the victims—corpses included—are uncannily similar to the more anodyne pictures made by (in some cases) the same individuals, such as those featuring PFC Sabrina Harman playing with an Iraqi child (fig. 4.2) and those depicting her mugging over the battered corpse

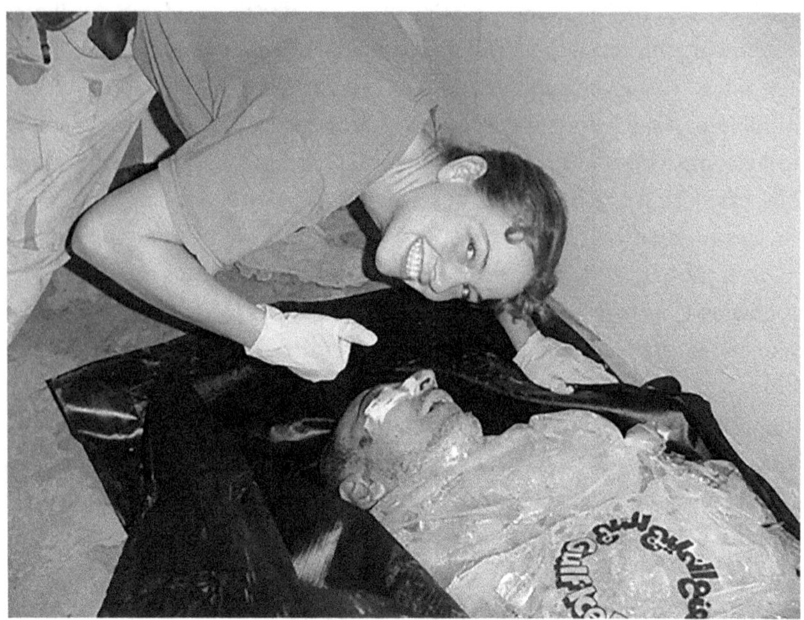

4.3 US Army specialist Sabrina Harman posing over the body of Manadel al-Jamadi, Abu Ghraib prison, Iraq, 2003.

of a prisoner (fig. 4.3). As such, the torture photo, like the touristic souvenir snapshot, is a visual trophy of a part of one's life that one wishes to be made visible, preserved, and remembered.

The photos from Abu Ghraib, as Sontag concluded, far from being the productions of a deviant fringe, or, as government apologists had it, "a few bad apples," were fully in keeping with a pornographic imaginary that constituted the underside of official US values and ideologies and that was further shaped by a global camera culture based on fantasies of imaginary possession and appropriation. It is also germane to note, as she did, that the actions and their documentation are equally shaped by the ideologies of militarism, military aggression, military occupation, and (although Sontag did not stress this) racism and anti-Arab prejudice. Her general conclusion was that the photographs are "representative of the fundamental corruptions of any foreign occupation and its distinctive policies which serve as a perfect recipe for the cruelties and crimes in American run prisons."[33]

In 2006, I taught an undergraduate seminar titled "Torture and Representation" that focused on the Abu Ghraib archive. For my students, some of whom had been largely indifferent to or even ignorant of the events at Abu Ghraib, reading Sontag and working with the photographic documentation permitted the question of photographic "inoculation" to be considered empirically. Several students testified to having become progressively inured to the content of the pictures merely because of having viewed them frequently. But, as was also evident, exposure to both these issues and to the images themselves, as well as the time spent in critical discussion, prompted a number of the students to consider the implications of both the war and the practice of torture, no less than the issues raised by the photographic representation of both.

In choosing to devote an undergraduate seminar to this subject, I was greatly inspired by Henry Giroux, specifically in this instance by his brilliant essay "What Might Education Mean after Abu Ghraib: Revisiting Adorno's Politics of Education."[34] In this essay, Giroux makes the crucially important observation that pedagogy is one of the discursive sites that allows for the critical interrogation of the meaning of photographs as they represent larger ethical and political circumstances:

> What is often ignored in the debates about Abu Ghraib, both in terms of its causes and what can be done about it, are questions that foreground the relevance of critical education to the debate. Such questions would clearly focus, at the very least, on what pedagogical conditions need to be in place to enable people to view the images of abuse at Abu Ghraib prison not as part of a voyeuristic, even pornographic, reception, but through a variety of discourses that enable them to ask critical and probing questions that get at the heart of how people learn to participate in sadistic acts of abuse and torture, internalize racist assumptions that make it easier to dehumanize people different from themselves, accept commands that violate basic human rights, become indifferent to the suffering and hardships of others, and view dissent as fundamentally unpatriotic.[35]

As Giroux argues with specific reference to the Abu Ghraib archive, it is the space of pedagogy that is useful in fostering those skills that enable students—citizens—to respond to the image world they live in with the requisite skills for analysis, with the ability to make connections between the politics of representation and the politics of the world they inhabit. Insofar as these are integrally, fundamentally linked, the possibilities of positive change and transformation require attention to both.[36] But the Abu Ghraib archive actually highlights two very different issues. As images, even if digital rather than analog, and notwithstanding the censorship that has prevented the release of material perhaps even more incendiary than what we have seen, they cause us to reflect on whether this unprecedented visual record of practices of torture, abjection, humiliation, and abuse has materially changed either policies or practices.[37] The second issue, around the failure to prosecute those who were ultimately responsible for the practice of torture—from John Woo, who provided the "legal" fig leaf, to Dick Cheney, who okayed many of the "enhanced interrogation" procedures, not only at Abu Ghraib, but at Bagram, at Guantanamo, and at "black sites" all over the world—does not suggest that the revelation of the Abu Ghraib images was particularly decisive in terms of actual existing policies. Finally, if I am correct in viewing the archive as both a kind of collective home movie, and as a self-representation of a certain strata of American society—the lower functionaries of the American imperium in its militaristic incarnation—there are many reasons to reflect on Sontag's succinct analysis of the imbrication of both aspects of the events: the photographs are "representative of the fundamental corruptions of any foreign occupation and its distinctive policies which serve as a perfect recipe for the cruelties and crimes in American run prisons." As the *New York Times* glossed her essay, "The photos are us."

# 5

## Harry Callahan

### GENDER, GENRE, AND STREET PHOTOGRAPHY

(2007)

The genesis of this essay was an invitation to participate in a conference on Harry Callahan held at the Center for Creative Photography in Tucson, Arizona, in 2008.[1] Having little interest in Callahan's photography, I took Callahan's work as itself the object of various discourses, rather than as a set of discrete images or series of images. These have served to open onto a number of issues, some of which are "proper" to artistic discourse, and others which open onto the social, political, and historical determinations that shape the nature and terms of cultural production in whatever time and place it occurs. In the specific case of Callahan, one can immediately identify a particular cluster of discourses and institutional coordinates, some in place during Callahan's working life, some previous to it, and some posthumous.

The most obvious discourse within which Callahan's work is embedded is that of art photography, a subset of photography as such, but one whose genealogy derives from art and aesthetic discourse. Here, the salient terms are those of modernist art photography (subcategory formalism). Formalist approaches to the medium, are, however, always more or less contaminated, as it were, by the fact that photography is predominantly referential, even when apparently self-reflexive. Thus, on the one hand, those pictures by Callahan that are relatively close to abstraction enable critics to employ an exclusively formal language; for example, "In Callahan's photographs of the store window, a stage-like spatial arrangement appears again. Figures are set in a narrow band layered between the picture plane and the storefront behind it, but here the foreground has been eliminated to heighten the flatness of the space. Callahan compresses the space still further by technical means. The prints lack the gray middle tones that would contribute to a description of roundness, depth and continuity among forms; the pictorial space is fractured and becomes jumbled areas of black and white that almost collapse into a single plane."[2] But, on the other hand, when the pictures are more figurative—say, those of Callahan's wife Eleanor—critical discourse shifts to another register entirely: "Emerging mysteriously from the water, Eleanor dominates his world. She is the center of his landscape: the woman among the trees, or the dunes, at rest in the sumac glade: the looming statue in the park, herself a natural fact. Similarly, she is the center of the domestic world, an object of infinite delight. . . . For Callahan, as for [the poet] William Carlos Williams, 'There is / no good in the world except out of / a woman.'"[3] To state the obvious, this a highly gendered discourse, one consistently unremarked by Callahan's critics in their invocations of the archetypal and the universal: "Callahan's power to create images that are mythic and meditative, that rise above the contingent and the specific to be universal statements of intensely felt observation, is clear in his later work: his pictures of his wife Eleanor come to mind. But this power to create universal imagery is present already in these early works."[4]

Unlike many other now canonized art photographers of his epoch (e.g., Walker Evans, Irving Penn, William Klein, Diane Arbus, etc.), Callahan's critics are spared the task of navigating between work for hire and personal expression; for most of his career Callahan supported himself by teaching. Accordingly, and from the perspective of American art photography discourse, Callahan has long been situated as a paradigm of purposeful creative self-invention, a modernist master with forebears and progeny. One of the most significant forbears was Walker Evans, whose photographs of the street are important precedents for Callahan's. As for progeny, one has only to look at Callahan's students' work—for example, that of Ray Metzger—to observe the transmission of both style and content. Relatively early in Callahan's career he was consecrated by the Museum of Modern Art's photography department, famously described by Martha Rosler as the "Kremlin of Modernism."[5] Callahan still features regularly in exhibitions, monographs, and symposia such as the one I attended in Tucson.

But even given the apparent unity of an oeuvre that is understood as wholly artistic, there is yet another set of discourses that are mobilized around Callahan's oeuvre. These hinge on the notion of genre, specifically photographic genres. Although certain of these—*the* nude, *the* landscape—are themselves derived from art theory and criticism, others, such as street photography, are medium specific (there exist hundreds of modern paintings of the street, or streets, but nothing called "street painting"). In this essay, therefore, I want to consider the notion of street photography as a presumed genre, what assumptions and conventions underlie it, and how issues of gender may figure within it. These in turn reveal how certain forms of photographic discourse function to obscure those historical, sociological, and indeed psychological formations that shape if not determine forms of cultural production, and do their own ideological work in transforming problems into givens.

Genres as such are a much-debated category and, as Jacques Derrida argued in his essay "The Law of Genre," possess in all senses a disciplinary function: "As soon as the word 'genre' is sounded, as soon as it is heard, as soon as one attempts to conceive it, a limit is drawn. And a when a limit is established, norms and interdictions are not far behind."[6] However, unlike beaux-arts categories such as nudes or landscapes, however problematic, what has come to be called street photography is, like other so-called photographic genres (for example, documentary), a twentieth-century invention. In its most literal sense, the term would more accurately describe either any or all photographs of city space or urban life, as well as a photographic *petit métier* begun in the later nineteenth century, pursued in cities the world over, in which itinerant photographers took pictures of pedestrians and then offered them for sale. These often-anonymous vernacular images are not, however, what is generally meant by street photography. And although it may now appear as a self-evident generic classification, the first English-language survey of street photography appeared only in 1994.[7] The geometrically increasing number of texts and exhibitions oriented to this form of production since then suggests that this was the formative decade in which the plural practices that might be justly designated by the term "street photography" (e.g., professional itinerant photographers in urban space) were refigured so as to produce a photography history with names—an art historical category that focuses on individual as opposed to collective production. Street photography, conceived *as* a genre, was therefore formulated to exclude, or perhaps repress, the overwhelming majority of photographs, from the 1840s on, that depict urban spaces with or without pedestrians. In sum, what has come to be known as street photography is a more or less "artistic"—or perhaps one could say, more "auteurist"—notion of this activity. That an art history of photography is generally confounded with a history of photography tout court is the inevitable consequence of how and why, and in the service of what interests and investments (in all senses), the boundless domain of photography is discursively organized.[8]

But my discussion here is oriented less toward issues of photographic aesthetics or connoisseurship than toward the kinds of questions that arise when we consider photography—of any stripe—as a social practice. Given this perspective, I am interested in how and why the practice of photographing people unawares within the modern city emerged when it did, why it did, and how such photography might be read in terms that exceed the individual intentions or subjectivity of the photographer. Such an inquiry raises other issues, including how perceptions of the urban environment are themselves subject to multiple determinations. It further serves to make us aware of changing conceptions about photographic protocols, conventions, and practices.

Inasmuch as the modern metropolis, initially Paris, has been a photographic subject continuously since the 1840s, it would be theoretically possible to construct a history of the medium using only images of the urban environment. And while such a project—beginning with the daguerreotype and the calotype; continuing through the era of wet collodion, dry plate, stereographic imagery, and snapshots; and concluding with digital images—would include every photographic technology and camera developed since the medium's invention, it would also span a considerable range of uses, contexts, and instrumentalities.

Such a venerable visual engagement with the metropolis is not surprising given the medium's historic implication with the transformative processes of industrialism, technology, and mass production. These have all contributed in various ways to the culture of modernity. In its artistic manifestations, however, one designates those works that employ the visual (or textual) expressions of modernity in innovative forms as modernist, and in this regard, the city as subject is as much a part of modernism as it is for painting and literature. A stereo card of crowds walking on Broadway or crossing the Pont Neuf is a document of the modern because the technology that created the picture and the desire to take (and, equally important, the desire to see or purchase) such a picture are themselves indices of modernity. But while such pictures are, by definition, modern, they are not necessarily *modernist*. A photograph by Ilse Bing, to choose an example almost at random, is a typical example of the syntax of modernist photography to the degree that it manifests the abstracting possibilities of photographic vision, emphasizing the expanded possibilities of perception produced by camera technology, and departing from "conventional" pictorial composition.

But the ways in which the city and its inhabitants have been photographically imaged are determined not only by the possibilities or limitations of the technology employed, and shaped not only by the individual photographer's subjectivity and practical or expressive purpose but equally by the various determinations operating upon a particular place and milieu in a particular time. With respect to those photographic histories that invent a presumptive tradition, there is reason to query the succession proposed. For Charles Marville to have photographed Paris both before and after Georges-Eugène Haussmann's transformations, or for Thomas Annan to have photographed the Glasgow slums, it was necessary that official governmental entities desired such documentation in the first place, and this was, even in the 1870s, unusual. For Eugène Atget to produce his massive record of Paris, it was necessary to have both a clientele for such imagery, as well as an existing discourse about the disappearance of "*vieux Paris*" in which, in this particular instance, he himself participated.[9] Like these earlier examples, the production of photographs manifesting the defamilarization or estrangement of vision by the photographic avant-garde of the 1920s was not merely a consequence of the technical means to produce such a vision. Accordingly, the *Octopus* of Alvin Langdon Coburn is a legacy of pictorialism, even though it depends on the same bird's-eye view and camera optics as does László Moholy-Nagy's *From the Radio Tower*. What each one looks like is the result of very different artistic goals and contrasting notions of camera aesthetics.

If the daguerreotypists or stereographic producers of the first and second generation were content to exploit the technical ability of the camera to faithfully represent the visual facts of the built environment, the envelope was pushed, so to speak, when the task became not only more interpretive but also inclusive of the city's inhabitants. While this capacity depended upon the development of portable cameras and faster film, it was not until the last two decades of the nineteenth century that photographers made pictures of theoretically identifiable pedestrians as opposed to distant views or undifferentiated crowds. Within the discourse of "street photography," it is these practices—documentary or artistic—that have been reckoned a genre, not, as I have indicated, the widespread activity of professional photographers making pictures of passersby for sale. If we reject a purely technologically deterministic approach to the medium (that is to say, the assumption that because technical improvements in photography permitted the taking of such pictures, they spawned them), we must then acknowledge those variously sociological, political, ideological, or even artistic motivations that also prompted or shaped their production. And once such an acknowledgment is made, the concept of street photography as a discrete genre is already put in question, for it requires a discursive shift in photographic practice for such an activity—the representation of individuals without their knowledge or consent—to become accept-

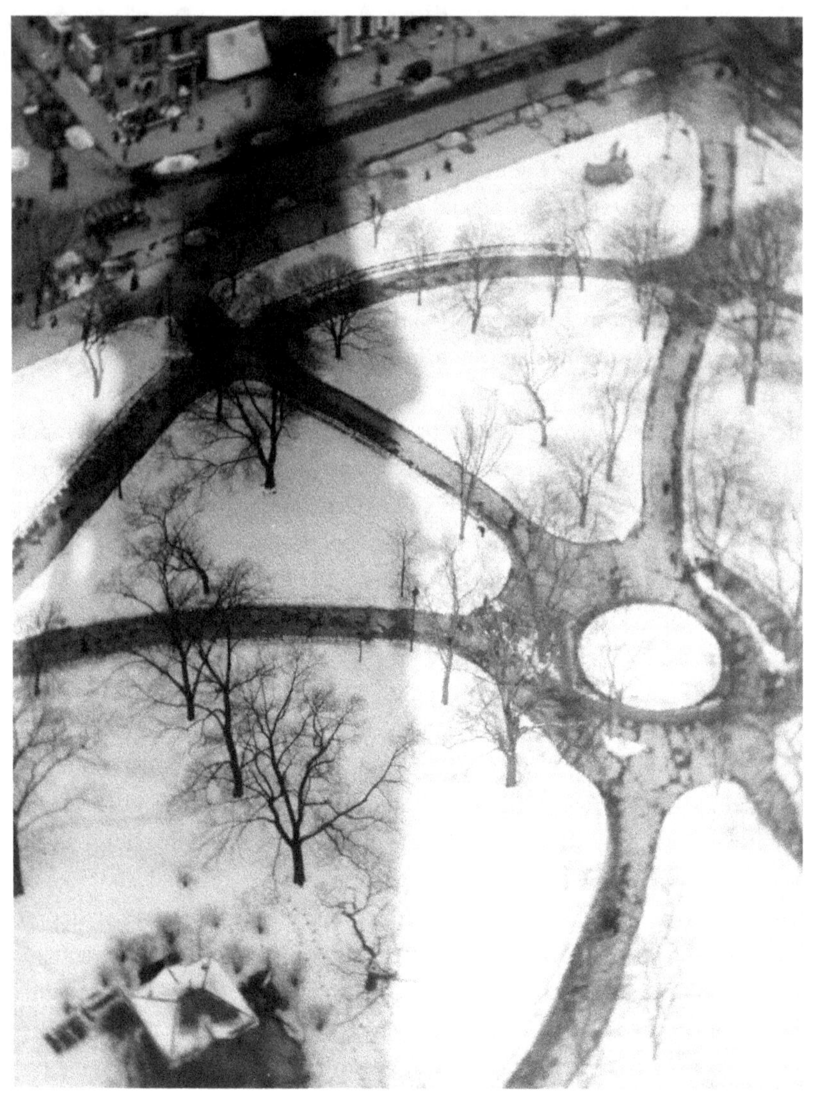

5.1 Alvin Langdon Coburn, *The Octopus*, New York, 1913. Gelatin silver print, printed ca. 1947. 12 3/16 × 9 1/8 in. COURTESY OF THE GEORGE EASTMAN MUSEUM.

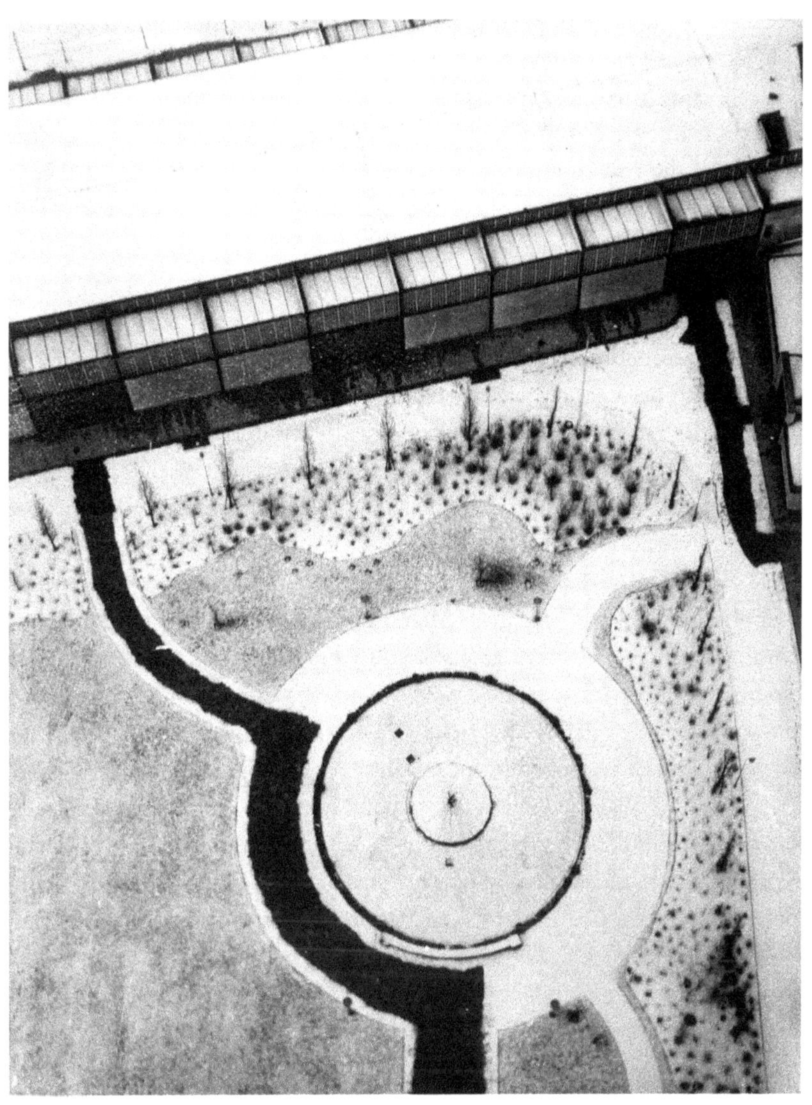

5.2 László Moholy-Nagy, *From the Radio Tower, Berlin*, 1928. Gelatin silver print, 11 ⅛ × 8 ⅜ in. Museum of Modern Art. Anonymous gift. 

able in the first place. In this regard, the photographic capture of the unaware subject was not without controversy.

In an essay titled "'Kodakers Lying in Wait': Amateur Photography and the Right of Privacy in New York, 1885–1915," Robert E. Mensel located one of the sources of the constitutionally guaranteed right to privacy in the challenge posed by amateur photographers photographing individuals in public space without their permission. As he argues, the legal evidence suggests that "amateur photographers played an important role in provoking the outrage among editorial commentators, judges, and legislators which eventually helped lead to the legal recognition of the right of privacy in New York," later enshrined in federal law.[10] Before it received legal protection and became acknowledged as a constitutional principal, the protection of privacy was considered a matter of etiquette rather than tort law. It was the extraordinary success of George Eastman's Kodak that produced the avalanche of amateur photographers whose perceived violations of privacy contributed to the establishment of privacy law. Contemporary journalistic accounts of the phenomenon describe amateur photographers as "positively Mephistophelean": they belonged to a class of minor demons known as "camera fiends," or "Kodak fiends," and were said "to be in league with some evil spirit."[11] The most uncompromising "among the photographers claimed the right to photograph anyone, and to do as they wished with the photographs, which they regarded as their personal property."[12] But, as Mensel demonstrates, many people felt a profound sense of exposure and violation upon being photographed, or upon finding their photographs displayed and sold in photo shops or used in advertisements, without their consent. The intrusive activities of amateur photographers were not, however, interdicted legally, even though the right to privacy became constitutionally protected in 1918.[13] The one exception was the use of a person's likeness without their consent for commercial purposes, a court case that turned on the use of a photograph of a young girl on a flour package. Restraining orders on photographers began only in response to the late-twentieth-century phenomenon of the paparazzi, and in that context, the plaintiffs have always been celebrities (e.g., Jacqueline Onassis). As it stands now, the law does not protect the photographing of subjects "in public space," although the *use* of such photographs may be subject to tort law.

The legal history of lawsuits made by those whose image was used without consent indicates how difficult it is for individuals to use issues of privacy in public space as the casus belli. In case after case, up to the present day, this meant that photographs of individuals in public space were not deemed to violate privacy laws, and use of such imagery in the press, for example, or as "artistic expression" is constitutionally protected.[14] The 2006 lawsuit of Erno Nussenzweig, an Orthodox Jew, against Philip-Lorca diCorcia and Pace/MacGill Gallery is a case in point. Having discovered by chance that a photograph of him featured in the diCorcia exhibition at Pace/MacGill, and was also reproduced in the catalogue, Nussenzweig sued to halt sales and publication of the photograph, requesting $500,000 in compensatory damages and $1.5 million in punitive damages for exhibiting and publishing the portrait without consent, and profiting from it financially. Moreover, Nussenzweig argued that use of the photograph interfered with his constitutional right to practice his religion, which prohibits the use of graven images. In rejecting Nussenzweig's claim, state supreme court justice Judith Gische ruled on First Amendment grounds that the making of such photographs is simply the price to be paid in a society in which information and opinion flow freely, and added that the photograph was indeed a work of art: "Defendant diCorcia has demonstrated his general reputation as a photographic artist in the international artistic community."[15] The question of why the use of the image as a work for sale, as was the catalogue, was *not* commercial or used for profit was not addressed, the assumption being that artworks and commodities have nothing to do with one another.

As these lawsuits demonstrate, the history of photographing people without their consent, often covertly, is not continuous with itinerant portrait photography, a more transactional and, indeed, democratizing practice, linked to the function of the studio. If we take into account those who have been most often unconsenting subjects depicted on the street, the borders between putative genres become so blurred that notions of photographic genre deconstruct themselves. For in providing a spurious lineage to an equally spurious genre, street photography readily collapses into documentary and reportage, and vice versa. But the more important point here is that much of what is currently designated street photography, or, for that matter, documentary photography, raises ethical questions to do with class, with gender, and with subject/object relations.[16]

What is significant here, therefore, is that when professional or amateur photographers—not the professional itinerants—first began photographing individual people in the street, it was often the disadvantaged—the poor—who served as photographic subjects. Moreover, there is a practical distinction to be drawn between photographs made for specific didactic, sociological, polemical, or ameliorative or moralizing purposes (as was the case with certain of John Thomson's photographs used in Henry Mayhew's *London Labour and the London Poor*, many of them posed; Jacob Riis's photographs of slum dwellers; and subsequent reformist projects such as those of Lewis Hine and the FSA). But there are further reasons to ask what prompts the desire to represent anonymous subjects as they go about their business unaware of being photographed. What, we might ask, was and is the interest of such pictures? For interest, by which I also mean psychological investment, does not come out of nowhere, but is itself implicated in a complex web of circumstance, ideology, and material determinations.

All these trouble the notion of street photography as a discrete genre, for it required a discursive shift for such practices to have become acceptable in the first place. Accordingly, while photographic representation of the urban subject was linked to technological advances, equally important was the change in the conventions of photographic practice, authorizing the photographer to depict subjects unawares, so they could serve unwittingly as representative of the photographer's "vision" of urban life. When such photographs first became commonplace in the early twentieth century, the photographer often attempted to establish himself as categorically distinct and apart from those he photographed, occupying a position analogous to that of the omniscient narrator common in fiction. For when subjects knowingly address the camera, they are equally addressing themselves to the photographer, whose presence is at least implicitly inscribed. When they are photographed unawares, the transactional or intrasubjective elements of the photograph accentuate the camera's voyeurism and obscure the aggressive features of the photograph "pounce" (Cartier-Bresson's term).

To take one early and less familiar example, consider a book of photographs and texts by Ilya Ehrenburg, titled *My Paris*, published in Moscow in 1933, although the photographs were probably taken in the late 1920s.[17] The cover depicts Ehrenburg himself, montaged against one of his photographs of Belleville, then as now one of the poorer parts of the city. Dwarfing the street, Ehrenburg stands holding his small Leica. It is a duplicitous instrument, one of the models that permitted the photographer to focus on an object while the lens appeared to be pointing away from it. Looking at the crudely reproduced pictures in the book, it is clear that Ehrenburg's Parisians—mostly old, a few very young, all poor—were unaware of being photographed. Even more suggestive, there are a number of photographs of clochards lying unconscious in the street or on park benches, a staple subject of both documentary and street photographers from the 1930s to the present. Although the book appears to be an "art book," it may well have meant to serve the needs of Stalinist propaganda. Ehrenburg, who did not return to Moscow until 1941, was a party faithful until his death in 1967. His emphasis on images of poverty and misery may well have been intended to expose the hidden squalor of the capitalist city of light.

Ehrenburg not only represents himself using the trick camera, but the first chapter of the book is titled "The Lateral Viewfinder," and in it one finds his *éloge* to the act of clandestine photography:

> A writer knows that to see people, he must remain unseen. The world changes when you stare straight at it: cowards become heroes, and heroes become puppets. This second world can be studied in the shop window of any provincial photographer. But the writer knows the arts of both cunning and pretence. He enters life under another's name. When he's looking at cars or at daisies, Comrade Pavlov or snub-nosed Valentina, they don't realize that he's looking at them.
>
> But what's one to do with a camera? A camera is clumsy and crude. It meddles insolently in other people's affairs. The lens scatters a crowd like the barrel of a gun.
>
> Ours is a guileful age. . . . For many months I roamed Paris with a little camera. People would sometimes wonder: why was I taking pictures of a fence or a road? They didn't know that I was taking pictures of them. Now and then, those in front of me would turn away or smarted themselves up: they thought they were being photographed. But I was photographing others: those to the side. I wasn't looking their way, but they were my subjects. It's an exceptionally cunning device. It bears the affectionate name, Leica. The Leica has a lateral viewfinder. It's constructed like a periscope. I was photographing at 90 degrees.[18]

Ehrenburg's description of both his activity (and his camera) manifests many if not all the characteristics, assumptions, and rationales endemic to so-called street photography. Cameras like Ehrenburg's that seemed to be focused elsewhere were used by Paul Strand in his photographs of New Yorkers, by Walker Evans for certain of his own New York pictures, and by Helen Levitt and many others. In her 1974 *Photography and Society,* Gisèle Freund refers to the Ermanox, "the first lightweight, compact camera [that] permitted photographers to venture indoors for candid pictures with the addition of a new lens. . . . Soon, the 'secret' photograph which caught public figures unawares at work or play would become the trademark of many newspapers."[19] Although the development of the technology for such cameras was fueled by the needs of photojournalists working for mass cultural publications, we should note the alacrity with which art photographers seized on these cameras for the purposes of making "personal," that is, artistic, work.

In some instances, notably in the cases of Erich Salomon, Walker Evans, and Henri Cartier-Bresson, the subterfuge was in hiding the camera. The smaller scale of newer cameras was perfectly suited for the "photographic pounce" as Cartier-Bresson described it: "I had just discovered the Leica. It became the extension of my eye, and I have never been separated from it since I found it. I prowled the streets all day, feeling very strung-up and ready to pounce, determined to 'trap' life—to preserve life in the act of living. Above all I craved to seize the whole essence, in the confines of one single photograph, of some situation that was in the process of unrolling itself before my eyes."[20] And, in the same vein, "The creative act lasts but a brief moment, a lightning instant of give-and-take, just long enough for you to level the camera and to trap the fleeting prey in your little box."[21] One can readily find similar statements made by photographers and by critics, whether as description or panegyric.

While such statements invoke the predatory, possessive, and aggressive aspects of the photographic act, rarely—if ever—have photographers acknowledged any ethical discomfort or indeed ethical self-consciousness about their activity. This suggests that by the 1930s, and even more so in the 1950s and 1960s, the visual appropriation of the urban subject in public space had become culturally permissible and, indeed, unremarkable. Just as the law permits the representation of subjects without their knowledge or permission because it occurs in public space (thereby affirming the absolute divide between the public and private spheres), so too does this photographic practice imply the absolute distinction between the photographer and his subject, the observing I/eye of the photographer as radically disjunct from what he photographs. I use the masculine pronoun because this type of photography has been largely, if not exclusively, a masculine preserve.[22] Just as the role of omniscient narrator "disappears" the actual author as a particular individual—the speaking subject—so too is the photographer absent from the nature or content of his imagery. As is already evident in *My Paris*—where the Russian Ehrenburg surveys the marginal, poor, and hapless residents of Belleville—photographs of blind people regularly appear in the work of canonical photographers of the urban scene. The photographer sees; the subject does not—this might be considered as a succinct expression of the social relations implicit in the form. Similarly, the action of photographing unconscious subjects, sleeping or drunk, is not unrelated to this power differential between the photographer who actively looks and shoots, and the subject who is incapable of even returning the look.[23] Such subjects obviate any need for discretion or secrecy, and, even more emphatically than others, secure and affirm the presiding worldview of the photographer—his "vision" of the urban landscape and its denizens. Despite the enormous amount of vaporizing in the photographic literature about the affirmation of the photographic subject's humanity, or, even more dubiously, claims for photographers' empathetic identification with their subjects, the visual evidence would suggest otherwise.

Turning now to Callahan's street photographs—begun in 1941 during wartime with the purchase of a 35-millimeter single-lens reflex camera, and continuing with the subsequent work of 1950–52 and the early 1960s—it is worth making an effort to reinsert the political and social context so conspicuously absent from most of the commentary and criticism devoted to his work. Formalist artmaking typically prompts formalist commentary (and vice versa), as the Callahan literature amply demonstrates when it is not openly hagiographic. But even the most abstract or seemingly "autonomous" cultural production is marked by its historical situation. The apparent absence of reference to social and political realities in Callahan's work does not mean that the work transcends or escapes its embeddedness in its historical, political, and ideological moment. While Callahan's photographs appear distant from the kind of sociopolitical reference that one finds, for example, in Robert Frank's *The Americans* (1958), or in William Klein's *Life Is Good and Good for You* (1956), one shared quality is their generally dystopic view of (American) urban life. But any serious analysis of Callahan's pictures should begin with the rejection of his celebrants' references to the timeless, universal, or archetypal features of his work. No matter how hermetic, insular, or even abstract Callahan's works may appear, they are the product of a white working-class American man producing his work during and after the cataclysm of World War II (Callahan was rejected for military service for health reasons), followed by the Cold War, a period characterized by anticommunist hysteria (which had an impact on many individual photographers, as well as Popular Front entities such as the Photo League), stifling conformity, social conservatism, and pervasive anxieties about the ongoing arms race.

With specific respect to Callahan's photographs of urban life, there is reason to consider not only obvious precedents and influences, such as Walker Evans and his colleagues Aaron Siskind and Arthur Siegel, but also the work of other of his contemporaries active from the 1930s through the 1950s. Among the legions of photographers to have depicted metropolitan street life were Ben Shahn, Sid Grossman, Leon Levinstein, Louis Faurer, Helen Levitt, Louis Stettner, Milton Rogovin, Max Yavno, John Gutman, and many others. Collectively, these photographers had already established a visual lexicon of the American city, whether or not their photographs were specifically known by Callahan.[24] Here it is apposite to note that many of Callahan's photographs featuring city dwellers focus on one, two, or a few individuals rather than depicting the collective bustle of crowds or animated social groupings. These bodies of work can be contrasted with much of the urban photography made in the same period. In the work of Shahn and others, the city exists far more as a social space in which human density, with or without social interaction, is apparent, as is the sense of bustle, energy, and actual or potential incident. This suggests that one aspect of Callahan's vision of the metropolis requires the suppression or avoidance of those aspects of the city that are communal, interactive, and productive of social space and social relations. Like Evans's clandestine pictures of subway riders or pedestrians, Callahan's photographs emphasize a sense of isolation, each passerby confined to the private space of the self, sealed off from the possibilities of interaction.

Often, however, Callahan depicts the city without inhabitants, as in those pictures representing the blank façades of apartment buildings or skyscrapers, whose rectangular geometries formally reiterate the picture plane. Sometimes these photographs of the built environment are jazzed up with superimpositions or multiple exposures, transforming them into quasi-abstractions. But Callahan's most characteristic photographs of urban spaces are those marked by dramatic contrasts of black and white, often featuring dark masses of architecture against which pedestrians are illuminated by shafts of sunlight. In these pictures, the urban landscape operates as a kind of stage in which solitary individuals are more or less dwarfed by their surroundings, evoking a no-man's-land of existential isolation, much discussed in the sociological literature of the time. In those pictures depicting his wife and daughter with architectural backgrounds, the presence of the two small figures dwarfed by weirdly empty expanses operates to reveal the environment as bleakly inhuman.

This particular conception of the city has, of course, historical precedents in American photography (for example, Paul Strand's *Wall Street* of 1915). In contrast to the urban views of, for example, the Soviet and Weimar avant-gardes that celebrated the modern city as a vital and dynamic locus of energy, it may well be the case that the predominant image of the metropolis in twentieth-century American art photography testifies to the general perception in American culture that cities are dubious and unnatural phenomena.[25] Moreover, it seems to be the case that even in work by photographers who were more socially or politically engaged than was Callahan, urban life was often depicted as joyless and inhospitable. Although it is a commonplace in writing about the photography of the 1950s to contrast it with more politically engaged projects (for instance, work associated with the Photo League or, later, with the FSA), it is by no means clear that the political orientation of the photographer determines how the city and its occupants are imaged. Thus, while the group psychology described in David Riesman's *The Lonely Crowd* (1950) is understood to describe postwar symptoms of alienation, the evidence of artistic street photography as early as the 1930s is not markedly different from that of the 1950s, although Callahan's has its own specificity.

Certainly, the most conspicuous aspect of Callahan's images of pedestrians is their gender; they are overwhelmingly women. In this regard, it is significant that in much of the street photography considered exemplary of the form (excluding scenes of mixed crowds), it appears that women are more frequently photographed then men, but then most of the photography made on the street is made by men. "Men look, women appear."[26] John Berger's observation from 1972 has lost nothing of its pithy truth, and it matters little if the subject thus captured is attractive or not.

Callahan's pictures of women on the street fall roughly into three chronological groups: 1943–45, made in Detroit; 1954–56, made in Chicago; and another series begun in 1961–65 and made principally in New York City and Providence, Rhode Island (where he had taken a teaching job at the Rhode Island School of Design). The Detroit pictures are of women's heads, and were made with a 35-millimeter single-lens reflex camera. Of the twenty-four, only one is of a male subject. Successive series rarely depict men, and then usually when there are multiple rather than single figures. Here we can locate one of the basic elisions in discussions of Callahan's photographs, for Callahan's pictures are rarely considered in terms of sexual politics. Many texts characterize these pictures as depictions of pedestrians, or shoppers, or city dwellers, as though the sex of Callahan's subjects were incidental. Most quote Callahan's own characterization of his pictures of women pedestrians as seeking to represent meditative and introspective states of consciousness. Where the occasional essay acknowledges that Callahan's subjects are women, it is rationalized, mythologized, or endorsed: "It seems significant that a majority of the pedestrians recorded by Callahan were women. His shyness may have drawn him to photograph persons who seemed equally reserved and therefore unlikely to confront or challenge him. On a deeper level this artistic predilection suggests an integral aspect of Callahan's vision."[27] Why should this "predilection" be considered integral rather than cultural? On the contrary, it would seem that the visual capture of female subjects, like that of unconscious drunks or children, speaks to a insistent but disavowed desire for mastery, manifesting the appropriative or aggressive attributes that are literally masked by the camera.

In Callahan's pictures focusing on the heads and faces of women, there is a strange tension produced by his telephoto lens, so that the physical proximity of the subject is counterpointed by her psychological distance, a dissonance further emphasized by Callahan's framing and cropping. Although the close-up of a face is not itself a guarantee of the illusion of intimacy or psychological access, it is in the very nature of clandestine views of the unaware subject that human relatedness or any form of personal exchange is blocked, since it is generally evident that the subject is unaware of being looked at. Among Callahan's pictures of women pedestrians, this effect is notable, especially in those of his pictures where a companion of the woman has been cropped out, so that the subject's expression, or rather, her act of speaking, appears oddly disjointed. And what should be made of those photographs that crop the face so that certain of the woman's attributes—the wrinkles produced by a frown, the excessive shininess of a varnished coiffure—are attenuated, suggestive of a kind of feminine grotesque? In Callahan's later work of the 1960s, one series combines pedestrians on the street with televisions viewed through glass fronts facing the street; many if not all of them show a female movie star. Collages made in the same period consist of hundreds of found images of women and their body parts.

Callahan's street photographs were begun in 1941 and continued through the 1960s but were paralleled by his other principle subjects: his wife and child, architecture and cityscapes (minus people), and landscape subjects. In this regard, it is necessary to consider his relatively limited range of subject matter horizontally and synchronically. The opposition between Callahan's vision of the city—inhuman, anomic, antisocial, and oppressive—and his depiction of Eleanor alone or with his daughter begin to reveal a set of structuring oppositions. These include the juxtaposing of domestic and "natural" space (i.e., the home, parks, trees, weeds) with public space; spouse versus stranger; elemental, sexualized body versus objectified alien body. Photographs that superimpose Eleanor's body on a landscape, or associate it with water and vegetation—woman as nature—testify to an atavistic fantasy that not only conflates woman and nature but implies that public life and social relations are the negative pole to which home (haven in a heartless world), nature, and spouse are the antidote. This perspective is very much in keeping with the quietist and individualistic ideologies of 1950s America.

But whether we are addressing Callahan's pictures or those of other art photographers discursively positioned under the genre umbrella of street photography, a further point should be made. What seems to be always at stake in the invention of this genre is a certain subject position for the photographer. I refer here to the art photographer, who in this context is producing not landscape, nude, still life, or abstraction—staple subjects of art photography that, by definition, declare their status as art. Instead of such duly consecrated aesthetic motifs, the photographer poaches, so to speak, on the territory of the photojournalist, the documentarian, the magazine photographer, and the commercial purveyor of urban views. Accordingly, for Callahan as for others photographers of this ilk, the work needs to distinguish itself from vernacular uses. In appropriating the mantle of the artist/observer, it is imperative that the observing consciousness be separate from what is observed, a convention that remains fully in place in more recent variants of this practice. The art of photographic capture is never innocent, is never an act of neutral bystanding. It cannot but manifest its mooring in relations of power and mastery that are variously articulated within the image itself. Such forms of photographic practices are, by definition, never an act of community or collectivity, of inclusion or identification. They reflect a relation to the social world that is, at best, the unengaged but endlessly curious stance of the flâneur. But the *flânerie* of the nineteenth century, defined by men such as Baudelaire, has developed in certain ways. Rather than the indifferently interested gaze of the man in the crowd, it can be now identified with the insatiability of both voyeurism and consumerism, the ever-mastering but ever-alienated gaze of the photographer at the subject as object.

# 6

## Caught Looking

### SUSAN MEISELAS'S *CARNIVAL STRIPPERS*

(2008)

In the consecutive summers of 1973, 1974, and 1975, the years of Gerald Ford's presidency, Susan Meiselas, then in her twenties, photographed the strippers, barkers ("talkers"), managers, bouncers ("roughies"), and audiences of several itinerant girl shows installed on the grounds of fairs and carnivals in rural New England and Pennsylvania. In addition to the photographs, Meiselas recorded many hours of audiotape, including conversations with the strippers and other workers, and comments from spectators. Thus, from very early in its inception, the project that became *Carnival Strippers* rejected the notion of the "purely visual" as adequate to its depiction of its subjects, their work, their place, and their milieu.[1] This expanded approach to photographic meaning, however, was hardly the norm in the 1970s, and it was doubtless Meiselas's departure from it that occasioned commentators to remark on her undergraduate major in anthropology and her youthful desire to become an ethnographic filmmaker.[2]

Be that as it may, both in its first edition (1976) and its revised reissue (2002), *Carnival Strippers* counterpointed the photographs with texts excerpted from transcripts of the recordings. When the project was first adapted to exhibition format at CEPA Gallery in Buffalo, Meiselas used the sound recordings throughout the exhibition space so that the voices of those photographed were part of the environment. In keeping with Meiselas's emphasis on the voices, the 2002 edition of the book also includes a CD consisting of commentary by one of the strippers (Lena) gathered over the course of four years, a collage of voices, and an interview with Meiselas made in 1977. Meiselas has also produced a fifteen-minute DVD, using the still images from the book with an added audio track.

Although the pictures are sometimes grim, they are less disturbing than some of the accompanying texts. And while pictures of the male customers (women were not permitted entry to the shows) reveal expressions ranging from rapt fascination to aggressive leering, the faces of the strippers (when not performing) mostly suggest boredom, introspection, or fatigue. It is only in the second part of the book, made up of relatively formal portraits in which the women themselves chose how to present themselves, that the occasional cheesecake pose or come-hither expression appears. But with the exception of a few pictures redolent of drunken hilarity, no one seems to be having a particularly good time.

These gritty, noir-esque pictures were—and are—unsettling in a number of ways. Part of this effect has to do with the project's subject matter, the bleak and tawdry domain of fairground striptease, a poor relation of the elaborately orchestrated floorshows of, say, Las Vegas. In the relatively low-end circuit of carnival stripping, the boundaries between performance and sex acts, depending on venue and law enforcement, might be significantly breached; "working strong" is the strippers' argot for letting customers perform cunnilingus during the show. "Lunch counter" is the term describing this activity from the customer's side of the stage.

Yet another discomfiting element is the way that Meiselas shot and cropped certain images to create the visual sensation of extreme proximity to the women's bodies. These bodies, moreover, are not likely to be confused with those of dancers, athletes, or models, whose very perfection functions as itself a kind of clothing. Fat or thin, the women's breasts, bellies, and thighs evoke the carnal in its most literal sense. As Deirdre English observes, their bodies bear the marks of mortality—pregnancies, nursing, age. Indeed, this is one of the ways one distinguishes between the unclothed human being—the naked—and the aesthetic concept that underpins the nude. There is, in fact, only a single photograph—remarked upon by English—that could pass muster *as* a nude, depicting the stripper named Lena asleep on a bed. In both editions of the book, this atypical photograph closes the first section.

The grainy, contrasting quality of the images, the blurred bodies in movement, the casual obscenity of much of the dialogue—all of these function to produce a sense of spontaneity, "real life" captured on the run. This, of course, is not to gainsay the *artifice* of Meiselas's work, for the artifice is precisely the art, and nothing could less resemble work made on the run than Meiselas's long-term engagement with her project. This deliberation is especially clear when one compares the 1976 version of the book with the later one. Although

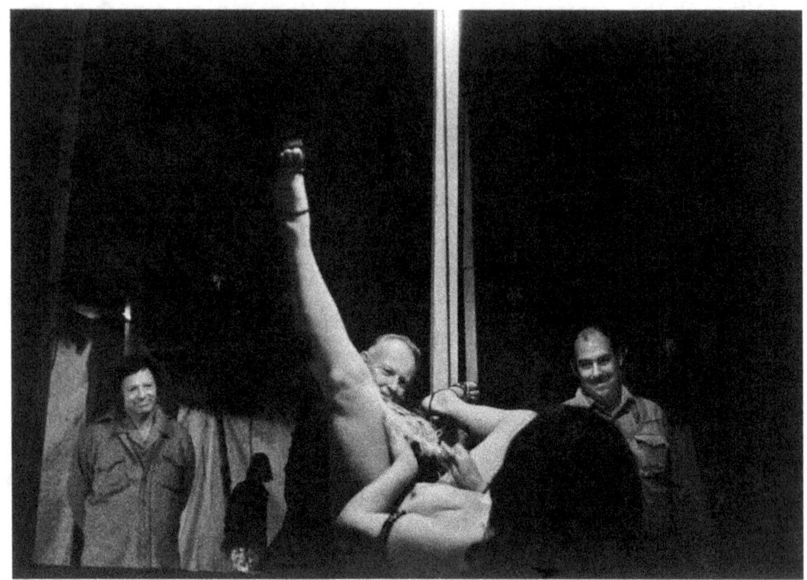

6.1 Susan Meiselas, *Playing Strong, Tunbridge, Vermont,* 1975. From *Carnival Strippers.* COURTESY OF SUSAN MEISELAS/MAGNUM PHOTOS.

only several photographs were dropped from the former or others added to the latter, the texts and images were variously resequenced. The new organization reinforces the perception of a spatial movement from outside to inside, and a temporal movement from early evening to late night. Sometimes the text appears to be generated by the person photographed, other times not. Although different girl shows, different places, and different years are intermingled, *Carnival Strippers* is not structured as a day-in-the-life narrative but rather as a virtual journey that begins with the bally call (*"Watch it! Watch it right now! Stop the music! You're gonna see burlesque, striptease, hootchie-kootchie, and daddy-o, it's all the way!"*) and ends with the dismantling of the show-in-a-truck that signals the itinerancy of the small world it has documented.

Most of the pictures—including those depicting the women dancing on the makeshift stages, lounging in their dressing areas, or lying on their motel beds—were made with a small, unobtrusive Leica and shot with ambient light and without a zoom lens. In certain of the close-ups, it seems extraordinary that Meiselas drew no attention to herself. It is as though the men—or boys—were so mesmerized by the strippers on the platform above them as to be unaware of the small young woman in the act of photographing them.

Framed in close-up and often shot in confined spaces, the women too ap-

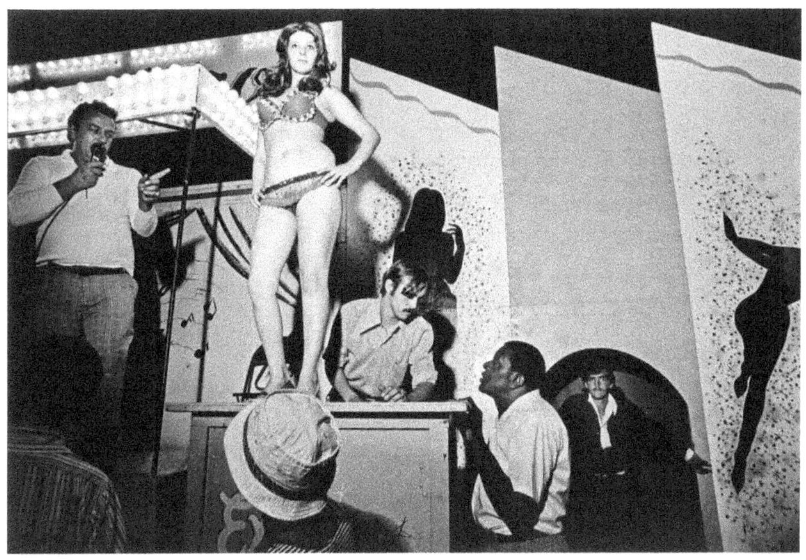

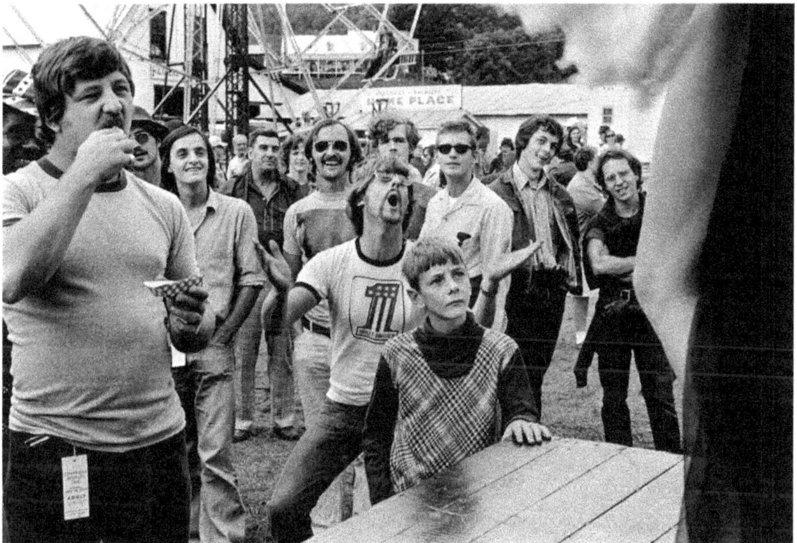

6.2 (*top*) Susan Meiselas, *Lena on the Bally Box, Essex Junction, Vermont*, 1973. From *Carnival Strippers*. COURTESY OF SUSAN MEISELAS/MAGNUM PHOTOS.

6.3 (*bottom*) Susan Meiselas, *Afternoon Tease, Tunbridge, Vermont*, 1974. From *Carnival Strippers*. COURTESY OF SUSAN MEISELAS/MAGNUM PHOTOS.

pear oblivious to the camera. In photographic practice, such spatial proximity is presumed to be a function of familiarity or intimacy with the subject(s). In the past few decades, this manner of working has become itself a topos of a certain genre of art photography and is often taken to be a kind of ethical immunization absolving the photographer of the charge of exploitation. Insofar as it signals the photographer's insider status in the world he or she depicts, the assumption is that the problems posed by the politics of representation are more or less resolved. But as is demonstrated, for example, by the work of Richard Billington and the purveyors of what might be termed "poverty porn," the photographer's intimacy with his or her subject matter guarantees nothing.[3] In fact, insider or outsider status in and of itself neither prevents nor facilitates empathetic or objectifying forms of viewing, does not in and of itself inculpate or exonerate the photographer. Viewing relations are, among other things, social relations, and what we might make of *Carnival Strippers* or how we respond to it depends on a multitude of factors. These include its discursive framing, the context of viewing, a host of cultural assumptions and beliefs, and our own subjectivity, conscious and unconscious. And it goes without saying that the meanings of any cultural object are more dependent on these determinations than they are on the photographer's intentions.

In regard to Meiselas's apparent "invisibility" as she made her pictures, a few further points might be made. Considering her documentary projects overall, from the *Strippers* to *Nicaragua* to the Kurdistan work and the extraordinary *Encounters with the Dani*, one cannot but be struck by a quality of discretion, of consistent self-effacement, which should not be confused with the furtive activity of the surreptitious street photographer or that of the workaday photojournalist. If Meiselas's photographs do not manifest a conspicuous signature style (as do a number of her contemporaries who are also Magnum photographers), it is perhaps indicative of a lack of artistic self-importance, a form of ethical *tact* before her subjects (in both senses of the word "subjects"). *Encounters with the Dani*, for example, contains a bare handful of Meiselas's own photographs; *Kurdistan: In the Shadow of History* is ongoing, exists in multiple forms (including its website), and is mosaic-like and receptive to all forms of documentation in addition to her own.[4] This ability to minimize oneself in the act of observing and photographing is a taken-for-granted attribute of professional photojournalism, but is less often the case with those who aspire to the mantle of "artist," or for those whose documentary projects are intended as recognizably "personal" productions (a generally hopeless enterprise in documentary practice).

In this context, although the "look" of the pictures in *Carnival Strippers* might resonate with certain kinds of documentary realist film practices (such as those of Frederick Wiseman), and inasmuch as black-and-white imagery now circulates in the mass media as a calculatedly retro style, it would seem more accurately descriptive to consider Meiselas's project as motivated by the desire to understand the subculture it depicts, even as one acknowledges the limits of such an enterprise, and, indeed, the limits of photography itself.

How and why these striptease road shows have disappeared, making *Carnival Strippers* a kind of historical artifact, has many determinations.[5] As English rightly observes, the eclipse of the girl shows had much to do with the advent of newer, glitzier, and more diverse forms of sexual entertainment as well (needless to say) as the "mainlining" of sexually explicit material in video and DVD formats. As an in-depth visual and aural documentation, *Carnival Strippers* might thus be considered a sociological or, given the passage of time, historico-sociological study. And, obviously, it can be approached as a significant example of the genre of photographic documentary; indeed, it was on the strength of this body of work that Meiselas, at the age of twenty-nine, became a member of the prestigious photographic agency Magnum, one of only two women to have been admitted by this date. Yet another way to situate and contextualize the book would be with reference to the more or less contemporary documentary photography books that appeared with increasing frequency from the late 1960s on. This is one of the reasons that the book form is so well adapted to photographic documentary projects in the first place: it permits narrative structures (either with or without text); it allows for the viewer or reader's reconsideration and reflection; and it is open to intimate as well as more social perusal.[6] Certain of these books are significant vis-à-vis Meiselas's work, not merely because she has indicated their importance for her but also because they exemplify certain qualities that distinguish the work of a documentary photographer from that of a professional photojournalist.[7] Martha Rosler's description of these differences is useful: "Documentary and photojournalistic practices overlap but are still distinguishable from one another. Photojournalists are primarily employed to work on specific journalistic 'stories,' supplying images while others provide copy, and their feelings and sympathies about what they are photographing remain unsolicited. In contrast, documentarians choose their subjects and treat them as they will, but with no guarantee of publication. In reality, however, many photographers engage in both practices, and the same images may function in both frames as well."[8]

As a professional photographer, Meiselas has operated on both sides of this putative divide. Moreover, the production of photographers such as Meiselas, who belong to photo agencies and often work on assignment, appears in different venues, at different times, to different ends. If not purchased outright by the magazine or newspaper that initially commissioned them, the pictures often end up in the agency's archives, where they can be reused in any number of contexts.[9] But the distinction Rosler draws here, however blurred in actual practice, is based on the notion of a photographer's *choice*. One might quibble with this insofar as during the heyday of picture magazines such as *Life*, canonized documentary photographers such as Eugene Smith might choose their subjects *and* be commissioned to shoot them *and* work with the feature's writer. But present-day practice probably conforms more to Rosler's distinction than not. What Rosler does not indicate (although it is implicit in her discussion) is that most photographic production designated as "documentary" and defined as an individually motivated rather than commercially commissioned project would seem to have been generated exclusively from the liberal end of the political spectrum. I can think of no well-known documentary photographer associated with conservative, much less reactionary, politics. Which is not to deny that many documentary projects intended as "progressive" are nevertheless politically problematic: this particular practice and the issues it raises (e.g., paternalism, careerism, exploitation, objectification, etc.) can be traced as far back as Jacob Riis's 1899 *How the Other Half Lives* and has long been the target of left critique.

This critique is worth mentioning in relation to *Carnival Strippers* (in any of its incarnations) because there is little if anything within it that permits one to identify a particular politics, a parti pris.[10] Which is to say that this is not a project that takes its place in the honorific role of reformist enterprises exemplified by Lewis Hine's documentation of child or sweatshop labor.[11] Nevertheless, the fact that the project originates at the historical moment of the reemergence of feminism is itself significant, although *Strippers* is not in any simple manner an obvious, that is to say, tendentious feminist enterprise. Which is by no means to suggest that it is antifeminist, or to deny that it is entirely compatible with feminist readings (as is clear from the essays by English and Wolf). If one is looking for an unambiguous political and feminist significance in the work, one can easily deduce that in the rural United States of the mid-1970s, uneducated and unskilled women had (and have) few vocational options; that it was possible for a woman to make more money stripping than working in a sardine factory; that women are subject to abuse from men; and that the world of what pundits like to call the "heartland" is remote from the metropolis. None of these conclusions is especially newsworthy, and none constitutes in any significant way the meanings that *Carnival Strippers* generates.

Part of the difficulty of identifying a clear and unambiguous point of view in *Carnival Strippers* (in contrast to Meiselas's justly famous *Nicaragua*, for example), is that it takes voyeurism as its central thematic, an activity that implicates subject, photographer, and, obviously, the viewer. This is the central point to be made, and is the source of the book's power to unsettle and disturb even though we know that *what* we are observing is long vanished. Photographic point of view is therefore a central problematic in the work, consistently if implicitly acknowledged through its emphasis on the activity of looking in its external and internal mechanisms, determinations, and significance. The word "stripper" itself is dense with associations even before we bring those to the viewing of the image. As such, and as Victor Burgin argued, there is no nonideological viewing position, no innocent eye, no possibility of visual perception or reception independent of already established meanings and connotations. "The structure of representation"—point of view and frame—is ultimately implicated in the reproduction of ideology (the "frame of mind" of our "point of view").[12] In the broadest sense, therefore, even the pictorial conventions of geometric perspective, or the constitutive acts of framing and cropping, are implicated in producing, or reproducing, social and psychic relations. Because it so directly engages with these aspects of photographic representation, *Carnival Strippers* raises issues about the activity of looking itself and the forms by which looking is bound up with gender, and with sex, by mechanisms of objectification, fetishism, and projection, especially when the depicted subject is that of the female body. Aside from the activity of striptease itself (to which I will return), many of the photographs in *Carnival Strippers* represent the act of looking itself, sometimes with the performers in the same frame as the spectators, and other times when the spectators are absent. Certain of the pictures depict the strippers observing the spectators from behind the curtain that separates offstage from onstage. Still others depict individuals looking at one another, in the midst of some kind of interaction. *Carnival Strippers* can therefore be described as a work about looking, voyeurism, and sexual difference. And insofar as the viewer's look replaces that of the photographer, Meiselas's original look through the lens of her Leica becomes structurally and necessarily our own.

Given the prevalence of the word "voyeurism"—a now commonplace term in film and photography criticism, and, for that matter, in everyday parlance—

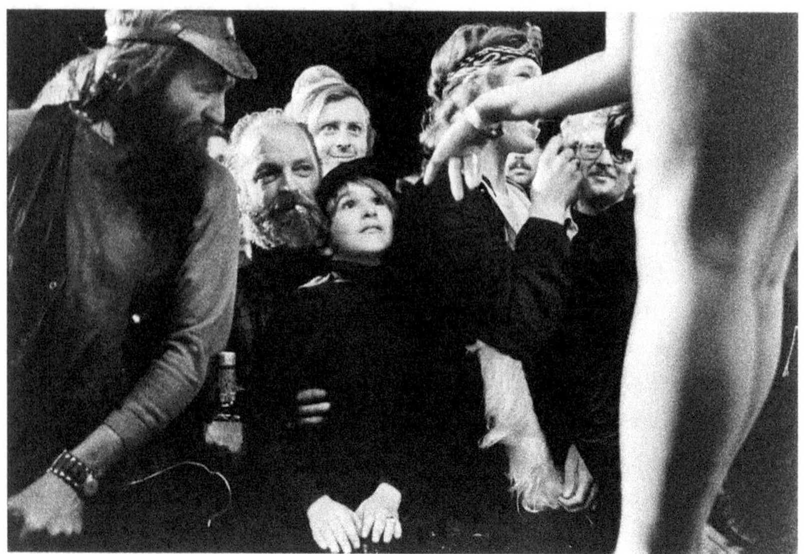

6.4 Susan Meiselas, *Before the Show, Tunbridge, Vermont,* 1974. From *Carnival Strippers.* COURTESY OF SUSAN MEISELAS/MAGNUM PHOTOS.

it is surprising to learn that its first appearance in English was as late as 1924. It appears first as an English translation of the second volume of Wilhelm Stekel's *Disorders of Instincts and Emotions,* where it duly repeats the definition first given it by Sigmund Freud in his "Three Essays on a Theory of Sexuality" (1905). Although he did not return to the subject until many years later, Freud maintained his basic assertion that voyeurism was an independent drive, identifiable in children's sexual curiosity, and characterized by the desire to see the body's "hidden parts."[13] Freud's use of the word is sometimes interchangeable with the more clinical-sounding "scopophilia," but in either locution, he considered it to occupy a spectrum in psychic life. In its extreme manifestation, Freud defined the activity as a perversion, exemplified by the activity of the Peeping Tom. Nevertheless, in keeping with the notion that modern Western culture is characterized by the production and consumption of images, and, more profoundly, that it conforms to Debord's theorization of the society of the spectacle, voyeurism has ceased to be limited to its designation as pathological behavior. This is reflected in the *Oxford English Dictionary*'s examples of the word's history, indicating that by 1976 it could be unremarkably employed as much as a social diagnostic as a form of pathology. Interestingly, one of the examples given in the *Oxford English Dictionary* refers to photography:

"1976, *Listener* 25 Nov. 682/3 A beggar's expression captured by a camera costing enough to feed, clothe and house him for maybe five years." Is this kind of photography good or bad? Is it just an obscene form of voyeurism, a record of what one privileged class finds quaint or interesting in another?

In terms of both voyeurism and sexual difference, striptease itself might well be considered an exemplary topic, for in most instances this type of performance is based on women removing their clothing, usually to music, and sometimes in the form of a dance. Thus, striptease is by definition a quintessentially voyeuristic entertainment in the way that tennis, for example, or tap dance is not. Although the dictionary definition of "striptease" allows for its performers to be of either gender—"1. A kind of entertainment in which a female (occas. a male) performer undresses gradually in a tantalizingly erotic fashion before an audience, usu. to music . . ."—the default meaning presumes a woman as the performer.[14] Notwithstanding the phenomenon of male striptease, the spectacle of striptease pivots on what Roland Barthes claimed to be a performance of *de*sexualization: "Striptease—at least Parisian striptease—is based on a contradiction: Woman is desexualized at the very moment when she is stripped naked. We may therefore say that we are dealing in a sense with a spectacle based on fear, or rather on the pretence of fear, as if eroticism here went no further than a sort of delicious terror, whose ritual signs have only to be announced to evoke at once the idea of sex and its conjuration."[15]

Given that Barthes' essay "Striptease" was written in 1956 and refers only to Paris, it does not necessarily apply to the kinds of performance depicted in *Carnival Strippers*. To state the obvious, the furs and furbelows, jewelry and other accessories, lighting, production values, and so on all operate, as Barthes observes, to occult the presence of a living female body: "The classic props of the music-hall, which are invariably rounded up here, constantly make the unveiled body more remote, and force it back into the all-pervading ease of a well-known rite: the furs, the fans, the gloves, the feathers, the fish-net stockings, in short the whole spectrum of adornment, constantly makes the living body return to the category of luxurious objects which surround man with a magical decor."[16]

As for the climax, as it were, of this type of theatricalized striptease—the baring (almost) of the entire body, Barthes's witty analysis makes very clear his debt to Freud's androcentric theory of fetishism: "The nakedness which follows remains itself unreal, smooth and enclosed like a beautiful slippery object, withdrawn by its very extravagance from human use: this is the underlying significance of the G-string covered with diamonds or sequins which is the very end of striptease. This ultimate triangle, by its pure and geometrical shape, by its hard and shiny material, bars the way to the sexual parts like a sword of purity, and definitively drives the woman back into a mineral world."[17]

"Smooth" and "firm," "the pure and geometric form," a "mineralogical universe"—here Barthes describes the female body magically and reassuringly transformed into the phallus itself. In arguing that fetishism was an unconscious formation produced by the little boy's traumatic misperception of the mother's body as castrated, a trauma perpetually denied (and therefore memorialized) by fixation on a substitute object, Freud based his conclusions on his analysis of actual fetishists. But like the word "voyeur," which, as I have indicated, has come to signify sociocultural as well as psychosexual phenomena, so too has "fetishism" come to far exceed the clinical meaning Freud first gave it.[18] Furthermore, the entirely conventionalized insignia of the eroticized female body (high heels, net stockings, garter belts, corsets, and the like) are fairly obvious examples of the banalization of what was once the purview of an erotic underworld, the subcultural domain of stag movies and men's magazines.[19]

Nevertheless, one difficulty with Freud's theory of fetishism is that it so insistently associates female genitals with lack and mutilation as to make it hard to understand why heterosexual men would wish to look at them at all, much less engage in oral sex.[20] Many feminist theorists generally deal with this contradiction by yoking together a wide array of responses as alternatives to the formation of a literal fetish object. These include, *pace* Barthes's striptease description, the transformation of the female body itself into a fetish (permitting its overvaluation or idealization no less than the denial of its supposed mutilation), obsessively investigating it, punishing it, and so forth.

As it happens, the strippers Meiselas photographed avail themselves of little in the way of accessories that might hide, much less transform, the visceral and carnal reality of the female body. In this respect, Meiselas's photographs of the strippers' "working strong," splaying their legs to display their sex, enticing or merely permitting clients to perform cunnilingus, might seem to belie the fetishistic structures of the masculine gaze. But certain pictures of male spectators—especially two pictures of seemingly spellbound young boys—remind us of what was so central, and still so disturbing, in Freud's work, namely his insistence on the irrational, that is, the unconscious mechanisms of sexuality and the difficulties that attend the negotiation of sexual difference. Certainly one of the many disturbing aspects of *Carnival Strippers* is its unflinching testimony to the violence to which women are subjected, be it the violence of social, familial, intimate, or professional relations. That the sex acts that occurred in the course of performance were so highly fraught, indeed violent—supporting Freud's contention that men's responses to the recesses of the female body are at the very least ambivalent—is amply demonstrated in one of Lena's horrifying accounts: "I have been pulled off the stage and beaten and I've been stepped on and I've had people cut me. I know that the guys that come in here have to be a little bit off—a lot of them are really sickies. Especially the ones who come in every show. . . . They say come down here and they bite your clit, the blood's running down your leg."[21]

Looking at these pictures, reading these texts so many years after they were made, and acknowledging the "pastness" that is the condition of all photography does not appreciably diminish their effects. Moreover, the knowledge of at least one of the women has died—Lena, so vividly alive when Meiselas photographed her at seventeen on the day she was hired as a stripper—provides its own somber coda. But the more important point is that the *Carnival Strippers* of today is not the *Carnival Strippers* of 1976, and not only because its form of presentation or exhibition is different from its earlier presentations. When Meiselas first decided to devote herself to the documentation of what was likely an utterly alien milieu, the reemergence of feminism and the various groupings and political formations of the women's movement were still relatively recent. And just as feminist theory and politics posed searching questions about real women in the real world (including complicated issues around sex work, pornography, and the commodification of women and their bodies), so too did it pose challenging questions about gender and representation, the politics of looking, and the mechanisms of dominance and subordination as these were played out in all aspects of women's lives. Within other subcultures—for example, professional documentary photography or the more rarified world of contemporary art photography—such questions were not wholly absent. Indeed, this was the period when critics and theorists of various stripes reanimated the field of photographic inquiry. Thus, if *Carnival Strippers* was considered controversial, or objectionable, or incomprehensible *as* the project of a young woman photographer, it was because so many of these issues, questions, and problems were newly situated within a political as well as a theoretical agenda. That these have apparently been wholly eclipsed by the infinite capacity of contemporary culture to neutralize or transform even the imagery of abjection into easily consumable spectacle should give us pause. As Martha Rosler has mordantly remarked, "Voyeurism as a naked motive for photography is increasingly expressed and rewarded, in art and mass culture, even in polite society."[22]

But it is not just voyeurism that is at stake; it is equally the case that an unapologetic fetishism—perhaps one should say an unembarrassed fetishism—seems not only ubiquitous but also possibly invisible as such. What else is one to make of the recent exhibition by Philip-Lorca diCorcia titled "Lucky Thirteen," a series of large-scale (5½ by 4 feet) color photographs of mostly nude pole dancers? These are tellingly described in the Pace/MacGill Gallery's press release: "DiCorcia's pole dancers are suspended in time and space within the theatrically transfigured environments of strip clubs. . . . 'Lucky Thirteen' is, at its essence, a series of psychologically penetrating portraits. Referred to by their stage names—Harvest Moon, Lola, Pepper, Sin—the women in diCorcia's photographs can be likened to sculpture insofar as they are simultaneously immortalized and monumentalized. The dancers' bodies are rigid and their expressions appear as if frozen; diCorcia abstracts the dancers into a realm that is larger-than-life." To characterize these as "portraits" is, needless to say, quite a stretch, but like the photographs themselves (significantly described by the press release as "rigid," "sculptural," and "monumental"), diCorcia's nudes are textbook examples of photographic fetishism. In terms of their lavish production values as well as their physical scale, they bespeak the grandiosity that is fully in keeping with the inflated and voracious art market that fostered their production. These are images that have little or nothing to do with the "psychology" of women pole dancers, notwithstanding the actual women who were photographed, and everything to do with the patriarchal imaginary. In this regard, *Lucky Thirteen* might well be considered a kind of epitaph to the complex and serious themes that Meiselas took on as her own. In this sense, the manifest *difference* between Meiselas's edgy, serious, deeply thoughtful, and complicated project of 1976 hardly needs elaboration, but it is perhaps the *distance*—political and ethical, no less than artistic—that separates these two bodies of work that is the most troublesome and disturbing issue of all.

# 7

# Framing Landscape Photography

(2010)

A working country is hardly ever a landscape. The very idea of landscape implies separation and observation. It is possible and useful to trace the internal histories of landscape painting, landscape writing, landscape gardening and landscape architecture, but in any final analysis we must relate these histories to the common history of a land and its society.
—RAYMOND WILLIAMS

## A Very, Very Short History of Nineteenth-Century Landscape Photography

Although many standard histories of photography assume the existence of a unified category of "landscape" photography inaugurated in the 1840s, this terminology is not always appropriate. Insofar as "landscape" is an *aesthetic* category in the visual arts that appeared in European painting only in the sixteenth century (although it appeared much earlier in China, where for millennia it was a highly privileged subject), the concept is premised on a complex schema of rules, conventions, formal structures, and motifs. To produce something visually recognizable *as* landscape was, therefore, to manipulate a set of pictorial devices that distinguished the natural world as such—*natura naturens*—from other related categories: forest, countryside, wilderness, garden, park, pasture, prospect, view, and so forth. This genre-fication of landscape, begun in the Renaissance, eventually permitted for the representations of particular kinds of landscape—mythological and classical, romantic and realist, rural and suburban, and, increasingly important in the nineteenth century, the identifiably national. The indispensable Harrison and Cynthia White inform us that during the midcentury, the prices for contemporary and classical French landscapes, which rose steadily, were eclipsed by the prices for seventeenth-century Dutch paintings.[1] But for the photographers seeking to produce landscapes in the 1850s, it was originally the paintings of Théodore Rousseau and his *école* from which they took their cue.[2]

In terms of its evolution in Western painting, the emergence of the category "landscape" was accompanied by its generic (and subgeneric) codification. By the 1660s, landscape—*paysage* in French, *paesaggio* in Italian—was officially, that is, institutionally, recognized as an independent genre with all that that implies; a system of rules and conventions understood by the artist and legible to the viewer.[3] But once established as a genre, landscape could nevertheless be inflected in various ways and made to signify different things, adapting itself to national cultures and to changing tastes, attitudes, and styles, and social, economic, and artistic values. It could, for example, be associated with republicanism, with democratic aspirations, or, at certain times, an implicit criticism of the empire and its cultural politics.[4] Nature could be made to serve conservative as well as democratic values. Thus, the portraits of British gentry posed out of doors were unambiguous celebrations of property and ownership.[5] But whatever the differences between Rousseau's dim marshes and Courbet's rugged Jura, Corot's misty pastorales and Monet's waterscapes—all are immediately identifiable to us, as they were to their contemporaries, as diverse incarnations of landscape. This malleability is part of landscape's durability, adapted as it was to classical idioms (the *paysage historique* à la Poussin); the homely rural scene (as in Dutch seventeenth-century art, or in the work of British artists such as Constable and Turner); the Romantic sublime (as in the work of the German Caspar David Friedrich or the British John Martin); the "realist" and regionally specific landscapes of nineteenth-century artists (including those of the Impressionists), and the many varieties of the picturesque purveyed in both elite and mass cultural forms, from grandiose painting to modest lithograph.

However, when, beginning in the later part of the 1850s, photographers turned their cameras on "nature," what they produced was not necessarily "landscape."[6] Their projects, often as not, originated in the service of government survey, architectural patrimony, topography, geology, botany, biblical studies, archeology, military strategy, and colonial conquest, as well as in the production of what were called "views." With respect to this latter term, and as Rosalind E. Krauss has demonstrated, the nineteenth-century "view" mobilizes its own lexicon of visual conventions and specific viewing circumstances (e.g., often in the form of the stereographic image and the apparatus to view it), as well as a range of discourses that cannot be collapsed into the modern aesthetic conception of landscape.[7] Thus, while it might be argued that all landscapes are "views," not all "views" are landscapes.

Descriptive rather than interpretive, many of these nineteenth-century photographic enterprises (the view and the panorama among them), reflect the diverse instrumentalities of the new medium. In fact, for the first twenty or so years of its existence, and irrespective of technology (i.e., daguerreotype, calotype, and, after 1851, wet-plate processes), there exists relatively little photographic imagery that can be fairly designated "pure" landscape, although landscape had by the 1840s become one of the most popular subjects of French painting.[8] The strikingly beautiful images produced between the late 1840s and 1870s by photographers such as Eugène Cuvelier, Alphonse Jeanrenaud, Gustave Le Gray, Henri Le Secq, or others should be understood as a very specific subcategory of nineteenth-century photography within which photographers (many if not most of them amateurs) attempted to represent what painters and printmakers had been producing en masse from the July Monarchy on.

In part, this was a consequence of landscape's generic aesthetic identity, which in turn determined the nature of its market. But absent a significant desire for such pictures in the new medium of photography, such imagery remained largely the province of the specialized milieu of gentlemen amateurs whose sorties in the genre were as likely to be informed by technical experiment (given the existing limitations of their medium) as by artistic intention. By the 1870s, landscape photographs were made by professionals, some of whom, such as Achille Quinet, made it one of their specialties. In the earlier days of photography, landscape subjects were for the most part produced, reproduced, circulated, exhibited, and (rarely) purchased within a circuit of artist-amateurs, specialized journals, photographic salons (in the later part of the century), and exclusive photographic societies.[9] In some cases (the larger, more visually detailed prints made by Alexandre Famin and Quinet), the pictures were sold to artists and students as aide-mémoires—the same market they supplied with nudes. Photographic landscape, *as* an aesthetic form distinct from topographic view or stereo for the tourist market (e.g., fig. 7.1), consequently existed on the fringes of the photographic industry at large, and remained so until after the 1880s. This tells us something about the marginality of artistic photography (at least in economic terms) in the broader context of visual culture in the Second Empire.[10] While landscape had long become dominant in the salons of the period and drew ever-increasing prices at auction, few landscape photographs were created, much less sold. Lithographic prints of landscape subjects commanded a large-scale market, but photography, practically speaking, was less adapted to its conventions and iconography in either its picturesque or romantic varieties.[11] In any case, to my knowledge, no French photographer of the nineteenth century made his or her living through landscape photography; many of the medium's artistically inclusive printers and publishers ended up bankrupt.[12] Hence photography's somewhat marginal status within the great industrial expansion that occurred after 1851 with Scott Archer's invention of the wet-collodion-on-glass process signaled the death knell for the paper negative and, eventually, the daguerreotype.[13]

It was only in the 1880s, when the British amateur Peter Henry Emerson produced his forty platinum prints included in his series *Life and Landscape on the Norfolk Broads* (1886) and, two years later, his series *Pictures of East Anglian Life*, that the "naturalistic" landscape became a staple subject of art photography.[14] But even as photographers such as Emerson rejected the concepts of the sublime or the picturesque, their landscapes were nonetheless highly aestheticized. Indeed, platinum printing, with its subtle modulations of tone and complicated printing and processing, was itself associated with the "art" of art photography.

While "pure" landscape photography had little market value, by the late 1850s and the widespread adaptation of Archer's positive/negative process, a significant market for photography rapidly emerged as an offshoot of the expanding tourist industry. Where scenic views that can be characterized as landscapes *were* commercially produced (for example, by the photographic firm of Adolphe Braun, or the Florence-based firm Fratelli Alinari), these usually represented those places that had long been established as sites of foreign travel—the Swiss Alps, Italy, and so on—and were surrogate or real souvenirs destined for the bourgeois sitting room and made to take their place alongside albums of portrait photographs, *cartes de visite*, and cabinets for stereographic cards with their stereopticon viewer.

What can also be referred to as photographic landscape had a brief flowering in the 1850s and 1860s in France and England, to reappear later within the context of pictorialism and symbolism in both countries, and, indeed, internationally. In its earliest avatar, landscape was one of the subjects adapted by French calotypists such as Henri Le Secq and Gustave Le Gray (who shifted to collodion in the mid-1850s), Henri-Victor Regnault, and a few others. By 1860, most landscape pictures were made from wet collodion on glass and printed on albuminized paper. In Britain, too, pictures of parks and trees had been made in the 1840s by the inventor of the positive/negative process on paper, Henry Fox Talbot.[15] Benjamin Brecknell Turner, who purchased rights to

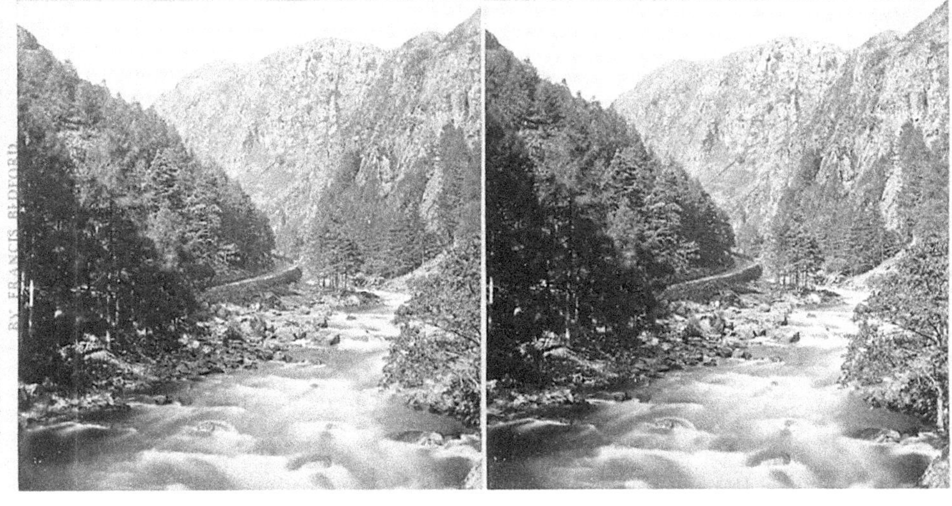


7.1 Francis Bedford, *Pass of Aberglaslyn—from the Bridge, No. 2*, ca. 1860. Stereograph 2779. 7.9 × 7.8 cm. (each) on 8.4 × 17.3 cm. mount. From Francis Bedford, *North Wales Illustrated Series*, ca. 1860.

Talbot's process, produced an album of sixty photographs, including trees and landscape views. Those producing landscape photographs from the 1840s on took their models less from the contemporary painting and lithographic prints influenced by romanticism (e.g., ruined abbeys and castles) or the picturesque than, as indicated, from the landscape painting of the Barbizon school.

Deriving their motifs from painters such as Narcisse de la Peña, Camille Corot, Théodore Rousseau, Charles Daubigny, Jean-François Millet, and many others, these photographers sought to produce equivalents of the painters' depictions of regional woodlands or parks, especially the forest of Fontainebleau.[16] These painters were considered to represent an informal "school" insofar as they painted this particular forest, repudiated the previous academic mode of the classical landscape (*le paysage historique*) as well as the forms of the sublime or the picturesque, and favored, instead, the depiction of the "natural" and the national. In some cases, painters were personal friends, worked side by side, lived in Barbizon or other forest villages in the summer, or were linked by crypto-environmental concerns for the forest and were instrumental in its preservation by the state.

But for the photographers who looked to these artists' works as pictorial models, the immediate problem was how to adapt precedents derived from paint or print to the specificities (and technical limitations) of the photograph.

These involved not only the absence of color (a viable color technology, autochrome, was not perfected until the 1880s) or limitations in scale (the largest landscape photographs, such as those of Eadweard Muybridge, exhibited in the 1882 Paris exhibition, were twenty by twenty-four inches, still a fraction of the size of most contemporary landscape paintings) but also the inability of their cameras to register clouds and sky (not possible until the development of panchromatic film in the 1880s), the problems of focus in relation to depth of field, and the optical challenge posed by halation effects and the slowness of exposure time that blurred the foliage when the wind blew.[17] Although these are effects that if anything enhance the surfaces of nineteenth-century photographs to our own eyes, it is doubtful that the blurred leaves or branches one sees in them were considered aesthetic benefits. Making a virtue out of necessity, several of the photographs of this period depict wintry landscapes and bare boughs. But, fundamentally and inescapably, photography far more than landscape painting was dependent on weather and light. Moreover, insofar as conventional, which is to say, academic or official, landscape practice, even in the epoch of Impressionism, still mandated a certain idealization of nature, including spatial arrangement and compositional structure, staffage, and the like, art photographers were hard put to replicate pictorial elements that painters took for granted (the staged figures placed strategically in photographs by Famin, Quinet, and others are their equivalents). But figures in the photographed landscape, by definition, had to have been there, usually posed and staged for the camera. Even though the Barbizon painters routinely made drawings and studies out of doors, landscape paintings were typically a product of the studio and could be variously composed and reworked; figures added or removed; tones, colors, and the relations between them subtly manipulated; and textures built up. Photography, however, was by definition dependent on what was quite literally there before the lens.

Despite concentrating on the commercially profitable production of photographic views, when professional photographers left their urban bases, their subjects tended to be "historical" (e.g., ruins, monuments, significant sites *within* landscapes in Europe, America, or in the non-Western world) or topographical (natural "wonders," exotic locales, colonial possessions, uncharted territories, and such), which could, of course, be themselves absorbed into the commerce of views, especially stereographic. In this respect, the advent of the Kodak camera eventually destroyed those establishments specializing in touristic scenery, a form of the art that survives today primarily in the manufacture of postcards, calendars, and reproductions in hotel rooms. And, of course, in our own photographic archives—analogue or digital—recording our tours, our vacations, and our days in the countryside.

Despite all this, it is the case that many standard photography histories seamlessly write these heterogeneous photographic practices into discussions of landscape photography, thereby not only obscuring the specificity of many nineteenth-century photographic genres and practices but also superimposing upon the extant record what is essentially a modernist conception of photography, oblivious to the historical contingencies of vision, viewing, and visual production. But in imposing a modernist aesthetic viewpoint on these photographs, what are also lost are the various meanings that such pictures conveyed to their viewers, and their role in producing modes of reception and consumption characteristic of urban modernity. If to contemporary eyes a photograph by Cuvelier says "tree" or "trees," to Cuvelier and to his pictures' viewers, it said "oak tree," a potent symbol of the Fontainebleau forest before and during the Second Empire. And in terms of how these photographs now deemed landscapes came into existence—even as we are struck and moved by their melancholy beauty—it is important to understand that they represent, among other things, the production of a cultivated elite who had the time, resources, and inclination to invent—to translate, as it were—the photographic equivalent of what had become the most popular form of painting of their epoch.[18] Perhaps even more significantly, the production of landscape photographs, like their prototypes in painting and print media, were instrumental in forging a quintessentially modern conception of nature as a refuge from modernity, a theme park *avant la lettre.*

## Making Virtues of Necessity: Landscape Photography in the Shadow of Painting

As we look more closely, what will come into focus is the way in which the experience of nature was moulded by those structures of looking that were peculiar to the contemporary city—by the fusion of consumerism and environmental awareness.
—NICHOLAS GREEN

A tree is an edifice, a forest a city, and among all the forests, the Forest of Fontainebleau is a monument.
—VICTOR HUGO

Of the photographs from the mid-nineteenth century now routinely exhibited in museums under the rubric of landscape, there are certain among them whose motifs are very close to those represented by contemporary painting. Gustave Le Gray's , *Forest of Fontainebleau* (1849–52), or Charles Famin/Achille Quinet's later *Rochers a Fontainebleau* (ca. 1870) (figs. 7.2 and 7.4) are relatives of Rousseau's and other artists' paintings of the same forest (for example, Corot's *Fountainebleau: Oak Trees at Bas-Breau*, 1832 or 1833; fig. 7.3). But, medium aside, it is important to be very clear about what constitutes the resemblances and what constitutes the differences between these representations of landscape. On the side of resemblance, it is preeminently the locale in all its geographic and symbolic specificity that links the work of photographers such as Cuvelier, Le Gray, Le Secq, and others to that of the painters. For the forest of Fontainebleau and its particular features—geological, geographical, botanical, economic, agricultural, and, hardly least, symbolic—were what determined its significance as a subject for painters and photographers alike. The significance of the forest in nineteenth-century French culture was itself inseparable from the transformations wrought by the mechanisms of urbanism and modernity that jointly produced what Nicholas Green called "the spectacle of nature."[19] In other words, the painted and photographed landscape of the nineteenth century is a view, a viewpoint, a point of view, a mode of viewing, and a viewing position, the elements of which are forged in and by metropolitan culture. What makes landscape a dominant genre in the nineteenth century, Green argued, has to do with its reconfiguration, its refurbishment of a familiar form, now adapted to high or low incarnations, from the elite language of oil painting to the mass-produced lithograph. In these various media, these new versions of a centuries-old genre produced new significations, shaping and reinventing its motifs to illustrate democratic and metropolitan leisure. In its aggregate forms, these fostered a consumerist attitude toward nature, just as they bred a profitable touristic or day-tripper industry, and the concomitant desire to possess pictures of it.

By 1850, the forest of Fontainebleau, and the village of Barbizon at its edge, was not only an established artistic colony, but because of the railroad link established in 1850, was also a well-known and much frequented site of urban leisure coexisting with rural poverty. By 1856, an estimated 150,000 visitors walked its allées and promenades, guidebooks in hand, aided by signs indicating the forest's most storied sites: ancient trees (many of which were named), hills that furnished views, bodies of water, and so on. These guides identified the particular rock formations, such as the Gorges d'Apremont, as well as discussing the forest's stands of oak, its named marshes, streams, and ponds. Originally a royal hunting preserve, the forest had been transformed into a national park under the Second Empire. As Véronique Chagnon-Burke demonstrates in her fascinating study of the economics, ecology, and symbolism of the forest in mid-nineteenth-century France, by the time the Barbizon painters had artistically claimed the site, it had also become variously contested.[20] Environmentally speaking, there arose conflicts over the area's reforestation using pine trees at the expense of its indigenous oaks and beeches. As Chagnon-Burke observes, the oak, due to its longevity, had long functioned as a symbol of French identity consolidating various myths of nation, land, and *terreau.* The mythic status of the oak was equally heterodox—it could connote Druidic worship, Saint Louis administering justice under its boughs, even the Liberty Trees planted during the 1789 Revolution.[21] Logging roads for the harvesting of the oaks and pines, allées cut through the forest for the promenading of increasing numbers of Parisian and foreign visitors, quarrying the stone used for paving Parisian boulevards—all menaced the singular ecology of the forest and the livelihoods of the forest's traditional inhabitants, the charcoal burners, wood gatherers, peasants, poachers, and small flock herders who scratched out their lives within its precincts.[22] Few photographs were made that illustrate any aspects of the economic exploitation of the forest. However, Le Secq's *Carrière* depicts a quarry near Saint-Leu-d'Essèrent, where he had gone to photograph l'Église Saint-Nicolas. His reasons for making this series are unknown. But, of course, those making photographs in the forest that were meant to function as analogues to paintings were no more interested in depicting the economic activities the forest supported than were the painters.

Following various calls for the preservation of the forest (including a petition prompted by Théodore Rousseau), in 1863, Napoleon III signed a decree setting aside 1,097 hectares of the Fontainebleau forest as a *réserve artistique,* protected from economic exploitation. As Chagnon-Burke observes, the petition "was not motivated only by what we would now call environmental concerns, but also by the fear of losing still more picturesque views to the pine trees, tourist paths, and woodcutters' saws."[23] Moreover, she also remarks how particular places within the forest—the Bas-Bréau, the Gorges d'Apremont and the Gorges du Loup, the Monts-Girard, the Plateau de Bellecroix, and other sites—had become especially significant for day-trippers, tourists, and artists, and these had been earlier celebrated by writers and poets.[24] The artistic defense of the forest, Chagnon-Burke reminds us, was not in itself a sign of a particular political orientation.

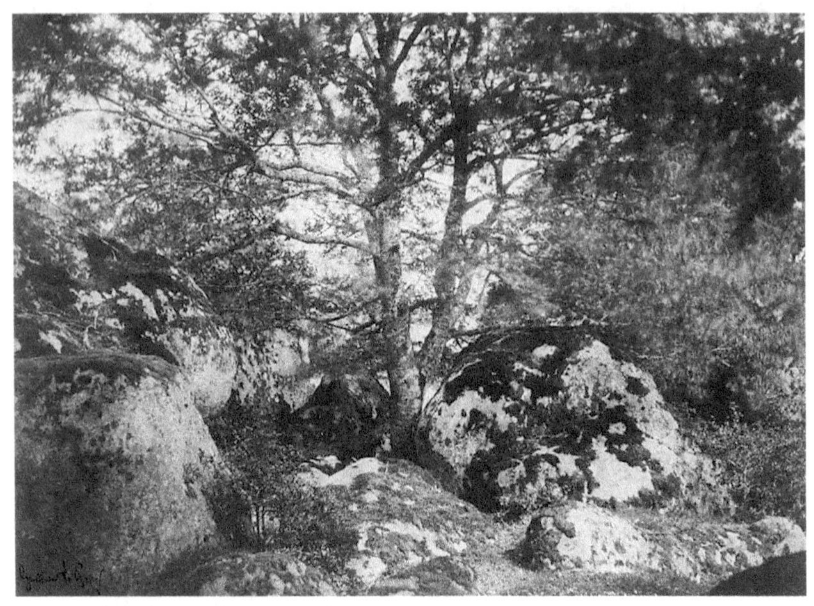

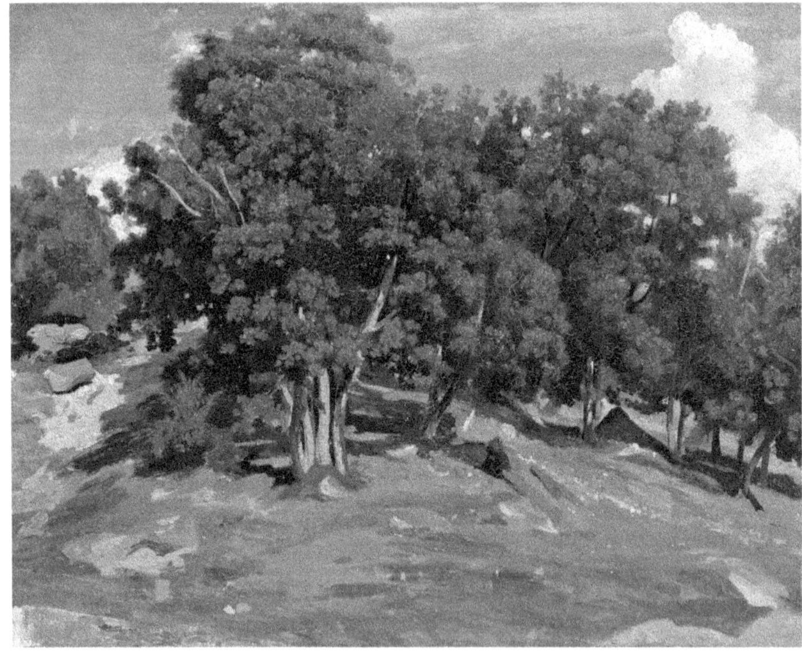

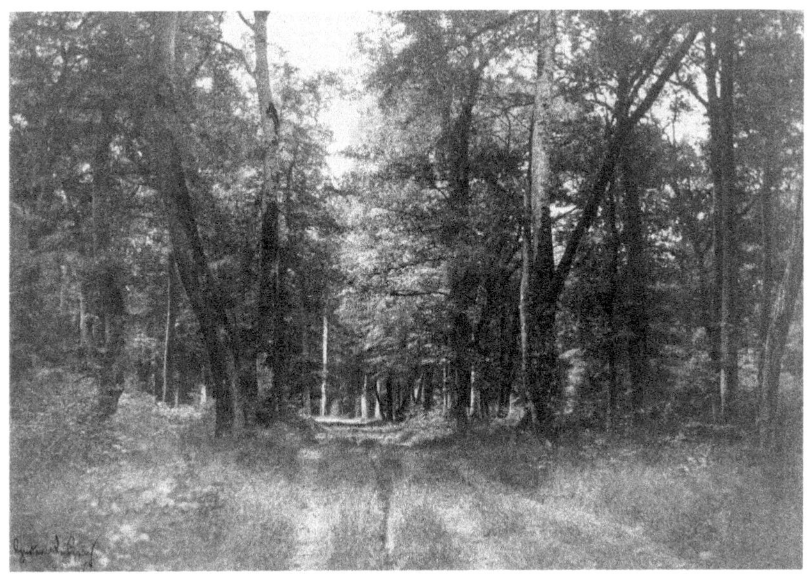

7.2 (*opposite, top*) Gustave Le Gray, *Oak Tree and Rocks, Forest of Fontainebleau,* 1849–52. Salted paper print from paper negative, 9 15/16 × 14 1/16 in. METROPOLITAN MUSEUM OF ART, NEW YORK. PURCHASE, JENNIFER AND JOSEPH DUKE AND LILA ACHESON WALLACE GIFTS, 2000 (2000.13). DIGITAL IMAGE © METROPOLITAN MUSEUM OF ART. COURTESY OF IMAGES FOR ACADEMIC PUBLISHING.

7.3 (*opposite, bottom*) Jean-Baptiste-Camille Corot, *Fontainebleau: Oak Trees at Bas-Bréau,* 1832 or 1833. Oil on paper, laid down on wood, 15 5/8 × 19 1/2 in. METROPOLITAN MUSEUM OF ART, NEW YORK. CATHARINE LORILLARD WOLFE COLLECTION, WOLFE FUND, 1979 (1979.404). DIGITAL IMAGE © METROPOLITAN MUSEUM OF ART. COURTESY OF IMAGES FOR ACADEMIC PUBLISHING.

7.4 (*above*) Gustave Le Gray, *Bas-Bréau, Forest of Fontainebleau,* 1849–52. Salted paper print from waxed-paper negative, 10 1/16 × 14 5/8 in. NATIONAL GALLERY OF ART, WASHINGTON, DC, PATRON'S PERMANENT FUND (1995.36.92). COURTESY OF THE NATIONAL GALLERY OF ART, WASHINGTON, DC.

In its earliest incarnation, however, photographic landscape was one of the subjects adapted by French amateur photographers such as Alphonse de Brébisson, Eugène Cuvelier, Gustave Le Gray, Alphonse Jeanrenaud, Henri-Victor Regnault, Henri Le Secq, and a handful of others. By the 1870s, however, even some professionals, such as Famin or Quinet, produced landscape subjects. In a number of cases, they called their pictures "études," which, like their nude *académies,* were marketed to artists and art students as aide-mémoires for their paintings. "Étude" was flexible as a designation; it meant that a given photograph was to be understood as just that, a "study," a preliminary work implying a certain spontaneity of execution. As a musical form, the étude was associated with Romanticism, but it had long existed as a type of artwork that showcased the artists' spontaneity and virtuosity while modestly defining itself as a sketch, not a finished work. But it is worth mentioning that an "étude," or *étude d'après nature,* designating a female or, more rarely, a nude male or child, escaped the prohibition of the censor, since the pictures were pitched to the needs of art students. "Étude d'après nature" could thus signify a nude or a tree or (more rarely) a landscape, but its use as a title of a photograph might also suggest a technical motivation, experimentation, or innovation.

The sites within the Fontainebleau forest favored by painters were those that featured in many of the contemporary guidebooks that predated the practice of realist landscapists. When photographers brought their cameras to the task of making landscapes, they chose the same or similar motifs, although, as I have indicated, their medium presented them with any number of technical problems and limitations. Certain of their pictures testify to their ability to perceive and express something we might call the life of trees, and is the product of an eye trained to read symbolic meanings in the botanical life of trees. Certain pictures, such as Le Secq's *Ruisseau en forêt cadre verticalement,* or his *Arbre mort en forêt,* suggest that the fallen beam over the small waterfall or the dead tree are of particular rather than general interest to him, although for what reason we cannot know. Trees locked in embrace, trees that are cloven, trees that shouldn't have survived but did, trees that are of great age, trees that are sometimes individually named, trees whose vulnerable roots are exposed to the air—all of these were signifying features of the Fontainebleau oaks and beeches captured in the photographs. Indeed, many of these photographs might be justly described as "portraits" of trees rather than as landscapes, a motif one can also identify in works by several Barbizon painters. One might think here of Courbet's *Le Chêne de Flagey* (1864), also known as the *Great Oak of Vercingetorix.* Such representations suggest a certain anthropomorphism, and the ability to imbue trees or rocks with a sense of their symbolic significance as venerable and living organisms. Anonymous's *Forêt de Fontainebleau, Le Jupiter* (fig. 7.5) depicts another individual (named) tree, and individual trees likewise figure in Cuvelier's *Chêne Bodmer,* Le Secq's *Étude de chêne,* and William Harrison's *Forêt de Fontainebleau.* Conversely, pictures such as those made by Joseph, vicomte Vigier in the Ardoise or the Pyrenees are closer to the touristic view, as are Anonymous's *Montigny, Vue sur le Loing,* Quinet's *Barque sur la berge,* or Famin's *La mare aux fées,* which include more of the landscape and are more "pictorial" in their organization. For us, viewing these photographs in our own context of environmental crisis, and detached as we are from either the nationalistic or the symbolic meanings of these objects and sites, what is most compelling is their formal and sober beauty, augmented by their subtle monochromic hues, subtle coloration produced by oxidation and other chemical transformations, and burnished patina of photographic age. Photography is nothing if not an elegiac art, even, or especially, in its most simple, straightforward, or stereotypical depictions. To our eyes, although these pictures may seem unmoored from any predetermined model or convention, like any cultural artifact, they are produced not only by their makers but also by the culture that provided their conceptual prototypes and the meanings that they communicated.

It is clear, however, that the medium of photography as *medium* had its own effects on the images that were made by these Second Empire photographers, and it is difficult to distinguish the formal effects of an image from what it represents, the core of the problem Barthes addressed in his famous essay on photographic rhetoric.[25] In other words, how do we distinguish between what is manifestly there in the photograph as subject, as content, as opposed to what kinds of messages and meanings were simultaneously generated at the time of their production and reception? If foliage presented a problem because of exposure time, this may have encouraged photographers to choose the starker scenes of winter, or the more close-up views of foliage, trunks, or roots.[26] Similarly, the problems caused by depth of field may have fostered a version of the "all-overness" that one sees in some of Cuvelier's pictures (*La chenaie*), or in Le Secq's *Taillis* or Le Gray's *Oak Tree and Rocks.* As for the effects of halation, if Aaron Scharf was correct, this was long considered to be a photographic "problem," although Corot was able to integrate it as a desired aesthetic effect into certain of his paintings.[27]

What is, however, consistent in the photographs, no less than the previous and contemporaneous paintings of the Fontainebleau forest, was the deliber-

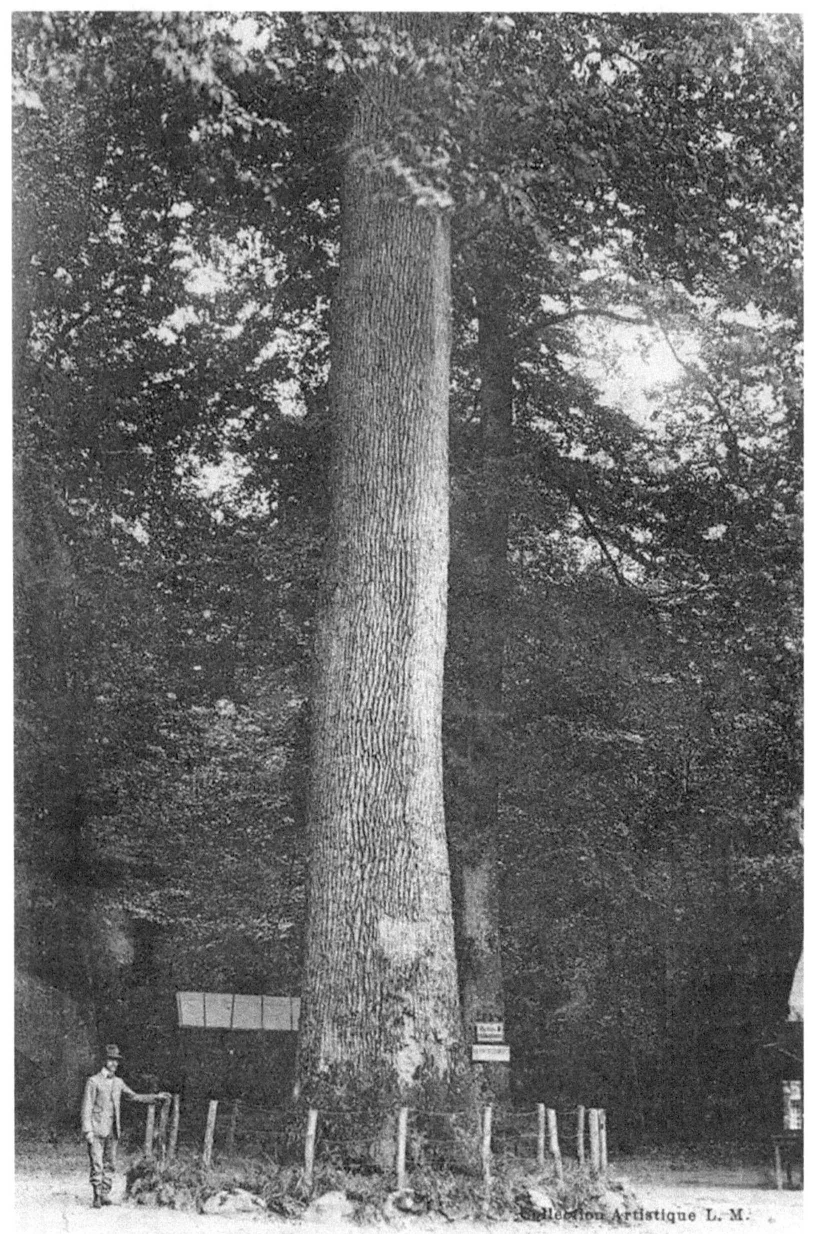


7.5 *Forêt de Fontainebleau—Le Jupiter, chêne de 6m50 de circumference.* Undated postcard. COLLECTION ARTISTIQUE L.M.

ate elision of its modern features, from signposts to tourists. There are certain exceptions, such as the paved road with stone edges seen in Anonymous's *Aprement la gorge aux Néfliers*, in the signpost just visible in the background of Le Gray's *Forest Crossroads*, and in the macadamized road in Le Gray's *Route de Chailly*. These, however, are exceptions, and whether intentionally included or adventitious is impossible to know. For the painters, most of whom maintained a parallel location in Paris (or a web of relationships there), or the gentlemen amateurs resolved to claim this particular artistic genre for photography, the forest's modern identity and its economic and recreational uses were to be edited out in the name of artistic effect. The contradiction that prompted this double consciousness of what was actually to be seen in the forest of Fontainebleau, as opposed to what was to be properly represented of it, was later to be resolved by the Impressionists, who deliberately included the signs of change and modernity in many of their works. Thus, factories, modern bridges, paved roads, and the like in suburbs and countryside, as well as newly available leisure activities outside of Paris (e.g., boating, picnicking, swimming) were frequently depicted in the art of the 1870s and thereafter; these had long featured in print culture well before becoming a subject in easel painting.

On the one hand, for the Barbizon artists, "nature" signified their artistic embrace, even their communion, with what was supposed to be untainted by modernity and modernization, while functioning as a sign of the artists' subjectivity, expressed through notions of their "sincerity" and "authenticity"—crucial terms in realist and Impressionist theory and criticism. On the other hand, it was industrialization and the processes of modernization that shaped the imagery—and experience—of nineteenth-century "nature." In this respect, the putative realism of Barbizon school landscapes, no less than the medium-specific realism of the photographic image, must be seen as the prototype for all of those touristic snapshots, generated in their millions, that are cropped to disappear the evidence of time and history, to create the very image of what one desires but what has already been lost, available in the present—ours or theirs—only as a cipher for something absent, elusive, and, in the final analysis, always mythological. And therefore always ideological. That the photographs produced in this period are as elegiac and melancholy as the paintings that predated them reminds us that the concepts of "nature" and attendant notions of the "natural" are themselves the products of culture, and that mid-nineteenth-century France, like any other country of the industrializing West, had to culturally and imaginatively negotiate the disenchantment of nature as one rite of passage into the culture of modernity.

This disenchantment of nature, however, as a historical process, is the knowledge that reanimates these pictures for us, making both the photographs and the paintings objects that signify for us in the present—whether in terms of democratic access to woodlands, to the human need for some kind of affective relation to the natural world, or, even better, to a heightened ecological consciousness about protection and preservation. While the forest or park of Fontainebleau could be considered a staging of nature, a scenography that established what nature was supposed to be (or look like), it ultimately produced viewers for whom preservation subsequently takes on an unanticipated ethical role, not merely a nationalist, privatized, or chauvinist one. The photographs point (as does any photograph) to a tree, a stand of trees, and a rock formation, and by so doing, implicitly assert their importance, their value, by virtue of the representation itself. Such images seek to elicit a gaze that affirms the worth of these "natural" entities, exceeding their economic or touristic value, and in this respect, the appreciation of landscape, as such, can have progressive as well as reifying implications, as was certainly the case in the formation of national park systems throughout the world. For we who now live with the knowledge of the ongoing catastrophe of environmental destruction on a global scale, the invention of landscape as an aesthetic category, first in painting and then in photography, might be grimly seen as its epitaph.

# 8

## The Ghosts of Documentary

(2012)

Every culture has its phantoms and the spectrality that is conditioned by its technology.
—JACQUES DERRIDA, *COPY, ARCHIVE, SIGNATURE* (2010)

What are the ghosts that haunt documentary? As is often the case with ghosts, these are figures of unresolved loss and mourning as well as bad conscience. They may represent, among other things, a variant of the return of the repressed, something disavowed or occluded in the past. Documentary's ghosts are, however, specific to its self-definition, even though, as I will argue, an entity dubbed "documentary" is itself a kind of phantasmatic formation. Recent writing on photography acknowledges that whatever illusions of truth were authorized by the indexical and evidentiary aspects of the medium, the replacement of analogue with digital modes of imaging has uncoupled this historic linkage.[1] And, as another instance of haunting, we might take as a symptom the obsessive investigations of the truth or deception involved in the making of such well-known (analogue) pictures as Roger Fenton's *Valley of the Shadow of Death*, Arthur Rothstein's bleached steer skull, or Robert Capa's death of a Republican militiaman. All have been subjected to scrutiny following challenges to their literal veracity (e.g., did Fenton or his crew reposition the cannonballs? Was the skull moved? Was the militiaman's death staged?), and have been recently subjected to painstaking reconstruction by the filmmaker Errol Morris in his recent book *Believing Is Seeing*.[2] Such a forensic inquiry is all the more surprising, as Morris's own documentary films freely employ simulations, atmospheric background music, reconstructions, and other forms of dramatization and narrative structuring.

Suggestively, if coincidentally, these three are funerary documents of a sort: a deserted battlefield, a bleached skull, a man struck by a bullet. The camera's instantaneous capture of time and movement has long been associated with mortality and petrifaction, recurring themes in the literature of the photographic medium. The notion of the photograph as a direct transfer or imprint of the real, a "certificate of presence," in Susan Sontag's formulation, has an equally venerable tradition in photography criticism. Although the argument for photographic realism depends on the camera's physical apparatus—the reflection of light rays from the object or scene "embalmed" on a light-sensitive emulsion—neither optically nor neurologically do photographic representations correspond to the mechanisms of the human eye.[3] Although by no means uncontested, much photography criticism and theory has nonetheless taken indexicality implicitly or explicitly as grounds for an ontological approach with which to theorize it.[4] But since the camera produces pictures, that is, representations, the photograph is an iconic as well as an indexical image, delimited by the crop, the photographer's point of view, and an array of other mediations. Moreover, the meaning of any given photograph is largely determined by its context and all the ancillary operations that form what Roland Barthes dubbed its "anchorage" and its "relays."[5] The division of camera-made images into a category of "art/expression" (aligned with the icon) is countered by those other uses—scientific, technological, and industrial—that align it more closely with the index. The indexical aspects of the medium were therefore those that historically authorized its use in journalism and documentary practice of all types and formats. And, of course, this attribute determined its use by the police, the courts, and the horse race (i.e., the "photo finish"). Even though the deliberate falsification of photographic imagery has its own interesting history, the fact that photographs could be doctored has been generally understood as a deviation from the norm and marginal to photography's typical uses and functions.[6]

Consequently, one of the ghosts that haunts contemporary photography is that of analogue technologies themselves, now become a residual if not yet altogether abandoned technique of image making. Accordingly, one manifestation of the haunting is a heightened interest in predigital production and an observable tendency among art photographers to adopt older techniques of analogue media. Technical developments that make some forms obsolete—for example, large-format cameras mounted on tripods, black-and-white film—may, of course, be precisely what recommends them to artists. Indeed, technical obsolescence, as Walter Benjamin maintained, has its own historical and cultural repercussions and its own uses in the present. This is why the use of black-and-white film, Polaroid cameras, artisanal printing procedures, or the use of view cameras such as the Linhof 4x5 or the Deerhof (cf., Joel Meyerowitz, Richard Misrach) have become signifiers of the "art" of art photography. In this respect, another ghost might be identified with the specter of obsolescence itself, accompanying the juggernaut of rapid technological transformation. This specter has a number of valences, few of them celebratory. As Rosalind Krauss observed, "Photography's apotheosis as a medium—which is to say its commercial, academic, and museological success—comes just at the moment of its capacity to eclipse the very notion of a medium and to emerge as a theoretical because heterogeneous object. But in a second moment, not too historically distant from the first, this object will lose its deconstructive force by passing out of the field of social use and into the twilight zone of obsolescence."[7] It thus follows that if one aspect of photography within contemporary art has been subject to criticism for its "deskilling" effects, these are paralleled by alternative artisanal, labor-intensive, or craftlike production. Where nineteenth-century pictorialist photographers used various forms on manipulation of the negative or print to secure their work's artistic status, photographers like Meyerowitz or Robert Adams, conversely, now stake their claims on the "classical" formats of "straight" photography, older cameras, and older processes with which to establish the aesthetic identity of their own production. This was earlier the language of photographic modernism, typified in the rhetoric of formalist criticism that allowed for both the photograph's indexical and expressive capabilities, icon and index, symbol and trace, in harmonious coexistence. Crudely stated, this approach acknowledged that while the camera recorded photochemically and photomechanically what lay before the lens, this was said to be artistically transformed by the photographers' subjectivity. That recent events such as the cleanup of the World Trade Towers or the devastation of Hurricane Katrina have been memorialized using old cameras and predigital techniques is therefore part of a larger phenomenon. This can be broadly defined as the migration of subject matter from the domain of photojournalism or documentary into artistic practices of various stripes that are now encountered in many different contexts—museums, galleries, art fairs, as well as in print media. Contemporary manifestations of such crossovers are readily found; we may take as examples the work of Simon Norfolk, Richard Mosse, and Luc Delahaye, and any number of other photographers whose work originated— photojournalistically —in theaters of war and sites of other disasters.

If one symptom of documentary's haunting is the more or less mournful nostalgia for analogical representation, especially in relation to its ethical and political role as witness, a reverse symptom is evident in the euphoric celebration of electronic media and its liberation from the constraints of analogue. Consequently, the fetishizing of archaic or residual modes of production (and reproduction) is paralleled by the fetishizing of those technological innovations whose perfections or capabilities are thought to surpass the merely human. In the most optimistic of these evaluations, digital imagery is redeemed as a Good Object, offering the prospects of expanded, more democratic access to representation and self-representation (e.g., the citizen-journalist with her iPhone).

With the advent of digitalization (whether within the camera itself, in the post facto digitalizing of an analogue original, or in printing techniques), controversies related to photographic realism therefore have paralleled the medium's technical developments. With digital imagery, the casus belli pivot on the betrayal of photography's truth claims, that is, the eclipse of its indexical warranty. For some, this is evidence of epistemic rupture. Fred Ritchin's recent book *After Photography* is symptomatic of the more dramatic assessments of the so-called digital revolution. "We have entered the digital age. And the digital age has entered us . . . We are no longer the same people we once were. For better or worse. We no longer think, talk, read, listen, see the same way. Nor do we write, photograph, or even make love the same way. It is inevitable. The changes in the media, especially media as pervasive as the digital, require that we live differently, with shifting perceptions and expectations."[8] And a few pages later, "For those who think of digital media as simply providing more efficient tools, what we are witnessing today is an evolution in media. . . . For those who see the digital as comprising a markedly different environment than the analog, what we are currently observing is no less than a revolution. This latter view is considerably more accurate."[9]

Aside from the technological determinism that underpins popular accounts such as Ritchin's, there has long existed a debate countering the Edenic truth claims of analogue against the fallen condition of the digital. Ritchin's examples of the slippery slope by which photography cedes its referential authority are those that have excited lively debate in the mass media but were initially ignited by unrelated pictures: the manipulation of the position of the Egyptian pyramids to fit the standard format of a *National Geographic* cover (1982); the darkening of O. J. Simpson's complexion for a *Time* magazine cover (1994); and the grafting of Oprah Winfrey's face to the body of Ann-Margret for a *TV Guide* cover (1989). Although these three have since become textbook emblems of manipulation-as-violation, they have thoroughly different vectors. Where the moving of the pyramids provides a viewpoint that is empirically impossible but of no particular consequence, the darkening of Simpson's skin color has racist political implications and effects. On the other hand, joining Winfrey's head to Ann-Margret's body, if taken as a breach of visual truth, implies that other mass media representations of Oprah are authentic and unmediated.

It is here that we may better observe some of the implications of an investment in photographic realism that pits the truth of the trace against the lure of the image. A recent book, *The New Media Invasion: Digital Technologies and the World They Unmake* by John David Ebert, symptomatizes the sense of loss and anger provoked by the digital.

> Right now, analogical images are disappearing into a pointillist universe of bytes and pixels. When photographs are plugged in and turned on via digital technology, they become dematerialized. They go directly from reality to take up residence inside the integrated circuits of computer chips, where they are stored as a form of virtual memory. The images attain the status of virtuality, that is to say, they are not real images, but computer memories subject, as are all human memories, to erasure, modification, information decay, or simple deletion. In doing so, the ontological status of photography shifts from that of a high art to a graphic art form and becomes capable of producing sophisticated images no more interesting than the nauseating illustrations that are displayed in the glossy pages of graphic design manuals. Real artists with visionary talents will turn to other media as film gradually and irretrievably disappears. The end of yet another art form as collateral damage in the tireless march of progress of technology.[10]

In fact, photographic imagery is often disembodied or dematerialized (e.g., slide projections, and all of cinema and video). Nor has photography ever been predominantly an art form. But, as Ebert continues, "The digital photo is so obscene precisely because it denudes the image of its tactile qualities: the graininess of the traditional photo, for example, the sense of texture that gives to the image its concreteness is gone, and along with it, the invisible yet mistakable presence of the shaping hand."[11]

Affirming that the chemical processes producing the analogue photograph records the presence of the maker in the physical object (as well as his or her hand in the resulting print) repeats the terms of the earliest photographic debates. Those who insisted on photography's expressive/subjective/artistic potential were defending the medium against the charge it was a soulless, godless copying machine. Now it is digitalization rather than the medium itself that usurps the importance of the maker's presence and the medium's putative purity. As one would expect, film theory and criticism has produced its own extensive bibliography around the topic of digitalization and the eclipse of analogue representation.[12]

Many of the more specialized discussions on the import of digitalization, especially those dealing with documentary film, tend to be far more nuanced, refusing a clear-cut opposition between the technologies by which camera-made images are generated.[13] For example, Philip Rosen sensibly observes that the digital camera image is itself a form of hybrid:

> . . . It is common for theorists to treat indexicality as the defining difference for the digital, so that the photographic image often becomes the most exemplary "other" of the digital image. Yet, digital often appropriates or conveys indexical images, and it is common for the digital image to retain compositional forms associated with indexicality. In practice, then, digital imagery is often (but of course not exclusively) constituted by being propped onto certain culturally powerful image codes that preexisted it. . . . The quest for digital mimicry has been one of the driving forces in the history of digital imaging. All of this means that, to a significant degree, digital imaging is not separable from prior histories of mediated representation on screen surfaces, but overlaps with them.[14]

This would seem to be the case with the development of the digital camera itself, whose first prototypes date back to the 1940s. In its equivalence to 16-millimeter, 35-millimeter, or 70-millimeter proportions, its rectangular frame, and the look of its image resolution, the digital photograph mimics a "better," improved—i.e., sharper, more resolved—conventional camera image. It is this that leads Rosen to speak of "digital mimicry," and also prompts the artist and theorist George Legrady to speak of the digital photograph as "a simulated photographic representation." The analogue camera was itself developed so as to replicate familiar forms of pictorial structure, including its perspective systems.[15]

In the case of contemporary cinema, animation aside, digital technologies are now the norm rather than the exception within the industry as a whole, including documentary filmmaking. This, however, has not transformed the material circumstances of the pro-filmic event (the actors or scenes positioned in front of the camera before it is activated). Nor has the integration of digital technologies destroyed the concept, experience, or even the phenomenology of cinema spectatorship. But perhaps an equally salient point is that digital cameras, outside of specialized applications (scientific, commercial, military, or artistic) are still employed in ways and for purposes that go back to George Eastman's Kodak. Like these earlier cameras, digital cameras are used for family snaps, for tourism, portraits of people, ID photos, and for various forms of information preservation. And of course, the staggering proliferation of the selfie. In all these respects, there is reason to concur with Mary Ann Doane's observation that, "In a sense, the digital has not annihilated the logic of the photochemical, but incorporated it. To take up the index today, as a theoretical concept, is to insist that the complexities of the issue of referentiality should not deter us from investigating and analyzing its force."[16] Similarly, her notion of an "indexical imaginary" is especially suggestive in thinking through the relations between digital imagery and the claims of or for photographic witness. Moreover, for those for whom photographic imagery was never coeval with truth, the either/or in the debates about digital imaging are inadequate to either form of representation.

Where these debates have been most intense, as one would expect, is in relation to those practices whose legitimacy was and is bound up with the camera's function as witness. But here, too, the ghosts are internal and specific to each variant of photographic practice. The photographic portrait, for example, is haunted by its invocation of mortality, a central theme in Roland Barthes's *Camera Lucida* and a recurring topos in the literature of photography from Benjamin and Bazin through contemporary theory. With documentary, however, the ghosts are not only those of its predigital authority, but also the shades of its own equivocal, ambivalent, and contingent histories. These are among those "chattering ghosts" that Allan Sekula identified in his now-classic essay of 1981, "The Traffic in Photographs," and these ghosts are as much a legacy of documentary practices as they are of his particular criminological, eugenicist, and Taylorist examples.[17] In this regard, documentary is haunted by that part of its history *as documentation* that was early on conscripted as an agent of domination and social control (ideological, colonial, racial, sexual, and so forth) in its many instrumental applications and its implication in the complex web of knowledge/power relations. Accordingly, Michel Foucault's observation that "the apparatus is thus always inscribed in a play of power; it is always linked to certain coordinates of knowledge which issue from it, but to an equal degree, condition it," has been a major influence in studies by Geoffrey Batchen, Christopher Pinney, John Tagg, as well as Sekula.[18]

To lay the ghosts to rest, we have not only to identify them but also to reckon with their particular manifestations. This means that a certain mapping of what documentary photography signifies now is useful, and, given the obvious imprecision of the term, this is no easy task. Indeed, the boundaries between something called "documentary," something called "social documentary," and something called "photojournalism" are themselves unstable (and permeable), although it is worth noting that these are all of twentieth-century vintage. We may well ask, however, whether these are coherent either as definitions, categories, genres, or merely loose and somewhat arbitrary designations that may shift position, blur into one another, or be positioned as subsets of broader definitions.

For John Grierson, who coined the term in 1926, "documentary," it merely designated nonfictional filmmaking, but within a decade or so it came to include still photography, and as its purview became increasingly inclusive, its meanings became increasingly amorphous. Certainly, and as I have argued elsewhere, the lateness with which the term entered the English language (and subsequently other languages) suggests that prior to the 1920s, the general assumption was that with certain exceptions (e.g., studio portraiture, the obviously staged image, art photography), *all* photographs were by definition visual documentations of their subject.[19] In fact, the documentary functions of photography were fully in place by the 1850s. If a new term became necessary, it was in response to the medium's ever-proliferating applications and, after the invention of halftone printing in the late 1880s, its adaptation to the printed page.[20] The exponential increase in photography-for-reproduction from the 1920s on, and a rapidly proliferating visual mass culture, was the context in which the category of documentary was summoned into discursive life. In an increasingly diversified and ubiquitous image world, where the new mass medium of cinema was itself divided between newsreel and fiction, the shaping forces of mass culture, national and cultural ideologies, identity formation, and, hardly least, advertising put pressure on those attributes of the camera image that had initially made it the warranty of empirical if not optical truth.

That the term was invented by a liberal intellectual suggests, however, that Grierson's formulation was prompted by political as opposed to formal or epistemological criteria. In fact, much of his writing and interviews emphasize the heuristic and democratizing goals of documentary production. Certainly, his directorial and production activities in the film units of the Empire Marketing Board (a governmental agency established in 1926 to promote British world trade and imperial solidarity), the British Post Office, and, later, his establishment of the National Film Board of Canada, indicates the institutional as well as nationalist context within which the concept of documentary was initially developed.

Well before Grierson, however, it was often the case that nineteenth-century productions (retrospectively defined as documentary) were of governmental origin, although there were also entrepreneurial initiatives.[21] Governmental commissions include the 1851 Missions Héliographiques, Auguste Salzmann's 1856 pictures of the Holy Land, Charles Marville's record of Haussmann's modernization of Paris (1858–70), Thomas Annan's 1863 pictures of the Glasgow slums, Timothy O'Sullivan's 1870s topographic survey projects, and so forth.[22] Among these, only Annan's photographs could be said to have had a reformist agenda, although this too was not without its contradictions.[23] These surveys are, of course, very well known and are often considered as precedents for twentieth-century practice. But my point here is that by the 1930s, this form of official commission was as much the rule as the exception, exemplified in the United Kingdom by Humphrey Spender's 1937 photographs for Mass Observation,[24] Roy Stryker's FSA photographic project in the United States inaugurated the same year, or Alexander Rodchenko's 1933 series on the building of the White Sea Canal made for *The USSR in Construction.*

That these were all more or less (mostly more) propaganda projects is not, needless to say, to imply a simple equivalence between what they represented and the authorities and purposes they served. But here one encounters another ghost of documentary; let us call it, following Foucault, the ghost of governmentality, an increasingly important agent in the manufacture of consent. This might be said to be an especially unwelcome ghost given documentary's subsequent discursive positioning as a reformist or progressive alternative to mainstream applications or to photographic aestheticism.

Moreover, it is also the case that the history of anthropological and ethnographic photographic representation logically falls under the rubric of documentary photography. Because ethnographic imagery belonged to "scientific" archives well before its assimilation into photographic histories, it has only recently figured in histories of photographic documentary. Significantly, this aspect of the "documentary factor" was largely absent from the historiography of the medium until the past fifteen or twenty years. In the work of British scholars such as Elizabeth Edwards and Christopher Pinney, for example, one sees how photography is implicated in those "sciences of man,"—anthropology and ethnography—that accompanied colonial rule while securing notions of white (and male) supremacy. Indeed, and as Pinney observes in passing, the words "stereotype" and "cliché" themselves derive from photographic language.[25] Which is finally to say that while documentary photography has occasionally functioned in ameliorative or progressive contexts, this should not obscure its parallel and far more significant functions as a technology of observation, surveillance, social control, and propaganda—in short, its normative ideological functions. Indeed, there seems every reason to consider a great deal of scientific photography as a part of the larger discourse of documentary consistent with what Tagg called "the archives of subjection."[26]

These factors are easily overlooked, in part because the adjectivally marked "social documentary" has been viewed as either a subspecies or alternative construction, and it is this formulation that is often considered synonymous with reformist or progressive practices. I can locate no hard-and-fast definition of this term, nor is it clear exactly when or by whom it was coined. But it does seems to be the case that in the Anglophone world, and sometime in the 1960s, the adjective "social" came to imply a Marxist, progressive, or reformist agenda (as in social art history). In fact, many of the exemplars of this type of photography—preeminently Lewis Hine—were important participants in Progressive Era reform politics, and were featured in publications such as *The Graphic* and the *Graphic Survey*. Forms of activist, i.e., engaged photography, appeared again in the 1930s and New York's Photo League was one of the hubs of such practices.[27] Similarly, in the United States, the late 1960s and 1970s were a period in which these modes of documentary photography, especially in book form, and preeminently in relation to the civil rights and antiwar movements, seem to have flourished.[28]

A number of historians situate the emergence of social documentary in the years of the Depression. William Stott, for example, in his classic study of 1973, remarks, "When people in the thirties spoke of documentary, they usually meant social documentary—and so do we today . . . social documentary . . . shows man at grips with conditions neither permanent nor necessary, conditions of a certain time and place, racial discrimination, police brutality, unemployment, the depression, the planned environment of the TVA, pollution, terrorism."[29] But a few pages on, he concedes, "Thirties social documentary in general is now as dead as the sermons of the Social Gospel."[30] Maren Stange, however, in her study of the subject, means the designation to refer to a broader array of practices, encompassing humanitarianism, reform movements from the 1890s on, corporate public relations (e.g., Roy Stryker at Standard Oil), and hardly least, social engineering. These practices, she observes "testified both to the existence of painful social facts and to reformers' special expertise in ameliorating them, thus reassuring a liberal middle class that social oversight was both its duty and its right."[31]

In his 2002 book *Le style documentaire,* Olivier Lugon makes a distinction between what he calls "documentary style"—an international photographic syntax already widespread in Western Europe the late 1920s—with the more tendentious mandate of the FSA photo section from 1935 to 1942.[32] For Lugon, prior to the 1920s, not only was documentary excluded as an artistic genre within photography, it was effectively considered its negation.[33] In his account, the privileging of sharp focus, frontal composition, clarity and detail of the visual field, lack of rhetorical or expressionist flourishes, straightforward attention to the object or subject, and the production of a sequence or narrative collectively characterize what he designates as a style, rather than a genre or a praxis. Contradicting the widespread assumption that twentieth-century documentary is implicitly or explicitly linked to reformist values and politics, Lugon considers this characterization as a retrospective (and specifically American) imposition. Citing various texts dating from the 1920s (e.g., Christian Zevros in 1928; Hans Windisch in 1928), Lugon effectively identifies modernist (that is, formalist) photography with the means if not the ends of documentary. Remarking on the retrospective identification of documentary with progressive causes, he notes, "The inflection of the notion of social reportage functions only belatedly, at the end of the decade, with the promotion of the FSA's images. It is around these, toward 1938–1940, that there is suddenly a wave of texts, all American, seeking not to invent the notion of documentary but, for the first time, to fix its meaning."[34]

Quoting from Stott's *Documentary Expression and Thirties America,* he locates this particular notion of documentary photography in the mandate of the FSA, as Stott himself defined it. "Simplifying, then: Documentary treats the actual unimagined experience of individuals belonging to a group (generally of lower standing in the society for whom the report is made) and treats this experience in such a way to try and render it vivid, human, and most often—poignant to the audience."[35] This class distinction between the situation or identity of the subject who is represented, and that of the viewing subject, is one of the most durable aspects of documentary photography, however defined, and from whatever period. It is in relation to these viewing relationships that the concept of a politics of representation emerged in the 1970s and from whence the critique of certain types of documentary took its cue.[36] Rhetorically, and even if considered *as* a style, these forms of depiction depend on pathos more than logos; affect, sensation, pity, and empathy are what galvanize its meanings. But as with photography in general, the framing context—textual, discursive, and temporal—are in the final analysis the most important factors in determining collective (as opposed to individual, that is, subjective) photographic meaning and significance. In this respect, it should be noted that while Stange too considers twentieth-century documentary as a form of style, this does not preclude her from distinguishing between its various applications, approaches, contexts, and instrumentalities.[37]

Be that as it may, for Lugon this more "politicized" form of documentary pursued in the United States elides or obscures the preexisting (European) syntax that would later come to be designated as "straight" photography. Lugon thereby affirms the familiar succession that has established an art history of documentary (for that is what it is), from Atget to Abbott, Evans, and Sander, with branches that genealogically connect these productions with European avant-gardes such as the Neue Sachlichkeit. As Lugon argues, this nontendentious, ostensibly nonideological discourse on the nature and terms of documentary has its own parallel history in the United States, but this, I would argue, is a history that has been more or less invented by curators, collectors, and museums and subsequently institutionalized.[38] Walker Evans is thus for Lugon, as for many others, *the* crucial figure, given the "classical" nature of his photographic production and his artistic ambitions before, during, and after his participation in the FSA. Consequently, for all its historicization and attentiveness to the photographic discourse of this period, Lugon's study nevertheless produces, or rather reproduces, the modernist lineage of photography as an autonomous and self-reflexive medium.

A further question about generic boundaries arises when one attempts to chart the distinctions between documentary and photojournalism. Lugon, like many others who have treated the subject of documentary, does not seek to distinguish the two, although however defined, individual photographers—especially now—may freely move between these practices.[39] Although some historians suggest that this distinction pivots on the difference between a discrete photograph reproduced in print, and a series or project orchestrated by the individual photographer, this seems hardly adequate as a workable definition. Photographs readily migrate between sites and usages: when a photograph by, say, Susan Meiselas, appears in the *New York Times,* it is the result of her work as a photojournalist; when she selects and presents her work organized under a specific subject in book or exhibition format, as in her book *Nicaragua,* it is considered as a documentary project.

As with documentary itself, and as Vincent Lavoie observes, "Current research on the history, semiotics, and aesthetics of photographic illustration shows that photojournalism is a category which is fundamentally unstable and continually in the process of being reconfigured by discourse. The ethics of the press image is a product of these historical reconfigurations."[40] In fact, the professionalizing of photojournalism established a range of structures, from unions to codes of ethics, and it was only after World War I that [some] photojournalists became salaried employees within the news industry. And it was only in 1945 that a national organization was formed in the United States—the National Press Photographers Association (NPPA)—one of whose goals was explicitly concerned with professionalization.[41] No less important was the institutionalization of the concept of "objectivity" as a core value for press photography (and news reporting), a value patently contradicted in actual practice. (However, and as a further example of the instability of all of these designations, it is worth mentioning that in 1990, the NPPA's members voted Joe Rosenthal's staged reenactment of marines raising the American flag in Iwo Jima the greatest news photograph of all time.[42])

Nevertheless, one might say that barring such actual staging, it was and is the case that while all photojournalism is implicitly documentary, not all documentary is journalistic. Insofar as the etymology of the word "journalistic" derives from the French *jour* (the root of the nouns *journal* and *journalisme*), the word "photojournalism" did not enter the English language until 1956, although the term *photoreportage* appeared in French in 1938. Accordingly, photojournalism, like *photoreportage,* was always identified with actuality—the news (French newsreels in the 1920s and 1930s were called *actualitiés*). This has remained a constant even as image technology has evolved from still photography through electronic media and live video feed. However, as this practice took on its modern form and meaning in the 1930s, documentary photography (and social documentary) often came to designate a collective project as opposed to a single reproduced image. Especially in picture magazines, photographs were presented as ensembles, sequences, and narratives.[43] As a multi-part and/or narrative series, the subject of documentary might have its origin in the initiative of the individual photographer (as a random example, Aaron Siskind's *Harlem Document,* the photographs for which were made in the 1930s), or, in the case of many illustrated magazines, a project commissioned and orchestrated by the editorial staff, but it was often their circulation as a multi-part of narrative series that signified their documentary function.

In the American print media, it is the professional (salaried or freelance) photojournalist whose photos are viewed by great numbers of people; documentary projects, on the other hand, as individual projects, have had no such mass audience since the glory days of the picture press. Dispatched by editors and agencies, photojournalists take pictures that are now immediately received, transmitted, downloaded, and disseminated by yet other circuits of reproduction. It follows that these more recent incarnations of documentary or journalistic subject are structured by different relations (including temporal ones). Still photography by definition suggests a pastness, an anterior moment, whereas live video feed implies an immediate presence and presentness.

Is there any real distinction to be drawn between one set of practices vaguely labeled documentary and another called social documentary? Whether or not documentary is best considered as a style, as Lugon and others argue, in most photographic histories, social documentary is generally considered as an offshoot or subcategory of documentary. For its partisans, social documentary is understood to constitute a form of praxis. It is to this putative tradition that those critics committed to the practice of contemporary social documentary (or its reconstruction) refer. This is apparent in Martha Rosler's discussion of the subject in her essay "Post-Documentary, Post-Photography?": "Of all photographic practices, social documentary—the self-professed truth-teller, implicated in modernity and part of its 'life world'—is the one in which the underlying issues of social power are accessible to contestation. . . . But over the past few decades, photography and photographic practices have been subject to attacks on all fronts."[44] This perception of social or documentary photography as both under attack and at risk of disappearance is shared by John Roberts, Steve Edwards, and other critics identified with the left. Like other commentators, Rosler locates one aspect of documentary's crisis with digitalization, but also connects its delegitimation to postmodernism's general skepticism about totalizing truth claims and its critique of realism. "Thus, post-structural and postcolonial discourses, along with digital technologies, have undermined the subject position of the photographer (and the cultural milieu into which the images are inserted) and the epistemological status of the image—its relationship to a phenomenologically present visual reality—denigrating its (metonymic) adequacy in relation to the situation it depicts and problematizing the ability of *any* image of a visual field to convey lived experience, custom, tradition, or history."[45] In the same essay, Rosler reflects on the new circumstances shaping documentary forms: "The tide of change poses its own particular threat to documentary, since 'post-photographic' practice at a minimum can be said to have abandoned any interest in indexicality and, perhaps just as importantly, in the privileged viewpoint of 'witness'—and therefore any embeddedness in a particular moment in time and space. The photographic seems poised to mutate into just another, relatively ephemeral, aesthetic form and its maker into an artist. What will determine the outcome of this unstable condition is not clear."[46]

For those committed to the goals of social documentary, what is thought to be lost, and subsequently mourned, in the digital age is ultimately the progressive political contexts within which it once (supposedly) flourished. John Roberts unambiguously links the demise of what he calls "documentary-image culture" with the demise of class politics: "From the 1920s to 1980s this documentary-image culture was the outcome of progressive triangulation of cultural and political forces: (i) the link between photographic truth and the power of photography to wrest some symbolic space from the specularity of capitalist culture; (ii) the link between photography and the democratic dispersal of counter-knowledge as part of working-class struggle and other struggles from below; and (iii) the link between access to photographic form and access to a common world of artistic skill."[47] Steve Edwards, like Rosler and Roberts, accepts that documentary practice is in self-evident decline, and also attributes this to a changed political climate. Citing Roberts, he concurs with his claim "that the decline of documentary—or at least the plummet of its prestige—has coincided with a retreat from class politics among the Western intelligentsia. Social class remains as powerful a determinant in our lives as it ever was . . . but they seem much less visible than they once were."[48]

As with documentary itself as a discursive entity, the kinds of practices that are eulogized or mourned by Rosler, Roberts, and Edwards are vague. What precisely is this practice whose eclipse is signified? Neither Rosler nor Edwards provides examples of which specific documentary practices are now mooted by contemporary critical theory. (Although Rosler, as an artist, is here writing as a critic and does not cite her own work.) What is meant by "documentary/image culture"? What is being referred to by Roberts's notion of "the democratic dispersal of counter knowledge as part of working class struggle and other struggles from below"? Is this the worker photography of the 1930s lauded by Walter Benjamin in his 1934 essay, "The Author as Producer"? If so, it is nearly a century since this was an actual (and short-lived) practice. Is there really a space "outside" of capitalist culture, and if so, where is it to be located? Do class politics accurately describe "documentary" photography in the present, much of it oriented to such issues as environmental destruction; violence against women; AIDS; civil, ethnic, or sectarian conflicts; other issues undreamed of by Marx?

Moreover, the invocation of a rise-and-fall model has a number of problems, not least of which is the fact that, however defined, there are now more "documentary" projects and more documentary photographers practicing than ever before in history, including legions in the non-Western world and the global south. In this respect, the digital age has fostered the growth of this practice just as it has with all other forms of imagemaking. There exist hundreds of websites devoted to various notions of documentary and, blogs and documentaries that are designed for web viewing. There are academic centers and other institutions devoted to it—journals, prizes, grants, and so forth. That many of these projects employ different technologies (digital cameras, obviously), take on subjects never treated previously, and are both supported and viewed differently from older systems of print media, may present different kinds of issues but contradict the assertions that documentary photography is an endangered species. Rather, it is a constantly mutating form of practices—not genres—that employ various techniques and procedures in various combinations for their fabrication before being launched into viewing space, reading space, exhibition space, or cyberspace.

As the unstable boundaries between different types of photographic practice (documentary, social documentary, photojournalism) become even less functional in defining or distinguishing forms of practice, subject matter previously associated with documentary or photojournalism has become an increasing presence in contemporary art exhibitions and, concomitantly, the international art market. This constitutes a new problematic, and requires an enlargement of the debates around the photographic politics of representation. What is at stake here is the phenomenon of documentary (or photojournalistic) subjects repurposed as art objects, where events or topics matter once perceived as the purview of documentation are now resignified (after various formal and contextual transformations) as images for aesthetic contemplation. One of the earlier controversies presaging these more recent manifestations can be located in polemics around the photography of Sebastião Selgado. In this respect, Selgado's formally beautiful black-and-white photographs of, for example, famine in the Sahel or migrant workers, and other instances of exploitation and misery in the global south, prompted criticism for their aestheticization of suffering.[49] In a certain sense, these debates symptomatize the erosion of boundaries between photographic "witness" and photographic "art," between the claims of historical evidence, ethical/political claims addressed to spectators, and the seductions of the image qua image. These go beyond the scope of this essay, but are relevant to the degree that they are further examples of how contemporary visual practices committed to "things as they are" are resistant to any consensus as to what such representations are expected to *do* and with what criteria they are to be accessed. Hence, yet another ghost of documentary is the belief that photographic witness in itself (and irrespective of its discursive and contextual embeddedness) might be sufficient in itself, that its referential grounding, *what* it represents, trumps ideology or spectacle.

Making a virtue out of necessity (i.e., the amorphousness of the category of documentary), a recent exhibition and catalogue, *Click / Doubleclick: The Documentary Factor*, is illustrative of the infinite elasticity of the documentary category. Prefaced with a series of (mostly) well-known photographs from the 1850s to the present, many of these would not have been assembled under this rubric even ten years ago. Beginning with Nadar's portrait of the mime Deburau, and continuing chronologically with Gustave Le Gray (a composite seascape), the sequence proceeds with a series of single photographs by August Sander, Bill Brandt, Walker Evans, Diane Arbus, William Eggleston, Thomas Ruff, Phillip-Lorca diCorcia, Thomas Struth, and Andreas Gursky. Leaving aside the scarcity of women photographers in the book and exhibition (seven out of forty-five), it seems as though the selection criteria were largely premised on the familiarity of the photographers and their market value.[50] That said, the apparent disregard for any definition of documentary, or, alternatively, the implicit claim that it is anything and everything, is explained by the exhibition's unabashed aesthetic orientation: "[The photographers'] works are not devoted primarily to the illustration of sociological, political, or anthropological subjects. Their works reflect these subjects, draw their material from the critical engagement with them, but must be understood as artistic self-expression that develops in a dialog. Their images do not have any evidential character; they do not put themselves in the service of science; they do not have any use. Rather, they formulate a belief in the artwork as an aesthetic object with its own laws."[51]

*Click / Doubleclick* (the title alludes to both camera and mouse) is, however, by no means unusual in its selection of photographers. Many exhibitions and catalogues now routinely group apparently unrelated works under the rubric of documentary, since there exist few if any criteria for exclusion.[52] Thus, the museumification of subject matter earlier confined to print, television, or informational media has eased the passageway of photographs originating in documentary or photojournalism into another discursive frame, that of contemporary art proper. Although photojournalists may now refashion themselves as artists, I do not know of any artist who has transformed herself into photojournalist. However, some of these crossover figures (e.g., Luc Delahaye and Simon Norfolk, et al.) who had made their reputations earlier as press photographers covering wars, have transformed the raw material of their photojournalism into wall-scaled art photographs. Nevertheless, it is interesting that critics such as Roberts, committed to counter-discursive practices, endorse this recent avatar of art photography, now fully assimilated into the emporia of contemporary art. As such, it has received its own generic designation, now referred to as "aftermath photography."

Here, however, I have tried to put these various photographic terms—documentary, social documentary and photojournalism—in historical perspective, for it is futile to establish fixed meanings for any of them. Rather, in placing them in some kind of relation to one another, and in the context of digital technology's liquidation of the indexical and the always vexed question of referentiality, it is more important to confront the new task of historicizing analogue representation. And while the evidentiary claims of analogue representation are inseparable from its indexicality, it is clear that there exists no general agreement as to what to make of documentary's recent circumstances, metamorphoses, technical transformations, and assimilation into other discursive frames. The question remains whether the categorical incoherence and/or mutability of the notion of documentary I have sketched should be celebrated or deplored. To what degree is a category called documentary now an epistemologically meaningful designation at all? Distinguishing between the concept of indexicality that guarantees the "real," as opposed to its digital incarnations presupposes that there exists in the former a warranty of truth, of historical presence, of witness that inheres within the image itself. But on the evidence, it seems that an entity designated "documentary photography" (and its subdivisions) that cordons itself from photography as such is itself an ideological, contingent, and wholly historical construction. As Jacques Derrida has taught us, all identity is internally divided, and contains within its putative boundaries the repressed and the excluded. It would seem to be the case that one of the most disruptive of ghosts that troubles our contemporary conception of photography is that which simultaneously subverts the imaginary category of documentary itself.

# 9

## Inventing Vivian Maier

### CATEGORIES, CAREERS, AND COMMERCE

(2013)

First she was found, as announced in the title of one of the two documentary films about her life and work (John Maloof's *Finding Vivian Maier* and an earlier film, the BBC documentary, *Who Took Nanny's Pictures?*). Now, only a few years after Vivian Maier's death and "discovery," her life and work are in the process of posthumous reconstruction, if not invention.[1] This enterprise is the result not only of Maier's work having recently come to light but also of its staggering quantity and remarkably swift entrance into the photographic marketplace. As for the work's "quality," the presumed reason for Maier's current fame, this is a question somewhat apart from the issues I wish to consider. The determination of artistic quality is not only subjective but perhaps less interesting to examine than the apparatuses by which artistic reputations are actually produced. In this respect, the nature and terms of Maier's invention are only two of several issues raised by her resurrection. As it happens, Maier's job as a nanny—an explicitly gendered profession—was itself an occasion for much of her photography. It also risks becoming a branding moniker: "Recluse Nanny Turns Out to Be Photography Genius," reads a recent headline in the *New York Post*. "Through the Nanny's Eyes" is the title of a *New York Times* article. And citing one of the now adult children Maier once minded, the news media have likened her to Mary Poppins.

Looking at Maier's many self-portraits reflected in mirrors and windows, there seems very little Poppins-like in her dour, impassive features.[2] Nevertheless, despite the unknowability of this deeply secretive woman and the many lacunae in her biography, her newfound fame as a so-called street photographer requires a story, a narrative, and a way to link this life with its massive, indeed obsessive, production of photos.

Art photography, now a subset of modern and contemporary art per se, has a very particular investment in the notion of genius. For one thing, as a medium not even two centuries old, the number of geniuses is relatively limited. Consequently, this honorific tends to be used somewhat promiscuously, although, it must be acknowledged, very rarely in the case of women. But the need for geniuses inevitably increases in relation to the growing market for photography. And, in the age of digital photography, there is a certain aura, a nostalgic one, that now attaches to analogue photography, an irony that must surely be noted by readers of Walter Benjamin. Nevertheless, the use of art historical terminology in relation to photography, analogue and digital, has always been a site of contradiction, if not of mystification. In other words, concepts of genius, masters and masterpieces, genres and signature styles are generally contradicted by the material realities of photographic production. Thirty years of criticism of these art historical paradigms have not appreciably diminished their influence. For example, in her 1984 essay "Landscape/View: Photography's Discursive Spaces," Rosalind Krauss addressed the complexities (and contradictions) of the art historical notion of "oeuvre" when applied to photographic production. As she observed, when photographic histories are constructed to conform to art historical models, they require equivalent concepts of authorship, intentionality, and some claim for the works' internal coherence or unity. Using as one of her examples the thousands of photographs made by Eugène Atget, Krauss questioned the validity of such concepts when applied to such a massive corpus:

> There are other practices, other exhibits, in the archive that also test the applicability of the concept *oeuvre*. One of these is the body of work that is too meager for this notion; the other is the body that is too large. Can we imagine an oeuvre consisting of one work? The history of photography tries to do this with the single photographic effort ever produced by Auguste Salzmann, a lone volume of archeological photographs . . . some portion of which are known to have been taken by his assistant. And, at the opposite extreme, can we imagine an oeuvre consisting of 10,000 works?[3]

This figure, however, based on Atget's extant archive, is more than dwarfed by the corpus of Garry Winogrand, who, when he died, left behind thousands of rolls of exposed but undeveloped film and unedited contact sheets—something like 250,000 exposures.[4] Vivian Maier's corpus, most of it undeveloped, is even larger.

In the case of Atget, Krauss's arguments were intended not just to demonstrate the misfit between the categories of art history as these are imposed on photographic history but also to interpret Atget's production in terms of the organizing logic of the archive. For Krauss, this approach was supported by Atget's own cataloguing system, which, as she observed, was adapted to the categories and requirements of his various clientele. And while it may be that Krauss's reading of Atget's motivations, their logic, and their embeddedness in use value (as opposed to exhibition value) is specific to Atget, the artistic, and indeed, epistemological issues posed by enormous photographic archives have by no means been resolved.

Consequently, the daunting number of recently excavated photographs, slides, negatives, Super 8 films, and audiocassettes made by Maier raise similar questions and many more. Moreover, because the Maier archives are all held in private collections and commercial galleries, the pictures now reproduced or exhibited, whether made by Maier or by those who now own them, beg the question as to whose "vision" (or aesthetic preference, or sensibility, or point of view) is actually being represented. But where the discovery (or rediscovery) of photographers over the last fifty years or so has usually played itself out through the relatively traditional apparatuses of connoisseurship and scholarship, or—increasingly—through markets and dealers, the speed with which Maier's work passed from oblivion to fame is indeed remarkable. Similarly, the ways in which her life is being reconstructed as additional information is unearthed provides a telling contrast with the stately pace required for the historical or biographical reconstruction of Eugène Atget and his eventual canonization.

About a month or so after I wrote a commissioned blog for the Jeu de Paume Museum in Paris that summarized what was then known of Maier and raised questions about the role of her collectors and the media in shaping her history, I met Pamela Bannos, a photographer and senior lecturer at Northwestern University in Chicago. For several years, Bannos has been researching the life and work of Maier, as well as that of her mother and grandmother and other biographical and contextual information. Unlike all the other actors in the Maier enterprise—I use the term advisedly—Bannos does not own any of Maier's work, and her research is scholarly rather than entrepreneurial. It was Bannos who organized one of the first exhibitions of Maier's work in Chicago in 2013, using photographs borrowed from one of Maier's first group of collectors, Jeffrey Goldstein.

In one of the lectures Bannos gives about Maier, she displays a slide featuring the logos of a range of social media sites. For, as she remarks, the rapid “invention,” if not branding, of Vivian Maier has profited from these new communications media, including eBay, Flickr, Facebook, Tumblr, YouTube, Kickstarter, and other websites, including those specific sites set up by owners of Maier’s work such as John Maloof. Bannos was given access to twenty thousand of Maier’s images by Goldstein, and it was from this cache of images that she organized her exhibition and began her research. She appears in the BBC documentary and the three Chicago Public Television programs that featured the earliest stories about Maier. Since then, Bannos has continued her research and is currently preparing a book-length study.

The dissemination of Maier’s work through electronic and social media is not without its ironies, inasmuch as few lives in the modern urban world have been lived so far under the radar as to produce only the barest traces of the subject, even after diligent research. For most of Maier’s adult life, she worked as a nanny, governess, or caregiver in the suburbs or towns around Chicago’s North Shore (ca. 1956–2000). Apparently, she seems to have discarded nothing she ever possessed; among her effects, beside the photographs, were found clothing, shoes, hats, old newspapers, books, albums, discarded cameras, memorabilia, and professional darkroom processing receipts. She never cashed in her tax reimbursements or social security checks, becoming effectively indigent by 2007. Thus, and with respect to her now celebrated photographs, it was only when the contents of her storage lockers were auctioned off for nonpayment that the story of her recovery properly begins.

Born in New York City in 1926, from the late 1940s until some time in the 1980s, Maier photographed her surroundings and their inhabitants obsessively—no other word adequately characterizes her activity. After 1956, when she moved permanently from New York to Chicago, while living in the homes of her various employers she maintained a vigilant personal privacy, all the more striking for its separation from the bustling family life that surrounded her. With neither family nor friends, and increasingly mentally disturbed, in her final years her sole financial support was provided by the Gensburg family, for whom she had worked longest and who paid her rent, hospital, and nursing home fees. In the end, one of the Gensburg brothers became her plenary guardian, assuming all responsibility for her care and finances. In 2008, already elderly, Maier slipped on the ice, and although she was expected to recover, after four months in the nursing home she died. It is thus significant that so soon after her death, there now exist two feature-length documentary films (and talk of a future biopic), three monographs, numerous websites (some with short videos), and a growing number of collectors and commercial galleries all functioning to catalogue, print, scan, publicize, exhibit, or sell Maier's work. Even more remarkable has been the reception of her photographs when exhibited, drawing large audiences in Chicago, New York, London, Tours, and Paris. In the wake of one of the recent exhibitions (drawn from Jeffrey Goldstein's holdings), a permanent Vivian Maier gallery is to be established as part of the Minneapolis Photo Center.[5] All of which is to say that we are looking at the ongoing labor of many players, with various investments, all engaged in the process of manufacturing a reputation and producing an oeuvre that must be culled from a staggering number of exposures, of which only a tiny fraction were ever printed by the photographer herself.

Accordingly, even as the biographical facts of Maier's life are fleshed out, the central questions raised by Krauss are even more dramatically foregrounded given the scale of Maier's extant archive, the total amount of which is still not known. The story of the passage of Maier's pictures from storage lockers to their current distribution between first and second purchasers, galleries, private dealers, stakeholders, and newly established foundations is not easy to reconstruct, nor, apparently, is it intended to be. Which is one of the most interesting but least chronicled aspects of the Maier phenomenon, for it can be taken as a case history of the marketing, branding, and complex capitalization of a virtually unknown photographer within a market constructed by new media and new players.

The first purchaser of the contents of Maier's storage lockers was Roger Gunderson, an auctioneer. In five "look but don't touch" auctions in Chicago, he sold the contents to half a dozen dealers for modest sums. At least one of the purchasers did not even know the contents of the boxes he acquired. Among the first three purchasers—John Maloof, Ron Slattery, and Randy Prow—it was Slattery who began posting and selling Maier's 35-millimeter slides on the web. John Maloof also made prints from some of Maier's negatives and posted and sold approximately two hundred individual negatives on eBay. It is Maloof who has been the most energetic and visible entrepreneur of the collection. He has produced three of the four monographs and the documentary *Finding Vivian Maier*, organized exhibitions, maintained a website, and established relations with galleries such as Steven Kasher and Howard Greenberg, both in New York City, to represent and sell Maier's work, both vintage prints and prints made from her negatives. (Only a small fraction of Maier's negatives were ever printed, either by Maier—who for several years had used her bathroom as a darkroom—or, later, by her commercial printers.) Neither Maloof's books nor his film acknowledge Bannos's research or the role of the other collectors. Recognizing the potential in Maier's work, Jeff Goldstein, a carpenter, purchased her work from Randy Prow, who purchased it from the first auction. Goldstein's collection now consists of approximately 18,000 negatives, including 225 rolls of undeveloped film, 1,500 color slides, 1,100 vintage prints, and 30 16-millimeter home movies. Goldstein has estimated that Maier produced about fifty thousand images for each decade of her active working life. From some of the interviews depicted in the documentary *Who Took Nanny's Pictures?* certain of these transactions sound like the plot of a B movie (meetings in abandoned warehouses, guns, bodyguards, all-cash exchanges). Slattery now has a selection of several thousand of Maier's original prints and an undisclosed number of negatives. The collection of Maloof, who purchased a lot of 30,000 to 40,000 negatives with an absentee bid, now consists of 100,000 to 150,000 negatives, over 3,000 prints, and also hundreds of still-undeveloped 35-millimeter Ektachrome film.

Inevitably and necessarily, what has thus far been reproduced or exhibited of Maier's work has been selected, and often printed, by its various owners, who are now, so to speak, its stakeholders.[6] This further begs the question of the definition of an oeuvre as a corpus of work expressing the preferences and choices—the presumed "vision"—of its maker. Putting aside for the moment all discussion of Maier's subject matter, including the dubious category of "street photography," it is an open question as to how those photographs printed from her negatives should look.[7] In *Who Took Nanny's Pictures?*, Joel Meyerowitz, one of the doyens of so-called street photography, raised this issue, expressing his concern about how Maier's work is being variously presented. Obviously, there is no way of knowing why Maier printed (or developed) those images that she did, or how she would have printed those that remained undeveloped. However, and as Bannos established by comparing full-frame digital scans with prints made by Maier, in many cases she cropped her prints, changing the square format of the view camera she had used to rectangular formats. Bannos makes a convincing case that Maier's cropping strategies were employed to bracket out what she considered peripheral to the contents of the image, but such cropping also produces the effect of greater proximity to its subject. (Although it should be kept in mind that, as with virtually all of her photographs, these were for intended only for her own viewing.[8]) The sole exception to the privacy with which Maier guarded her photographic production was her occasional sale of pictures to the parents of the children who were in her charge. Bannos has also persuasively argued that far from being a kind of idiot savant of photography, Maier was technically skilled and informed about current photography, especially by the time she started shooting with a Rolleiflex.

Without endorsing the fetishism of certain types of photographic connoisseurship, it is nevertheless the case that choices in printing, cropping, and paper do materially affect the appearance of photographs, especially in black and white. This is equally the case with book or catalogue reproductions, as can be readily seen by comparing the reproductions in Maloof's *Vivian Maier: Street Photographer* (2011) and Richard Cahan and Michael Williams's *Vivian Maier: Out of the Shadows* (2012). The photographs in the Maloof book were printed from high-quality scans of the negatives, and are crisp, sharp, and tonal. They are full-page reproductions but not full-page bleeds, as are many of the photographs reproduced in Cahan and Williams's catalogue. Which of the photographs are more accurate or faithful to the negative is impossible to judge; the (relatively) limited numbers of prints made by Maier provide the only sense of her own formal preferences. Bannos, however, claims that neither book fairly represents the qualities of Maier's large vintage prints, which she thinks were printed on Kodak Ektalure paper, characterized by soft, low contrast and warm tones. But what if the prints made by scans or by reprinting from Maier's negatives are of markedly "better" quality than the ones Maier made herself? (I suspect this will turn out to be the case; had Maier been concerned with the quality of her prints, there would be many more of them.) This suggests that for Maier, it was the *act* of photographing, rather than the production of a discrete image, that was the psychological imperative. A negative, one might say, is an *unrealized* image. Inescapably, the questions that arise with the posthumous reconstruction of a photographic reputation reveal problems that are only distantly related to the art history of printmaking, but are endemic to the fabrication of photographic histories.

I have written elsewhere about the problematic category of "street photography," a label invented in the 1970s and so broad as to be effectively meaningless. While there exist hundreds, if not thousands, of photographers, many anonymous, who have made pictures on the street since photography's earliest years (and for many different reasons and purposes), this does not in and of itself constitute a coherent genre. As a term invented within art photography discourse, the notion of "street photography" has been deployed to consecrate work by a very limited number of (mostly) art photographers (Walker Evans, Henri Cartier-Bresson, and Robert Frank are a few paradigmatic examples). Be that as it may, among the ranks of those taking pictures of passersby in public space, women are significantly rare.[9] In this respect, one of the most remarkable aspects of Maier as, in a sense, a compulsive photographer, is her gender. Certain of Maier's commentators have invoked the precedents of Lisette Model and Helen Levitt, whose work Maier may well have known. Nevertheless, many if not most of Model's published photographs are oriented toward the grotesque, and Levitt mostly photographed neighborhood children. In any event, despite her distance from photography as a professional métier, Maier's lifelong picture taking, done primarily in public space, was anything but the hobby of an amateur, despite its private motivation.

On her return to New York City from her second visit to Saint Bonnet-sur-Champsaur in the 1950s (her mother's natal French Alpine village), Maier corresponded with at least one proprietor of a local photographic studio about the possibility of his printing her negatives for sale as postcards. However, and with another possible exception indicated below, it appears that she made no attempt to sell or publicize her photography, although its pace did not slacken for decades. But as to the question of whether Maier's compulsive photographing was a deliberate form of art making, a kind of compulsion, an expression of madness, a function of her asocial existence, or a symptom of sociocultural and psychological unbelonging, who can really say?

Bannos suggests that it was only after leaving New York City for Illinois in 1956 that Maier abandoned any thought of selling or exhibiting her work, although the existence of the portfolios Bannos has studied might be taken as evidence of her intention to obtain magazine or editorial work.[10] Like so much else of Maier's life and work, this remains an open question. What one can say is that in some mysterious and, indeed, poignant way, Maier lived her adult life through the camera's lens, a vicarious existence in which the camera "eye" and the subjective "I" were inextricably linked. I know of no other such example in the history of photography.

But one of the important points to be made is that like professional photojournalism, photographing on the street is and has been a quintessentially masculine preserve. The reasons for this are many, and include the masculine prerogatives of active looking, the gendered attributes of public space, the relative vulnerability of women within that space, and the aggressive aspects of photographing unwitting subjects. Consequently, sexual difference, as well as gender—both inescapable facts of human psychic and social existence—cannot be immaterial or irrelevant in Maier's photographic practice. It may have determined how she photographed (the Rolleiflex is far more discreet than a camera held to the eye), what she photographed (much of her subject matter relates to suburban children who were the source of her livelihood), and how she photographed herself (as an isolated figure disconnected from other human beings).

Be all this as it may, and in keeping with Maier's professional employment, one major aspect of her work from the 1950s on is the manner with which she recorded the life of children (her charges included) with little sentimentality or condescension. Depicted outdoors in parks, beaches, backyards, and schoolyards, her children living in the well-to-do suburbs of North Shore are interestingly paralleled by her pictures of inner-city children and adults of color, as well as the working class, the poor, and the down-and-out. These raise interesting questions as to how and why this Franco-American, spinsterish woman would be so drawn to depict the urban margins. Was it voyeurism? Curiosity? Empathy? Identification? Reference is made by some of her employers to her identification with or espousal of "liberal" or "left" politics, but no concrete details are supplied. Moreover, to have photographed then vice president Richard Nixon greeting crowds in Chicago, or to have photographed newspaper headlines about John Kennedy's and later Robert Kennedy's assassinations are not indices of any particular political orientation. Apparently, there exist many photographs made during Maier's extensive international travels, which included South Asia, the Philippines, Cuba, and Egypt, as well as other places. Few of these photographs have thus far been published or exhibited. If nothing else, these far-flung voyages during which, as always, Maier photographed constantly, suggest that she was utterly fearless (in the 1950s, few women would have hazarded such journeys alone, just as they would have avoided the Bowery or Chicago slums).

From Bannos's research and other sources, one knows that when Maier and her mother, Marie Jaussaud, returned from France to New York City in 1938, the two moved into the apartment of a French-born portrait photographer named Jeanne Bertrand (they were listed as living there in the 1940 census). Whether Bertrand and her profession had any bearing on Maier's future activities as a photographer is, yet again, unknowable. Maier's mother had separated previously from her husband, Charles Maier (an Austrian émigré), shortly after Maier's birth in New York City in 1926, but Charles Maier disappears from the record after 1940. It has been established that in 1940 Maier's brother was then living with his paternal grandparents in the Bronx. From the information given in the documentary *Finding Vivian Maier*, Bertrand was at some point institutionalized, but little is known about the time that Maier and her mother shared the apartment with her.

Bannos is herself fascinated by this multigeneration succession of French women living in improvised households in New York City and placing themselves outside of "conventional" sexual or familial structures. Not the least interesting of Bannos's sleuthlike discoveries is Maier's consistent mystification or falsification of everything from her place of birth (she claimed it was France, although it was New York) to the date of the death of her mother (Maier said 1943, but, in fact, it was 1975) and other deceptions. As with many outsider artists or photographers—that is, those outside either professional or artistic practice—reconstituting a life is even more difficult than reconstituting an archive.

In 1950, at the age of twenty-five, Maier returned from New York to Saint Bonnet-sur-Champsaur to claim a legacy from the sale of a family property, and it was there that she produced her first known photographs. From what has been so far reproduced, these are unremarkable but accomplished pictures of the Alpine scenery and the residents of the village and its environs. It seems evident, however, that when photographing these subjects, Maier was within a familiar milieu, and her pictures made with the cooperation of her subjects. With the proceeds of the sale of her inherited property Maier made her first independent travels in the south of France. Although Maloof has claimed that these photographs made in France were taken with a simple box camera, Bannos's research suggests otherwise. Based on her examination of the analogue proof sheets and an assortment of negative scans from the Goldstein collection, Bannos is convinced that they were made with a more sophisticated camera, as evidenced by the variety of exposures and manipulations of shutter and aperture. These pictures are mostly of landscapes and inhabitants of the village, "postcard" types that also include portraits of villagers, and even some street work, presaging Maier's interest in photographing sleeping people.

In her passport application of 1950, Maier described herself as a factory worker (her passport says "machine operator," which could mean anything). In July of 1952, she replaced her earlier camera, which produced rectangular negatives, with a medium-format Rolleiflex, and possibly used other cameras she might have acquired. The Rolleiflex, with which she produced so much of her subsequent work, produces two-and-a-quarter-inch square negatives, twelve exposures to a roll of film. Aside from the square format of the negative (which in turn influences an image's formal composition), the exposure is made as the photographer looks down through the viewfinder, where the image appears reversed. It may have taken Maier some time to master this more complicated camera, but by 1953 she was using the Rolleiflex exclusively.[11] One of the other characteristics of this camera is that the making of the exposure requires no eye contact with the subject. Once the exposure is set, the photographer could be looking anywhere, and as such, the subject on the street may be altogether unaware of their visual capture. Indeed, in many of the self-portraits in which Maier looks up, sideways or frontally, the camera usually remains at waist level.

The pictures in which her subject is clearly aware of the camera and willing to be photographed seem to be overwhelmingly of children, the elderly, and minority or marginal adults (e.g., skid row denizens, the very poor, etc.). This is not unproblematic. Although photography critics and historians frequently argue for the photographer's empathetic identification with the subject and other alibis for "street photography," at least since Martha Rosler's classic essay of 1981 there has existed a rigorous critique of the implications of posing the camera downward.[12] In other words, issues of power, of subject-object relations, social relations, and class are aspects of what might be called the ethics as well as the politics of photographic representation. Photographing the down-and-out in the urban landscape has been a staple of photography at least since the 1920s, from Ilya Ehrenburg and Germaine Krull in 1930s Paris to the present. How should we consider Maier's practice in relation to such issues?

Of what has thus far been seen of Maier's pictures (and this qualification should be kept in mind), there appear to be very few pictures of beautiful women or handsome men (there are some exceptions, but they are exceptions, unless this itself reflects editorial choices). However, there are many pictures of unconscious subjects (as well as unwitting ones), many back views, and many fragmented bodies. Bannos has noted the frequency with which Maier photographed the backs of legs. These might also suggest the gendering of photographic practice, inasmuch as it requires a certain assertiveness, if not aggression, to photograph people without their permission. The expression of affront or annoyance on the face of certain of the bourgeois elderly women in Maier's pictures makes evident their displeasure at being so taken, as it were, off guard. Such pictures of women are also a frequent subject in the photography of the 1930s and after. Thus, while certain of Maier's photographic subjects can be said to be participating in a social transaction, there are also numerous instances of what Henri Cartier-Bresson characterized as the camera's "pounce." ("I prowled the streets all day, feeling very strung-up and ready to pounce, determined to 'trap' life—to preserve life in the act of living."[13])

It is here, however, where we might distinguish between Maier's self-portraits and her self-representations, for while all portraits are self-representations, not all self-representations are self-portraits. Specifically, I refer here to the many photographs in which Maier's unmistakable shadow looms across the foreground before her viewfinder. This is, as is well known, a recurring trope in modernist photography; indeed, Lee Friedlander produced an entire book around this device—other examples are legion. Which in turn suggests that Maier may have been far more aware of the photography of her contemporaries than her "Mary Poppins" or "Nanny" characterizations imply. Among her archives were a number of photography books, including a selection of the *Time/Life* photography books, and during her residence and subsequent visits to New York City she apparently frequented exhibitions at MoMA and other venues where photography was regularly exhibited. Perhaps the assumption of her unfamiliarity with contemporary work, even her supposed ignorance of it, is thought to further burnish her reputation, as though her presumed lack of technical virtuosity or knowledge of her contemporaries were further evidence of artistic accomplishment. Many of Maier's photographs of women, both aware and unaware of the camera, are similar to Harry Callahan's photographs, who likewise lived in Chicago and was often exhibited. Excluding Maier's often striking and quite singular self-portraits, her posthumous construction as a naive and intuitive genius of street photography should not be taken at face value. During Maier's most active photographic period, and before and after it, photographing anonymous people in urban settings was a common practice of amateurs and professionals alike. From the city scenes made by members of the New York Photo League to official government documentary projects to the artfully artless production of Winogrand and his epigones, up to and including such recent photographers as Beat Streuli and Philip-Lorca diCorcia, the "spontaneous" capture of metropolitan street life has long been the photographic coin of the realm. In fact, Maier's photographs made on the street are strikingly similar to those of other photographers active in the period. Sid Grossman, Leon Levinstein, Louis Faurer, Max Yavno, Ben Shahn, and legions of others could well have been the work of Maier, and vice versa. What distinguishes Maier's work from theirs is first her gender, and then her work's astounding quantity, and her apparent indifference to printing what she shot.

As for the self-portraits, it is their implacable opacity, and occasionally striking formal invention, that places them in a different category from the more conventional imagery Maier made in the street. Looking at those so far published or exhibited, most of which appear to have been made between the 1950s and the 1970s, it would seem that most are shot by Maier, although a number of her former charges recall that she asked them to make the exposures, and it does seem evident in certain photographs that someone else made the exposure. But those photographs made in Maier's various bedrooms in the homes of her employers, and those made in front of mirrors and other reflective surfaces, are striking in their lack of expressivity or suggestion of a "personality." Maier was by no means an ugly woman, but rather one essentially conforming to the notion of "plain-looking."

With respect to these self-portraits, it was as though Maier used the camera to confirm her very existence to and for herself, as though she were detached from the human community around her. Somewhat poignantly, what emerges in Maloof's documentary film is what can only be termed Maier's increasing madness. Previous employers (including the television personality Phil Donahue) made mention of her maniacal hoarding: thousands of newspapers and magazines, scavenged garbage, flea market purchases, and boxes and boxes of papers, as well as her lifetime accumulation of photographs and negatives and cameras. This hoarding was such that in one household, the weight of Maier's belongings required the structural reinforcement of the ceiling below her floor. Even more disturbing are some of the reminiscences of Maier's now adult charges, certain of which resemble a kind of sadism (why would one take small children to a slaughterhouse?). One anecdote, recounted by one of the mothers who had employed Maier, describes an incident in which her son was knocked down by a car, and Maier stood by to photograph the fallen child rather than assist him. But as stories accumulate of Maier's secrecy (if not paranoia), nocturnal wandering, aggressive outbursts, social isolation, and hoarding, one wonders how and why what seems a descent into mental illness was not only ignored by her employers but thought irrelevant to her responsibilities as the caretaker of their children. Which is to say that these are anecdotes not only illustrating eccentricity but something far more somber and disturbing: a woman's social isolation and intensifying madness that provoked no alarm, and prompted no intervention. So much for Mary Poppins. Which in turn raises yet another question, and that has to do with if, or how, Maier's mental illness was related to her photography, for both the hoarding and the photographing suggest an obsessive-compulsive disorder. Is this a photographic analogue to the production of "outsider" artists? While such artists have typically worked with painting, drawing, fabric, or even three-dimensional structures, photographic production cannot take place in isolation, be it private or institutional. One way or another, the photographer is in the world, must master the apparatus, buy and process film, deal with other people, and navigate social space. Perhaps it is here that Maier's singularity is most in evidence, for given the scale of the archive, it seems that the act of photographing the life around her was a substitute for having a life of her own. The accumulating pictures, like Maier's later accumulation of *stuff*, suggest a terrible vacuum that she somehow tried to fill.

In the present, however, perhaps Maier fills another vacuum. I have mentioned the institutional and commercial need for photographic geniuses. And given the underrepresentation of women photographers in photographic history and in exhibitions, the posthumous recognition of Maier can hardly be criticized. Also, as I have indicated, the new dominance of digital media, which permits any and all forms of manipulation, creates forms of nostalgia for the analogue, just as it subverts older although imaginary notions of photographic truth. But any real knowledge of what passes for "street photography" should caution against an inflated notion of Maier's "originality," which, it seems to me, is largely represented by her unsentimental representation of children, her dystopic vision of both middle- and lower-class life, and, preeminently, her strange and wholly solipsistic practice of self-portraiture. Finally, that almost all of what we are given to see of Maier's work has been, so to speak, "preprocessed" by her works' owners, gallerists, and other stakeholders, and thus mediated though their own aesthetic, marketing, or other preferences, should remind us that photographic discourse, especially that which pertains to some notion of art photography, is moored in social relations, in burgeoning markets, and in a profound ideological investment in the individuality, originality, and intentionality of cultural producers.

## Afterword

Recently in the *New York Times*, an article by Randy Kennedy was published with the clever title "The Heir's Not Apparent: A Legal Battle over Vivian Maier's Work."[14] According to the *Times*, a former photographer and now lawyer, David C. Deal, filed a case in 2015, claiming to have located a French relative of Maier's who might be the legitimate heir (or co-heir) of the Maier estate. Motives, stakes, genealogies, various payments to various principals, copyright law, and much else are not only highly ambiguous but certainly up in the air. It seems at least a possibility that as this saga unfolds it might become a Fog of Chancery perfectly updated to the new realities of the (art) photographic marketplace, and with potentially damaging effects on Maier's current market (or even exhibitions). Whatever might happen in what promises to be a lengthy process, I dare not predict. Queried by the *Times* on his reaction to these untimely events, Maloof responded more in sorrow than in anger: "It's kind of sad. I have a very emotional attachment to her work and I'm very protective of it. And I've never let anything happen to it that's not been of the highest quality."

# 10

## Robert Mapplethorpe

### WHITEWASHED AND POLISHED

(2014)

In the spring of 2014, a large retrospective of Robert Mapplethorpe's work opened at the Grand Palais in Paris. It was coupled with another Mapplethorpe exhibition at the Musée Rodin in which Mapplethorpe's photographs—I am not joking—were displayed with various sculptures by Rodin.

As it happens, Mapplethorpe did photograph sculptures (torsos, heads, and backs) in ways not so different from those in which he photographed living bodies, although it seems not to have mattered if the sculptures were authentic, copies, classical, neoclassical, or kitsch. Somewhat perversely (I use the term advisedly), the photographs in the Grand Palais show were of sculptures, whereas the photographs in the Musée Rodin were mostly of living bodies (or body parts), as well as the miscellaneous self-portrait or still life. More to the point, what the latter exhibition really demonstrated is that for good or ill, Rodin's sculptures, plasters, or small studies have *nothing* whatsoever to do with Mapplethorpe's work and vice versa. Why would they?

The press release for the Musée Rodin exhibition makes no reference to Mapplethorpe's sculptural choices or artistic preferences, perhaps implicitly acknowledging that any given sculpture, as an integral whole, was not what interested him. Much is made of the photographer's stated admiration for Michelangelo. But for Mapplethorpe, a part of a sculpture, like a part of a body, was the raw material with which he worked. Be that as it may, the Musée Rodin's press release provides the institutional rationale for the exhibition:

> There would appear to be little similarity between these two renowned figures, even though Mapplethorpe continually sought to sculpt the body through photography and Rodin used photography throughout his career.

> Robert Mapplethorpe sought the perfect form, while Rodin attempted to capture a sense of movement in inanimate materials. There is no spontaneity in Mapplethorpe's work, everything is constructed, whereas Rodin retains the traces of his touch and takes advantage of the accidental. One was attracted to men, the other to women, obsessively in both cases. But this did not stop Mapplethorpe from photographing female nudes, or Rodin from sculpting many male bodies. Here, however, the differences between these two artists are instantly transformed into an unexpected dialogue.

This dialogue, however, might be better characterized as overdetermined rather than unexpected, since the point of this curatorial exercise is to burnish, sanitize, and heroize Mapplethorpe. Yet again, we can observe, in real time, the cranking up of the apparatuses of canon formation, the mechanisms by which that totem of elite culture, the Great Artist, is collectively forged.[1] This is hardly necessary for Rodin or his work, housed in its consecrated museum, and *Mapplethorpe-Rodin* is displayed in that part of the renovated museum aptly called the Chapel. Moreover, the aims, approach, and presentation of Mapplethorpe's work is by no means simply the result of a few individuals' choices, because both exhibitions are collective endeavors involving different institutions (most importantly, the Robert Mapplethorpe Foundation, the source of most of the exhibited work), corporate sponsors, and curators from the foundation and from the two museums. But the nature and terms of the framing discourse within which both exhibitions are conceived, consciously or not, are such as to minimize if not obscure what is arguably Mapplethorpe's most significant work. In privileging a great deal of his blandest production a "great artist" is manufactured conforming to the hoariest and most sterile notions of art photography, with the addition of some racial spice to supply a more edgy frisson.[2]

By blandness, I refer, to Mapplethorpe's highly stylized, glacially chic, knowingly retro pictures of flowers and still lives, and his artfully crafted objects, such as folding screens, triptychs with moiré silk panels, mirrored panels, and other *objets de luxe* for interior decoration. Also in this category are the impeccably printed, tastefully abstracted nudes (male and female), black-and-white photographs that could easily have come from the darkrooms of Edward Weston and his descendants. In his use of platinum printing and other avatars of the fine print, the exotic wood frames, and the objects themselves, it is difficult not to see the influence of Mapplethorpe's various dealers, such as the Robert Miller Gallery, if not the influence of his lover and companion of twenty years, Sam Wagstaff, himself a collector first of painting, then of photography, and later, silver.[3] Additional instances of the bland include many of his portraits of artists (some of them friends of Wagstaff and artists he had exhibited during his curatorial career), socialites (also from Wagstaff's milieu), fashion designers, actresses, singers, and so on. (Mapplethorpe's portraits of drag queens and more marginal individuals are not on view). Judging from the pictures, it seems unlikely that Mapplethorpe shared with these subjects the kind of intimacy or friendship that inspired the portraits of Patti Smith and a few others.

But dwarfing in notoriety these sorts of photographs are those of black men. All of which is to say that without the sorts of photographs Mapplethorpe chose for his X, Y, and Z Portfolios, or certain of the pictures reproduced in his *Black Book*, Mapplethorpe is merely another art photographer with a good eye for framing and composition, a perfectionist's regard for print quality, and a savvy notion of his market. Without the brutal, gritty, and still shocking photographs of New York City's (and San Francisco's) pre-AIDS gay underworld of bars, drugs, orgies, and S/M practices—in all of which Mapplethorpe was a participant-observer—one has a very partial sense of what made him such an important witness of his time and place.

Be that as it may, at the Grand Palais, those pictures deemed too dangerous for the eyes of minors are sequestered in a separate, very dark, and smallish room painted a blackish-purple. When I went, there was a cautionary notice posted at the entrance to the room, and the room itself was respectfully hushed, except for the muffled titters of a couple of elderly women. But aside from close-ups of heroically sized penises and one photograph of analingis, the hard-core photographs made by Mapplethorpe were not on view. Although pictures depicting fist-fucking, water sports, and various S/M activities, as well as Mapplethorpe's well-known self-portrait with a whip inserted in his rectum, have been reproduced in various monographs and exhibited in such venues as the Los Angeles County Museum in 2013, these were conspicuously absent from this exhibit. Yet the no-less-notorious *Man in Polyester Suit* was on view in the main exhibition, as were photographs of other nude men, mostly black, all freely on display for the impressionable eyes of minors.

Had Mapplethorpe not been struck down by AIDS in the prime of life, as were so many of his contemporaries—Sam Wagstaff and his other lovers included—one could have said he had lived a charmed life, at least professionally and materially. Wagstaff, who died of AIDS a year before Mapplethorpe, was not only independently wealthy but also generous: after he became involved with Mapplethorpe in 1972, he purchased a loft for him (as well as a Hasselblad), and was also in a position to help orchestrate Mapplethorpe's career. A year earlier, Mapplethorpe had become friends with John McKendry, a curator at the Metropolitan Museum of Art, and thus linked to a more uptown and wealthy network. Mapplethorpe became successful relatively early on, and, as should be obvious, his photographs had several niche markets. At thirty-one, he was invited to exhibit at Documenta 6. That same year, the Holly Solomon Gallery gave him a one-person show. In 1978, the Robert Miller Gallery became his "official" gallery. And so on.

In the obscenity trial of 1990 that charged the Cincinnati's Contemporary Arts Center and its director, Dennis Barrie, with "pandering obscenity" and therefore breaking antipornography laws, it was the task of the defense team to prove to the jury that Mapplethorpe's photographs were art with a capital "A" and thus constitutionally protected as free speech (Mapplethorpe had died the previous year of AIDS at the age of forty-two). To make these arguments, the defense enlisted the testimony of "expert witnesses." These included Janet Kardon, the original curator of the exhibition; Jacquelynn Baas, then director of the University of California Berkeley Art Museum; and Robert Sobieszek, then senior curator at the International Museum of Photography in Rochester, New York. By the time the trial began, only seven of the 175 photographs in the exhibition were designated as obscene or pornographic. Two of these were of little girls whose genitalia could be seen, although their mothers' testified that the pictures were made with their knowledge and permission and that they had tacitly assumed the pictures might be exhibited or reproduced (none of Mapplethorpe's pictures of children are on view in the Paris exhibitions). The other five were of *white* men engaging in sexual activities. To the prosecution's question as to whether these passed muster as art, Sobieszek argued, "If it's in an art museum, it is intended to be art and that's why it's there."[4] This we might call the Duchampian or nominative defense, and there is no reason not to take it seriously. But it was the aesthetic arguments made by Kardon and others, couched in the terms of a formalist aestheticism that approached parody, that actually carried the day: "'Would you call these sexual acts?' Mr. Prouty [the prosecuting attorney] asked. 'I would call them figure studies,' Mrs. Kardon said. Mr. Prouty then asked her, picture by picture, what was artistic about each work. 'What are the formal values of the picture where the finger is inserted in the penis?' Mr. Prouty asked in a straightforward manner. 'It's a central image, very symmetrical, a very ordered, classical composition,' she said, noting that Mr. Mapplethorpe once commented on how 'beautiful' the hand gestures were."[5] In the end, both the museum and Barrie were exculpated, but despite the apparent victory of "free speech" as a condition for unfettered cultural production, this was a Pyrrhic victory, insofar it heralded the end of US government funding for anything remotely controversial in the visual arts.[6] Nevertheless, it is within the sanitizing and mystifying realm of such abstractions as "Art," "Beauty," and "the Nude" that the Grand Palais and, presumably, the Musée Rodin framed their exhibitions—by which I refer to everything from the signage and the epigraphic quotations from Mapplethorpe stenciled on the walls to the physical organization of the show and the basic gist of the two accompanying catalogues.

The issues raised by Mapplethorpe's work are as large as they are troubling—and both exhibitions work strenuously to occlude them—but among those that require consideration are the work's various contexts including its viewing contexts; its place in the photographic canon; the role of marketplace, museum, and the stakeholders of an oeuvre; and the various backstories (biographical and institutional) that surround both artist and work, as well as, in terms of its artistic claims, the complex issue of "content" and "form" in photographic production. Such issues inevitably lead to questions about spectatorial reception, the representation of marginal communities, the psychic and social components of desire in looking, and, by no means least, issues of fetishism (both commodity and psychic). Finally, such a body of work requires a difficult discussion about the politics of racial representation as these are enacted and staged in Mapplethorpe's photographs of black men, his lovers, and others.

In this respect, and as the most incisive critical writing on Mapplethorpe attests, the work of Frantz Fanon provides an indispensable counter-discourse to the formalist babbling (or apologetics) that passes for commentary on Mapplethorpe's pictures of black men: "When one reads this passage [from *Martinique* by Michel Cournot] a dozen times and lets oneself go; that is, abandons oneself to the movement of its images—one is no longer aware of the Negro but only of a penis; the Negro is eclipsed. He is turned into a penis. He is a penis."[7]

By no means the least ironic aspect of the Mapplethorpe enterprise is the way in which the fetishism that is so prominent a feature within the work is replicated in its celebratory discourses as well as its exhibition formats.[8] If we accept Freud's model of the structure of fetishism in which the male subject recognizes a physical fact (i.e., women do not have penises) and simultaneously rejects, denies, or represses this disturbing observation by investing a surrogate object with compensatory significance, a number of contradictions in the discourses generated by Mapplethorpe's oeuvre are clarified. Indeed, one of the reasons that this model of (psychic) fetishism is useful in critical thinking is that it helps account for logical contradictions, famously encapsulated in Octave Mannoni's "Je sais bien, mais quand même" (I know, but nevertheless).

Here, for example, are some of the contradictions one might glean from the Grand Palais' exhibition catalogue as well as from the two exhibitions themselves:

1. Yes, one knows that there are any number of photographers both prior to and contemporary with Mapplethorpe where nude men are photographed as aesthetic objects (including Mapplethorpe's friend the New Orleans artist George Dureau [fig. 10.1] or his contemporary Peter Hujar) but . . . Mapplethorpe is singular in his artistry and originality vis-à-vis the male body.
2. Yes, one knows that first through his relationship with John McKendry, and shortly after, in his long-term relationship with Sam Wagstaff (then in the midst of amassing an enormous collection of nineteenth- and twentieth-century photographs and mentoring Mapplethorpe's work and career), Mapplethorpe assimilated—I would say, mimicked—the style and the forms of "classic" photographers such as Brassaï, Edward Weston, Imogen Cunningham, Edward Steichen, Herbert List, and George Hoyningen-Huene, among many others, but . . . his "inspiration" comes from Michelangelo, Piero della Francesca, Caravaggio, Francis Bacon, and so forth . . .
3. Yes, one knows that Mapplethorpe was ferociously ambitious and his work and career were managed and shaped by Wagstaff, the Robert Miller Gallery, and other art world professionals, but . . . like any great artist, he possessed a singular vision (genius will win out).
4. Yes, one knows that various biographers have documented Mapplethorpe's appallingly racist comments about black men's minds and bodies, his obsession with black men's genitalia, but . . . he elevates his subjects to the empyrean of art, and even titles the pictures with their first names, and sometimes their surnames.[9]
5. Yes, Mapplethorpe's black lovers and models were primarily from what is called the underclass, but . . . he gave each of his models a signed print.

6. Yes, except for creating his foundation a year before his death Mapplethorpe manifested no interest in racism, gay rights, or AIDS militancy, but . . . he and his work can be somehow aligned with that of Jean Genet, whose political activism was unceasing and a central preoccupation in his later writing. In other words, it is not bad faith that underpins both the whitewashing of Mapplethorpe's character and the sanitizing of the racial—if not racist—fantasies that are the sine qua non of his representations of black masculinity.

It is rather the combined force of investment in their various senses (ideological, psychic, and economic) that shape the museological treatment of Mapplethorpe's work. One might also note the increasing dependence of institutional art spaces such as the Grand Palais on corporate financial support and blockbuster attendance. Last, and in the specific case of Mapplethorpe's life and death, he incarnates a particular role, (variant) totem of art photography; *l'artiste maudit* whose "scandalous" subjects assure an audience (or purchasers) of its sophistication, tolerance, and connoisseurship.[10]

In 1993, on the occasion of the Whitney Museum's Biennial exhibition, Glenn Ligon presented his serial work *Notes on the Margin of the Black Book* (1991–93), in which ninety-one photographs of black men cut from Robert Mapplethorpe's *Black Book* were framed and sequenced in the same order as the publication (figs. 10.2 and 10.3).

Accompanying the photographs were approximately seventy quotes and citations that Ligon had collected during the two years of the work's production. Mounted and framed between the two rows of images, these included excerpts from literary texts, quotes from the civil rights movement, Christian evangelical tracts, comments by other artists, statements made by the models, "found" texts, and observations by random men Ligon had queried in gay bars. What determined Ligon's placement of the texts in relation to the images I do not know, but even if randomly positioned, they served to reframe Mapplethorpe's pictures, both as individual images *and* as a collective ensemble.

This reframing, however, revealed little about Ligon's own opinion of Mapplethorpe's work (Ligon is black and gay).[11] Instead, it reframed the pictures as a kind of open question to the viewer. Insofar as the short texts embraced race and racism, desire and sexuality, domination and subjection, and history and political struggle, as well as individual responses, the spectator was enjoined to interrogate her own responses to the imagery in far more complex ways than the pictures, on their own, might prompt. Moreover, in addition to the com-

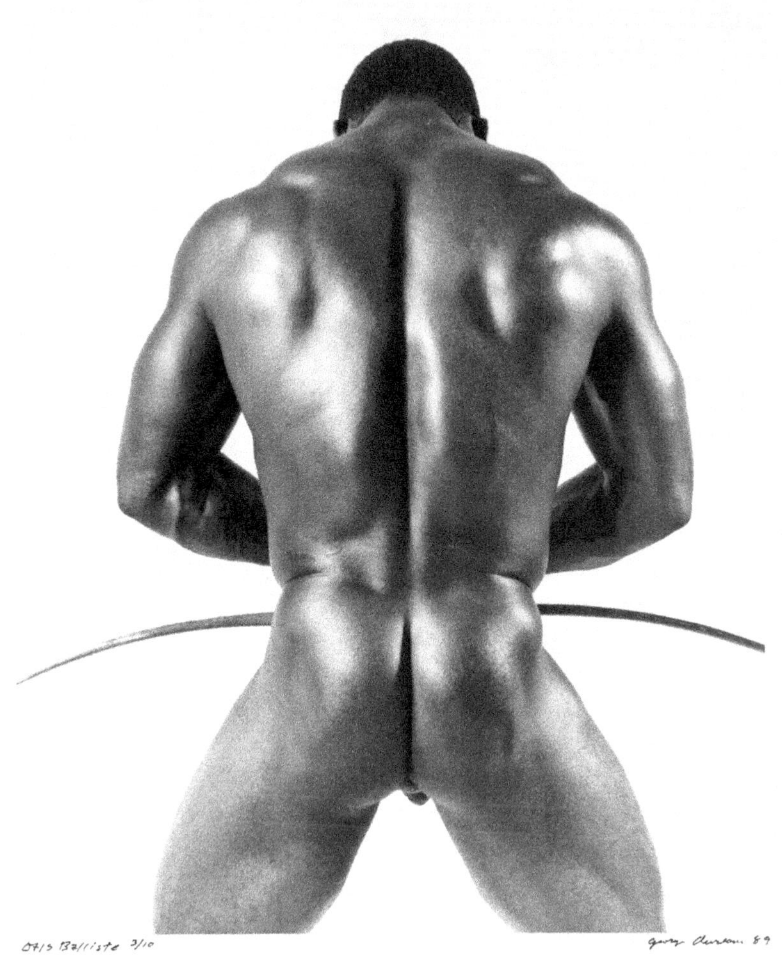


10.1 George Dureau, *Battiste with Bow #2*, 1989. Gelatin silver print, 20 × 16 in. © 1989 George Dureau. COURTESY OF THE ARTHUR ROGER GALLERY, NEW ORLEANS.

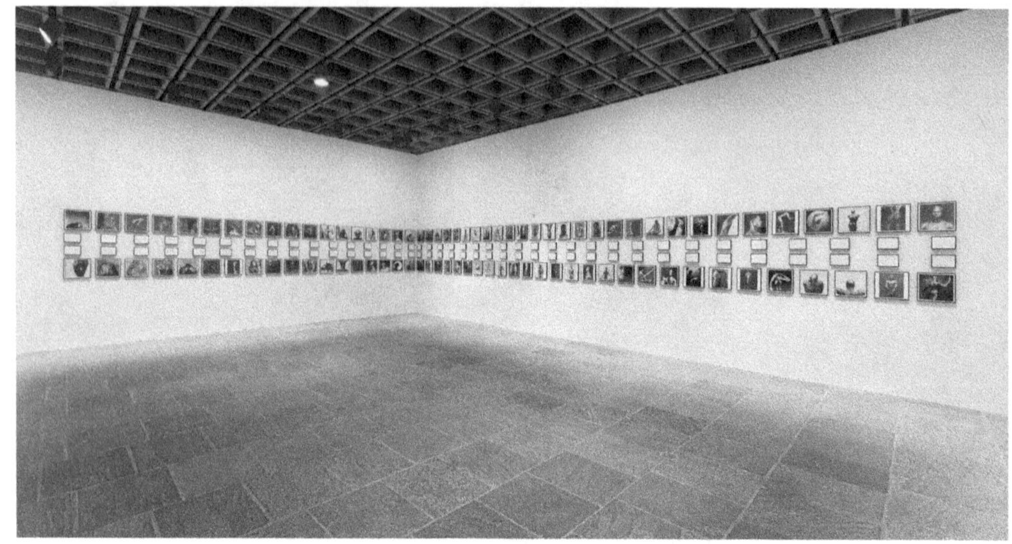

10.2 Glenn Ligon, *Notes on the Margin of the Black Book,* 1991–93. Ninety-one offset prints, 11 ½ × 11 ½ in. each (framed); seventy-eight text pages, 5 ¼ × 7 ¼ in. each (framed). Installation view, *Glenn Ligon:* AMERICA (March 10 to June 5, 2011), Whitney Museum of American Art, New York City. SOLOMON R. GUGGENHEIM MUSEUM, NEW YORK; GIFT OF THE BOHEN FOUNDATION. © 1993 GLENN LIGON. COURTESY OF THE ARTIST AND LUHRING AUGUSTINE, NEW YORK; REGEN PROJECTS, LOS ANGELES; AND THOMAS DANE GALLERY, LONDON. INSTALLATION PHOTOGRAPH © 2011 SHELDAN C. COLLINS. COURTESY OF THE ROBERT MAPPLETHORPE FOUNDATION AND THE WHITNEY MUSEUM OF AMERICAN ART, NEW YORK.

10.3 (*opposite*) Glenn Ligon, *Notes on the Margin of the Black Book,* 1991–93 (detail). Installation view, *Glenn Ligon:* AMERICA (March 10 to June 5, 2011), Whitney Museum of American Art, New York City. SOLOMON R. GUGGENHEIM MUSEUM, NEW YORK; GIFT OF THE BOHEN FOUNDATION. © 1993 GLENN LIGON. COURTESY OF THE ARTIST AND LUHRING AUGUSTINE, NEW YORK; REGEN PROJECTS, LOS ANGELES; AND THOMAS DANE GALLERY, LONDON. DETAIL PHOTOGRAPH © 2011 GEOFFREY CLEMENTS. COURTESY OF THE ROBERT MAPPLETHORPE FOUNDATION AND THE WHITNEY MUSEUM OF AMERICAN ART, NEW YORK.

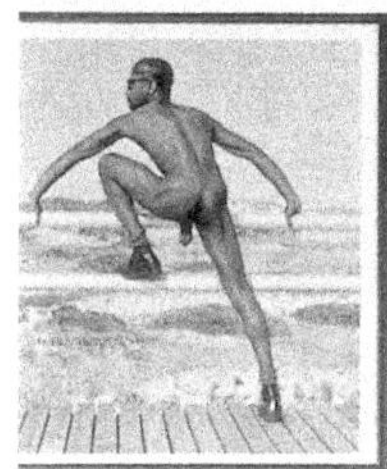
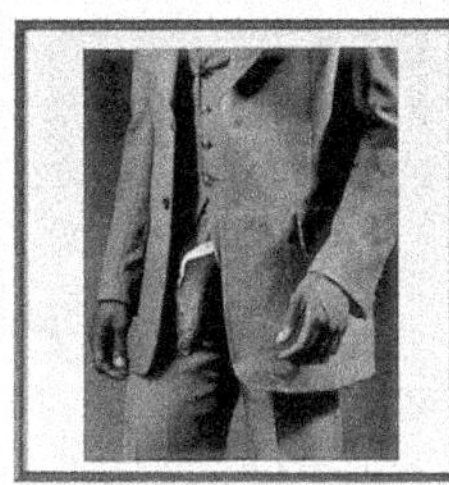
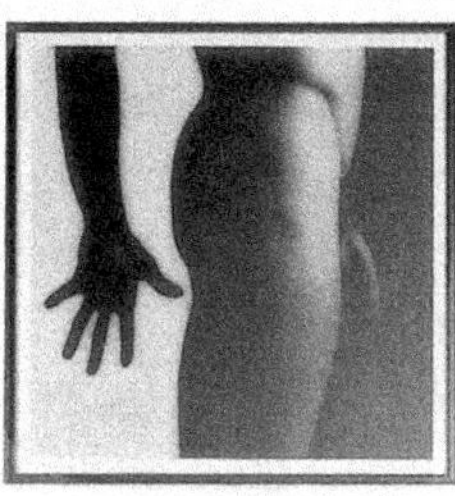
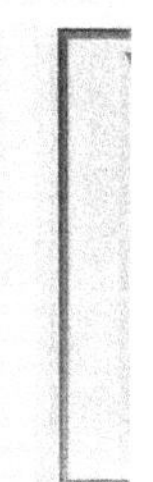
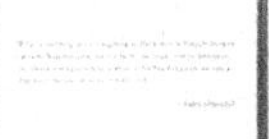
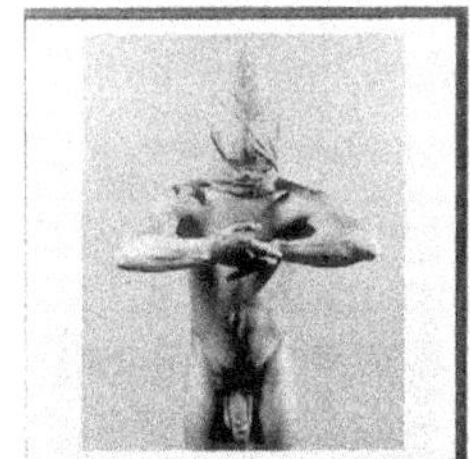
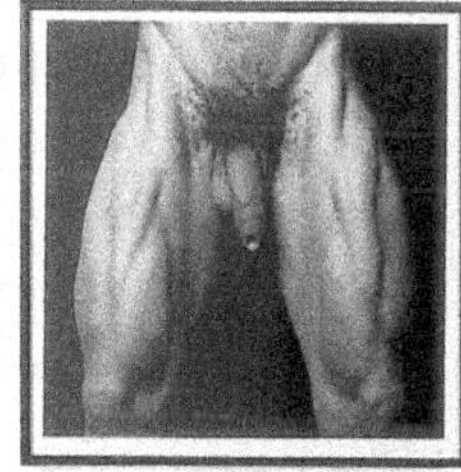
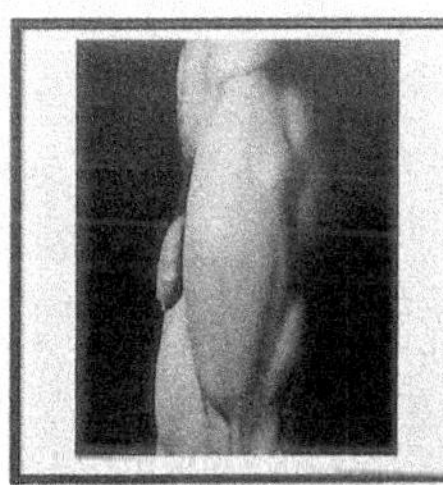

plicated interaction of form and content in photography (as well as the no less complicated issue of authorship—not for nothing is Ligon a Whitney Program alumnus), *Notes on the Margin* implicitly acknowledged that the bedrock of each and every response is located in individual subjectivity, in the elements that constitute the personal, including racial and sexual identity—and possibly—the politics of the viewer. An important aspect of Ligon's project was thus the way that it opened for question rather than adjudicated the politics of representation as they are raised by Mapplethorpe's unapologetically aestheticized, fetishized, and objectivized photographs of black men as icons of his own desire.

More than a decade after Ligon's *Notes on the Margin,* and nearly thirty years after *The Black Book*'s publication, the exhibitions at the Grand Palais and the Musée Rodin (and the catalogue accompanying the former) gave little indication that there might be any real problem with the Mapplethorpe oeuvre other than its sexually explicit subject matter (which are not, in any case, on view). I refer again to the issue of race, the elephant in the living room, an issue unmistakably evident in Mapplethorpe's photographs of black men but apparently invisible to French critics or viewers (as always, the indispensable Élisabeth Lebovici, conscience of the French art world, is the exception).[12] Although Michel Guerrin's review in *Le Monde* is bracingly shrewd about the self-censorship so apparent in the Grand Palais, as well the mutually reinforcing apparatuses of scandal and market, nevertheless, the political and ethical stakes that arise in the domain of race and representation were unremarked.[13] As one would expect, the visitors at both exhibitions were overwhelmingly white; security staff and other low-level personnel were (mostly) people of color. This is perhaps neither here nor there; the art world in France, as in the United States, is overwhelmingly white, and even those artists resolved to invent new kinds of public spaces, new forms of address, engage new publics, or contrive new approaches to democratize culture are often trumped by the more powerful determinations of class and the power differentials among the museum, the space of elite culture, and the street.[14]

Even at the time of their initial exhibition and publication as a book, Mapplethorpe's photographs of black men provoked considerable controversy. Aside from the more predictable outrage originating in homophobic, right-wing, or antipornography camps, some of the most substantial critique was produced by black intellectuals, for whom the issues raised by racial representation were anything but academic.[15] Kobena Mercer's 1986 essay "Reading Racial Fetishism" is a case in point, a scathing analysis of how Mapplethorpe's photographs operate on racial, sexual, and political levels:

Approached as a textual system, both *Black Males* (1983) and the *Black Book* (1986) catalogue a series of perspectives, vantage points, and "takes" on the black male body. The first thing to notice—so obvious it goes without saying—is that all the men are *nude*. Each of the camera's points of view leads to a unitary vanishing point: an erotic/aesthetic objectification of black male bodies into the idealized form of a homogeneous type thoroughly saturated with a totality of sexual predicates. We look through a sequence of individual personally named Afro-American men, but what we *see* is only their sex as the essential sum total of their meanings signified around blackness and maleness. It is as if according to Mapplethorpe's line of sight: Black + Male = Erotic/Aesthetic Object. Regardless of the sexual preferences of the spectator, the connotation is that the "essence" of black male identity lies in the domain of sexuality. Whereas the photographs of gay male S/M rituals invoke a subcultural sexuality that consists of *doing* something, black men are confined and defined in their very *being* as sexual and nothing but sexual, hence hypersexual.[16]

Drawing on a number of theorists, including Homi Bhabha, Stuart Hall, and Frantz Fanon, Mercer scrutinized the works from many perspectives, including the codes of art photography and sculpture, the mechanisms of fetishism, the binary structure of the racist imaginary, and the function of the racial stereotype, among many others. Among the most incisive of his arguments is his discussion of Mapplethorpe's treatment of skin, what Frantz Fanon had called the "epidermalization" of (colonial) racist projection:

As each fragment [of the body] seduces the eye into ever more intense fascination, we glimpse the dilation of a libidinal way of looking that spreads itself across the surface of black skin. Harsh contrasts of shadow and light draw the eye to focus and fix attention on the texture of black men's skin. According to Bhahba, unlike the sexual fetish *per se*, whose meanings are usually hidden as a hermeneutic secret, skin color functions as "*the most visible of fetishes*" (Bhabha 1983: 30). Whether it is devalorized in the signifying chain of "negrophobia" or hypervalorized as a desirable attribute in "negrophilia," the fetish of skin color in the codes of racial discourse constitutes the most visible element in the articulation of what Stuart Hall (1977) calls "the ethnic signifier." The shining surface of black skin serves several functions in representation: it suggests the physical exertion of powerful bodies, as black boxers always glisten like bronze in the illuminated square of the boxing ring; or, in pornography, it suggests intense sexual activity

> "just before" the photograph was taken. . . . In Mapplethorpe's pictures the specular brilliance of black skin is bound in a double articulation as a fixing agent for the fetishistic structure of the photographs. . . . Here, black skin and print surface are bound together to enhance the pleasure of the white spectator as much as the profitability of these art-world commodities exchanged among the artist and his dealers, collectors and curators.[17]

Mapplethorpe's production is now retrospectively inseparable from the history of AIDS in the United States, and almost all contextual discussions of his work include references to its devastations in the New York City cultural world. It was the cause of Mapplethorpe's death, and that of Sam Wagstaff as well as many of his lovers, friends, and models. In a certain sense, therefore, this makes of his work a form of memento mori for a particular milieu, one that encompassed different classes and races—lives all brutally cut short. But for many of the middle-aged or elderly survivors of the halcyon days of pre-AIDS sexual underworlds who now write about Mapplethorpe, his milieu and imagery, there exists an element of nostalgia that suffuses the writing, thereby muting, when not foreclosing, the more troubling considerations of racial stereotyping within gay (and straight) white culture.[18] One element of this nostalgia is the utopian notion of a heterogeneous and polymorphous—although primarily gay—sexuality as an agent of liberation, in which forms of sexual expression are believed to subvert what I would call patriarchy but which others now refer to as "heteronormativity." Both nostalgia and gay identity politics operate to paper over issues of race and class that were not then, much less now, resolved by interracial sexual relations or particular sexual practices.

As was already evident at the time of his first posthumous exhibitions, Mapplethorpe's photographs provided fodder for an increasingly powerful right-wing reaction, fueled by vicious homophobic wellsprings (a frequent accompaniment to fascist and other authoritarian politics), within which Mapplethorpe's life and work could be viewed—as was the epidemic itself—as the just punishment for wild, promiscuous, and perverse sexuality (and drugs, but that is another story). This coalescing of a moral panic, the ascendancy of the religious right, the so-called culture wars of the 1980s and 1990s, and a wide-scale sociopolitical backlash led to a certain rethinking by Mapplethorpe's earlier critics. This is apparent in Ligon's comment in endnote 11, but is discussed at length in Mercer's revision of his argument written in 1989, three years after his initial essay. "This chain of events," Mercer remarks, "has irrevocably altered the context in which we perceive, evaluate and argue about the aesthetic and political value of Mapplethorpe's photographs."[19]

Basically, Mercer puts a somewhat different emphasis on Mapplethorpe's homosexuality and his works' address to a gay black male spectator, insofar as the continuous ascendancy of right-wing politics and intensifying homophobia make Mapplethorpe's work signify *differently*. In this later reading, Mercer affirms his own desire and identifications with respect to Mapplethorpe's imagery, arguing that the affirmation of the beauty and desirability of these men legitimizes the viewing position of the gay, black male subject. Mercer here modifies his earlier analysis of the imagery as trafficking with the most pernicious racist stereotypes. Certain aspects of his rethinking are echoed by other celebrants of Mapplethorpe's pictures, such as Edward White. In these considerations of the work, emphasis is variously placed on Mapplethorpe's having been a sexual partner of the men he photographed, his status as a subordinated subject as a gay man, his act of making black men aesthetically present, his transgression of barriers between high and low, and so forth. As Mercer argues, "Once grounded in the context of an urban gay male culture, as one of the many subcultures of modernity, Mapplethorpe's ironic juxtaposition of elements drawn from the repository of high culture—where the nude is indeed one of the most valued genres of the dominant culture—with elements drawn from below—such as pornographic conventions or commonplace stereotypes—can be seen as a subversive recoding of the ideological values supporting the normative aesthetic ideal."[20]

That Mercer's reconsideration of his earlier essay is longer than the initial one (which is, obviously, far more polemical) is suggestive. Much of the argumentation is strained, circuitous, hard to pin down, and, as he freely concedes, personal. But asserting that the nude (sex unspecified, but surely he means the female nude) is ipso facto a sign of elite culture obscures the fact that the beautiful nude is largely dead as an artistic genre (for good reason) and, more to the point, that it is precisely feminist theory, criticism, and practice that helped to make it obsolete (I am not here referring to the naked body as such, whether in performance or other media, but the nude-as-genre in Mercer's argument). In other words, if feminism teaches us anything in terms of the politics of corporeal representation, especially photographic representation, it is that relations of domination and subordination, and ideologies of gender, voyeurism, objectification—and, preeminently, affirmations of fetishistic desire—are inevitably sustained if they are not subverted, desublimated, or otherwise "ruined." Mercer's argument *as* a gay male subject who finds his desire affirmed in Mapplethorpe's images is thus perhaps analogous to those gay women who find erotic or pornographic representations of women pleasurable or arousing and celebrate it as such. My point is not that they shouldn't, much less that such imagery is "bad" and should be censored, but that how such imagery operates for gay women or women of any erotic proclivity has little to do with how it operates in the spheres of consumer culture, mass media, visual culture in general. Here, as elsewhere, context counts, but the context of Mapplethorpe's contemporary exhibitions in Paris, or, better, its total absence of context other than its museological finery, that is, its mode of *address,* is a major problem. A serious presentation of Mapplethorpe's production, instead of exhibiting his kitsch religious artifacts or juvenilia, might well have included his contemporaries working with similar subjects in a similar milieu (e.g., Hujar, Dureau, Mark Morrisroe, etc.), possibly some Tom of Finland graphics and gay magazines to link with mass cultural forms, and, crucially, the programming of such works as Marlon Riggs's *Tongues Untied,* Isaac Julien's *Looking for Langston,* and mixed media from activist collectives such as ACT UP and other organizations.

All of which is to say that the ethical and political issues that arise around certain types of representation of black bodies by white photographers should not be willed away, and Mapplethorpe's status as participant observer in a particular time, place, and milieu should not exempt his work from critical analysis—especially in France, where debates and discussions about race and representation, so important within Anglo-American contexts, appear disappointingly absent.

# 11

## Body Double

(2014)

In 1986, on the occasion of the first retrospective of the work of Francesca Woodman, I was invited by Ann Gabhart, then director of the Wellesley College Art Museum (now the Davis Museum at Wellesley College) and Rosalind Krauss, then a professor at Hunter College and the Graduate Center, CUNY, to write one of the three essays for the catalogue. It was Gabhart, a friend of Francesca Woodman's parents, who inaugurated the project, showing some of the photographs to Krauss, who immediately recognized Woodman's importance. Quite soon, they determined on an exhibition that would open at the Hunter College Art Gallery and then travel to the Wellesley College Art Museum.[1] Thus it was that in the fall of 1985 the Woodmans presented us with numerous boxes of Woodman's photographs, containing everything from contact sheets to large-scale diazotypes, work prints to exhibition prints, pictures made as series, pictures made as discrete images, artists' books, and prints annotated with Woodman's handwritten phrases or sentences. Since then, we have learned that Woodman experimented with other media, including video, and her personal correspondence indicates that she was painting (at least during her years at the Rhode Island School of Design) and producing drawings throughout her career. It still remains unclear as to which of her works were student assignments and which were made at her own initiative, but certainly the majority of her work was done while an art student. It also seems possible that Woodman occasionally approached her projects conceptually in terms of performance art. Although it isn't known if or when Woodman might have seen any actual performances, it was an artistic practice in which women were especially prominent, and which often deployed the female body itself as the medium.

As for Woodman's videos, of whose existence we were then unaware, although they are obviously connected to her photographic work, it does not seem that Woodman considered them to be finished works.[2]

But with respect to this much-expanded volume of work in several media, there arose questions about how an "oeuvre" is posthumously constituted. In 1986, we assumed the works to number in a few hundreds; later essays from the 1980s refer to approximately 500 works; those from the 1990s refer to approximately 600; and in a catalogue from 2010, the number has climbed to over 900. This increase is based not only on new caches that have come to light but also the fact that the estate has authorized additional printings from negatives (the estate affirms that all new prints are based on existing positives and duplicate the original size).[3] This expanded archive of Woodman's work helps identify and contextualize those photographs she did print and also facilitates their dating. Nevertheless, the process of assembling this oeuvre reminds us that *pace* Michel Foucault, the construction of authorship is by no means a self-evident enterprise.[4]

Since that first retrospective, Woodman has become remarkably well known, far beyond what any of us could have then anticipated. Indeed, and as many have observed, Woodman has become something of a cult figure for reasons that exceed the formal and aesthetic aspects of her extant production. The particular circumstances of Woodman's work, made between the ages of thirteen and twenty-two, no less than the resonance of her characteristic themes and their affective power, make Woodman's artistic trajectory from obscurity to fame somewhat singular. Now that more of her work has been widely exhibited and reproduced—now that there exists a daunting bibliography of monographs, catalogues, essays in several languages, a documentary film (C. Scott Willis's *The Woodman: The Haunting Story of Late Photographer Francesca Woodman and Her Family*), a fiction film (Elisabeth Subrin's *The Fancy*), a book of poetry Carolyn Carlson dedicated to her, a scholarly book positioning her work in relation to the Kantian sublime, and at least two doctoral dissertations—it is difficult to recover something of the astonishment felt by those, myself included, who saw Woodman's work for the first time. One aspect of this initial astonishment was the works' precocity, for whatever subsequent critical revisions or arguments have been made, this remains one of its remarkable features. Moreover, Woodman's youth as well as gender remain relevant insofar as these were significant determinations of her subject matter and how she explored it. It is unlikely that a middle-aged woman, or a man, even a young man, would have created such pictures. How these are interpreted, and how they are seen to shape the nature and terms of Woodman's work has been treated by critics in contrasting, even conflicting, ways.[5]

One consequence of Woodman's posthumous renown is the Sammlung Verbund's gradual acquisition of seventy-seven works by the artist. Accordingly, it was in relation to the preparation of this monograph that the Sammlung's curator, Gabriele Schor, invited me to contribute an essay. One purpose was to consider some of the major books and essays devoted to Woodman's work that have appeared since 1986, and another was to reflect on whether or how my perception of Woodman's art has changed since the essay I wrote so long ago.

This has turned out to be a somewhat difficult task for a number of reasons, some general, and some personal. Among the more general reasons is the fact that in 1986 much less of Woodman's work was available. Second, the sheer volume of Woodman's bibliography made a complete retrospective reading impossible. A third general problem was geographical: the lack of access to the actual photographs. Aside from the Verbund's collection, the last time I saw Woodman's work on display was in 2011 at an exhibition in San Francisco. This is regrettable, as many of Woodman's pictures require close examination; even in high-quality reproductions they can be difficult to decipher. Sometimes it isn't clear if it is Woodman or another model that is depicted (I shall explain below why this matters; see fig. 11.1).

More personally, however, to revisit an essay superseded by the many contributions of subsequent critics and scholars inevitably required acknowledging my own errors of fact and interpretation. This is never pleasant for a critic or art historian, and is one reason why I rarely reread my own writing. Of factual errors, I found several—perhaps there are more. For example, there is the erroneous attribution of the 1909 novella *The Yellow Wallpaper* to Olive Schreiner instead of to Charlotte Perkins Gilmore (I cringe). Even worse was my misreading of Woodman's photo *I could no longer play / I could not play by instinct* (Providence, Rhode Island, ca. 1977), where I described the necklace of photos as a "reptilian object" instead of identifying it correctly as a strip of photographic portraits. And while I suggested that Woodman might have been aware of precedents in Surrealist photography, possibly through her friendship with the dealer Timothy Baum, it now appears that Woodman was indeed familiar with Surrealist art and literature. Aside from what Woodman might have seen in exhibitions or learned in art history classes or through her own reading, during her 1977–78 residency in Rome she frequented the Libreria Maldoror, a bookstore where she could have found books, catalogues, loose pictures and photos, postcards, and journals relevant to Surrealism and other European avant-gardes, and whose proprietors (and their larger circle) befriended her.

In terms of interpretation, I think I erred in the assumption that it was primarily Woodman who featured in her pictures, an assumption that still dominates most of the literature. Viewing so many images I had not previously seen, albeit mostly in reproduction, there seems to be a pervasive aspect of Woodman's method that turns on her use of "surrogacy." Not only is it the case that a number of photographs thought to be of Woodman herself are those of friends or models, but there are also many that stage two figures. This recurring incidence of doubling or twinning of female bodies (i.e., *Me and my roommate*, Boulder, Colorado, 1976; *Yet another day alone i wake up in these white chairs*, Stanwood, Washington, 1979; *Quaderno dei dettatti et dei temi, an artist's book thought to date from 1979–80*; and Woodman's pictures made in New York City featuring two models) puts in question the frequent characterization of her work as an extended exercise in self-portraiture. This aspect of Woodman's practice has been noted by several writers.[6] In some instances, especially *yet another day alone i wake up in these white chairs*, the paired bodies are strikingly similar. In others, in which the figure is cropped at the neck, the body could be Woodman's or a similar one. In this regard, a suggestive example is the much-reproduced picture Woodman made in Providence depicting three similar female bodies sporting identical masks bearing the image of Woodman's face, and a fourth, somewhat different portrait, pinned to the wall. (This too is a recurring topos in Woodman's work, counterpointing different modes or registers of representation—graphic, photographic, indexical, iconic—within the same visual field.) Although Woodman's body is recognizable from her knee socks and Chinese slippers, the stress is on the interchangeability of the bodies, so similar morphologically. In her essay on Woodman's videos, Jennifer Blessing has also remarked on this orchestration of similar bodies: "The picture [a photo taken by one of Woodman's friends] not only documents her studio as the space of female activity but demonstrates the way that Woodman uses other bodies to mirror hers. Their uncannily similar figures stand in for, and become interchangeable with, the artist's."[7] This further unsettles any too-easy reading of Woodman's work as a more or less direct imprint of her subjectivity through the medium and the image of an individualized body.

In 1986, among other omissions, I did not reflect on the scarcity of Woodman's pictures of male subjects. Pictures of her lovers or male friends are strikingly rare.[8] However, if one looks very closely, even in reproduction, it seems there are male bodies that in somewhat ghostly fashion inhabit some of the

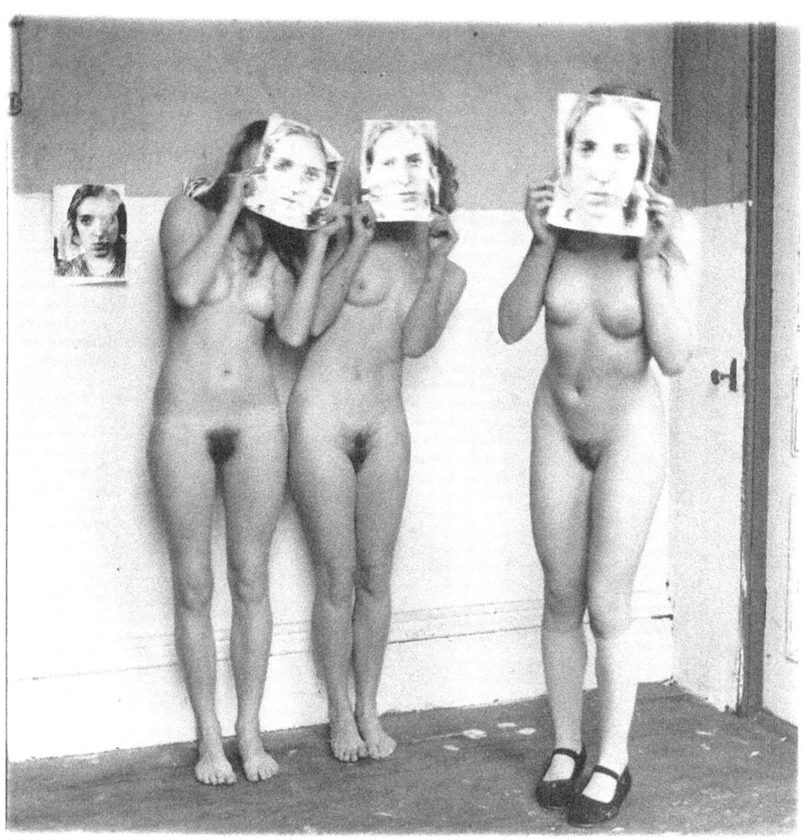

11.1 Francesca Woodman, *About Being My Model*, Providence, Rhode Island, 1976. Black-and-white gelatin silver print 5 5/16 × 5 3/8 in. COURTESY OF GEORGE AND BETTY WOODMAN.

series. But aside from Woodman's well-known series of Charlie the model, several of those that do feature male subjects are explicitly "feminized" (*Untitled* [Providence, Rhode Island, 1976; fig. 11.2] and *Untitled* [New York, 1979–80]). Thus, in two photographs a young man is shown in a Victorian woman's nightdress, a shell at the neckline; in another, a supine and slender (headless) male body (possibly that of Benjamin Moore, a boyfriend) is partially covered, including his sex, with a flufflike substance that I can't identify. Another photograph of Benjamin, taken during Woodman's visit to him in Stanwood, Washington, is especially notable in relation to Woodman's use of handwritten legends on some of her pictures (fig. 11.3). Here, the text on the print ("Yet another day alone I wake up . . . ") is visually contradicted by

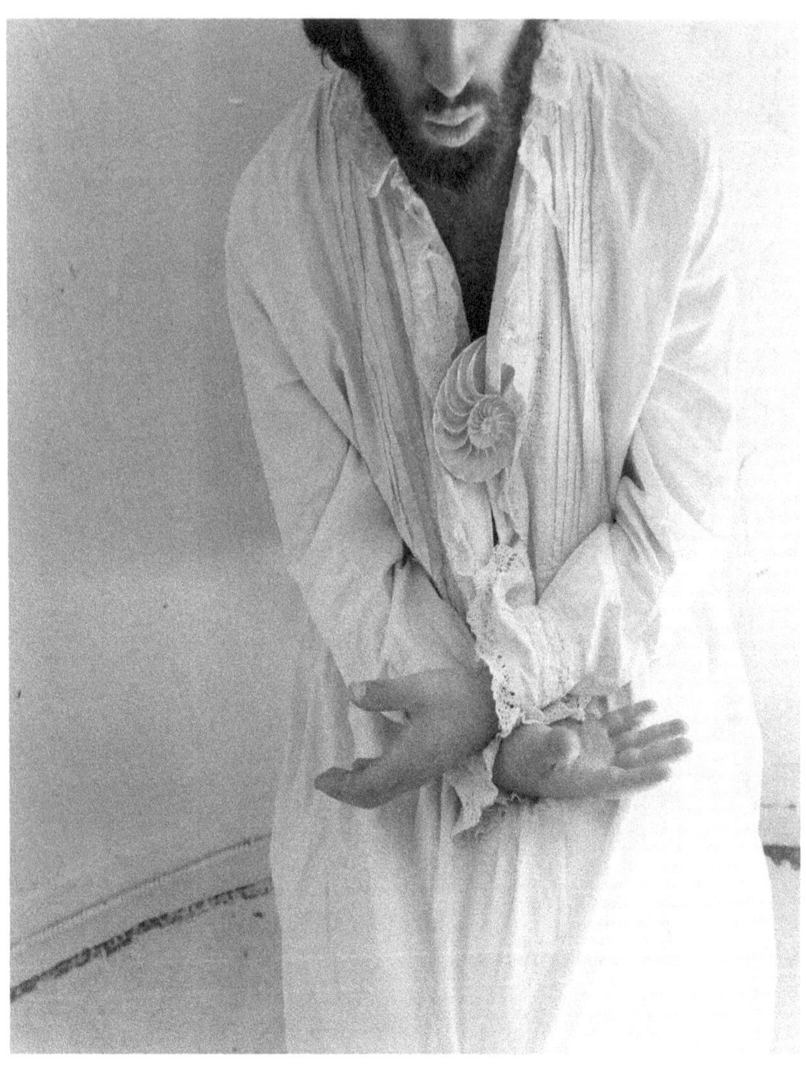

11.2 Francesca Woodman, *Untitled*, Providence, Rhode Island, 1976. Black-and-white gelatin silver print on barite paper 5 ½ × 5 ⅜ in. COURTESY OF GEORGE AND BETTY WOODMAN.

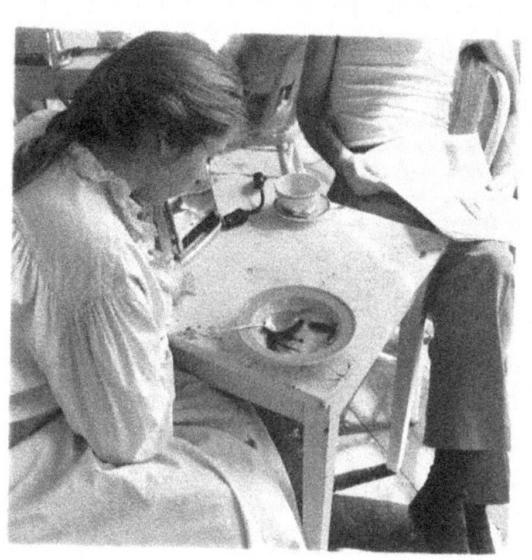

yet another day alone i wake
up in these white chairs.

11.3 Francesca Woodman, *yet another day alone i wake up in these white chairs*, Stanwood, Washington, 1979. Black-and-white gelatin silver print on barite paper 4 ¼ × 4 ¼ in. COURTESY OF GEORGE AND BETTY WOODMAN.

the fact that Woodman is seated at the table with her companion. A great of deal of the exegeses of Woodman's handwritten phrases are curiously literal, as though text and image directly referred to one another or were reciprocally explanatory, which is clearly not the case.[9] As it happens, Benjamin's visage is reproduced on the saucer (and it seems that the same photo appears on the wall behind Woodman's bed in *Untitled*, Antella, Italy, 1977–78). It is as though in Woodman's art there is no satisfactory way in which masculinity can be represented as such, as though only femininity can be imaged—although very significantly, in the fraught forms of apparition, fetish, or ephemeral illusion.

In any case, Woodman's internal doublings and reiterations, her placing of images *en abyme*, are a reminder that Woodman was keenly attentive to the various "frames" of representation, and, good formalist artist that she (also) was, her deployment of mirrors, reflections, and different types of representation within a single frame are, among other things, an acknowledgment of both the mediations of the image and the self-reflexivity of the medium, just as her series *Space 2* describes the square format of her negatives. Finally, what many critics have brought to the foreground in their discussion of the work, namely, Woodman's constantly inventive explorations of pictorial space, architectural space, illusionistic space, spaces of confinement and imprisonment, and, obviously, photographic space, is as susceptible to feminist reading as is Woodman's representation of female bodies.

With respect to my reading of the literature (by no means in its entirety), it seems that aside from methodological differences, there is a fundamental divergence in the writing of critics and art historians. Crudely stated, this division is based on the extent to which gender and sexual difference (as both content and significance) are acknowledged, minimalized, or disregarded. In foregrounding gender and sexuality when I first addressed Woodman's work, I was not suggesting that all bodies of work by all women artists require this specification. However, insofar as Woodman's art is so centrally, indeed obsessionally, focused on the young female body, often nude, her own as well others', to proceed as though these are incidental aspects of the work is to disregard its most insistent and consistent motif. That said, in considering the nature and terms of Woodman's bibliography, a few more observations are in order.

Because thirty-five years have passed since Woodman's last works were produced, current interpretations necessarily exist at the intersection of art history (a discipline with particular protocols and models) and art criticism, a far more fluid and more pluralistic discourse. While these are not hard-and-fast distinctions, it is generally the case that this latter practice fosters more subjective and personal approaches. Each approach has particular discursive consequences that often constellate around the relationship of an artists' work to her life. This can be observed in the ways a writer deals with Woodman's suicide. For certain writers, Woodman's suicide is the central element of and for the reading of her work.[10] For others, the suicide provides one more reason to view the work as a continuous activity of self-representation, even of self-portraiture, conceived as recording—almost diaristically—the artist's subjectivity. Those of her pictures in which Woodman is blurred, obscured, or otherwise physically effaced, those made in decrepit or ruined architectural spaces, and those sequences alternating the figures' appearance and disappearance are taken to be indices of the artist's psychology.

Woodman's work clearly incites very powerful impulses of projection, identification, and empathy, especially in its reception by women and young women artists. This is doubtless the reason several writers refer to her familiarly as Francesca.[11] Manifestly, a life willfully cut short and an art so bound to the female body strikes many women in intensely personal ways. A recent blog post by the poet Ariana Reines is exemplary of this intense form of investment: "I look at her pictures I identify with them completely and therefore resent analyzing them as I resent mere praise or critique, and she is a problem because I cannot deny that I identify not only with her images but with real and documented aspects of her despair."[12] In other instances, Woodman's work (or a fanciful version of Woodman-the-woman) functions as a kind of mirror for narcissistic male fantasies. Thus, when Philippe Sollers (to take an especially egregious example) titles his short essay "The Sorceress" ("farewell, refined sorceress!"[13]) and recounts his flirtatious hash-enhanced encounter with a "young film actress, brunette and extremely attractive," who dares him to throw himself out the window "to see if it makes her come," we have reason to wonder how and why Woodman fosters such excesses of free association.

The force of these projective responses is another one of the reasons that Woodman's work overall is taken to be a career-long enterprise of self-portraiture. There exist many essays that make this assertion, some more nuanced than others. I choose these two almost at random: "Straight away then, Francesca Woodman clearly declares in her photographs that the basis of every action, every image she produces, every thought she expresses through the images is nothing but her own self"[14] and "The whole of Francesca Woodman's journey as an artist can be essentially enclosed within the category of the self-portrait. This premise is only apparently unambiguous, and is in fact consciously formulated with a degree of approximation . . . right from the beginning, Francesca Woodman appointed herself as the almost exclusive subject of her works. *Self portrait at thirteen,* the first of her photographs to come to us, appears today almost as a declaration of intents perhaps still to be fully developed but at least already delineated in their main features."[15]

But while there may well be photographs within Woodman's archive that are intended (and may possibly be read) as self-portraits, there are far more in which her identity is variously obscured. These include the many pictures cropped at the head or obscured by hair, the back views, fragments of the body, the blurring of the figure, and other varieties of effacement (wallpaper, fabric, plastic sheeting, and so forth). While it is important to acknowledge the distinction between the self-portrait and self-representation (all self-portraits are self-representations, but not all self-representations are portraits), what is at stake in a number of debates about Woodman is the enduring belief that an artist is, by definition, somehow present or immanent in their work. The self-portrait as (originally) an art historical genre implies the prior existence of an individual person, whose subjectivity, psychology, and indeed biography are bound up with its rendering. (The other modality of the portrait, such as the ceremonial or symbolic representation of a monarch, for example, does different work.) However, artistic self-representation, especially in modern media, may be equally construed as collective, allegorical, symbolic, or metaphorical. These distinctions are not exclusively medium specific, although it is still necessary to take account of the specificity of the photographic medium. In analogue photography, the subject is indeed literally present before the lens, but as the work of Cindy Sherman—or for that matter, that of Claude Cahun, Marcel Moore, Ana Mendieta, Hannah Wilke, or Birgit Jürgenssen—so eloquently demonstrates, the material presence of the author/artist/subject is by no means identical to their existential presence. Hence, the suggestive aspect of the use of body doubles as it operates to destabilize notions of the unique individual.

Returning now to the summary of Woodman's bibliography after 1986, there are as well examples of the inverse of excessive projection and identification. In certain instances, these seem to take the form of a willful refusal to see or critical blindness to the specificity of Woodman's artistic projects. Rosalind Krauss's essay in the catalogue from 1986 was a characteristically elegant and eloquent formalist reading of Woodman that avoided all considerations of gender and sexual difference. As such, it has functioned as a kind of template in which Woodman's work may be read in terms of spatial preoccupations and her use of classroom exercises as specific "problems" in photographic representation to the exclusion of its pervasive subject matter. But the more subtle aspects of the repression of difference has to do with the conscription of Woodman's oeuvre into an art or photographic historical discourse that is severed from any relation to women artists, to the efflorescence of feminist practices, or to the feminist politics that were so much a part of artistic and political culture in the 1970s. Obviously my point here is not whether Woodman defined herself personally as a feminist or was making "feminist" art but rather to consider the cultural and political environment in which she came of age and where many of her own preoccupations were writ large.

In this regard, it is instructive to look at the lineup of putative influences that efface the problematics of sexual difference in the service of a normative art and photography history. For Chris Townsend, the author of a major monograph on the artist, the assumption is that we will better understand Woodman's work if we view it in the context of the art and photography of the period. Woodman's work has thus been compared by Townsend and other critics, such as Benjamin Buchloh, to a diverse list of (significantly) mostly male artists such as Gordon Matta-Clark, Francis Bacon, Cy Twombly, and Bruce Nauman, as well as to a host of 1970s art photographers. Among the art photographers, Townsend lists Duane Michals (serial sequences, narrative structures, handwritten texts on the prints); Clarence John Laughlin (gothic allusions, abandoned Southern mansions, ghostly effects); Jerry Uelsmann (manipulated prints, oneiric effects); Ralph Eugene Meatyard (masked figures, vernacular Surrealism); Ralph Gibson (an illuminated hand opening a door); and, one of the few women on the list, Barbara Jo Revelle. Townsend concludes that Michals and Laughlin in particular should be seen as having provided the "stylistic and thematic lineage for Woodman's work."[16] While her awareness of Michals's work, for example, may have authorized or even inspired Woodman to handwrite phrases or sentences on her prints or work with serial or narrative forms, Michals's work takes as one of its major subjects gay male sexuality, which, needless to say, is not one of Woodman's themes. Uelsmann's work does not center on the female figure and involves elaborate darkroom manipulation. Moreover, Michals's use of narrative is quite literal, indeed, conventional, telling a story with a beginning and an end. None of Woodman's series conform to this type of narrative structure. Surrealist precedents are likewise marshaled to ostensibly contextualize Woodman's work in relation to ancestors as well as art photographers. That this ends up as a primarily masculine legacy is not surprising. When critics such as Buchloh invoke as Woodman's predecessors such figures as Vito Acconci or Bruce Nauman, they neutralize and indeed efface the very notion of difference that is precisely what establishes her historical importance.[17] And when Townsend pairs Richard Serra's *Strike: To Roberta and Rudy* (1969–71) with Woodman's *Untitled* (Providence, Rhode Island, 1976), duly noting that Serra was a friend of the Woodmans, there is reason to wonder about the writer's motivation in proposing such a pairing. But this question of what imagery Woodman knew, saw, admired, was influenced by, assimilated, or appropriated is not an especially enlightening or even useful enterprise. It is, first of all, a model of inquiry derived from conventional art history (referred to in my graduate school days as "source-mongering"). As such, it involves the relentless and potentially infinite tracking of what any given artist saw, admired, was influenced by, assimilated, or appropriated. Also, putting aside the question of whether a method employed to investigate the iconography of Renaissance painting is appropriate to the work of a modern or contemporary photographer who has doubtless been exposed to millions of images since birth, we must ask what such inventories actually reveal or illuminate about an artist's work. There exists also the risk of what the art historian Erwin Panofsky memorably characterized as "pseudomorphism," the way that two works that might visually or morphologically resemble each other may, in reality, have no relation whatsoever, as would seem to be the case in Townsend's pairing of Serra's sculpture and Woodman's photograph.

Let me give one more example of the deceptive nature of "source." Even in 1986, Gabhart, Krauss, and I were well aware of Woodman's great admiration for the fashion photographer Deborah Turbeville. This was evident from photos Woodman made when she settled in New York City, in which one could see her attempting to develop a Turbeville-like style (and not merely because she had hoped to get a job as Turbeville's assistant). Does this mean that Woodman's work, in the broadest sense of a corpus—its themes, preoccupations, formal concerns, even stylistics—is in any significant way *like* Turbeville's (or vice versa)? Even those pictures made by Woodman that are now classified as "fashion" work are far more unsettling, more edgy, more *strange* than any work by Turbeville. And, finally, inasmuch as fetishism is an integral aspect of fashion photography, can Turbeville's work, in contrast to Woodman's, be said to adopt a critical relation to it?

Similar problems arise in the frequent references to Surrealist photography from the 1920s as a decisive influence on Woodman's practice. Overwhelmingly the production of men, Surrealist imagery privileges an eroticized and phantasmatic femininity that was its central fetish.[18] Woodman's work, as I read it in 1986 and still, perhaps stubbornly, read it now, makes fetishism visible as a *problematic.* Woodman parses it, anatomizes it, mimics it, mocks it, plays with it, and sometimes exposes it, as in *No. 4* and 5 (New York, 1979–80), featuring garter belts, or *Face* (Providence, Rhode Island, 1976; fig. 11.4), in which a plaster mask is placed in front of the model's crotch. Although I believe this attentiveness to fetishism to be a recurring trope in the work of modern and contemporary women artists, it is hardly their exclusive prerogative; René Magritte, Man Ray, and Brassaï, to take three examples, were as adept in elaborations of the fetish as any woman artist. Nevertheless, in comparing Woodman's picture of her own cellotaped body with Hans Bellmer's photograph of the trussed body of Unica Zürn, as has been done by several writers, says little about Bellmer's art and even less about Woodman's. For a male artist to bind and photograph his female companion cannot be reasonably analogized to a woman artist binding and photographing herself for her own artistic purposes fifty years later.

Many of the pictorial strategies of Surrealist photography (the use of mirrors, reflections, doubling, and shadows) as well as its iconography (gloves, hands, masks, the *corps morcelé,* and sexual symbolism) are frequently seen in Woodman's pictures. Woodman's orchestration of both phallic and vaginal symbols (eels, conch shells, fur boas, lilies, and so forth) is, needless to say, a culturally available lexicon that is anything but esoteric. Which is only to say that even without reference to the Surrealist repertoire, these objects belong to a venerable semiotics of the sexual body. Similarly, Surrealist art and letters provide numerous deployments of the *acéphale*—the headless body. Does this mean that we should conclude that Woodman's many photographs in which the head is cropped out manifest a similar meaning?

Much has been made of the relevance of an 1881 print cycle, *Paraphrase on the Finding of a Glove,* by Max Klinger, a narrative that turns on a woman dropping her glove, and the compulsive pursuit of the woman by the man who picks it up.[19] Apparently, Woodman was familiar with this print cycle, and because of the frequent deployment of gloves in certain of Woodman's pictures—sometimes very strategically placed, as in *No. 36 Horizontale* (Providence, Rhode Island, 1976–77)—again there is the assumption that we may better understand Woodman's pictures in the light of Klinger's. Without refuting Woodman's knowledge of, or indeed, the "influence" of Klinger's cycle, the erotic and fetishistic connotations of women's gloves, from the time of Shakespeare and probably earlier, are, like that of shoes, culturally ubiquitous.

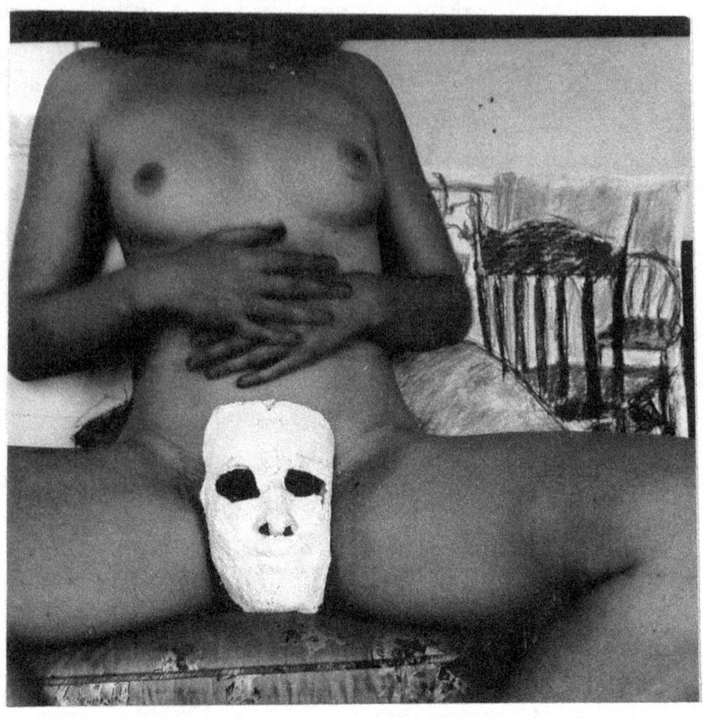

11.4 Francesca Woodman, *Face*, Providence, Rhode Island, 1975–76. Black-and-white gelatin silver print 3 13/16 × 4 7/8 in. COURTESY OF GEORGE AND BETTY WOODMAN.

Moreover, the Libreria Maldoror had even proposed an unrealized project about gloves for which Woodman would have been one of the commissioned artists. And while it is perhaps interesting to identify iconographic precedents by way of establishing an artist's knowledge and even use of them, the more important question hinges on how these references are to be subsequently interpreted.

Much the same issues arise in discussions linking Woodman's photographs to work by Julia Margaret Cameron and by Lady Clementina Hawarden, an aristocratic Victorian amateur who between 1857 and 1868 produced hundreds of pictures of her daughters in their home, often in what the Victorians called "fancy dress," or in modest dishabillé, in languishing poses before windows and mirrors, or in tableau-type stagings of two or three figures. It is possible

Woodman saw the 1974 monograph by Gerry Badger (the only one in print before Hawarden was resurrected from obscurity in the 1990s), and she probably knew at least some of Cameron's pictures. Both women have become the object of feminist readings (or rereadings), informed by Freudian, Lacanian, or other psychoanalytic theories.[20] One aspect of their revival has to do with a turn in feminist theory toward the exploration of the maternal, the relationships of mothers and children, and the psychosexual bonds between them—all of which falls under the discursive umbrella of "inscriptions" of the feminine.[21] In the case of Cameron, her sentimental soft-focus staging of toddlers and infants as cupids and angels has fueled discussion of how Woodman might have yet again been influenced by this imagery. But while it is one thing to read and reinterpret the past through the present (we view Hawarden's and Cameron's work *differently* in the light of contemporary women's photography as well as feminist revisions of psychoanalytic theory), to read the present through the past is an essentially regressive move. For where the discussions of Hawarden's and Cameron's photography vis-à-vis the work of Woodman assumes the task of exploring the legacies of women *in* photography and *as* photographers (and, until the twentieth century, there were very few), how should we evaluate the ever-increasing list of photographers who are now taken to have shaped or informed Woodman's work? More to the point, to sidestep Woodman's unmistakable preoccupation with the female body (as subject), femininity (as topos), and the representation of both is less obscurantism than mystification. In the final analysis, the evidence suggests that Woodman, like most artists before and after her, took what she needed from whatever sources were available or congenial to her and used them for her own purposes. Which is simply another way of saying that in our age of mechanical and postmechanical reproduction, in our post-Malraux imaginary museum, and within the image world that is the ether we breathe, the modern or contemporary artist inherits a staggering image repertoire available as raw material to draw upon and to work with as they wish.

The more interesting approach to the notion of "influence" is to compare works and artists that Woodman in all likelihood *never* knew or saw, including photographs made well before her time as well as those made by her contemporaries. I would here again refer to pictures by artists such as Claude Cahun and Marcel Moore (only a few photographs were known in Woodman's lifetime); Woodman's older contemporaries, Suzanne Santoro (whom she did know) and Valie Export (whose work she probably did not know); and her close contemporaries, Helen Chadwick, Ana Mendieta, Birgit Jürgenssen, and others. This way of considering the influence of cultural, social, and psychological determinations is not limited to who saw what or to what any two works look like, although actual resemblance is not necessarily excluded. Thus the rationale for pairing Cahun/Moore's photograph of Cahun confined in a pantry, to Woodman's photograph of herself in *Untitled* (Providence, Rhode Island, 1975–78), indicates that the visual metaphorization of feminine constraint or sequestration are intuitive and shared concerns, although entirely separated by time and space. Similarly, we might compare those photographs by Ana Mendiata in which she presses a glass pane against her body with those of Woodman who likewise manipulates a sheet of glass, both artists playing with the notion of photographic as well as the evocation of bodily vulnerability or harm. Or, in yet another example, we might compare Woodman's torso pinched with clothespins to one of Jürgenssen's *Korper* projections. In other words, rather than accumulating vast lists of artists of works who serve as source or influence, there is reason to acknowledge a strain or current in twentieth-century art by women, international in scope, that hinges on both the politics and the poetics of gender as these are mediated within forms of representation.[22] Similarly, there is reason to speak of the concept of the *inscription* of sexual difference such that a comparison of Acconci photographing himself as "castrated" should be distinguished from the work of those women artists who intuited that possession or lack of a penis involves more than staging or theatricalizing their putative castration.

Another way to consider the issue of sexual difference is to pose the question of how our readings of Woodman's art might be altered if we hypothesize a female spectator. I do not mean to say that Woodman intentionally or deliberately had such a goal in mind, but such unprecedented notions of female spectatorship were very much in the air in the 1970s. Barbara Kruger in particular, defined one of her artistic goals as the task of constructing and addressing a female spectator. And, in fact, first-wave feminist practices were profoundly shaped by this supposition—or invention—of a feminine "sphere of reception" outside the constraints or oppressions of a patriarchal and often misogynist art world. However speculative it may be, thinking of Woodman's work in its literal context of women's space and women's relationships situates her work in intriguing ways among that of her avowedly feminist contemporaries, with whom she may or may not have been familiar.

But perhaps more important, the perception of Woodman's various studios as feminine spaces where women friends and models came and went, worked and chatted, and slept over from time to time is possibly a more insightful way of considering gendered space in Woodman's work. However, her studios that functioned, as a space of and for the feminine is counterpointed by the more menacing or devouring features of Woodman's *House* series.[23] Despite this more "gothic" mode, as Blessing observes, "At the heart of Woodman's performances for the camera is a sense of play, of fun which may have been solitary at times but often involved other people, specifically female friends, suggesting a kind of feminine if not feminist utopia."[24] Often someone operated the camera as Woodman performed, or served in front of the camera as surrogate.[25] The videos clearly demonstrate the presence of others in the production of Woodman's work, an engagement emblematic of the dynamic between the director of the image and her subject, something that is less obvious in the still photography.[26] Moreover, given the intensity of Woodman's friendships with women, many of them artists themselves (in Sloan Rankin's case, also a fellow art student and roommate in Rome), why should the perception of certain of Woodman's works as collaborative be ruled out entirely? Very rarely does one see in Woodman's still pictures the cable necessary for a time-release exposure, and many of Woodman's poses seem far too complicated or too improvisational for her to have adjusted her view camera and then placed herself in the desired position.[27] Nevertheless, those of her friends who also modeled for her, such as Sabina Murri and Sloan Rankin, are quite certain that sequences were made as time-release exposures.

With respect to my impressions of the overall tenor of the Woodman literature, these must be said to raise complex questions about the task of criticism and interpretation. Which in turn prompts such fundamental questions as to how one grasps the work of the work, and how to understand what it tries to accomplish. How is meaning to be gleaned from a work, and with what critical apparatuses? In certain of the criticism devoted to Woodman, there is an implicit or explicit rejection of interpretation, viewed as somehow dated, parochial, or partisan. The premise here, as is always the case in critiques of "political" criticism, is that the writer is him or herself free of ideology, and it is the feminist who is blinded by or fails to adequately comprehend the work because of her political commitments. In any number of these essays, feminism is conceded to be one of the factors to consider when addressing Woodman's work, but is deemed neither necessary nor sufficient in itself. In this manner, a great deal of the writing on Woodman either skirts feminist issues entirely, invokes them only to dismiss them, or invokes them and goes on immediately to change the subject. "To my eye," writes Meaghan Thurston, "the transgressive, boundary-pushing spatial relationship of Woodman's work transcends feminist readings."[28] The use of the verb "transcends" is telling, derived as it is from the Latin *transcendĕre*, which the *Oxford English Dictionary* gives as "to climb over or beyond, surmount." Have we truly surmounted or transcended feminism because we have entered the brave new world of sex and gender parity? Are the sexual and gender politics of the representation of the female body in whatever medium an ancillary rather than central problematic in all aspects of the visual including elite culture?

In reflecting on this disturbing aspect of Woodman's bibliography, I wonder whether this should be considered—pace Raymond Williams—as a residual, dominant, or emerging consensus? For this legacy of feminist thought, which in all its forms is unapologetically political, not only links Woodman to her historical moment (the years between 1973 and 1981) but helps account for the great power and accomplishment of her work, even as it rescues both her art and life from the trivialities of sentimentalism and mythology.

# 12

## The Coming of Age

### CINDY SHERMAN, FEMINISM, AND ART HISTORY

(2014)

What you are looking at in fig. 12.1 is *not* a photograph by Cindy Sherman. It is a photograph I came upon by chance on the London *Guardian*'s web page, and it depicts Ellie Goulding, a British pop singer, on the occasion of her just-released music video. If you thought it was by Sherman, then you have not looked that closely at Sherman's so-called centerfold photos that this photo closely resembles. Aside from the nominal subject—a young blonde woman seen from above—the resemblances lie in the theatrical lighting, the horizontal format, the close-up view, and the minimal number of objects within the frame: a sheepskin fur throw on the bed and a fur rug on the floor.

In the twelve photos that Sherman made on a commission from *Artforum* in 1981 (but that were rejected for publication), none of the figures addresses the spectator. Although engaging the spectator is a familiar photographic trope employed in everything from photographic portraiture to fashion photography to pornography, the illusion produced in Sherman's centerfolds is that the subject is unobserved in her interiority and inwardness. The viewer thus fictively intrudes, more or less voyeuristically, on the subject's privacy. Furthermore, with the exception of certain of her earlier black-and-white film stills, few of Sherman's photographs depict a woman or girl who might be described as especially glamorous or seductive. On the contrary, the female subjects who returned to her work in the so-called fashion photographs of 1993 (commissioned by *Harper's Bazaar* and individual dress designers) are extravagantly grotesque, and those depicted later in the so-called Hollywood/Hampton series produced after 2000 are victims, or so it seems, of their own clumsy (and failed) self-fashioning. Finally, in the centerfold pictures, the female figures are staged so as suggest states of anxiety, apprehension, and grief.

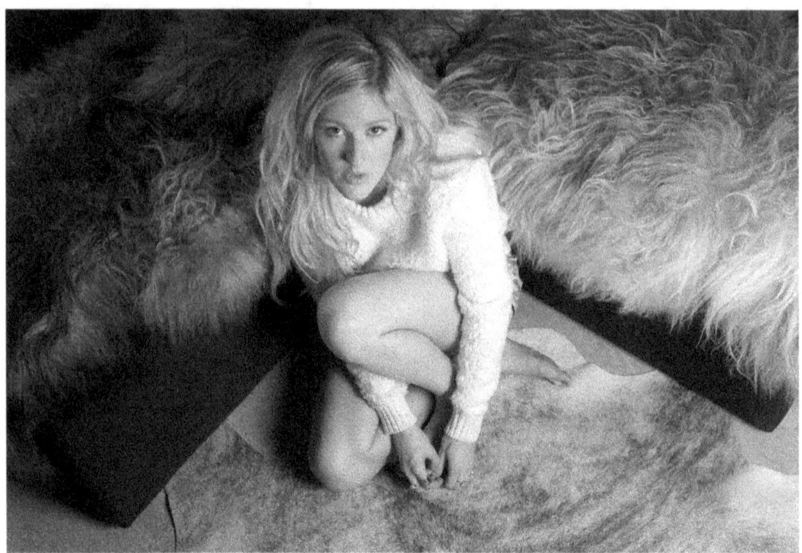

12.1 "I felt a pull towards electronic music": Ellie Goulding at her home in West London, November 2013. Photograph by Richard Saker for the *Observer* © 2013. COURTESY OF THE PHOTOGRAPHER AND GUARDIAN NEWS AND MEDIA.

And following from that (as in Sherman's previous film stills and subsequent color series using rear-screen projections), there is invariably an evocation of narrative in keeping with each photograph's cinematic connotations and mise-en-scène.

However, for those who might have taken Ellie Goulding's photograph for a Cindy Sherman, there are good reasons for such a misrecognition. This misrecognition goes to the heart of Sherman's work as it developed from the late 1970s through the early 1990s, almost all of it featuring female protagonists. In my view, these photographs pivot precisely on the problematic of recognition/misrecognition, a viewing relationship that has particular implications for the female spectator. For what is at stake in the couplet recognition/misrecognition in the psychic register opens up to the processes of projection, identification, disidentification, and introjection. On the sociocultural register these refer also to ideologies of gender, to what Louis Althusser famously called "interpellation." By this he meant how the ideological positioning of the subject functioned as a form of "hailing" and effectively reacting "Yes, that's me." During the same period that Sherman was working in this manner, Barbara Kruger explored this interpellation process more polemically and programmatically with her texts addressing "you" or "we," an address that the viewer either accepts or rejects, and with which Kruger intended to both locate and affirm the existence of a female spectator.

When we look at the photo of Goulding, nothing seems particularly odd in either its form or its context. Yet it somehow conveys an erotic charge. Where is the eroticism to be located? Is it simply that a pretty young woman is always and already a signifier of eroticism? (This was one of Laura Mulvey's theses in her classic essay "Visual Pleasure and Narrative Cinema" of 1972, and was referred to in both Mulvey's and Judith Williamson's essays on Sherman.) Is the eroticism implied by the fact that she is doing nothing other than appearing to engage the viewer's gaze? True, part of her thigh is exposed, and there is also a bed. And then there is her unkempt "bedhead" hair. The picture has a certain geometry, a triangular area with the head at its apex, and shiny rose-colored and partly opened lips. As for the spectator's point of view—created, of course, by the photographer—one looks down at the woman, a position that by definition is the dominant (i.e., active) viewpoint, and, according to Freud, the masculine position. Which is to say that, whether looking at the image as a male or female viewer, the photographic point of view is an important determination of meaning, although how and if one occupies that position "correctly" is another question. And, finally, there is all that fur, animal fur and blonde hair, the latter framed by the former. Why all that fur?

In 1992, Sherman produced a series of pictures that have come to be referred to as the "sex pictures." Like all references to Sherman's nominal subjects this is something of a misnomer; for one, because Sherman never titles her work, but also because no human subjects are involved. The pictures were produced with combinations of anatomical models, freely reassembled, extravagantly modified, and staged, as always, within Sherman's studio. The period in which Sherman produced these aggressive and often violent pictures was during the censorship wars in the United States, a point worth mentioning because Sherman's series are in fact frequently linked to larger sociopolitical as well as cultural phenomena.

Among this series, certainly one of the most disturbing, if not repellant, photographs is *Untitled #250* (1992; fig. 12.2), a picture that might be said to "unveil" the repressed material that structures the idealized, usually eroticized convention of the female nude. This particular legacy informs all "artistic" and aestheticized renderings of the female body, from classical antiquity to the present, and all mass media incarnations of ideal femininity. Thus (and I speak here only of the Western tradition) from the invention of the female nude in Athens in the fifth century BC through the early twentieth century, the idealized female body has neither vulva nor pubic hair. Hair may be copious on the head but nowhere else, and female genitalia are conventionally effaced by the unmarked triangle of the pubis or elided with hand or drapery. Accordingly, on the most immediate level, Sherman's *#250* represents the monstrous female body of the patriarchal imaginary, the frightening presence that is the flip side of the intact perfection of the artistic nude. Instead of the reassuring image of desire, Sherman presents the viewer with an obscene concatenation of a witchlike crone with an ancient wrinkled face and straggly strands of gray hair, prosthetic red-nippled breasts and swollen belly, and, as a detached body part, a groin, amputated at the thighs, featuring a conspicuously hairy and gaping vagina from which emerges a string of turdlike sausages (see Freud on infantile fantasies of feces = baby.) This nightmare figure reclines (as do a vast proportion of the female nudes in European painting), but here it reclines on a bed of hair, the very excess of which emphasizes its scarcity on the head and, needless to say, invokes one of the typical guises of fetishism. But *#250* is, of course, an antifetish assemblage, undoing precisely the mechanisms of sublimation and denial that make the fetish a memorial of castration fear. Which is also to say that in many of the sex pictures of 1992, it is sexual difference (in its psychoanalytic sense) rather than gender (a sociocultural construction) that is at stake. But this topos is evident in earlier work too; *Untitled #143* (1985) is especially interesting; not only is it a virile figure—note the beard and executioner- or S/M-type costume—but one that appears decapitated, revealing also, on the right cheek, two unmistakably vaginal slits.

Like a number of Sherman's so-called history paintings made in 1989 after several months in Rome, Sherman's litmus-like sensitivity to codes of representation enables her to reveal, dissect, and desublimate them, what Roland Barthes called the work of demythologizing, which remains a necessary element of critical practice. That Sherman would take on, so to speak, the artistic canon of Western painting from the Renaissance to the early nineteenth century in her photography is itself a significant move. In a certain sense, one might see it as the equivalent of the feminist art historical work initiated by Linda Nochlin's manifesto-like essay "Why Have There Been No Great Women Artists?" of 1971. Nochlin's essay, which inaugurated the practice of feminist art history, has since inspired three generations of feminist art historians to revisit the history of art, including its conventions of representation as well as its forms of discourse. Although I doubt that Sherman intended to claim the role of the great woman artist who would disprove the stereotype, her series referring

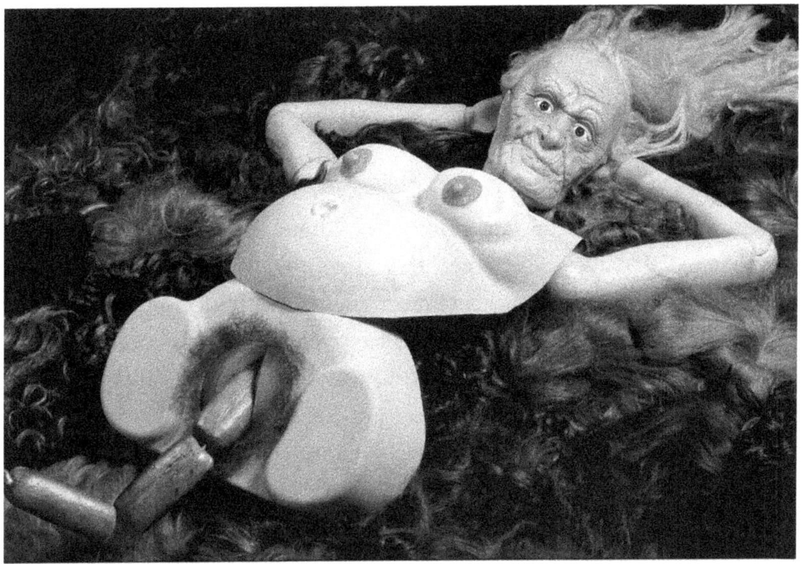

12.2 Cindy Sherman, *Untitled #250*, 1992. Chromogenic color print, 50 × 75 in. Edition of 6. 

to museum art is nevertheless an intervention (as well as analysis) of what generally passes unremarked in conventional scholarship. Generally speaking, her revision of certain types of portraiture, of men and women both, focuses on the specific meanings of pictorial conventions, so commonplace as to be overlooked, such as the various signifiers of power, luxury, learning, and material possessions in portraiture. Here, the issue of masquerade, already evident in earlier series such as Sherman's film stills, is revealed as integral to historical portraiture as such, as much an attribute of masculinity as of femininity. Nevertheless, it is in Sherman's pastiches of female portraits that certain general characteristics in the representation of femininity are made fully visible. One of these characteristics has to do with a certain vacancy of expression in the female face, often attributed by scholars to the painter's attempt to idealize. In other words, where much portraiture attempts to convey the power, individuality, and character of the male sitter, this has been rarely a goal, much less an ideal, in depicting the female sitter.[1] In other cases, conventions of depiction, such as the profile view common in quattrocento painting, is mimicked for the profile view—often of a marriageable woman whose portrait was commissioned for her prospective husband—elides the subject's gaze as a signifier of the women's modesty and virtue. In Sherman's pictures, prosthetic parts are always used in interesting ways, often but not always in relation to secondary sex characteristics or, in the sex pictures, genitalia. In this regard, Sherman's use of prosthetic breasts is as insightful as it is witty. For, as all art historians know, like the unmarked pubis, the youthfully small, round, and separated breasts are a kind of template of corporal perfection. Even the nursing breast, sometimes visible in representations of the Virgin, is closer in size to a baseball than to its anatomical referent; there are no Dolly Partons in art history. Comparing one of Sherman's history paintings as it relates closely to its model, Raphael's *La fornarina* (figs. 12.2 and 12.3), reveals her shrewd awareness of precisely those aspects of Raphael's painting most relevant to feminist analysis in her transformation of the youthful torso into a plastic bulging carapace. Where Raphael inscribes his signature on the golden armband of his model, declaring both authorship and sexual possession, Sherman attaches to the model's arm a tacky garter, itself a fetish-like accessory. Recognizing the formal and semiotic function of the diaphanous and transparent veil that accentuates the erotic charge of nudity, Sherman uses a bargain-basement scrap of woven curtain to demonstrate its function.

I first saw Cindy Sherman's work—a selection of the black-and-white film stills—exhibited at Metro Pictures in 1980, shortly after the gallery first opened. Over the next ten years, I often referred to Sherman's work in my essays, for, like a number of other women artists who were my US contemporaries—for example, Barbara Kruger, Louise Lawler, Sherrie Levine, Silvia Kolbowski, Martha Rosler, Mary Kelly, and Sarah Charlesworth, all born in the late 1940s and early 1950s—Sherman's work influenced my own work as a feminist art critic and art historian. Moreover, the critical enterprise within art criticism and theory that could be retrospectively called the formulation of a feminist postmodernism (or perhaps a postmodern feminism) involved a complex interaction between artists, theorists, and critics, a relationship caricatured in the 1980s by those who claimed such art practices merely "illustrated" certain postmodernist theories. It was only, however, in 1991 that I wrote an essay dealing exclusively with Sherman. The essay, written for *Parkett,* was titled "Suitable for Framing; The Critical Recasting of Cindy Sherman" and was less a study of Sherman's work than a reading of some of its criticism, all of it laudatory. Basically, what I sought to demonstrate was that as Sherman became ever more artistically celebrated, those aspects of her work that could be said to engage with the representation of femininity, with feminine stereotypes, with gendered subjectivity, with sexual difference, with the visual politics of femininity-as-spectacle-or-masquerade, with issues of fetishism and specularity—all of those elements that might logically require reference to feminism, or, for that matter, women—were significantly absent or only marginally noted. In other words, in the process of Sherman's ascendance to the status of great artist, the particularism of gender was dissolved into the universality of genius, for, as the saying goes, genius has no gender. Accordingly, for critics as diverse as Peter Schjeldahl, Jean-Pierre Criqui, Régis Durand, Rosalind Krauss, Norman Bryson, Hal Foster, and many, many others, Sherman's art was understood to address itself—variously—to the human condition, the mutations and aporias of self and identity, mass media stereotypes, the workings of abjection, the *informe*, and so on and so forth. Alternatively, as in the case of Peter Schjeldahl, one could identify a form of perverse mimeticism, as in his excited observation: "As a male, I also find these pictures sentimentally, charmingly, and sometimes pretty fiercely erotic: I'm in love again with every look at the insecure blonde in the nighttime city. I am responding to Sherman's knack, shared with many movie actresses, of projecting feminine vulnerability, thereby triggering (masculine) urges to ravish and/or to protect."[2] But while these responses manifest a failure to distinguish signifier from signified, the more problematic commentaries are those in which the political, that is, the feminist, implications of Sherman's work were significantly minimized.

Certainly, and as is clear in Sherman's recent retrospectives, from the late 1970s to the present, from the early black-and-white film stills to the recent large-scale wall pieces, a major part of all of Sherman's work has focused on the modalities of woman-as-image (as opposed to images of women, a crucial distinction made by Griselda Pollock in the early 1980s). At the same time, each new body of work has engaged with various issues, social, political, and artistic, even as Sherman's working methods have remained generally unchanged (I refer to her studio-based practice in which working alone, she is the exclusive model and director, even as she has shifted from analogue to digital photography and from modest to mural-sized scale). This is not to deny that issues such as abjection or the fluidity of identity are *not* elements in any given series, but rather to insist that these accompany or are part of Sherman's career-long preoccupation, engagement, and intervention with ideologies of gender, with Woman as a phantasm (or symptom) of patriarchy, with violence and aggression in sexual relations, and with conventions of representation that determine and fix subject positions.

In 2006, Johanna Burton compiled an anthology of essays on Sherman's work in which my own essay was reproduced, but what struck me then is that

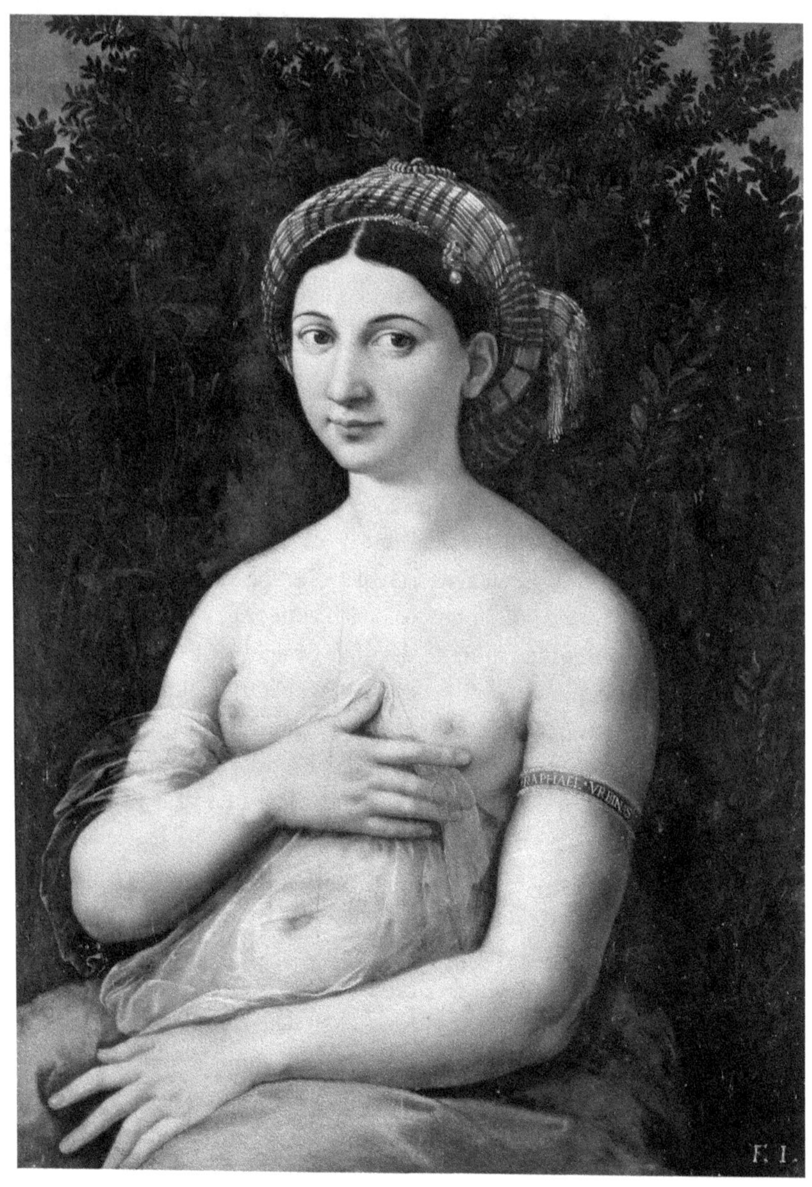


12.3 Raffaello Sanzio, *Portrait of a Young Woman (La fornarina)*, ca. 1518. Oil on wood, 33.46 × 23.62 in. GALLERIA NAZIONALE D'ARTE ANTICA, ROME. DIGITAL IMAGE © 2006 SCALA, FLORENCE / ART RESOURCE, NY.

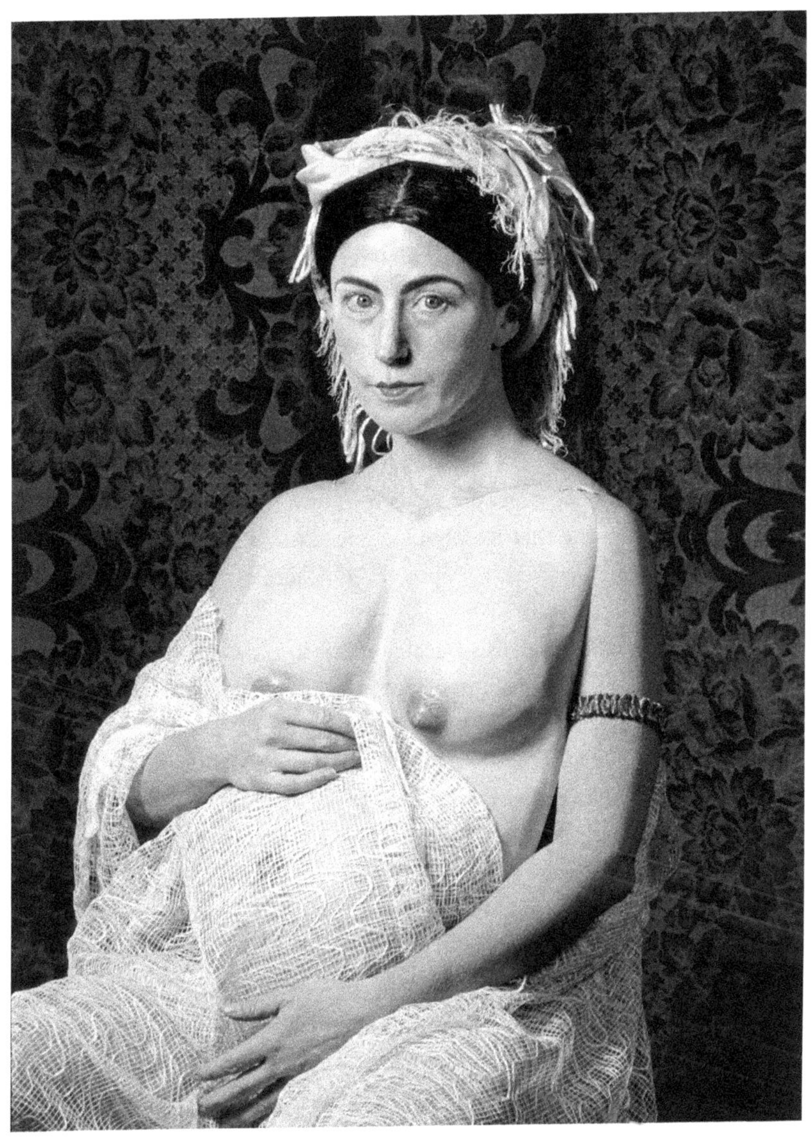

12.4 Cindy Sherman, *Untitled #205*, 1989. Chromogenic color print, 53 ½ × 40 ¼ in. Edition of 6. © Cindy Sherman. COURTESY OF THE ARTIST AND METRO PICTURES, NEW YORK.

the explicitly feminist readings of Sherman's pictures—notably those of Laura Mulvey and Judith Williamson—were written in the 1980s. And while subsequent feminist interpretations of Sherman's work appeared in the 1990s—for example, those of Amelia Jones, Elisabeth Bronfen, and the recent catalogue raisonné of Sherman's work up until 1984 by Gabriele Schor and others—by and large, the tendency to neuter, so to speak, the sexual politics of Sherman's work is if anything even more pronounced. And while it is true that certain of Sherman's series, such as the history paintings, feature male figures, and certain others do not feature human figures at all, in the majority of her pictures, there is usually *some* avatar of femininity at play. In this respect, and considering the many critical responses to her retrospectives—enthusiastic as they are—the elision of feminism appears as alternatively a symptom of repression or one of denial. This denial, however, or nonrecognition, of the constitutive significance of feminism as it informs Sherman's art is part of a larger problematic, one that Rosalyn Deutsche has discussed (in relation to Mary Kelly's recent work) as the "forgetting" of feminism in art theory, criticism, and indeed art history.

There is some irony in all this, because it was in 2006–8 that in Europe and the United States a number of important exhibitions took place featuring art, in all media, influenced by feminism in various ways. And, in the wake of such shows as *WACK*, *Global Feminism*, Judy Chicago's *Sexual Politics*, *Elles*, *Rebel Rebel*, *Female Trouble*, and *Gender Check* there appeared a number of monographic retrospectives of woman artists. These in turn were accompanied by symposia and conferences, and were followed by reviews and essays and even coffee table books. One might then have concluded that the first decade of the twenty-first century in Europe and the United States was marked by a kind of institutionalization of the art generated or influenced by the women's movement as it emerged in the late 1960s and its subsequent and plural developments. But reading recent Anglophone and Francophone contemporary art criticism and art history, and despite the recent elevation and coming-into-visibility of impressive numbers of women artists, it seems as though outside of explicitly feminist venues and publications, feminist critical thought is less frequent, having become simply one possible critical option among others. It is as though the urgency and militancy of feminist critique, especially in the visual arts, has been blunted or diminished. For this and other reasons, I take the tenor of the recent writing on Sherman as a disturbing sign of what I am calling "the coming of age," the title of Simone de Beauvoir's book on the subject.

By this "coming of age" I am referring to different but possibly related phenomena. On one level, this refers to the process of maturing, a term with far more positive connotations for good wines than for women (the "mature woman" is usually a euphemism). There is also the aging of what is usually called "second-generation feminism," meaning that which emerged from the women's movement in the late 1960s and 1970s. In relation to the visual arts—art history and criticism, cinema studies, and film theory—many of feminism's foundational texts in English were first produced in the early 1970s and 1980s (e.g., Mulvey, Nochlin, and Pollock) and flourished through the 1980s. Artists defining themselves *as* feminists and intent on inventing declaredly feminist forms of art, like the women's movement itself, were a fully international phenomenon. The aging of feminism in turn has given rise to the media invention of something called "postfeminism." Be that as it may, whether one wishes to retain a category called "feminist art" in contemporary production is another issue. But the point is that in terms of age, feminist politics and feminist thought parallel the lives of Sherman and her contemporaries, and thus feminism is a movement that came of age as they did. For this reason, the coming of age of feminism, like any aspect of the life world, is susceptible to the still-revolutionary insight (however trivialized in mass culture) that the personal is political.

Between 2000 and 2002, Sherman produced a series of works that have come to be known as the Hollywood/Hampton pictures (or alternatively the West Coast/East Coast series). And in 2008, when Sherman was fifty-four, she made a series sometimes referred to as the society portraits. Although there is a six-year interval between these series, they are both related to the process of aging, and in a number of the society pictures, the subjects appear to be close to Sherman's age at the time they were made.

In this respect, although everyone ages, as does every social and political movement, the aging of women and of the women's movement have themselves been subject to feminist inquiry and analysis. This, as it happens, was the subject of two major works by Mary Kelly; the first, *Interim*, was completed in 1989 and first shown in its entirety at the New Museum in New York City; the second, her more recent *Love Songs*, was shown at the Postmasters Gallery (a larger version of which was shown in Documenta 12). *Interim* was an extended multipart project produced over a four-year period, whose central theme was precisely that of aging, more specifically the experience, contradictions, conundrums, and anxieties of (mostly) middle-class white women. Feminist and psychoanalytic theory provided Kelly with a form of conceptual architecture that enabled her to explore the aging process in several ways. In the section called *Corpus*, these conflictual processes are articulated between women as they are situated (or situate themselves) in relation to the maternal, to sexual identity, and to the loss of visibility and desirability that accompanies their aging, often experienced as painful loss. *Historia* addresses the history of the women's movement and its impact on the everyday life of women. This section included personal histories told by four generations of feminists since 1968, as well as historical episodes in the history of feminism itself.

With *Love Songs*, Kelly returned to the history of the women's movement and the vicissitudes of feminism. As the title suggests, the installation and its complex interweaving of texts similarly encompass multiple generations. In her eloquent essay on the work to which I referred above, Rosalyn Deutsche remarked on *how* the radical implications of feminism are variously "forgotten": "Kelly's exhibition treated the political event of feminism as also a personal one, an amorous passion, giving new meaning to the slogan of the Women's Liberation Movement, 'the personal is political.' This slogan challenged both mainstream and traditional critical conceptions of the public sphere, conceptions that draw a rigid divide between public/political and private/nonpolitical space. Whereas the public/private division once forced women's issues into privacy, now the division is shored up by left melancholics who exclude feminist explorations of subjectivity from the public sphere."[3] But what is also underscored in Deutsche's consideration of *Love Songs* are affective identifications and projections that operate for women in relation to the changing and always complex modalities of feminist thought and politics. Deutsche takes account of the existence of a certain nostalgia for the utopian promises of the early movement, what was then called "women's liberation," one of whose mottos was "sisterhood is powerful." In fact, the house that is the architectural center of the installation bears the text "Sisterhood is POW" a locution that abbreviates "powerful" but indicates the sense of revelation that many women experienced encountering the feminist movement. Yet one of the most interesting aspects of the work is its refusal to elegize or romanticize a "past" of feminism, even as it interweaves statements by contemporary young women who do not necessarily identify with, or find relevant, feminism's plural histories. Even as it restages, photographically, a feminist protest demonstration from 1971 in front of the Albert Hall (a protest against the Miss World pageant) with a reenactment by Kelly's students, it acknowledges the importance of the "not-forgetting" of the event (Deutsche is using the word "event" in the sense that the philosopher Alain Badiou uses it).

I refer to these works by Kelly, both of which are far too complex to fairly summarize, for two reasons. First, to indicate that coming of age, both politically and personally, is an inescapable problematic for feminists *and* women artists of a certain age. Second, and without meaning to make invidious comparisons, to point out that Sherman's pictures of aging women, the so-called Hollywood/Hampton or East Coast/West Coast series, are a disturbing departure from her previous and subsequent production. In the former series, and unlike her repertoire of feminine types from earlier work (excluding the so-called fashion series and fairy-tale series, neither of which invoke the portrait genre), these are broadly satirical. *Untitled #353* (2000 fig. 12.5), for example—definitely West Coast—is exemplary of how the series "works." Aside from the improbably jutting breasts and the very wiglike appearance of the wig, other telling signifiers have to do with the subject's taste or style (i.e., bad; note the neckerchief, the gold embroidery on the kaftan, the gold buckled belt featuring clasped hands). This image is an amalgam of sex and class. But what is uncomfortable here are the ways that female aging (and its denial) are so artfully articulated. Note the slackening of the jaw under the rouged cheekbone, the frown lines stretching from the nostrils and around the mouth, the forehead lines just below the wig. Note as well the barest suggestion of a moustache, and the puffy area below the eyes imperfectly concealed with highlighting makeup. Sherman's unobtrusive use of makeup for the film stills, rear-screen, or centerfold pictures to style her subjects is here dramatically reversed, for there is a way in which, with the exception of those few figures with no visible makeup (and thus even more grotesque-looking), one might say that the subject is makeup itself. Moreover, it is makeup that derives from the up-to-the-minute fashionable face as purveyed by the beauty/cosmetics/entertainment media industry—consequently, the plumped-up, collagen-swollen lips, often with excessive lip liner (as in *Untitled #360* and *Untitled #397*); overly plucked or overly thick eyebrows, almost all over or under the natural brow (*Untitled #354* and *Untitled #355*), excess of highlighter or concealer (*Untitled #400*), inappropriate coiffures (*Untitled #398* and *Untitled #399*), overuse of Botox, and so forth. Hence, the various feminine types in this series are as typological as those in the earlier works, but in a disturbing way, they seem like agents of their own absurdity (or worse). Which is another way of saying that where Sherman's woman-as-image series insists on the essential absence of a "real" female subject, these appear to be parodic indictments—caricatures—of actual women who vainly, and pitiably, attempt to deny the depredations of age and who equally vainly attempt a self-fashioning based on mass media images of desirable femininity.

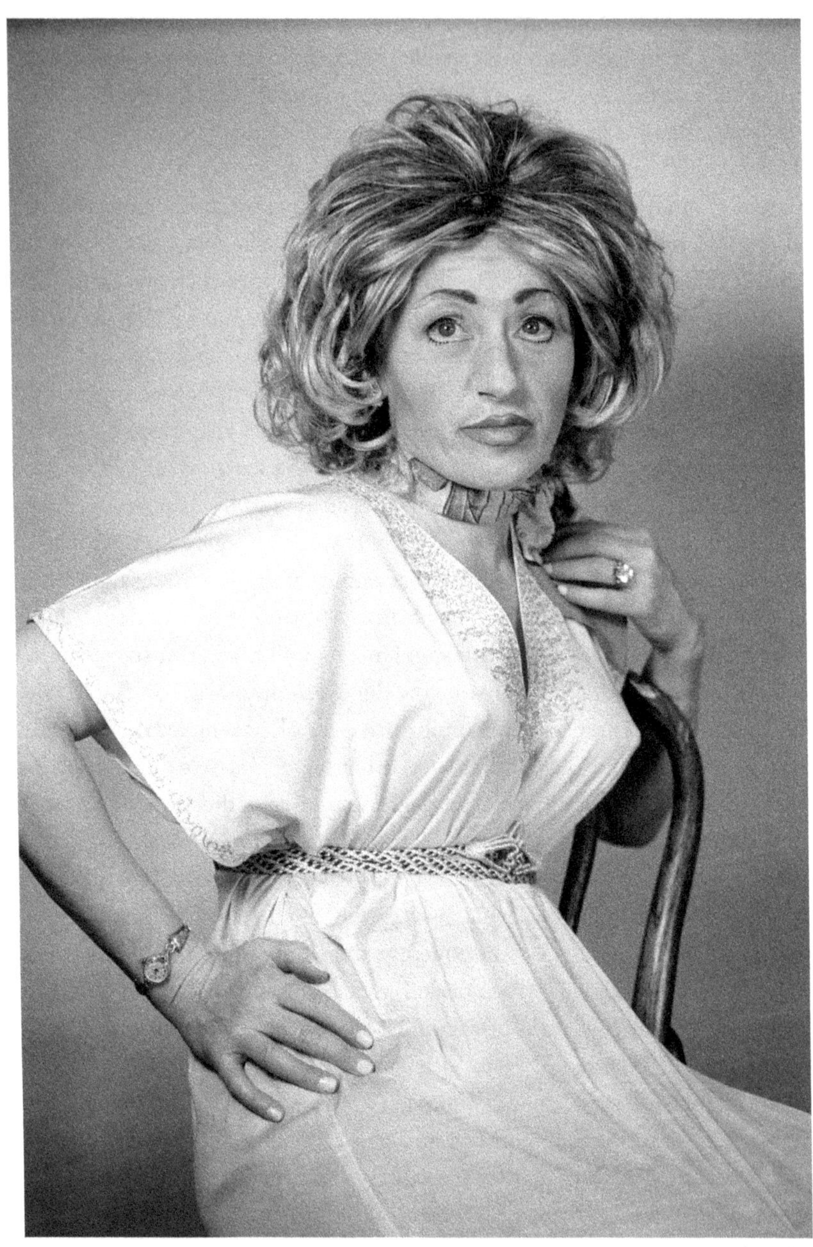

12.5 Cindy Sherman, *Untitled #353*, 2000. Chromogenic color print, 36 × 24 in. Edition of 6. © 2000 Cindy Sherman. COURTESY OF THE ARTIST AND METRO PICTURES, NEW YORK.

By the time Sherman produced the so-called society portraits, tours de force in which she employed computerized backgrounds from such places as Central Park and the Cloisters, certain of the women depicted seem to have been literally modeled on actual society women, such as Brooke Astor, a major New York City philanthropist. Moreover, there is some reason to think that others were based on wealthy women who might even be collectors of Sherman's work. Certain of the art critics reviewing the exhibition remarked on the resemblance of the women at the opening to the personages in the photographs. Be that as it may, what is troubling in this series is the shift from (broadly stated) demonstrations of the fantasmatic and often-misogynist aspects of representations of femininity to the far easier practice of social satire and parody. In other words, the implication is that it is the woman herself who is responsible for her own decadence, vanity, vulgarity, and absurdity. Which is, in effect, akin to blaming the victim. Vanity thy name is Woman.

In her extremely interesting essay in the Museum of Modern Art catalogue, Burton introduces the Hollywood/Hampton series of 2000–2002 and the society portraits of 2008 with an anecdote recounted by Calvin Tomkins in a *New Yorker* profile about Sherman from 2002. In Tomkins's telling, on the occasion on Sherman's exhibition at the Gagosian Gallery in Los Angeles, a woman described by him in no other detail than as wearing a mink stole, remarks to him that she finds the portraits to be "without empathy."[4] It is clear, although Tomkins does not elaborate, that this woman's response has to do with her recognition that in some way these avatars of middle-aged or older women, all of whom aspire to an ideal that they fail to incarnate, are subjects of mockery, insofar as she herself has some identification with the portraits on view. Here arises the issue of identification/misidentification that was so central in Sherman's earlier work. For Burton—as for Eva Respini, Ingrid Sischy, and other commentators—both series are understood to invoke empathetic, more or less poignant responses to what one might well call the spectacle of aging (white) women. Burton articulates this problem as a largely formalist question, that is to say, a question that devolves to where one locates expressivity and affect in a staged photograph, all of whose elements are fictive: choreographed, orchestrated, and within which there is no "real" whatsoever. Drawing on Rosalind Krauss's essays on Sherman that criticized feminist readings of Sherman for their naive fixation on the signified ("images of women"), Burton seeks to conscript the notion of "abstraction" in Sherman's work, thereby avoiding the specifically feminist problems that arise in these two bodies of work. "In the mid-1990s," Burton writes,

> I was fully convinced both of Sherman's work as performing the ongoing analysis—unveiling the vicissitudes of signification—and the necessity of removing Sherman entirely from the expected role of expressive "actress" or "performer" in those scenes she produced. Yet, nearly twenty years later, and with works such as the Hollywood/Hamptons series in mind (as well as attending questions of empathy the works provoke), I find myself wanting to complicate some aspects of these terms. Indeed, if Sherman's "abject" period ushered in the very elements that might be said to trouble representation where it commonly ceases to accommodate and in ways that point to its aporias and antagonisms . . . one might argue that Sherman's "return" to her own work over the last decade enacts a kind of revenge on a culture that wills women to slowly disappear as they age, or to render them desexualized but campy, comic-relief characters. But such a reading would merely replace the problematic figure of "The Girl" with that of "The Crone" and reinscribe the telos such images might otherwise displace.[5]

My own response to both the 2000–2002 and the 2008 series is far more ambivalent. Much depends on how one identifies/disidentifies with Sherman's imagery. For many years, at least since the rear-screen and centerfold pictures, issues of identification and projection were not particularly in play in Sherman's work. Certainly those works in which no image of femininity appears, or in those employing dolls or anatomical models, there is little question of projection. But in both of these "portrait" series, which feature only female subjects who are either the approximate age of Sherman or older, there is a significant change from Sherman's earlier imagery as codified in cinema and mass media, in folkloric traditions, in the patriarchal imaginary, in the unconscious, and in fantasies that reveal the structures of fetishism. But what strikes me is that where earlier work demonstrates that femininity is an empty signifier, such as to imply that there is and cannot be no "real woman" in the image, these other series imply that these are indeed in some fashion "realistic" representations of a certain type of woman.

That Cindy Sherman is the best-known living woman artist is, from the perspective of a feminist art critic and art historian, an entirely positive development. Moreover, if we think about Sherman's male contemporaries working in photography whose fame might be equivalent—Andreas Gursky or Jeff Koons, for example—there is even more reason to celebrate Sherman's critical prominence. Nevertheless, it would be naive to think that Sherman's deserved success in the new globalized, media-saturated, and hypercommodified emporium of contemporary art is merely the inevitable recognition of the quality of her production. Success and fame in the international art world is overdetermined, and within the terms of this global emporium, the list of determinations grows ever longer. "Name recognition" of a woman artist is subject to somewhat different determinations than those of male artists, and in this respect, it is suggestive to note that the most well-known, most famous dead woman artist is Frida Kahlo, and not merely because she was the subject of a Hollywood movie or because Madonna collects her work. There is reason to suspect that these two women artists have become brand names in modern and contemporary art because of their perceived "presence," insofar as they are, in albeit in very different ways, visible in their works. Thus, Kahlo's extensive use of her own face and variously represented body in her painting, and the public knowledge that Sherman is the model in her photographs, provide, however illusionistically, the desired "presence" of the artist who is also the woman. Where the work of Kahlo is popularly read through her biography, and where her self-representations are considered to be, moreover, icons of "exotic" beauty, Sherman's work is obviously more resistant to such readings, given that, unlike Kahlo, Sherman is only a multitude of appearances, including grotesque and monstrous ones, none of them anchored in a "real" Sherman. Nevertheless, because of the knowledge that Sherman is "in" her pictures, license is given to a reading of her work that links her "dressing up," her "masquerades," her "role playing" either to an exploration of "self" or to "narcissism" and leads to endless speculation as to who is the "real" Sherman beneath the masks and personae (quite a few journalistic writings about Sherman seek, repetitively, indeed obsessively, to make this distinction).

In making these observations, I do not wish to imply that Sherman's artistic reputation is unwarranted because it is based on false assumptions, but only to suggest that insofar as artistic reputations are themselves gendered, ascension into the category of "major artist" may require either an insistence on femininity (e.g., Diane Arbus, Sylvia Plath, Virginia Woolf, and, of course, Kahlo) or, in other recent instances, an erasure of gender, and indeed of feminism. This latter has demonstrably accompanied Sherman's ascent as *the* major woman artist of her generation, inasmuch as this elevation *required* the minimization of its feminist implications. But if part of my argument is concerned with demonstrating the ways that Sherman's work is integrally linked to the critical project of feminism in the visual arts, the broader argument, to which my title alludes, has to do with the aging of feminism, and its "forgetting" within the discourses of art criticism. For those of us for whom the aging of feminism is an element of our lived history, the critical reception of Sherman, as it reflects the "place" of feminist criticism, cannot but be an ambivalent phenomenon.

# NOTES

## Preface

1 Solomon-Godeau, "Going Native," 118–29.
2 In 2012, Rebecca Solnit reposted her 2008 essay "Men Explain Things to Me: Facts Didn't Get in Their Way" with a new introduction, "The Archipelago of Arrogance," on *TomDispatch*, August 19, 2012, http://www.tomdispatch.com/blog/175584/.
3 Dyer, "Academic Author's Unintentional Masterpiece," *New York Times*, July 22, 2011.
4 Solomon-Godeau, "Ontology, Essences, and Photography's Aesthetics," 269.
5 Giroux, "What Might Education Mean," 3–22.
6 Long, *W. G. Sebald*, 48–49. See also Hesford, *Spectacular Rhetorics*, 57.
7 Carrabine, "Just Images," 463–89.
8 Margolis, "Looking at Discipline," 72–96.
9 Brevik-Zender, "Interstitial Narratives," 91–123.
10 Andrews, "Excavating Michael Jordan" 186.
11 Scott, "Gender," 1053–75.
12 Derrida, "Law of Genre," 55–81.
13 Phelan, "Returns of Touch," 357.
14 Solomon-Godeau, *Photography at the Dock*, xxxi. And yet few photography scholars focus on these questions. New Media scholar Wendy Hui Kyong Chun examines the new cultural circuits of power engendered (in both senses of the term) by new technologies. "Habits of Leaking: Of Sluts and Network Cards," *differences: A Journal of Feminist Cultural Studies* 26, no. 2 (2015): 1–28, cowritten with Sarah Friedland, analyzes the innate leakiness of social media through several cases, including the case of Canadian teenager Amanda Todd. After a year of requests, a stranger convinced Todd to flash her breasts during a webcam chat when she was twelve. The man took a screenshot and circulated the photograph, which was eventually used to cyberbully and slut shame her. After years of trying to escape the abuse, Amanda Todd committed suicide at the age of fifteen.

15 Beyoncé quoted in Amy Wallace, "Miss Millennium: Beyonce," *Gentleman's Quarterly*, January 10, 2013. http://www.gq.com/story/beyonce-cover-story-interview-gq-february-2013.

16 As Solomon-Godeau acknowledges, her arguments have been influenced by the pioneering texts of Rosalind Krauss (e.g., "Photography's Discursive Spaces: Landscape/View") and by Douglas Crimp's "The Museum's Old/The Library's New Subject," both of which forcefully demonstrate the transformation of photographic production in the nineteenth century (and after) from discourse value to commodity value.

17 Green, *Spectacle of Nature*.

Introduction

1 See Fried's *Why Photography Matters* and Krauss's somewhat different definition of and brief for medium specificity, *A Voyage on the North Sea*; "Reinventing the Medium"; and also *Perpetual Inventory*, in which Krauss states, "The abandonment of the specific medium spells the death of serious art" (xiii). For a detailed discussion of how medium specificity has figured in recent photography theory, see Costello, "On the Very Idea of a 'Specific' Medium." A recent exhibition and catalogue reflecting on the durability of formalist approaches to photography is Chéroux, *Photographie*.

2 "A soon as the word 'genre' is sounded, as soon as it is heard, as soon as one attempts to conceive it, a limit is drawn. And when a limit is established, norms and interdictions are not far behind." Derrida, "Law of Genre," 202.

3 Notwithstanding the logical absurdity of this designation (all photographic imagery is an "aftermath" of the moment represented), this term has come to refer to a form of practice that blurs boundaries between photojournalistic imagery, often made in theaters of war (initially intended for mass media reproduction and dissemination) and art photography. Exemplified by photographers such as Simon Norfolk, Luc Delahaye, and Sophie Ristelhueber, among others, its characteristics are scale (large and very large) and emphasis on the physical terrain rather than human subjects. Such work tends to minimize action or dramatic event and is without any textual support or information relating to its subject. See, in this regard, Campany, "Safety in Numbness"; Roberts, "Photography after the Photograph"; James, "Making an Ugly World Beautiful"; and Tello, "Aftermath Photography."

4 As for "tableau," like other aesthetic mystifications that cluster around photographic production, this concept aligns camera-made imagery not merely with the history of easel painting but, even more extravagantly, with history painting itself. Olivier Lugon traces the invention and development of this putative genre in "Avant la forme Tableau." His genealogy includes Chevrier and Lingwood, *Une autre objectivité*; Chevrier, "Aventures de la forme tableau"; Chevrier and David, "Actualité de l'image"; and Chevrier, "Tableau and the Document of Experience." Chevrier's notions have thus born fruit in Anglophone criticism, especially in Fried's *Why Photography Matters*.

5 Jeff Wall, possibly the most famous figure among Canadian artists *ever*, is unquestionably the major protagonist in this development. His commanding position in contemporary art and photography criticism (theoretical, aesthetic, philosophical, academic, etc.) has been facilitated by his own writing and interviews, which have provided a form of an "authoritative" vade mecum to his own production. And while there have been other (but few) artist/theorists in photography (e.g., Victor Burgin, Allan Sekula, and Martha Rosler), none has had the same kind of legitimation, either discursively or in the market.

6 Thus, when Bernd Stiegler writes in the first sentence of his essay "Photography as the Medium of Reflection" that "photography is the technical medium of realism," he implies that there is no structural contradiction between concepts of realism and all the complex mediations of representational media, analogue photography included. In any case, the issue of photographic realism, given its best-known twentieth-century formulation in Bazin's "The Ontology of the Photographic Image," has itself a lengthy bibliography, both supporting and contesting the medium's realist definitions. With regard to the fortunes of specialized periodicals devoted to photography as a discrete medium, these of course continue to exist, whether in the form of specialized publications (e.g., *History of Photography, Aperture, Afterimage, Eikon, Études Photographiques, Camera Austria, Foam, Fotogeschichte*, etc.) or in popular mass media journals. As for the concept of photography as a medium based on analogue representation, Kaja Silverman's recent book, *The Miracle of Analogy*, posits that *every* aspect of the medium, including its chemistry, its physical properties, and its psychological affects, is not to be located in its semiotic status (i.e., the photograph as both index and icon) but springs from its *essential* identity as analogical.

7 "Visual turn" and "pictorial turn" are generally associated with the writing of W. J. T. Mitchell, in, for example, "Picture Theory," and in many related essays that have appeared in the journal *Critical Inquiry* and elsewhere. But there exist similar and more or less contemporary versions in German and French theory as well.

8 William J. Mitchell seems to be one of the first to have coined the term "post-photographic" in his book *The Reconfigured Eye*, still one of the basic texts for understanding the shift to and consequences of electronic media.

9 Two recent books on photographic theory can stand as examples, although the bibliography drawing on Barthes and Benjamin in German, French, and English is enormous. See Elkins, *What Photography Is*, which duplicates the exact form of *Camera Lucida*, including short, numbered meditations on individual photographs, and Silverman, *Miracle of an Analogy*. Other influential studies include Cadava, *Words of Light*, and Batchen, *Photography Degree Zero*.

10 Enthusiastic reception to Flusser's work occurred earlier in Germany, in the early 1980s. See van der Meulen, "Vilém Flusser's Media Theory," 110.

11 See Krauss, "Reinventing the Medium."

12 One significant exception has to do with Walter Benjamin's use of the historical research of his friend Gisèle Freund in her doctoral thesis in *Photographie en France dans le XIX siécle*. Her significant contribution to photographic history is rarely

given its due. An English-language version of her dissertation was published in 1982 with the title *Photography and Society.*

13 To take one symbolic example, the orange uniforms used by the État Islamique (E. I., or Daech) for their prisoners were deliberately copied from the American military ones used in Guantanamo, Iraq, and Afghanistan.

Chapter 1. Inside/Out

Originally published as "Inside/Out" in the exhibition catalogue *Public Information: Desire, Disaster, Document* (San Francisco: San Francisco Museum of Modern Art, 1995).

1 Sontag, *On Photography*, 41–42.
2 Rosler, "In, Around, and Afterthoughts," 78. Sontag, *On Photography*, 12.
3 Sontag, *On Photography*, 42.
4 Benjamin, *A Short History of Photography*, 206.
5 Sontag, *On Photography*, 42.
6 SFMOMA, *Public Information: Desire, Disaster, Document.*
7 Goldin, *Ballad of Sexual Dependency*, 6. It is, however, important to note that the original format of *The Ballad of Sexual Dependency* was a slide/audio work involving more than seven hundred images. The specific nature of this format; the sound track that organizes, accompanies, and counterpoints the images; the darkness in which the work is viewed by the spectator; the speed with which the images flash by; its temporal, evanescent structure; and, lastly, its intentionally "spectacularizing" form all decisively distinguish it from the book version of the same project. Nevertheless, in exploring the modalities of the inside/outside opposition, and given my emphasis on the medium of still photography, I have based my discussion of Goldin on the book versions of her projects.
8 L. Clark, *Tulsa*, n.p.
9 L. Clark, *Teenage Lust*, n.p.
10 L. Clark, *Perfect Childhood*, n.p.
11 "Le film commencerait dans l'eblouissement de l'été, en Allemagne de l'Est, puis en Pologne. Juste le regard de quelqu'un qui passe, quelqu'un qui n'a pas totalement accès a cette réalité, Peu a peu, alors qu'on pénètre plus avant dans le pays, l'été s'éteint pour faire place a l'automne, un automne sourd et blanc, recouvert par une masse de brouillard. Dans la campagne, des hommes et des femmes presque couchés sur la terre noire d'Ukraine, se confondant avec elle, ramassent des betteraves. Non loin d'eux, la route défoncée par le passage continuel des camions déglingues dont s'échappe une lunée noire. Et c'est l'hiver en Moscou ou le film se resserrera. Laissera sans doute percevoir quelque chose de ce monde déboussole avec cette impression d'après-guerre ou chaque jour passe semble être une victoire. Cela peut sembler terrible et sans poids, mais au milieu de tout cela, je monterai des visages, qui des qu'ils sont isolés de la masse, expriment quelque chose d'encore intouché et souvent le contraire de cette uniformité qui parfois nous frappe dans le mouvement des foules, le contraire de notre uniformité a nous aussi. Sans

faire trop de sentiment, je dirais que ce sont des visages pas gâtés et qui s'offrent; se donnent comme ils sont, et effacent par moment sentiment de perte, de monde au bord du gouffre qui parfois vous étreint lorsque vous traversez l'Est comme je viens de le faire."

## Chapter 2. Written on the Body

Originally published as "Written on the Body," in *Visible Light: Photography and Classification in Art, Science and the Everyday*, ed. by Chrissie Iles and Russell Roberts, 69–81. Exhibition catalogue, (Oxford: Museum of Modern Art Oxford, 1997).

1 Breton, *Surrealism and Painting*, 1.
2 Foster, "Preface," ix.
3 The term is W. F. Haug's. See Haug, *Critique of Commodity Aesthetics.*
4 These are all titles of books that have appeared in the past decade; the list could, of course, be expanded.
5 Valéry, "Nude," 48.
6 Pacteau, *Symptom of Beauty*, 16.
7 Rose, "Sexuality in the Field of Vision," 228.
8 Contemporaries of von Gloeden who constructed thematically similar tableaux (for example, naked boys, pastoral settings, Greek togas, etc.) are Thomas Eakins, working in Philadelphia, and F. Holland Day, working in Boston. See for example, Danly and Leibold, *Eakins and the Photograph;* and the exhibition catalogue edited by Fritz Clattenburg, *Photographic Work of F. Holland Day.*
9 Barthes, *Taormina*, n.p.
10 Burgin, "Photography, Phantasy, Fiction," 189–90. See, too, in this regard, Metz, "Photography and Fetish," 80–90.
11 Baudry, "Basic Cinematographic Apparatus," 28.
12 Marx, "Eighteenth Brumaire of Louis Bonaparte," 608.
13 Von Gloeden did in fact on occasion use a paste of oil, milk, and glycerine as a form of "body makeup" on his models, masking imperfections and approximating the flesh to marble. See Pohlmann, *Wilhelm von Gloeden.*
14 Freud did not believe that male or female genitals could be perceived as beautiful: "'Beauty' and 'attraction,'" he wrote, "are originally attributes of the sexual objects. It is worth remarking that the genitals themselves, the sight of which is always exciting, are nevertheless hardly ever judged to beautiful; the quality of beauty seems, instead, to attach to secondary sexual characters." Freud, *Civilization and its Discontents*, 32. For a discussion of the reasons for the small genitals of the idealized male nude, see Solomon-Godeau, *Male Trouble.*
15 See, in this regard, Barthes, *Taormina.*
16 Foucault, *History of Sexuality*, 107.
17 Kuhn, "Lawless Seeing," 22.
18 The anonymous photographs in the exhibition are from the Kinsey Institute Archive. The circumstances under which Kinsey collected, organized, and classified what eventually became an archive of over 75,000 images is a striking confirmation

of Foucault's arguments in *The History of Sexuality*. As James Crump has described this archive, "Kinsey's methodology of taxonomically ordering human sexual behaviours and their visual analogues was rooted in a lifetime of collecting that reached its apogee during his career as a scientist. The immense archive of photography should be seen in this context—of ordering, collecting, and assembling a paradigmatic visual resource that reflects usefully upon its subject, in this case human sexuality." Crump, "Kinsey Institute Archive," 1–12. Compare with Foucault's description: "'Sexuality': the correlative of the slowly developed discursive practice which constitutes the *scientia sexualis*. The essential features of this sexuality are not the expression of a representation that is more or less distorted by ideology, or of a misunderstanding caused by taboos; they correspond to the functional requirements of a discourse that must produce its truth. Situated at the point of intersection of a technique of confession and a scientific discursivity, where certain major mechanisms had to be found for adapting them to one another . . . sexuality was defined as being 'by nature'; a domain susceptible to pathological processes, and hence one calling for therapeutic or normalising interventions; a field of meaning to decipher; the site of processes concealed by specific mechanisms; a focus of indefinite causal relations; and an obscure speech . . . that had to be ferreted out and listened to." Foucault, *History of Sexuality,* 68.

19 On the conditions and market for such photographs, see McCauley, *Industrial Madness*. For a discussion of some of the larger implications of nineteenth-century erotic and pornographic photography, see my essays "Reconsidering Erotic Photography" and "Legs of the Countess."

20 Freud, "Fetishism," 155.

21 Willemen, "Letter to John," 178.

22 Willemen, "Letter to John," 179.

23 Kuhn, "Lawless Seeing," 23.

24 L. Williams, "Film Body," 507–34.

25 L. Williams, "Film Body," 509.

26 L. Williams, "Film Body," 512.

27 Williams's recognition of the excessive marking of difference in the human section of Muybridge's *Animal Locomotion* has a lengthy iconographic tradition. For example, certain of the seventeenth-century anatomical Venuses modeled in wax are embellished with necklaces in addition to long hair; in one of William Hunter's obstetrical drawings of the gravid uterus, a book is propped at the vagina; wax models of the faces of women with skin diseases at the Hôpital Saint-Louis in Paris are provided with wigs or lace caps.

## Chapter 3. The Family of Man

Originally published as "The Family of Man: Refurbishing Humanism for a Postmodern Age," in Jean Back and Viktoria Schmidt-Linsenhoff, *Family of Man, 1955–2001: Humanism and Postmodernism: A Reappraisal of the Photo Exhibition by Edward Steichen* (Marburg, Germany: Jonas Verlag, 2005), 28–55.

1 With some significant omissions, however. Eric J. Sandeen makes a great deal of the fact that the photograph of the atomic bomb mushroom cloud positioned prominently toward the end of the original exhibition at MoMA was not reproduced in the exhibition catalogue. See Sandeen, *Picturing an Exhibition: The Family of Man and 1950s America* (Albuquerque: University of New Mexico Press, 1995).

2 Allan Sekula, who saw the reconstituted version in Luxembourg in 2001, has interesting things to say about it in his essay, "Between the Net and the Deep Blue Sea (Rethinking the Traffic in Photographs)," *October* 102 (autumn, 2002), 3–34.

3 Barthes, "Great Family of Man," 12.

4 Schmidt-Linsenhoff, "Banalität des Guten."

5 See Sandeen, *Picturing an Exhibition,* as well as Whitfield, *Culture of the Cold War.*

6 Schmidt-Linsenhoff, "Banalität des Guten," 70.

7 Wollen, "Introduction," 10.

8 Wollen, "Introduction," 10.

9 Second comes Rapho with thirteen pictures, Black Star with ten, Pix with seven, and Brackman with four. Then there are perhaps half a dozen other agencies represented by one photo, with the exception of Sovfoto, which had three. Added to the Magnum photographs, this comes to something like 13 percent of the total show. *Vogue* was represented by nine, *Fortune* by seven, *Argosy* by seven (all by Homer Page), *Ladies Home Journal* by four; *Popular Photography* by three, *Seventeen* by one, *Glamour* by one, *Harper's Bazaar* by one, *Time* by one, the British magazine *Picture Pos*t by one, and *Du,* the only European picture magazine included, by one. This is about 22 percent of the exhibition.

10 These were as follows: Robert Doisneau, Helen Levitt, Manuel Álvarez Bravo, Bill Brandt, Édouard Boubat, Harry Callahan (two), Nat Farbman (five of Bechuanaland, in addition to his *Life* pictures), and Robert Frank (four). Lastly, there are three photographs of Eskimos from the book *Three Lions* by Robert Harrington.

11 Althusser, "Ideology and Ideological State Apparatuses," 172.

12 This central principle in the exhibition's conception and organization has been noted by numerous critics. But see the excellent essay by Segalen, "Family of Man."

13 Benjamin, "Author as Producer," 234.

14 Phillips, "Judgment Seat of Photography."

15 Phillips, "Judgment Seat of Photography," 223.

16 Phillips, "Judgment Seat of Photography," 246.

17 Phillips, "Judgment Seat of Photography," 246.

18 "Que peut enseigner un père sinon la fleur de la culture de son pays? . . . La place du Père dans les photos-titres de la famille, au coeur de l'exposition, n'est pas innocente: toujours à l'arrière, debout, la tête dépassant légèrement celle des femmes, mères ou enfants. Le Père, c'est le sommet de la pyramide, la source de vie, le coeur existentiel du noyau famille, de la société, de la nation, de la grande famille des hommes. " Melon, "Patriarchal Family," 56–57.

19 See, for example, Ehrenreich, *Hearts of Men*; and Modleski, *Feminism without Women*. Modleski's discussion of *The Incredible Shrinking Man* is especially interesting.

20 Wylie, *Generation of Vipers*; Riesman, *Lonely Crowd*; Whyte, *Organization Man*.

21 Sekula, "Traffic in Photographs," 95.

22 Rogoff, "Subjects/Spaces/Places," 172.

23 This work was exhibited at the Galerie Metropole, Vienna in 1993 and exists as a catalogue: *The Family of Austrians* (Stuttgart: Sammlung Karola Grässlin, 1993).

24 Barthes, "Great Family of Man," 163.

## Chapter 4. Torture at Abu Ghraib

Originally published as "Torture à Abou Ghraib: les médias et leur dehors," *Multitudes* 1/2007 (No 28), 211–31.

1 In this essay, I use the term "torture" to characterize much if not most of the violence—physical and psychological—employed against prisoners at Abu Ghraib. However, the term used in official government language from the White House on down to the military, as well as in the American press (i.e., the *New York Times*, the *Washington Post*, etc.), is "abuse," or, in bureaucratese, "enhanced interrogation techniques." This usage is clearly determined by political rather than ethical considerations. In an article by Tom Wright, the word "torture" appears only once, and that is because it figures in the document's name. See Tom Wright, "U.S. Defends Rights Record before U.N. Panel in Geneva," *New York Times*, May 6, 2006. International covenants and other human rights documents of necessity use the most general definitions of torture, so there is no universal consensus as to whether waterboarding does or does not constitute torture. Nowhere is the politics of language use more evident than in the differing views on the appropriateness of the word "torture" to describe what happened at Abu Ghraib, Bagram, and Guantanamo ("torture" would be a violation of the human rights agreements to which the United States is a signatory). See Giles Hewitt, "Treading a Torturous Path around the 'T' Word," *Agence France-Presse*, May 30, 2004. The US government and military have been concerned, however, since 2001, to redefine the accepted meanings of the word. See the appendices in "Torture and Truth in Words and Pictures," in Danner, *Torture and Truth*.

2 The pornographic aspects of the torture have been much commented upon, with left and right drawing (predictably) very different conclusions. As reported by Frank Rich, for example, Charles Colson, a former Watergate felon born again as a Christian preacher, attributed the torture to "a steady diet of MTV and pornography." See Frank Rich, "It Was the Porn That Made Them Do It," *New York Times*, May 30, 2004.

3 There is a substantial bibliography on the psychology and sociology of torture, but with respect to the "ordinariness" of those who abused or tortured detainees in Abu Ghraib prison, see especially Conroy, *Unspeakable Acts, Ordinary People*.

4 There are, of course, numerous precedents for these collective photographic portraits; soldiers, communards, and concentration camp personnel—all have produced visual documentation of their activities. But, as I will argue, the pictures from Abu Ghraib are fundamentally different from their predecessors.

5 See Human Rights Watch annual reports at http://www.hrw.org. As a recent article demonstrates, however, both the rationale and the practice of prisoner abuse, if not torture, were originally developed for the interrogation of prisoners held in Guantanamo Bay. On December 2, 2002, secretary of defense Donald Rumsfeld gave his formal approval for the use of "hooding," "exploitation of phobias," "stress positions," "deprivation of light and auditory stimuli," and other coercive tactics ordinarily forbidden by the Army Field Manual. See, in this respect, and with regard to other aspects of the White House and Defense Department's legal rationales for torture, Jane Mayer, "Annals of the Pentagon: The Memo," *New Yorker,* February 27, 2006.

6 See, for example, US Dept. of Justice, Office of Legal Counsel, "Memorandum for Alberto Gonzales," August 1, 2002: "Physical pain amounting to torture must be equivalent in intensity to the pain accompanying serious physical injury, such as organ failure, impairment of bodily function, or even death." Danner, *Torture and Truth,* 115.

7 Rush Limbaugh, for example, compared the torture at Abu Ghraib to fraternity hijinks. During his May 4, 2004, broadcast, he commented, "This is no different than what happens at the Skull & Bones initiation. . . . I'm talking about people having a good time. These people—you ever heard of emotional release? You ever heard of needing to blow some steam off?" Maureen Dowd, "Shocking and Awful," *New York Times,* May 6, 2004.

8 The primary sources I have used in this essay with respect to actual events, investigations, etc., are Danner, *Torture and Truth*; and Strasser, *Abu Ghraib Investigations.*

9 Tom Wright, "U.S. Defends Itself on Inmate Abuse," *New York Times,* May 9, 2006. In the Abu Ghraib case, as of this writing—July 2014—only eleven low-ranking military personnel involved have ever received prison sentences, ranging from ninety days to six and a half years served of a ten-year sentence (i.e., Charles Graner).

10 The photographs exhibited at the New-York Historical Society were drawn from the collection of James Allen and were later published in Allen, *Without Sanctuary.* See, for example, Apel, "Torture Culture."

11 Eisenman, *Abu Ghraib Effect.*

12 And, I would add, made by digital rather than analogue cameras. For while in theory the digital cameras used in Abu Ghraib are by definition technically distinct from the indexical properties of analogue representation, the cameras and videos were used no differently than analogue cameras, nor, apparently, were they manipulated.

13 This is clearly the case with the photographs made by Sabrina Harman, one of the protagonists in the Abu Ghraib torture archive whose images include Iraqi children at play and her own mugging for the camera over the corpse of a dead prisoner. Philip Gourevitch, whose original essay on Harman in the *New Yorker* was expanded into the book *Standard Operating Procedure,* coauthored with Errol Morris, strives mightily to exculpate Harman from the general sadism she photographed, and considers her touristic snaps of Iraq and others of children as indices

of her ethical distance from the others of her cohort. Morris's film of the same title, made in 2008, reiterates this position.

14 See Kosofsky Sedgwick, *Between Men.*

15 The notion that rape is an act of power rather than sexuality as such was the thesis of Susan Brownmiller's groundbreaking study *Against Our Will: Men, Women, and Rape.* For many, one of the most shocking aspects of the Abu Ghraib visual archive appears to have been the role of women within it. But why should the existence of women torturers be so shocking? In part, the dismay occasioned at the sight of wholesome-looking young white women mugging over corpses testifies to cherished beliefs about women's putative moral sensibilities. However, in the locus classicus of pornographic literature, namely de Sade's novels, the importance of women as participants or even orchestrators of torture is a central feature. Indeed, the role of women as torturers is a subject that the greatest "pornographic" writers have explored, doubtless for its subversion of traditional myths of femininity. See Norberg, "Libertine Whore." Similarly, the complex reworking of the erotic in Georges Bataille and Angeles Carter include "de-sublimatory" approaches to the representation of both female sexuality and sensibility.

16 See Apel, "Torture Culture"; Hazel Carby, "A Strange and Bitter Crop: The Spectacle of Torture," *Open Democracy,* October 11, 2004, https://www.opendemocracy.net/media-abu_ghraib/article_2149.jsp; and Susan Sontag, "Regarding the Torture of Others," *New York Times Magazine,* May 23, 2004.

17 *Final Report of the Independent Panel to Review DoD Detention Operations (The Schlesinger Report)* by James R. Schlesinger, Harold Brown, Tillie K. Fowler, and General Charles A. Horner (USAF-Ret.), August 2004. Reprinted in Danner, *Torture and Truth.*

18 Danner has discussed the ways in which the defense of the Abu Ghraib soldiers, MPs, and others sought to distinguish between what he calls the "celebrity abuses" and other interrogation techniques: "The key strategy of the defense is both to focus on the photographs and to isolate the acts they depict—which, if not the most serious, are those with the most political effect—from any inference that they may have resulted, either directly or indirectly, from policy. Thus, the dogged effort to isolate these acts as 'violence/sexual abuse incidents' that originated wholly in the minds of sadistic military police during the wee hours, and that, above all, had nothing whatever to do with what was done 'to set the conditions' for interrogation—even though this division is quite artificial and many of the latter activities . . . were conducted by precisely the same people and were equally, or more, disgusting, sadistic and abusive." Danner, *Torture and Truth,* 40.

19 That these are in part deeply misogynistic (as in the analogous case of Orthodox Judaism, in which menstrual blood or menstruating women are "unclean") is in the present context irrelevant.

20 A POW, under international covenant, is required to give only name, rank, and serial number. It was, needless to say, a central feature of the Bush administration's "war on terror" to deny Afghani or Iraqi insurgents the status of POWs, who would,

as such, normally be covered by the Geneva Conventions. Hence the category of "unlawful combatant." See Danner, *Torture and Truth.*

21 "Whether the sexual acts were performed or simulated, the prisoners were forced into the position of pornographic 'actors.' Significantly, the hundreds of pictures seen by Congress after the scandal erupted included not only acts of torture upon prisoners but (reputedly) acts of sexual intercourse among the guards themselves. The soldiers who took the pictures knew that in both instances, they were making porn (albeit in different subgenres). There was no other reason to record the tortures; it was, in fact, self-incriminating and stupid by all practical standards. Except that the idea of recording the acts of torture was, to a significant extent, the inspiration to commit them." Alessandro Camon, "American Torture, American Porn," *Salon,* June 7, 2004, http://www.salon.com/2004/06/07/torture_37/.

22 A selection of the Abu Ghraib pictures was exhibited at the International Center of Photography in New York City (September 17–November 28, 2004). See the thoughtful review by Heartney, "War and Its Images."

23 W. J. T. Mitchell has discussed the symbolic resonance of the hooded Iraqi tricked out with wires and the reasons for its iconic status. See Mitchell, "Sacred Gestures," 18.

24 See Mitchell, *Cloning Terror.*

25 Debate continues about the actual identity of the hooded man. See Kate Zernicke, "Cited as Symbol of Abu Ghraib, Man Admits He Is Not in Photo," *New York Times,* March 18, 2006.

26 These Freedom of Information Act lawsuits were first filed in October 2003, for the purpose of documenting the abuse of detainees held in US custody abroad, well before the release of the first set of images from the prison nearly seven months later. These lawsuits resulted in the release of more than ninety thousand pages of government documents on issues of detainee treatment in Iraq and Afghanistan, and at the US military prison in Guantanamo Bay, Cuba.

27 *Salon* obtained the files and other electronic documents from one of the investigators involved with (or close to) the army's Criminal Investigation Command (CID). The material, which includes more than 1,000 photographs, videos, and supporting documents from the CID, may not represent all of the photographic and video evidence that pertained to that investigation. According to the army's own accounting, the "review of all of the computer media submitted to this office revealed a total of 1,325 images of suspected detainee abuse, 93 video files of suspected detainee abuse, 660 images of adult pornography, 546 images of suspected dead Iraqi detainees, 29 images of soldiers in simulated sexual acts, 20 images of a soldier with a Swastika drawn between his eyes, 37 images of military working dogs being used in abuse of detainees, and 125 images of questionable acts." Based on time signatures of the digital cameras used, all the photographs and videos were taken between October 18, 2003, and December 2003.

28 Sontag, *On Photography.*

29 This argument was one of the central themes in the Situationist critique of mass media in capitalist society. See Debord, *Society of the Spectacle.*

30 Sontag, *On Photography*, 20.

31 The war that provided the immediate context for her discussion of recent war photography was the war in Bosnia.

32 Sontag, *Regarding the Pain of Others*, 310.

33 Sontag, "Regarding the Torture of Others," n.p.

34 Giroux, "What Might Education Mean," 3–22.

35 Giroux, "What Might Education Mean," 6.

36 Giroux, "What Might Education Mean," 6. "Photographs demand an ability to read within and against the representations they present and to raise fundamental questions about how they work to secure particular meanings, desires, and investments. As a form of public pedagogy, photographic images have the potential to call forth from readers modes of witnessing that connect meaning with compassion, a concern for others, and a broader understanding of the historical and contemporary contexts and relations that frame meaning in particular ways. Critical reading demands pedagogical practices that short-circuit common sense, resist easy assumptions, bracket how images are framed, engage meaning as a struggle over power and politics, and as such refuse to posit reading (especially images) exclusively as an aesthetic exercise, positing it also as a political and moral practice."

37 The latest report gives little cause for optimism. See Siems, *Torture Report*. See as well the ongoing searchable website by the American Civil Liberties Union, http://www.aclu.org/blog/national-security/torture-report, as well as the relevant chapters in Danner, *Stripping Bare the Body*.

## Chapter 5. Harry Callahan

This essay was first presented at a conference on Harry Callahan held at the Center for Creative Photography in Tucson, Arizona, in 2008.

1 The conference on Harry Callahan for which the first version of this essay was written was actually more a celebration of the photographer than anything else. It was the first conference I had ever attended consecrated to a single photographer. It was chaired by John Pultz, who at that time worked for the Center for Creative Photography and who subsequently published his study of Callahan's street pictures in the period 1941–43. Among the participants were several photographers, now middle-aged, who had been Callahan's students, many of whom reminisced fondly about him, and elegized his gifts as a teacher. I was the only woman speaker, and the only one who did not share in the celebratory spirit of the others. But, as I have remarked elsewhere, art photography discourse is descriptive, informational, and euphoric; it is not what one could call a critical discourse. For the present version of the essay, aside from some rewriting, I have added to the bibliography extensively, in order to give the reader a much more encompassing set of references, some of which appeared only after my essay was first published. Since it was first written, exhibitions, catalogues, monographs, and articles on street photography have continued to increase, and there has been with street photography, as with other types of photography, an integration with contemporary art as such (e.g.,

Beat Streuli, Philip-Lorca diCorcia, and many others). Despite differences in scale (the latter forms are always big, often very big) and technology (e.g., digital imaging), it does not seem to me that the basic arguments made here have been made irrelevant to current practice.

2 Pultz, *Harry Callahan*, 35.

3 Sherman, "Introduction," 7.

4 Bunnell, *Harry Callahan*, 42.

5 His first exhibition at MoMA was in 1949; before that he was featured in a four-person show in 1948. MoMA owns 250 of Callahan's photographs.

6 Derrida, "Law of Genre," 56.

7 Westerbeck and Meyerowitz, *Bystander*.

8 See as well Geoffrey Batchen's essay "Vernacular Photographies," which makes an argument very similar to mine: "As a *parergon*, vernacular photography is the absent presence that determines its medium's historical and physical identity; it is that thing that decides what proper is not. Truly to understand photography and its history, therefore, one must closely attend to what that history has chosen to repress." Batchen, *Each Wild Idea*, 59.

9 See de Thezy and Debuison, *Charles Marville*; Annan, *Photographs*; Nesbit, *Eugène Atget*.

10 Mensel, 'Kodakers Lying in Wait,' 25.

11 Mensel, 'Kodakers Lying in Wait,' 29

12 Mensel, 'Kodakers Lying in Wait,' 32.

13 Sarah Parsons traces the history of privacy laws in relation to photography in her fascinating account "Privacy, Photography, and the Art Defense." Discussing the *Harvard Law Review* essay of 1890 written by Samuel Warren and future United States Supreme Court justice Louis Brandeis, titled "The Right to Privacy," Parsons notes that their concept of "the right to be left alone" was prompted by their awareness of "instantaneous photographs and newspaper enterprise" that invaded "the sacred precincts of private and domestic life." She notes that Warren and Brandeis worried that "since the latest advances in photographic art have rendered it possible to take pictures surreptitiously, the doctrines of contract and of trust are inadequate to support the required protection, and the law of tort must be resorted to." Her essay appears in *Revealing Privacy*. See as well Richardson, "Candid Camera"; and Zeronda, "Street Shootings," 1131.

14 The case of Arrington vs. The *New York Times* Company is also relevant here. As Philip Gefter outlined, "Clarence Arrington, whose photograph, taken without his knowledge while he was walking in the Wall Street area, appeared on the cover of the *New York Times Magazine* in 1978 to illustrate an article titled 'The Black Middle Class: Making It.' Arrington said the picture was published without his consent to represent a story he did not agree with. The New York Court of Appeals held that The *Times*' First Amendment rights trumped Arrington's privacy rights." See Philip Gefter, "Street Photography: A Right or Invasion?," *New York Times*, March 17, 2006. For an excellent survey of the issues raised in street photography, see Gross, Katz, and Ruby, *Image Ethics*.

15 Gische, J. Nussenzweig v DiCorcia 2006 NY Slip Op 50171(U) [11 Misc 3d 1051(A)] Supreme Court, New York County February 8, 2006 (http://www.courts.state.ny.us/reporter/3dseries/2006/2006_50171.htm).

16 A number of the essays in *Image Ethics* address these issues in depth.

17 I am indebted to Mary Panzer for reference to this book. See Ehrenburg and Lissitzky, *My Paris*. See also Wolf, "Author as Photographer."

18 Ehrenburg and Lissitzky, *My Paris*, n.p.

19 Freund, *Photography and Society*, 119. The first English edition of the book was published in 1980.

20 Cartier-Bresson, *Decisive Moment*, n.p.

21 Cartier-Bresson quoted in Zeronda, "Street Shootings," 1132. This highly informative article traces the history of legislation and lawsuits in the United States that have to do with "unauthorized" photography in public space.

22 There have, of course, been women photographers who photographed on the street (i.e., Berenice Abbott, Helen Levitt, and the FSA photographers, as well as Europeans such as Ilse Bing and the newly rediscovered Eva Besnyö [1910–2003]. See Besnyö, *L'image Sensible*. In the work of Lisette Model, however, it is significant that most of her subjects are fully aware of being photographed, although there are exceptions. I have discussed this phenomenon elsewhere, but here it is sufficient merely to indicate that, at least historically, it is far more difficult for women to occupy the kind of subject position implicit in this kind of photographic practice. Nevertheless, the (posthumous) rediscovery of thousands of pictures made on the street by Vivian Maier, a French-born governess who spent most of her life in Chicago, raises the question as to whether there are other women photographers who produced such work but whose work has not yet come to light. See Maloof, *Vivian Maier*.

23 See Rosler's classic essay, "The Bowery in Two Inadequate Descriptive Systems." With respect to the unconscious subject, see Stein, "Making Connections with the Camera."

24 On these photographers, see the following monographic studies: Shamis, Kozloff, and Levinstein, *Moment of Exposure*; Tucker et al., *Louis Faurer*; Tonelli, Faurer, and Gossage, *Louis Faurer*; Stettner, *Early Joys*; Stettner, *Louis Stettner's New York*; and Stettner, *American Photographer*. See also Shahn, *Photographic Eye of Ben Shahn*; Shahn and Weiss, *Ben Shahn, Photographer*; and Faurer and Alexander, *Louis Faurer*. Recent exhibitions under the rubric "street photography" include *The Streets of New York, 1938–1958*, National Gallery of Art, Washington, DC (September 17, 2006–January 15, 2007); and *Street and Studio*, Tate Modern, London, and Museum Folkwang, Essen (May 22, 2008–January 31, 2009).

25 Obviously, there are many possible "visions" of the American city that have been expressed in photography—overwhelmingly (or so it seems) depicting New York City. For example, one might identify "pastoralized" images, such as those made by Alfred Steiglitz in the teens (*Two Towers–New York*, 1911), or those in Paul Strand's film *Manahatta*. There exists as well an elegiac vision exemplified by Berenice Abbott's *Changing New York* (after the example of Eugène Atget's memorialization

of old Paris). One might also make a category in which the skyscraper or, more generally, the modern built environment, is the focus of attention (like the Eiffel Tower for French photographers and émigrés such as Germaine Krull). One might make further subcategories: the city of the racial other (i.e., Aaron Siskind's *Harlem Document*), the city of poverty (i.e., Bruce Davidson's *East 100 Street*), the city of aggression or violence (i.e., William Klein, *Weegee*), and so forth. Moreover, if one factors in the tens of thousands of commercial stereo cards made of American cities nationwide from the 1870s until well after World War I, no generalization about subjective "vision" is either possible or desirable. Here, my observations are oriented toward very specific—that is, artistic—as opposed to vernacular photography. But what seems specific to the representation of this latter expression of the American metropolis is its fundamentally dyspeptic vision.

26 Berger, *Ways of Seeing*.

27 Davis, "Rhythms of the City," 16.

## Chapter 6. Caught Looking

Originally published as "Caught Looking" in the exhibition catalogue *Susan Meiselas: In History*, edited by Kristen Lubben (Göttingen, Germany: Steidl / International Center of Photography, 2009), 90–99. Text by Caroline Brothers, Edmundo Desnoes, and Abigail Solomon-Godeau.

1 As Victor Burgin long ago remarked, "Treating the photograph as an object-text, 'classic' semiotics showed that the notion of the 'purely visual' *image* is nothing but an Edenic fiction . . . whatever specificity might be attributed to photography at the level of the 'image' is inextricably caught up within the specificity of the social acts which attend that image and its meanings." Burgin, "Looking at Photographs," 145.

2 For a detailed history of the history and development of the project, see the excellent essays by Sylvia Wolf, "Behind the Ballyhoo," and Deirdre English, "Stripped Bare: Nude Girls and Naked Truths," in Meiselas, English, and Wolf, *Carnival Strippers*.

3 This genre can be traced from Larry Clark's 1971 *Tulsa* recording of the alcohol-drugs-and-guns lives and occasional deaths of his teenage friends through the more recent careers of Nan Goldin, Richard Billington, Wolfgang Tillmans, Jack Pierson, and many others. I have discussed the question of the photographer's relation to his or her milieu in the essay "Inside/Out." See also Rosler's withering discussion of Billington's work in her essay "Post-Documentary, Post-Photography?"

4 Meiselas and van Bruinessen, *Kurdistan*; Meiselas and International Center of Photography, *Encounters with the Dani*.

5 See English's essay "Stripped Bare" in Meiselas, English, and Wolf, *Carnival Strippers*.

6 In the introduction to *Carnival Strippers*, Meiselas analogizes the structure of the book to that of the performance it represents: "Any book allows its reader to distance himself. The curtain closing on the girl show stage is replaced by the page turning over. Like the show, the book represents coexistent aspects of a phenome-

non, one which horrifies, one which honors." Meiselas, English, and Wolf, "Introduction," *Carnival Strippers*.

7 According to Wolf, Meiselas felt a particular kinship with photographers such as Larry Clark, whose book *Tulsa* was published in 1971, and Danny Lyon, whose book *The Bikeriders* was published in 1968 (New York: Macmillan). Both books (neither of which employs text) are meant as collective portraits of marginal groups. Especially in the case of *Tulsa*, the photographer was himself part of the milieu he photographed. I would, however, also mention such a remarkable photographic book of the period as Eugene Richards, *Few Comforts or Surprises: The Arkansas Delta* (Cambridge, MA: MIT Press, 1973). The point here being that whatever the strengths or weaknesses of these forms of photographic documentary, the period seems to have witnessed a revival of this particular genre, a development linked to the relative vitality of leftist, progressive, or reformist politics.

8 Rosler, "Post-Documentary, Post-Photography?," 225.

9 For example, pictures shot by Meiselas in Nicaragua during the US-supported Contra War were deposited in the Magnum library. Once there, *Time* magazine, for example, could use a picture Meiselas took of people lined up at a Managua supermarket to receive free milk from the Sandinista government with a caption stating that the image depicted food shortages.

10 English notes that when Meiselas first brought her pictures to the recently founded *Ms.* magazine, the editors were not interested. This suggests that since *Carnival Strippers* did not function as a type of exposé reportage, it was unclear what the work was intended to *mean*.

11 This absence of an identifiable political position within the forms of photographic documentary has long been a target of left photographic criticism, a critique first developed in Walter Benjamin's well-known essay of 1936, "The Author as Producer." Many others, including Roland Barthes, Susan Sontag, and so on, have subsequently seconded Benjamin's criticism. But because *Carnival Strippers* departs in so many ways from the conventional forms of documentary, including its use of narrative structure and its deployment of the protagonists' voices, it is, as I have suggested, closer perhaps to the cinema verité of Frederick Wiseman than to those documentaries predicated on the silent image with or without explanatory captions.

12 Burgin, "Looking at Photographs," 146.

13 Freud, "Three Essays," 156.

14 The term is itself of modern coinage, the current meaning dating only to 1937, as the *Oxford English Dictionary* indicates (i.e., *Daily Telegraph*, [April 29, 1937]: "Can anything be said in defense of the present public interest in 'strip-tease' and nudist or semi-nudist displays on stage?").

15 Barthes, *Mythologies*, 84.

16 Barthes, *Mythologies*, 85

17 Barthes, *Mythologies*, 85.

18 Freud, "Fetishism," xxi.

19 See the classic essay by Mulvey, "You Don't Know What's Happening, Do You Mr. Jones?"

20 Apropos of heterosexuality, in his essay on fetishism Freud hypothesized that recourse to fetishism operates to prevent men from becoming homosexual. To state the obvious, it must be said that Freud was a man of his time, class, religion, and so on. He considered everything except heterosexual vaginal intercourse as more or less a deviation from the norm (even as he relativized the very concept of the normal), and in a number of his writings indicated his opinion that "no one" was spared the fright of their first perception of women's genitalia and "no one" could possibly find genitals "beautiful."

21 Meiselas, English, and Wolf, *Carnival Strippers,* 85.

22 Rosler, "Post-Documentary, Post-Photography?," 229.

## Chapter 7. Framing Landscape Photography

Originally published as "Framing Landscape Photography" 85–95 *From Corot to Monet: The Ecology of Impressionism* Edited by Stephen F. Eisenman. Milano: Skira and New York: Distributed by Rizzoli International Publications, 2010.

1 White and White, *Canvases and Careers.*

2 This group, called "amateurs" in photographic literature, needs to be distinguished from the ranks of professionals, for despite the occasional overlap, the first appearance of "landscape" in French photography is largely the work of amateurs.

3 Defined as a genre, landscape was also eligible for prizes. In France, however, it remained a secondary genre in the academic hierarchy of genres. It was not until 1817 that landscape painters were eligible for the prestigious Prix de Rome, but the form of landscape thus recognized was the classicizing *paysage historique.* Outside of academic hierarchies, however, and especially in England and the Netherlands, landscape paintings of all types and formats were copiously produced and collected.

4 Thus the enthusiasm of politically liberal art critics such as Théophile Thoré for the homely Dutch landscapes of the seventeenth century — art produced in a republic, not a monarchy; art that ostensibly celebrated the "real," not the ideal.

5 See John Berger's classic reading of the Gainsborough landscape *Mr. and Mrs. Andrews* in *Ways of Seeing,* and the major studies of British landscape by John Barrell and Anne Bermingham.

6 For example, in her essay "The Landscape in French Nineteenth-Century Photography," Françoise Heilbrun claims that "the first known French photograph is a landscape, a view of Gras taken by Joseph Nicéphore Niépce from his window in 1826." Aside from the fact that this picture shows Niépce's cobblestoned yard and a group of houses and walls, these first *essais* with the medium are more experimentally than aesthetically motivated. Here, Niépce merely photographed what was outside his window. Heilbrun, "Landscape," 349.

7 Krauss, "Photography's Discursive Spaces," 131–70. Krauss also points out in this essay that photographic views were attributed to the publisher, not to the photographer who had produced them. With respect to the enormous produc-

tion of stereographic imagery, see Earle, *Points of View*. The principle of the stereoscopic view was known in the eighteenth century, and there exists a pre-photographic tradition of such stereos made on glass or paper.

8 In photography's first twenty years, the technical deficiencies of the medium with respect to the registering of sky and clouds, or the limitations of orthochromatic as opposed to panchromatic negatives to register tonal differences, were given as reasons for its perceived limitations, as well as its inability to register color. See Lady Elizabeth Eastlake's summary of the state of photography in 1856, "Photography," 39–69.

9 Photographic journals of this period included *La Lumière* founded in 1851, which was founded by the Société héliographique (later the Société française de photographie, or SFP); the *Bulletin de la Société française de photographie,* founded in 1855; *Photographische Mitteilungen,* founded in 1864; and numerous others. In my context, amateur status does not indicate any lack of expertise but rather the distinction between the professional who did work for hire and maintained a commercial business, and those who were able to pursue photography without any commercial considerations. Commercial photographers were formally banned from membership in the SFP. In this respect, the structure of photographic societies mimicked that of the original art academies. All of which is to say that these photographers—mostly men (and a few women)—were people of independent means whose production should (but rarely is) be considered in relation to class privilege.

10 See McCauley, *Industrial Madness.*

11 Beginning with Isadore Taylor and Charles Nodier's twenty-four-volume *Voyages pittoresques et romantiques dans l'Ancienne France* (1820–78), there was a long tradition of publishing lithographically illustrated volumes featuring landscapes; wood engravings of landscapes featured as well in the art magazines of the period.

12 The photographic printing firm Blanquart-Evard, as well as the studio launched by Gustave Le Gray—both of which were intended to produce and distribute artistic photographs, including landscape—went bankrupt relatively quickly, indicating the absence of a viable market.

13 See Janis, *Art of French Calotype.*

14 See the exhibition catalogue and essay by Panzer, *Philadelphia Naturalistic Photography.*

15 Indeed, Talbot wrote that the impetus for his investigations derived from his desire to be able to "draw" the landscape views he was only imperfectly able to render in front of the motif.

16 Barbizon was the small village on the fringe of the forest where a number of the painters lived and worked. By the 1850s, it was a popular site for landscape tourism, and thus became the blanket designation of the artists who painted the forest of Fontainebleau.

17 To produce the effect of sky and clouds, photographers had recourse to combina-

tion printing (using two different negatives) or retouching. These were exemplified in Gustave Le Gray's seascapes made in the 1850s.

18 As these photographs have aged, especially the calotypes, they are transformed in their visual properties as much as in their referential ones. These features have been a significant factor in their recent rise in aesthetic, and thus market, value. Where the albumen print made from a collodion negative tends to fade uniformly to a paler version of itself, the calotype's aging can produce more variegated visual effects. As Grace Glueck observes in her article on Cuvelier, "The tonal richness and subtlety of Cuvelier's prints were heightened by his use of salted paper, paper coated with a sodium chloride emulsion that seemed to soak the image deep into the fibers. It was a slow technique that had already been replaced in his day by the more commercial albumen process. The salted paper also allowed for a range of subtle print colors, from eggplant to lavender and even blue-black." Glueck, "Capturing Fontainebleau Forest's Myriad Moods." The physical decay of the photograph, as the writer indicates, is part of its formal beauty. This means that we are looking at a quite different version of the picture now that it has acquired a patina of age, which heightens the effect of pastness, the aura of the elegiac. See also Malcolm Daniel's 1996 essay "Eugène Cuvelier: Photographer in the Circle of Corot."

19 Green, *Spectacle of Nature*, 79.

20 See Chagnon-Burke for an analysis of the different economies involved. The profits of the forest's lumber went directly into the household funds of the emperor, who in turn maintained the large number of workers necessary for the harvesting of trees and other kinds of forest and park management.

21 "Denoncourt gave the ancient oak trees of the Fontainebleau Forest names such as *Le Rageur, Le Sully, Le Henri IV, Le Déluge,* and *Le Gutenberg*. By 1893 there were 276 named trees, and 323 by 1916. The oldest still standing is named *Le Jupiter*. In Fontainebleau, *Le Rageur,* Corot presented the oak tree as a survivor, growing wild out of the boulder. While this tree embodied the symbolic qualities of longevity and endurance, it was also one of the most threatened species of the forest. In Fontainebleau, *Le Rageur,* Corot confronts the audience with a piece of nature, as if seized by a traveler on the move; the oak dominates, while the human presence lets us measure the real size of the tree. In one of the earliest articles on the School of Barbizon published in 1866 in *L'Artiste,* Hector Callias stressed the connection between the Barbizon painters and primordial France, comparing the painters to druids worshipping the oak tree." Chagnon-Burke, 75–76.

22 These were, however, themes addressed by Millet. Later, Pissarro's work in the forest was also focused on the laborers and peasants who lived off its wood and game.

23 Chagnon-Burke, "The Politicization of Nature," 103.

24 With respect to this subject in relation to painting, see the indispensable work of Robert Herbert, especially the essays on the Barbizon and peasant painters.

25 Barthes, "Rhetoric of the Image" and "Photographic Message," in *Image, Music, Text.*
26 French firm Ziegler and Company's close-up of tree roots might have been shot with artists' needs in mind.
27 Scharf, *Art and Photography*.

Chapter 8. The Ghosts of Documentary

Originally published in *Heterotopien: Perspektiven der intermedialen Ästhetik*, edited by Nadja Elia-Borer, Constanze Schellow, Nina Schimmel, Bettina Wodianka (Bielefeld: Transcript, 2013), 303–26.
1 This observation is anything but new, and virtually all reflections on contemporary photography take this uncoupling as their point of departure. One area of debate, however, is whether digital modes constitute a different medium from analogue forms, or indeed whether the very notion of medium specificity has now been dissolved or overcome. "Photography is somehow an anachronism now. It's disappearing while we talk. We are going to lose it soon and we are going to replace it with something that is still images but something very, very different. Photography: to draw in light. It's not that anymore, it's electronic." Tacita Dean quoted in Godfrey, "Photography Found and Lost," 91.
2 Morris, *Believing Is Seeing.*
3 Snyder and Allen, "Photography, Vision and Representation," 143–87.
4 Most recently, in Silverman's *The Miracle of Analogy or The History of Photography, Part I.* See, for example, the special issue of *differences*, "Indexicality: Trace and Sign," especially Doane's essay "Indexicality and the Concept of Medium Specificity," 128–50; Mulvey, "Index and the Uncanny"; and the discussions among the contributors in Elkins, *Photography Theory*.
5 Barthes, "Photographic Message" and "Rhetoric of the Image."
6 Altered, simulated, montaged, and other forms of photographic manipulation are the subject of a recent exhibition at the Metropolitan Museum of Art titled *Faking It: Manipulated Photography before Photoshop* (October 11, 2012–January 27, 2013).
7 Krauss, "Reinventing the Medium," 69.
8 Writing from a liberal political perspective, Ritchin proposes many ideas about the new possibilities offered by electronic media, including its uses in social media and for documentary and journalistic purposes. Ritchin, *After Photography*, 9. A more judicious evaluation is found in Mitchell's now standard study *The Reconfigured Eye*.
9 Ritchin, *After Photography*, 9.
10 Ebert, *New Media Invasion*, 134
11 Ebert, *New Media Invasion*, 135.
12 For example, Doane cites a similar comment by Paul Willemen: "An image of a person in a room need no longer mean that the person was in that particular room, or that such a room ever existed, or indeed that such a person ever existed.

Photochemical images will continue to be made, but the change in the regime of 'believability' will eventually leech all the resistance that reality offers to 'manipulation' from even those images [....] The digitally constructed death mask has lost any trace [...] of the dialectic between index and icon." Willemen, "Reflections on Digital Imagery," cited in Doane, "Indexicality and the Concept of Medium Specificity," 132.

13 See, for example, Mitchell's *The Reconfigured Eye*, as well Manovich's rebuttal to Mitchell, "Paradoxes of Digital Photography."

14 Rosen, *Change Mummified*, 314. From a quite different perspective, one more concerned with the processes of photographic reception, see Burnett, *Cultures of Vision*.

15 Snyder, "Picturing Vision."

16 Doane, "Introduction," *differences*, 5

17 "Photography is haunted by two chattering ghosts: that of bourgeois science and that of bourgeois art. The first goes on about the truth of appearances, about the world reduced to a positive ensemble of facts, to a constellation of knowable and possessable objects. The second specter has the historical mission of apologizing for and redeeming the atrocities committed by the subservient—and more than spectral—hand of science. This second specter offers us a reconstructed subject in the luminous person of the artist. Thus, from 1839 onward, affirmative commentaries on photography have engaged in a comic, shuffling dance between technological determinism and *auteurism*, between faith and the objective powers of the machine and the belief in the subjective, imaginative capabilities of the artist." Sekula, "Traffic in Photographs."

18 See Foucault, *Power/Knowledge*, 96; Tagg, *Burden of Representation*; Batchen, *Burning with Desire*; and Sekula, "Body in the Archive."

19 See my essay "Who Is Speaking Thus? Some Questions about Documentary."

20 "All in all, then, Grierson's phraseology appears to have become current almost as soon as he proposed it. This suggests less his own importance than a cultural conjuncture requiring some designation of the field he named: an arena of meaning centering on the authority of the real founded on the indexical trace, various forms of which were rapidly disseminated at all levels of industrial and now postindustrial culture." Rosen, "Document and Documentary," 66.

21 A number of important exceptions were those projects that were entrepreneurial and speculative. These are exemplified by Francis Frith's photographs of Egypt, and Matthew Brady's commissioned photographs of the American Civil War, for which he employed a team of photographers (notably Timothy O'Sullivan and Alexander Gardiner). It is possible that Roger Fenton's photographs made during the Crimean War were commissioned by William Agnew of the publishing firm Thomas Agnew & Sons.

22 The Missions Héliographiques were organized by the Commission of Historical Monuments; Salzmann was commissioned by the Ministry of Public Instruction; Charles Marville by the Administration of Public Works; Annan by the Glasgow City Improvement Trust; and O'Sullivan by the US Geological Survey, an agency of the US Department of the Interior.

23 As with John Thomson (another problematic conscript into the history of nineteenth-century documentary), it is necessary, as always, to retain the context of production: bourgeois anxieties about the dangerous classes, and the threat of their disorder, disease, and contagion. See Tagg, *Burden of Representation*; Stein, "Making Connections"; and Stange's discussion of Jacob Riis in Stange, *Symbols of Ideal Life*.

24 Mass Observation was a large-scale investigation into the habits and customs of the people of Britain, initiated in the city of Bolton in 1937 to monitor its "public morale." Between 1937 and 1938, Spender took over nine hundred pictures of the city and its residents. The official website of the project is http://boltonworktown.co.uk.

25 See, for example, E. Edwards, *Raw Histories*; and Pinney, *Photography and Anthropology*.

26 Tagg, *Burden of Representation*.

27 See the catalogue for the New York Jewish Museum's exhibition, Klein and Evans, *Radical Camera: New York's Photo League, 1936–1951*.

28 See, for example, Leonard Freed, *Black in White America* (1969); Lorraine Hansbury and James Baldwin, *The Movement* (1965); Magnum Photos, *America in Crisis 1969*; Herbert Cole, *House of Bondage* (1967); Phillip Jones Griffith, *Vietnam Inc.* (1971); Bruce Davidson, *East 100th St.* (1971); and Danny Lyon, *Conversations with the Dead* (1971).

29 Stott, *Documentary Expression*, 18. The reference in this list to the TVA (not then associated with environmental depredation but rather with electrification and the provision of clean water) is curious, but, as I have already suggested, neither documentary nor social documentary is a coherent category.

30 Stott, *Documentary Expression*, 25.

31 Stange, *Symbols of Ideal Life*, xiii.

32 Lugon, *Style documentaire*. Lugon, however, is not the only scholar to consider documentary as a style. "Documentary photography is an aesthetic mode or a style. Often the champions of documentary deny this, claiming their work is style-less, objective, and direct. Nevertheless, this work is always an approach to photography; a mode of representation predicated on the form of the document." S. Edwards, *Photography*, 28.

33 My translation. "Si [l'idée de document photographique] apparaît dans la littérature artistique, ce n'est que comme antonyme du terme 'art', les deux catégories s'excluent l'une l'autre. . . . Avant les années vingt, non seulement le documentaire ne constitue pas un genre esthétique mais il en est la négation." Lugon, *Style documentaire*, 15.

34 My translation. "L'inflexion de la notion de reportage social ne s'opère que de façon tardive, à la fin de la décennie, avec la promotion des images ce FSA. C'est autour d'elles que s'ordonne, vers 1938–1940, une soudaine vagues de textes, tous américains, cherchent non pas à inventer la notion de documentaires mais, pour la première fois, à en fixer solidement le sens." Lugon, *Style documentaire*, 10.

35 Stott, *Documentary Expression*, 62.

36 The landmark work here is Rosler, "The Bowery in Two Inadequate Descriptive Systems." For a recent summary of such critiques, see Entin, "Modernist Documentary."

37 Stange, *Symbols of Ideal Life*, xiv. Moreover, as she observes, "For the sponsor and the audience of the documentary exhibition or publication, the photograph necessarily took on meaning within a particular rhetorical framework created by its interaction with caption, text, and agency, even though the photographer and his or her subject did not always intend such a meaning or share its ideology."

38 On MoMA's aesthetic ideologies, see Phillips's indispensable and widely anthologized essay "The Judgment Seat of Photography," first published in *October*.

39 The introductory essay in *Things as They Are: Photojournalism in Context since 1955* summarizes some of photojournalism's various definitions, although Panzer and Caujolle's own subject is limited to photo stories in illustrated magazines. For a more thorough account beginning with the first uses of pictures in the illustrated press, see the exhibition catalogue by Lemeck and von Dewitz, *Kiosk*.

40 My translation. "Le photojournalisme est une catégorie fondamentalement instable et constamment reconfigurée par les discours. L'éthique de l'image de presse s'inscrit dans la perspective de ces reconfigurations historiques." The changing shape of photojournalism, especially as a salaried profession, is traced in Lavoie's fascinating account "La rectitude photojournalistique: Codes de déontologie, éthique et définition morale de l'image de presse." Lavoie, "Photojournalistic Integrity," which forms a chapter in his book *Photojournalismes*.

41 In addition to Lavoie, see Schwartz, "Objective Representation"; and Griffin, "Great War Photographs."

42 Griffin, "Great War Photographs," 153.

43 Although the reproduction of FSA photographs—like Lewis Hine's earlier photographs of child labor, recent immigrants, or sweated labor—could range from single images to narrative sequences depending on the requirements or specifications of the given publication. It must be noted, too, that in the even earlier production of Jacob Riis, the images did service as lantern slides in public presentations and lectures, as well as in books and pamphlets. See Stange, *Symbols of Ideal Life*.

44 Rosler, "Post-Documentary, Post-Photography?," 209–10.

45 Rosler, "Post-Documentary, Post-Photography?," 211. Italics in source.

46 Rosler, "Post-Documentary, Post-Photography?," 211. This critique is echoed by John Roberts in his book *The Art of Interruption*. Like Rosler, Roberts associates poststructuralism with the crisis of documentary, noting that "questions of social reference have been suppressed in the interests of privileging the avant-garde critique of representation" (3).

47 Roberts, "Photography," 284.

48 S. Edwards, *Photography*, 37.

49 See, for example, Stallabrass's sympathetic account, "Sebastião Salgado and Fine Art Journalism"; and Sassen, "Black and White Photography."

50 The small number of women photographers in these categories requires little explanation, and, with a few major exceptions, professional women photojournalists

on the battlefield are rare, despite the active presence of women photographers between and during the two world wars.

51 Weski, "Documentary Factor," 36.

52 See, for example, *Photography: New Documentary Forms* (Tate Modern, May 11, 2011–April 10, 2012); the artists included were Luc Delahaye, Mitch Epstein, Guy Tillim, Akram Zaatari. In the case of *Engaged Observers: Documentary Photography since the Sixties* (J. Paul Getty Museum, 2010), the criteria seems to have been some notion of parti pris, as the title implies. However, the inclusion of Larry Towell's black-and-white series on a Mennonite community, and Lauren Greenfield's series of adolescents at a weight-loss camp and well-to-do teenage girls in LA seem not entirely in keeping with such an agenda. My point here, however, is that any current group exhibition in a museum that bears the word "documentary" in its title will be equally random.

## Chapter 9. Inventing Vivian Maier

A version was originally published as "Inventing Vivian Maier" in the online magazine *Jeu de Paume*, September 16, 2013, http://lemagazine.jeudepaume.org/2013/09/vivian-maier-by-abigail-solomon-godeau/.

1 *Finding Vivian Maier* is a feature film documentary produced and directed by John Maloof and Charles Siskel. First shown at the Toronto Film Festival in 2013 and now in general release, it is one of several productions by Maloof, one of the principle holders of the work of Maier.

2 The most recent of the three books devoted to Maier is *Vivian Maier: Self-Portraits*, edited by John Maloof.

3 Krauss, "Photography's Discursive Spaces," 311–19. A somewhat revised version of her essay is reprinted in Krauss, *Originality of the Avant-Garde*.

4 See the recent exhibition and the monograph by Leo Rubenfien published in connection with the San Francisco Museum of Modern Art's exhibition *Garry Winogrand*.

5 According to the press release, "Record attendance at our recent Vivian Maier Exhibition, and continued interest from the Minneapolis community, inspired owners Orin and Abby Rutchick to open a permanent Vivian Maier gallery installation and theater dedicated solely to Maier's work. In the future, the MPLS Photo Center will feature additional Maier exhibitions, screen associated films and continue to offer print and book sales." http://www.vita.mn/crawl/249955231.html.

6 The Howard Greenberg Gallery advertises its wares as follows: "Our contemporary prints [of Maier] are made on request by master printer Steve Rifkin who also printed for Lisette Model and verified by the Maloof Collection. Prints are made with high quality archival paper, stamped on verso and are available in 12×12 inch in an edition of 15. Vintage Prints are also available for purchase. By definition, 'vintage' means original prints that are made at or around the time of the shooting of the image. From its archives, the Maloof Collection offers you the chance to acquire an original vintage print by Vivian Maier depending on its availability."

7 The principle holders of the archive, Maloof and Goldstein, are clearly earnest about their recognition of Maier's importance to the history of photography, and their desire to preserve her "legacy," but it would be also naive to ignore the fact that Maier's work has entered the marketplace well before entering into photography history. Therefore, it is the market, which has determined what gets printed, how it is printed, what subjects are privileged, and so forth. Certainly Maloof has become the most active entrepreneur of Maier's photographs, having produced two of the three monographs and the recent documentary. Somewhat ironically, according to Maloof, it was the late Allan Sekula, by no means a celebrant of the commodification of photography, who after seeing some of Maier's pictures posted on the web urged Maloof to preserve the negatives and to prevent disbursal of the collection.

8 Having learned recently of the existence of four "lost portfolios" (11×14 spiral-bound books containing vintage prints from the 1950s), Bannos thinks this conclusion might be premature. These portfolios were purchased at the 2007 auctions by an unnamed buyer who put them aside, unaware of the growing interest in Maier's work and persona. This purchaser put all portfolios up for sale at yet another auction in 2011, retaining one mounted print and six unmounted ones. Bannos recognized three of the prints when she saw them, raising the question of whether Maier had separated her "portfolio" negatives from the rest, possibly with some commercial intention in mind.

9 Until the 1920s, itinerant or studio photographers were invariably men, although there are exceptions. By the 1930s, there were a few women photographers working in public space (e.g., Ilse Bing, Germaine Krull, Marianne Breslauer, and others) and, in the United States, several women also employed by the WPA and FSA as professional photographers (e.g., Esther Bubley, Dorothea Lange, Marion Post Wolcott, Margaret Bourke-White, etc.). Nevertheless, even now, very few women photographers have taken urban streets as their photographic territory while any number of men, including contemporary photographers such as Beat Streuli and Philip-Lorca diCorcia, have made their reputations as art photographers with this type of photography.

10 On the basis of the descriptions provided by the previous owner of the portfolios, Bannos thinks that the four portfolios were organized into four subject categories: children, street photographs, European sites, and unconscious drunks.

11 Maier was in the New York area from the time she returned from Europe in April 1951. She worked in Southampton and in Brookville, New York, until her employment with a family on Riverside Drive from spring 1952 through 1953. It is clear that she was in New York City for at least some of that year, as she photographed Salvador Dalí in front of the Museum of Modern Art and dated the back of the print January 24, 1952—at the time the museum mounted an exhibition titled *Five French Photographers* (Henri Cartier-Bresson, Robert Doisneau, Brassaï, Willy Ronis, and Izis). Bannos thinks that Maier's exposure to this form of photography may have been a decisive influence.

12 Rosler, "In, Around, and Afterthoughts." This is why the history of the putative

genre of street photography exhibits so many examples of hidden cameras, surreptitious shooting, "detective cameras," and other deceptive practices that enable the photographer to shoot undetected.

13 Cartier-Bresson, *Mind's Eye,* 22.

14 Randy Kennedy, "The Heir's Not Apparent: A Legal Battle over Vivian Maier's Work," *New York Times,* September 5, 2014.

Chapter 10. Robert Mapplethorpe

Originally published as "A Tale of Two Mapplethorpes," http://blog.fotomuseum.ch/2014/04/3-a-tale-of-two-mapplethorpes/; and "Whitewash: Artist and Models," http://blog.fotomuseum.ch/2014/05/4-witewash-artist-and-models/, two blog entries for Fotomuseum, *Still Searching,* in spring 2014.

1 "Vingt-cinq ans après sa mort, l'événement est une occasion unique d'élever le célèbre photographe au rang des plus grands artistes de l'histoire, qui l'ont tant inspiré: Titien, Michel-Ange, Piero della Francesca, le Bernin, David, Dali, Duchamp, etc." Aubin, *Robert Mapplethorpe,* n.p. "Twenty-five years after his death, [this] event is a unique occasion to elevate the famous photographer to the rank of the greatest artists in history who so much inspired him: Titian, Michelangelo, Piero della Francesca, Bernini, David, Dali, Duchamp, etc."

2 As all art historians know, when producing the totem of the Great Artist, early work, if not juvenilia, *counts.* Thus, as part of the treatment, early prephotographic works were included from Mapplethorpe's time at the Pratt Institute, as well as some Joseph Cornell–like boxes (e.g., *Lamb*), collage works, drawings, and early Polaroids.

3 As curator of contemporary art at the Wadsworth Atheneum, and later at the Detroit Institute of Art, Wagstaff acquired 20th century art for his personal collection, which he subsequently sold for a considerable profit. Shortly after meeting Mapplethope, he began collecting nineteenth- and twentieth-century photography in the early stage of what became a boom market in the 1980s. This collection he eventually sold to the Getty for an undisclosed amount that is said to have been around five million dollars. After that, Wagstaff started collecting silver.

4 Isabel Wilkerson, "Clashes at Obscenity Trial on What an Eye Really Sees," *New York Times,* October 3, 1990.

5 Wilkerson, "Clashes at Obscenity Trial."

6 In 1989, the Institute of Contemporary Art at the University of Pennsylvania received thirty thousand dollars from the National Endowment for the Arts (NEA) to organize the retrospective *Robert Mapplethorpe: The Perfect Moment* to be held at the Corcoran Gallery of Art in Washington, DC. The exhibition was ultimately canceled as the gallery became involved in a larger attack on the funding of several controversial artists and their works, most notably photographer Andres Serrano's *Piss Christ* of 1987. The NEA's conservative opponents petitioned the agency to end its sponsorship of "morally reprehensible trash"; by the next year, a growing num-

ber of representatives were calling for a total phase out of the NEA. Vance, "War on Culture," 107.

7 Fanon, *Black Skin, White Masks*, 169–70.

8 I mean "enterprise" in the dictionary sense, insofar as the name Robert Mapplethorpe encompasses his foundation, his galleries, the individual dealers, the museums that exhibit or acquire his work, its auction market activities, the corporations that sponsor or own his work, the (vast) publishing of monographs or coffee table books dedicated to his work, and so forth.

9 See, for example, Morrisoe, *Mapplethorpe: A Biography*. See as well the Fritscher interview "Take 17: Mapplethorpe Mentor George Dureau."

10 The corporate funding for the Grand Palais show came from Aurel BCG, an investment firm, with the "cooperation" of the Robert Mapplethorpe Foundation (which I assume means its loan of Mapplethorpe's work).

11 "I asked myself if those photographs were racist. I realized then that the question was too limiting, that it was more complicated. Can we say that Mapplethorpe's work is documentary or fetishistic? Maybe, but at the same time he put black men into a tradition of portraiture to which they've never had access before." Ligon quoted in Berwick, "Stranger in America: Glenn Ligon."

12 See Lebovici's blog *Le Beau Vice* and her essay on the Grand Palais exhibition (http://le-beau-vice.blogspot.ca/2014/03/dix-minutes-douche-comprise-lexposition.html).

13 Michel Guerrin, "Le mauvais Mapplethorpe," *Le Monde*, April 19, 2014.

14 The concurrent exhibition of Thomas Hirschhorn's installation/space *Flamme Éternelle (Présence et Production)* at the Palais de Tokyo is an apt example. The security staff and fire-prevention personnel (because of the eponymous flame) are men of color; the cleaning staff (each day produces a huge mess) is a specially contracted Portuguese cleaning company; the visitors appeared to be overwhelmingly white and young.

15 It needs also be acknowledged that black women artists and intellectuals, notably Ntozake Shange, have endorsed Mapplethorpe's photographs of black men. See, for example, Mapplethorpe and Shange, *Black Book*.

16 Mercer, "Reading Racial Fetishism," 174. Italics in source.

17 Mercer, "Reading Racial Fetishism," 183–84.

18 See, for example, Edmund White's remarkably ingenuous essay "Génération Mapplethorpe,"139–61.

19 Mercer, "Reading Racial Fetishism," 189.

20 Mercer, "Reading Racial Fetishism," 198–99.

## Chapter 11. Body Double

Originally published as "Body Double," in *Francesca Woodman, Works from the Sammlung Verbund*, ed. Gabriele Schor and Elisabeth Bronfen (Cologne, Germany: Verlag der Buchhandlung Walther König and New York: Artbook/D.A.P 2014).

1 The exhibit went on to travel to the University of Colorado Boulder (where Woodman's father George taught, and where Woodman grew up), then to the Krannert Museum of the University of Illinois and elsewhere.

2 According to Katarina Jerinic, the curator of Woodman's archive, the extant videotapes in their entirety make up only an hour's worth of material. Jerinic notes, "Much of what one sees in the tapes seem to be fragments, unfinished pieces, additional tapes, etc." Cited in Blessing, "Geometry of Time."

3 Previously unpublished work was also reproduced in the exhibition catalogue *Francesca Woodman, Roma, 1977–1981*, eds. Casetti and Stocchi. This includes work in the possession of Casetti and others. As to the increasing number of works, an article in the *New York Times* gives this account: "Woodman produced more than 800 different images in her lifetime, and there are thousands of negatives on hand. . . . The [Woodmans] enlisted a powerful ally in 2004 when they chose the gallerist Marian Goodman to represent Woodman's vintage photographs: those printed in her lifetime, which are most prized among collectors. (The gallery sells images only if the archive also has an original version of it.) On their own the Woodmans also create, sell and lend so-called estate prints, in editions of 40, from their cache of negatives." Ted Roos, "Sharing a Guarded Legacy," *New York Times*, December 1, 2011.

4 Foucault's witty example in his well-known essay of 1968, "What Is an Author?," rhetorically asks if the oeuvre of Hegel should include his handwritten laundry lists. In Michel Foucault, *Language, Counter-Memory, Practice*, 113–38.

5 For example, within the critical literature devoted to Woodman there is some disagreement as to whether her youth is a necessary qualification in evaluating her work or her achievement; in other words, whether the body of work can or should be considered as aesthetically "realized." Krauss's essay, however, takes the circumstances of Woodman's art school assignment as both structural and enabling facets of her art. See Krauss, "Problem Sets."

6 "Woodman's preferred subject was herself: from the first time she picked up a camera as a teenager she used it to thoroughly plumb—and, more importantly, complicate—the genre of self-portraiture. Even when others appear in the frame, they are clearly stand-ins for the artist." Keller, "Portrait of the Artist," 169. Or, from another perspective: "Although thoroughly embedded within this performative art world context, Woodman's practice is primarily photographic, and within this series she tries to explore the ways in which the medium functions as a highly codified system. By failing to offer up the 'reality' of artistic presence, Woodman upsets the seductive promise of indexical proximity, as she performs a bodily displacement that re-stages the total 'self-absence' precipitated in the photographic act, reflected in the way her body gradually slips out of sight." Riches, "Disappearing Act," 103.

7 Blessing, "Geometry of Time," 203.

8 It goes without saying that any or all of my generalizations as to content are based on what has been reproduced or exhibited.

9 Some commentators profess to see the fugitive marks of piano keys on the wall

where Woodman places her hands ("I could no longer play the piano . . ."). In reproductions, this is not evident to me, but it is the desire to see an objective referent to the text that is at issue here.

10 The most extreme deployment of Woodman's suicide as a kind of hermeneutic key is found in Phelan, "Francesca Woodman's Photography." Phelan proposes that Woodman's body of work is both proleptic and an *artistic* realization of her eventual self-destruction: "This redemptive move . . . is common enough, particularly in regard to the suicides of young women artists, but it risks betraying something vitally important in Woodman's work and in her life and death. Are we certain that her suicide is a tragedy? What might we gain if we considered it, however tentatively, as a kind of an achievement, even, as I will suggest shortly, as a kind of gift?" 984.

11 This is fairly unusual in the discussion of modern or contemporary artists, but it is significant that when and where the first name is used, it is often women who are thus addressed. Needless to say, art historians do not refer to "Pablo" or "Jackson."

12 Ariana Reines, "An Hourglass Figure: On Photographer Francesca Woodman," *Los Angeles Review of Books*, April 4, 2013, https://lareviewofbooks.org/article/an-hourglass-figure-on-photographer-francesca-woodman/.

13 Sollers, "Sorceress," 9–13.

14 Tejeda and Pierini, *Francesca Woodman,* 37.

15 Tejeda and Pierini, *Francesca Woodman,* 37.

16 Townsend, *Francesca Woodman,* 8.

17 Buchloh, "Francesca Woodman."

18 A sizeable number of feminist readings on surrealist photography exists now, beginning with the classic Xavière Gauthier, *Surréalisme et Sexualité*, 1971. See also Susan Rubin Suleiman's essays in *The Body in Western Art,* ed. Carol Armstrong; Suleiman, "Dialogue and Double Allegiance, Some Contemporary Women Artists and the Historical Avant-Garde," in *Mirror Images–Women, Surrealism and Self-Representation,* ed. Whitney Chadwick; and Chadwick, "Women Artists and the Surrealist Movement."

19 Harriet Riches provides a detailed and ingenious demonstration of how Klinger's print cycle (1876–81) manifests a number of themes that Woodman explores. Thus, in addition to the glove and its plural symbolism, Riches sees other iconographic elements in Woodman's pictures that turn on absence/presence, positive/negative, appearance/disappearance and relate to the formal features of photography and their psychological equivalents. See Riches, "Disappearing Act."

20 For example, Armstrong, "Cupid's Pencil of Light"; and Mavor, *Becoming.*

21 This was the conceptual framework employed by de Zegher in her important exhibition and accompanying book, *Inside the Visible.*

22 See de Zegher's introduction in *Inside the Visible, An Elliptical Traverse of 20th Century Art in, of, and from the Feminine.*

23 "Woodman marks almost all of her photographic spaces, whether inside or outside, inhabited by herself or other bodies or not (they are often both at once) as 'feminine': the windowed house, the dark cellar, the gash in the ground, the dry-

adic tree, often with attendant ghosts. But she begs the question of whether those spaces are essentially or discursively 'feminine.' And she does so by inhabiting and investigating the zone *between* those two ways of thinking about gender, by constituting herself within a series of fissured, enfolded spaces of fleeting appearance and disappearance, in which she models a series of metaphors." Armstrong, "Ghost in the House," 350.

24 Blessing, "Geometry of Time," 203.

25 In a very short but suggestive memoir of 1985, "G. M." describes how she and Woodman, an intimate friend, worked together: "When she photographed me, I usually contributed to the pictures and it became fun, and she forgot that she was working hard to make a picture, which is why she liked me as a friend and model." The writer goes on, "We spent a lot of time in an abandoned house in Providence. . . . I was often there when she was making pictures of herself. She'd hate me to admit it, but sometimes I would help her or handle the camera if it didn't go off automatically." And adds, "When she couldn't use herself as a model, I stood in for her. In any of the pictures we couldn't tell ourselves apart because she managed to make my features photograph like her own." Quoted in Malanga, *Scopophilia*, 116–17.

26 Malanga, *Scopophilia*, 103.

27 Looking at different exposures made at the same time might confirm or refute this observation.

28 Thurston, "At Home in the Dust," n.p.

## Chapter 12. The Coming of Age

First presented as "The Coming of Age: Cindy Sherman, Feminism and Art History," at the National Museum of Iceland on February 3, 2014.

1 For example, the striking difference in the way Jean-Auguste-Dominique Ingres depicts his male and female portrait subjects is an especially vivid example of how the physiognomic idealization of female sitters overwrites any attribute of personality or character. This is also the case in the portraits of artists as different as Thomas Gainsborough, John Hoppner, and John Singer Sargeant.

2 Burton, "Introduction," 9.

3 Deutsche, "Not-Forgetting," 26–37.

4 Calvin Tomkins, "Her Secret Identities," *New Yorker*, May 15, 2000, 74–83.

5 Burton, "Cindy Sherman," 63.

# BIBLIOGRAPHY


Allen, James. *Without Sanctuary: Lynching Photography in America*. Santa Fe, NM: Twin Palms, 2000.

Althusser, Louis. "Ideology and Ideological State Apparatuses (Notes towards an Investigation)." In *Lenin and Philosophy and Other Essays*, translated by Ben Brewster, 127–86. London: New Left Books, 1971.

Andrews, David L. "Excavating Michael Jordan: Notes on a Critical Pedagogy of Sporting Representation." In *Sports and Postmodern Times*, edited by Genevieve Rail, 185–220. Albany: State University of New York Press, 1998.

Annan, Thomas. *Photographs of the Old Closes and Streets of Glasgow, 1868–1877*. New York: Dover, 1977.

Apel, Dora. "Torture Culture: Lynching Photographs and the Images of Abi Ghraib." *Art Journal* 54, no. 2 (2005): 88–100.

Armstrong, Carol. "A Ghost in the House of Photography." In *Women Artists at the Millennium*, edited by Carol Armstrong, 347–69. Cambridge, MA: MIT Press, 2001.

———. "Cupid's Pencil of Light: Julia Margaret Cameron and the Maternalization of Photography." *October* 76 (spring 1996): 114–41.

Aubin, Jean-Pierre, ed. *Robert Mapplethorpe*. Exhibition catalogue. Paris: Editions de la Réunion des Musées Nationaux–Grand Palais, 2014.

Barrell, John. *The Dark Side of the Landscape: The Rural Poor in English Painting, 1730–1840*. Cambridge: Cambridge University Press, 1980.

Barthes, Roland. *Camera Lucida: Reflections on Photography*. New York: Hill and Wang, 1982.

———. "The Great Family of Man." In *A Critical and Cultural Theory Reader*, edited by Antony Easthope and Kate McGowan, 12–14. 2nd ed. Toronto: University of Toronto Press, 2004.

———. *Mythologies*. Translated by Annette Lavers. Herts, UK: Paladan, 1976.

———. "The Photographic Message." In *Image, Music,* Text, translated by Stephen Heath, 15–31. New York: Hill and Wang, 1977.

———. “The Rhetoric of the Image.” In *Image, Music, Text,* translated by Stephen Heath, 31–51. New York: Hill and Wang, 1977.

———. *Taormina: Wilhelm Von Gloeden*. Translated by Angus Whyte. Santa Fe, NM: Twelvetrees Press, 1997.

———. *Wilhelm Von Gloeden*. Naples: Amelio Editore, 1978.

Batchen, Geoffrey. *Burning with Desire*. Cambridge, MA: MIT Press, 2001.

———. *Each Wild Idea: Writing Photography History*. Cambridge, MA: MIT Press, 2001.

———, ed. *Photography Degree Zero: Reflections on Roland Barthes'* Camera Lucida. Cambridge, MA: MIT Press, 2009.

Baudry, Jean-Louis. “Ideological Effects of the Basic Cinematographic Apparatus.” In *Apparatus,* edited by Theresa Hak Kyung Cha, 25–37. New York: Tanam Press, 1981.

Bazin, André. “The Ontology of the Photographic Image.” *Film Quarterly* 13, no. 4. (summer 1960): 4–9.

Benjamin, Walter. “The Author as Producer.” In *Understanding Brecht,* translated by Anna Bostock, 85–103. London: Verso, 1998.

———. “A Short History of Photography,” in *Classic Essays on Photography,* ed. Alan Trachtenberg (New Haven, Conn.: Leete's Island Books, 1980)

Berger, John. *Ways of Seeing*. London: Penguin, 1972.

Bermingham, Ann. *Landscape and Ideology: The English Rustic Tradition, 1740–1860*. Berkeley: University of California Press, 1989.

Berwick, Carley. “Stranger in America: Glenn Ligon.” *Art in America,* May 2011, 121–30.

Besnyö, Eva. *L'image Sensible*. Edited by Marion Beckers and Elisabeth Moortgat. Amsterdam: Somogy éditions dart / Paris: Éditions du Jeu de Paume, 2012.

Blessing, Jennifer. “The Geometry of Time: Some Notes on Francesca Woodman's Video.” In *Francesca Woodman,* edited by Corey Keller, 197–203. Exhibition catalogue. San Francisco: San Francisco Museum of Modern Art; New York: in association with D.A.P./Distributed Art Publishers, 2011.

Brennen, Bonnie, and Hanno Hardt, eds. *Picturing the Past: Media, History, and Photography*. Urbana: University of Illinois Press, 1999.

Breton, André. *Surrealism and Painting*. Translated by Simon Watson Taylor. New York: Harper & Row, 1965.

Brevik-Zender, Heidi. “Interstitial Narratives: Rethinking Feminine Spaces of Modernity in Nineteenth-Century French Fashion Plates.” *Nineteenth-Century Contexts: An Interdisciplinary Journal* 36, no. 2 (2014): 91–123.

Brownmiller, Susan. *Against Our Will: Men, Women, and Rape*. New York: Simon and Schuster, 1975.

Buchloh, Benjamin H. D. “Francesca Woodman: Performing the Photograph, Staging the Subject.” In *Francesca Woodman: Photographs, 1975–1980,* 40–50. Exhibition catalogue. New York: Marion Goodman Gallery, 2004.

Bunnell, Peter. *Harry Callahan*. New York: International Exhibitions Committee of the American Federation of Arts, 1978.

Burgin, Victor. “Looking at Photographs.” In *Thinking Photography,* edited by Victor Burgin, 142–53. London: Macmillan, 1978.

———. "Photography, Phantasy, Fiction." In *Thinking Photography*, edited by Victor Burgin, 189–90. London: Macmillan, 1982.

Burton, Johanna. "Cindy Sherman: Abstraction and Empathy." In *Cindy Sherman*, edited by Eve Respini and Johanna Burton, 54–67. New York: Museum of Modern Art, 2012.

Burnett, Ron. *Cultures of Vision: Images, Media, and the Imaginary*. Bloomington: University of Indiana Press, 1995.

Cadava, Eduardo. *Words of Light: Theses on the Photography of History.* Princeton, NJ: Princeton University Press, 1998.

Campany, David. "Safety in Numbness: Some Remarks on Problems of 'Late Photography.'" In *The Cinematic*, edited by David Campany, 185–94. Cambridge, MA: MIT Press, 2007.

Carrabine, Eamonn. "Just Images: Aesthetics, Ethics and Visual Criminology." *British Journal of Criminology* 52, no. 3 (2012): 463–89.

Cartier-Bresson, Henri. *The Decisive Moment*. New York: Simon and Schuster, 1952.

———. *The Mind's Eye: Writing on Photography and Photographers.* New York: Aperture, 1999.

Casetti, Guiseppe, and Francesco Stocchi, eds. *Francesca Woodman, Roma, 1977–1981.* Rome: Agma Publications, 2011.

Chagnon-Burke, Véronique. "The Politicization of Nature: The Critical Reception of Barbizon Painting During the July Monarchy," PhD dissertation, The Graduate Center of the City University of New York, 2000.

Chéroux, Clément, ed. *Qu'est ce que c'est la Photographie*. Paris: Centre Georges Pompidou, 2015.

Chevrier, Jean-François. "Les aventures de la forme tableau dans l'histoire de la photographie." In *Photo-kunst: Du xxe au xixe siècle, aller et retour / Arbeiten aus 150 Jahren*, 47–81. Exhibition catalogue. Stuttgart: Staatsgalerie Stuttgart, Verlag Cantz, 1989.

———. "The Tableau and the Document of Experience." In *Click Doubleclick: The Documentary Factor*, edited by Thomas Weski, 51–61. Exhibition catalogue. Munich: Verlag der Buchhandlung Walther König, 2006.

Chevrier, Jean-François, and Catherine David. "Actualité de l'image." In *Passages de l'image*, edited by Raymond Bellour, Catherine David, and Christine Van Assche, 17–36. Exhibition catalogue. Paris: Centre Georges Pompidou, 1990.

Chevrier, Jean-François, and James Lingwood. *Une autre objectivité*. Exhibition catalogue. Paris: Centre National des Arts Plastiques, 1989.

Chun, Wendy Hui Kyong and Sarah Friedland. "Habits of Leaking: Of Sluts and Network Cards," *differences: A Journal of Feminist Cultural Studies* 26, no. 2 (2015): 1–28.

Clark, Kenneth. *Landscape into Art*. London: John Murray, 1949.

Clark, Larry. *The Perfect Childhood*. Zurich: Scala, 1993.

———. *Teenage Lust: An Autobiography.* New York: Larry Clark, 1983.

———. *Tulsa.* New York: Lustrum Press, 1971.

Conroy, John. *Unspeakable Acts, Ordinary People: The Dynamics of Torture.* 1st ed. New York: Knopf, 2000.

Costello, Diarmuid. "On the Very Idea of a 'Specific' Medium: Michael Fried and Stanley Cavell on Painting and Photography as Arts." *Critical Inquiry* 34, no. 2 (winter 2008): 274–312.

Crimp, Douglas. "The Museum's Old/The Library's New Subject." In *The Contest of Meaning: Critical Histories of Photography*, edited by Richard Bolton, 3–14. Cambridge, MA: MIT Press, 1989.

Crump, James. "The Kinsey Institute Archive: A Taxonomy of Erotic Photography." *History of Photography* 18, no. 1 (spring 1994): 1–12.

Daniel, Malcolm. "Eugène Cuvelier: Photographer in the Circle of Corot." In *Eugene Cuvelier: Photographer in the Circle of* Corot, 3–16. New York: Metropolitan Museum of Art, 1996.

Danly, Susan, and Cheryl Leibold, eds. *Eakins and the Photograph: Works by Thomas Eakins and His Circle in the Collection of the Pennsylvania Academy of the Fine Arts.* Washington, DC: Smithsonian Institution Press / Philadelphia: Pennsylvania Academy of Fine Arts, 1994.

Danner, Mark. *Stripping Bare the Body: Politics, Violence, War.* New York: Nation Books, 2009.

———. *Torture and Truth: America, Abu Ghraib, and the War on Terror.* New York: New York Review of Books, 2004.

Davis, Keith F. *Harry Callahan: New Color Photographs, 1978–1987.* Albuquerque: University of New Mexico Press and Hallmark Cards, 1988. See "The Rhythms of the City: Continuity and Change in the Work of Harry Callahan," 8–27.

Debord, Guy. *The Society of the Spectacle.* Detroit: Black and Red, 1983.

Derrida, Jacques. *Copy, Archive, Signature.* Translated by Jeff Fort. Stanford, CA: Stanford University Press, 2010.

———. "The Law of Genre." *Glyph* 7 (spring 1980): 202–12.

de Thezy, Marie, and Roxane Debuison. *Charles Marville, 1816–1879.* Paris: Hazan, 1994.

Deutsche, Rosalyn. "Not-Forgetting: Mary Kelly's *Love Songs*." *Grey Room*, no. 24 (summer 2006): 26–37.

de Zegher, Catherine. *Inside the Visible: An Elliptical Traverse of Twentieth-Century Art in, of, and from the Feminine.* Cambridge, MA: MIT Press, 1996.

Doane, Mary Ann. "Indexicality and the Concept of Medium Specificity." Special Issue, "Indexicality: Trace and Sign," edited by Mary Ann Doane, *differences: A Journal of Feminist Cultural Studies* 18, issue 1 (spring 2007): 128–50.

———. "Indexicality: Trace and Sign: Introduction." Special Issue, "Indexicality: Trace and Sign," edited by Mary Ann Doane, *differences A Journal of Feminist Cultural Studies* 18, issue 1 (spring 2007): 1–6.

Dyer, Geoff. "An Academic Author's Unintentional Masterpiece." *New York Times*, July 22, 2011. http://www.nytimes.com/2011/07/24/books/review/an-academic-authors-unintentional-masterpiece.html?_r=0.

Earle, Edward W., ed. *Points of View: The Stereograph in America: A Cultural History.* Rochester, NY: Visual Studies Workshop, 1979.

Eastlake, Elizabeth. "Photography." In *Classic Essays on Photography*, edited by Alan Trachtenberg, 39–69. New Haven, CT: Leete's Island Books, 1980.

Ebert, John David. *The New Media Invasion: Digital Technologies and the World They Unmake.* Jefferson, NC: McFarland, 2011.
Edwards, Elizabeth. *Raw Histories: Photographs, Anthropology, and Museums.* Oxford: Berg, 2001.
Edwards, Steve. *Photography: A Very Short Introduction.* London: Oxford University Press, 2006.
Ehrenburg, Ilya, and El Lissitzky. *My Paris.* Translated from the Russian by Oliver Ready. Photomontage and design by El Lissitzky. Gottingen, Germany: Steidl [1933] 2005.
Ehrenreich, Barbara. *The Hearts of Men: American Dreams and the Flight from Commitment.* Garden City, NY: Anchor Press, 1983.
Eisenman, Stephen F. *The Abu Ghraib Effect.* London: Reaktion Books, 2007.
Elkins, James. *Photography Theory.* London: Routledge, 2007.
———. *What Photography Is.* New York: Routledge, 2011.
Entin, Joseph. "Modernist Documentary: Aaron Siskind's Harlem Document." *Yale Journal of Criticism* 12, no. 2 (1999): 357–82.
Fanon, Frantz. *Black Skin, White Masks.* London: Pluto Classics, 1986.
Faurer, Louis, and Stuart Alexander. *Louis Faurer: Photographies.* Paris: Centre National de la Photographie, 1992.
Foster, Hal. "Preface." In *Vision and Visuality,* edited by Hal Foster, ix–xiv. Seattle, WA: Bay Press, 1988.
Foucault, Michel. *The History of Sexuality.* Translated by Robert Hurley. New York: Pantheon Books, 1978.
———. *Power/Knowledge.* New York: Pantheon, 1972.
Freud, Sigmund. *Civilization and Its Discontents.* Translated by James Strachey. New York: W. W. Norton, 1961.
———. "Fetishism." In *The Standard Edition of the Complete Psychological Works of Sigmund Freud,* vol. 21, edited and translated by James Strachey, 147–57. London: Hogarth Press, 1953–74.
———. "Three Essays on a Theory of Sexuality." In *The Standard Edition of the Complete Psychological Works of Sigmund Freud,* vol. 7, edited and translated by James Strachey, 135–245. London: Hogarth Press, 1953–74.
Freund, Gisèle. *La photographie en France au dix-neuvieme siècle.* Paris: La Maison des Amis des Livres, 1936. Translated and partially integrated into Freund's English-language *Photography and Society.* Boston: David R. Godine, 1980.
———. *Photography and Society.* Boston: David A. Godine, 1980.
Fried, Michael. *Why Photography Matters as an Art as Never Before.* New Haven, CT: Yale University Press, 2011.
Fritscher, Jack. "Take 17: Mapplethorpe Mentor George Dureau." In *Mapplethorpe: Assault with a Deadly Camera.* San Francisco: Palm Drive, 1994.
Fritz Clattenburg, Ellen. *The Photographic Work of F. Holland Day.* Wellesley, MA: College Museum, 1975.
Giroux, Henry. "What Might Education Mean after Abu Ghraib: Revisiting Adorno's Politics of Education." *Comparative Studies of South Asia, Africa and the Middle East* 24, no. 1 (2004): 3–22.

Glueck, Grace. "Capturing Fontainebleau Forest's Myriad Moods." *New York Times*, November 29, 1996.

Godfrey, Mark. "Photography Found and Lost: On Tacita Dean's *Floh*." *October* 114 (2005): 90–119.

Goldin, Nan. *The Ballad of Sexual Dependency*. New York: Aperture, 1986.

Gourevitch, Philip, and Errol Morris. *Standard Operating Procedure*. New York: Penguin Press, 2008.

Green, Nicholas. *The Spectacle of Nature: Landscape and Bourgeois Culture in Nineteenth-Century France*. Manchester, UK: Manchester University Press, 1990.

Griffin, Michael. "The Great War Photographs: Constructing Myths of History and Photojournalism." In *Picturing the Past: Media, History, and Photography*, edited by Bonnie Brennen and Hanno Hardt, 122–57. Urbana: University of Illinois Press, 1999.

Gross, Larry, John Stuart Katz, and Jay Ruby, eds. *Image Ethics: The Moral Rights of Subjects in Photographs, Film, and Television*. New York: Oxford University Press, 1988.

Haug, W. F. *Critique of Commodity Aesthetics: Appearance, Sexuality, and Advertising in Capitalist Society*. Minneapolis: University of Minnesota Press, 1986.

Heartney, Eleanor. "A War and Its Images." *Art in America*, October 2004, 51.

Heilbrun, Françoise. "The Landscape in French Nineteenth-Century Photography." In *A Day in the Country: Impressionism and the French Landscape*, edited by Richard R. Bretell, Scott Schafer, Sylvie Gache-Patin, and Françoise Heilbrun, 349–62. Art Institute of Chicago and Los Angeles County Museum of Art. New York: Harry N. Abrams, 1984.

Hesford, Wendy. *Spectacular Rhetorics: Human Rights Visions, Recognitions, Feminisms*. Durham, NC: Duke University Press, 2011.

James, Sarah. "Making an Ugly World Beautiful: Morality and Aesthetics in the Aftermath." In *Memory of Fire: The War of Images and Images of War*, edited by Julian Stalleybrass, 12–15. Brighton, UK: Photoworks, 2008.

Janis, Eugenia Parry. *The Art of French Calotype*. Princeton, NJ: Princeton University Press, 1984.

Keller, Corey. "A Portrait of the Artist as a Young Woman." In *Francesca Woodman*, edited by Corey Keller, 169–85. Exhibition catalogue. San Francisco: San Francisco Museum of Modern Art; New York: in association with D.A.P./Distributed Art Publishers, 2011.

Klein, Mason, and Catherine Evans, eds. *The Radical Camera: New York's Photo League, 1936–1951*. New Haven, CT: Yale University Press, 2011.

Kosofsky Sedgwick, Eve. *Between Men: English Literature and Male Homosocial Desire, Gender, and Culture*. New York: Columbia University Press, 1985.

Krauss, Rosalind E. *The Originality of the Avant-Garde and Other Modernist Myths*. Cambridge, MA: MIT Press, 1985.

———. *Perpetual Inventory*. Cambridge, MA: MIT Press, 2013.

———. "Photography's Discursive Spaces: Landscape/View." *Art Journal* 42, no. 4, *Crisis in the Discipline* (winter 1982): 311–19.

———. "Problem Sets." In *Francesca Woodman: Photographic Work*, edited by Ann Gabhart, 41–51. Exhibition catalogue. Wellesley, MA: Wellesley College Art Museum and Hunter College Art Gallery, 1986.

———. "Reinventing the Medium." *Critical Inquiry* 25, no. 2, Special issue. *"Angelus Novus": Perspectives on Walter Benjamin* (winter 1999): 289–305.

Kuhn, Annette. *The Power of the Image: Essays on Representation and Sexuality*. London: Routledge & Kegan Paul, 1985. See chapter 2, "Lawless Seeing," 19–47.

Lavoie, Vincent. *Photojournalismes: Revoir les canons de l'image de presse.* Paris: Hazan, 2010.

———. "Photojournalistic Integrity: Codes of Conduct, Professional Ethics, and the Moral Definition of Press Photography." *Écrits Photographiques* 26 (2010): 190–212.

Lemeck, Robert, and Bodo von Dewitz. *Kiosk: A History of Photojournalism*. London: Thames & Hudson, 2002.

Long, J. J. *W. G. Sebald: Image, Archive, Modernity*. New York: Columbia University Press, 2006.

Lugon, Olivier. "Avant la forme Tableau: Grand format photographique dans l'exposition 'Signs of Life.'" *Etudes Photographiques* (May 2010): 6–41.

———. *Le Style documentaire: D'August Sander à Walker Evans, 1920–1945*. Paris: Macula, 2001.

Malanga, Gerard, ed. *Scopophilia: The Love of Looking*. New York: Alfred van der March Editions, 1985.

Maloof, John, ed. *Vivian Maier: Street Photographer.* Chicago: Powerhouse Books, 2011.

Manovich, Lev. "The Paradoxes of Digital Photography." In *Photography after Photography: Memory and Representation in the Digital Age,* edited by Hubertus von Amelunxen et al., 57–65. London: G&B Arts, 1997.

Mapplethorpe, Robert, and Ntozake Shange. *Black Book.* New York: Saint Martin's, 1986.

Margolis, Eric. "Looking at Discipline, Looking at Labour: Photographic Representations of Indian Boarding Schools." *Visual Studies* 19, no. 1 (2004): 72–96.

Marx, Karl. "The Eighteenth Brumaire of Louis Bonaparte." In *The Marx-Engels Reader,* edited by Robert C. Tucker, 594–617. New York: W. W. Norton, 1978.

Mavor, Carol. *Becoming: The Photographs of Clementina, Viscountess Hawarden.* Durham, NC: Duke University Press, 1999.

McCauley, Elizabeth Ann. *Industrial Madness: Commercial Photography in France, 1848–1871.* New Haven, CT: Yale University Press, 1994.

Meiselas, Susan. *Encounters with the Dani: Stories from the Baliem Valley*. New York and Gottingen: International Center of Photography; Steidl, 2003.

Meiselas, Susan, and Martin van Bruinessen. *Kurdistan: In the Shadow of History*. 1st ed. New York: Random House, 1997.

Meiselas, Susan, Deirdre English, and Sylvia Wolf. *Carnival Strippers*. 2nd ed. New York: Whitney Museum of American Art/Gottingen, Germany: Steidl, 2003.

Melon, Marc-Emmanuel. "The Patriarchal Family: Domestic Ideology in *The Family of Man.*" In *Family of Man 1955–2001: Humanism and Postmodernism: A Reappraisal of the Photo Exhibition by Edward Steichen*, edited by Jean Back and Viktoria Schmidt-Linsenhoff, 56–79. Marburg, Germany: Jonas Verlag, 2004.

Mensel, Robert E. "'Kodakers Lying in Wait': Amateur Photography and the Right of Privacy in New York, 1885–1915." *American Quarterly* 43, no. 1 (March 1991): 24–45.

Mercer, Kobena. *Welcome to the Jungle, New Positions in Black Cultural Studies.* New York: Routledge, 1994. See chapter 6, "Reading Racial Fetishism: the Photographs of Robert Mapplethorpe."

Metz, Christian. "Photography and Fetish." *October* 34 (fall 1985): 81–90.

Mitchell, W. J. T. *Cloning Terror: The War of Images, 9/11 to the Present.* Chicago: University of Chicago Press, 2011.

———. "Picture Theory." In *Essays on Verbal and Visual Representation,* 11–35. Chicago: University of Chicago Press, 1994.

Mitchell, William J. *The Reconfigured Eye: Visual Truth in the Post-Photographic Era.* Cambridge, MA: MIT Press, 1992.

———. "Sacred Gestures: Images from Our Holy War." *Afterimage* 34, no. 3 (2006): 18–23.

Modleski, Tania. *Feminism without Women: Culture and Criticism in a Postfeminist Age.* New York: Methuan, 1991.

Morris, Errol. *Believing Is Seeing: Observations on the Mystery of Photography.* New York: Penguin, 2011.

Morrisoe, Patricia. *Mapplethorpe: A Biography.* New York: Random House, 1995.

Mulvey, Laura. "The Index and the Uncanny." In *Time and the Image,* edited by Carolyn Bailey Gill, 139–48. Manchester, UK: Manchester University Press, 2008.

———. *Fetishism and Curiosity.* Bloomington: Indiana University Press, 1996. See preface.

———. *Visual and Other Pleasures.* Houndmills, UK: Macmillan, 1989. See chapter 2, "Fear, Fantasies and the Male Unconscious or You Don't Know What's Happening, Do You Mr. Jones?"

Nesbit, Molly. *Eugène Atget: Interieures Parisiens: Un Album du Musée Carnavalet.* Paris: Éditions au Carré and Paris-Musées, 1992.

Norberg, Kathryn. "The Libertine Whore: Prostitution in French Pornography from Margot to Juliette." In *The Invention of Pornography: Obscenity and the Origins of Modernity, 1500–1800,* edited by Lynn Hunt, 225–52. New York: Zone Books, 1993.

Pacteau, Francette. *The Symptom of Beauty.* London: Reaktion Books, 1994.

Panzer, Mary. *Philadelphia Naturalistic Photography, 1865–1906.* New Haven, CT: Yale Art Gallery, 1984.

Panzer, Mary, and Christian Caujolle. *Things as They Are: Photojournalism in Context since 1955.* London: Chris Boot and World Press Photo, 2005.

Parsons, Sarah. "Privacy, Photography, and the Art Defense." In *Revealing Privacy: Debating the Understandings of Privacy,* edited by Margherita Carucci, 105–18. New York: Peter Lang Publishers, 2012.

Phelan, Peggy. "Francesca Woodman's Photography: Death and the Image One More Time." *Signs* 27, no. 4 (summer 2002): 979–1004.

———. "The Returns of Touch: Feminist Performances, 1960–1980." In *WACK!: Art and the Feminist Revolution,* edited by Cornelia Butler and Lisa Gabrielle Mark, 346–61. Cambridge, MA: MIT Press, 2007.

Phillips, Christopher. "The Judgment Seat of Photography." *October* 22 (autumn 1982): 27–63.

Pinney, Christopher. *Photography and Anthropology*. London: Reaktion Books, 2011.
Pohlmann, Ulrich. *Wilhelm von Gloeden: Sehnsucht nach Arkadien*. Berlin: Nischen, 1987.
Pultz, John. *Harry Callahan: Early Street Photography, 1943–45*. The Archive Research Series 28. Tucson, AZ: Center for Creative Photography, 1990.
Respini, Eva. *Cindy Sherman*. Exhibition catalogue. New York City: Museum of Modern Art, 2012.
Riesman, David. *The Lonely Crowd*. New Haven, CT: Yale University Press, 1950.
Richardson, Meghan. "Candid Camera." *Meanjin* 66, no. 3 (2007): 83–87.
Riches, Harriet. "A Disappearing Act: Francesca Woodman's *Portrait of a Reputation*." *Oxford Art Journal* 27, no. 1 (2004): 97–113.
Ritchin, Fred. *After Photography*. New York: W. W. Norton, 2009.
Roberts, John. *The Art of Interruption: Realism, Photography, and the Everyday*. Manchester, UK: Manchester University Press, 1998.
———. "Photography after the Photograph: Event, Archive and the Non-Symbolic." *Oxford Art Journal* 32, no. 2 (2009): 281–98.
———. *Photography and Its Violations*. New York: Columbia University Press, 2014.
Rogoff, Irit. "Subjects/Spaces/Places." In *Family Nation Tribe Community* SHIFT: *Zeitgenössische künstlerische Konzepte im Haus der Kulturen der Welt*, 171–74. Exhibition catalogue. Berlin: Neue Gesellschaft für Bildende Kunst, 1996.
Rose, Jacqueline. "Sexuality in the Field of Vision." In *Sexuality in the Field of Vision*, edited by Jacqueline Rose, 225–35. London: Verso, 1986.
Rosen, Philip. *Change Mummified: Cinema, Historicity, Theory*. Minneapolis: University of Minnesota Press, 2001.
———. "Document and Documentary: On the Persistence of Historical Concepts." In *Theorizing Documentary*, edited by Michael Renov, 58–89. New York: Routledge, 1993.
Rosler, Martha. *Decoys and Disruptions: Selected Writings, 1975–2001*. Cambridge, MA: MIT Press, 2004. See "Post-Documentary, Post-Photography."
———. *3 Works*. Halifax: Nova Scotia School of Art and Design, 1983. See "The Bowery in Two Inadequate Descriptive Systems" and "In, Around, and Afterthoughts (On Documentary Photography)."
Rubenfien, Leo. *Garry Winogrand*. New Haven, CT: Yale University Press, 2013.
San Francisco Museum of Modern Art, *Public Information: Desire, Disaster, Document*. San Francisco: San Francisco Museum of Modern Art/New York: Distributed Art Publishers, 1994.
Sandeen, Eric. J. *Picturing an Exhibition: The Family of Man and 1950s America*. Albuquerque: University of New Mexico Press, 1995.
Sassen, Saskia. "Black and White Photography as Theorizing: Seeing What the Eye Cannot See." *Sociological Forum* 26, no. 2 (2011): 438–43.
Scharf, Aaron. *Art and Photography*. Harmondsworth, UK: Penguin, 1968.
Schmidt-Linsenhoff, Viktoria. "Die Banalität des Guten: Zur fotografischen Re-Konstruktion der Menschlichkeit in der Ausstellung *The Family of Man*." In *Wiener Jahrbuch für jüdische Geschichte, Kultur und Museumswesen* 3, (1997/1998): 59–74.

Schwartz, Dona. "Objective Representation: Photographs as Facts." In *Picturing the Past: Media, History, and Photography*, edited by Bonnie Brennen and Hanno Hardt, 158–81. Urbana: University of Illinois Press, 1999.

Scott, Joan W. "Gender: A Useful Category of Historical Analysis." *American Historical Review* 91, no. 5 (December 1986): 1053–75.

Segalen, Martine. "The Family of Man oú la Grande Illusion." In *The Family of Man: Témoignages et Documents*, edited by Jean Back and Gabriel Bauret, 117–28. Luxembourg: Ministry of Cultural Affairs, 1994.

Sekula, Allan. "Between the Net and the Deep Blue Sea (Rethinking the Traffic in Photographs)." *October* 102 (autumn 2002): 3–34.

———. "The Body in the Archive." In *The Contest of Meaning*, edited by Richard Bolton, 343–89. Cambridge, MA: MIT Press, 1992.

———. *Photography against the Grain*. Nova Scotia: College of the Nova Scotia College of Art, 1984. See "The Traffic in Photographs."

Shahn, Ben. *The Photographic Eye of Ben Shahn*. Cambridge, MA: Harvard University Press, 1975.

Shahn, Ben, and Margaret R. Weiss. *Ben Shahn, Photographer: An Album from the Thirties*. New York: Da Capo Press, 1973.

Shamis, Bob, Max Kozloff, and Leon Levinstein. *The Moment of Exposure*. New York: Museum of Modern Art, 1995.

Sherman, Paul. *Harry Callahan*. New York: Museum of Modern Art, 1967. See introduction.

Siems, Larry. *The Torture Report: What the Documents Say about America's Post-9/11 Torture Program*. New York: OR Books, 2012.

Silverman, Kaja. *The Miracle of Analogy, or The History of Photography, Part 1*. Stanford, CA: Stanford University Press, 2015.

Snyder, Joel, and Neil Walsh Allen. "Photography, Vision and Representation." *Critical Inquiry* (autumn 1975): 143–87.

Sollers, Philippe. "The Sorceress." In *Francesca Woodman*, edited by Hervé Chandés, 9–13. Exhibition catalogue. Paris: Fondation Cartier, 1998.

Solnit, Rebecca. "The Archipelago of Arrogance." *TomDispatch*. August 19, 2012. http://www.tomdispatch.com/blog/175584/.

———. *Men Explain Things to Me*, Chicago: Haymarket Books, 2014. See "Men Explain Things to Me, 2008."

Solomon-Godeau, Abigail. "Going Native: Paul Gauguin and the Invention of Primitivist Modernism." *Art in America* July 1989, 118–29.

———. "Inside/Out." In *Public Information: Desire, Disaster, Document*, 49–61. San Francisco: San Francisco Museum of Modern Art/New York: Distributed Art Publishers, 1994.

———. "The Legs of the Countess." *October* 39 (winter 1986): 65–108.

———. *Male Trouble: A Crisis in Representation*. London: Thames & Hudson, 1997.

———. "Ontology, Essences, and Photography's Aesthetics: Wringing the Goose's Neck One More Time." In *The Art Seminar: Photography Theory*, edited by James Elkins, 256–67. New York: Routledge, 2007.

———. *Photography at the Dock: Essays on Photographic History, Institutions, and Practices.* Minneapolis: University of Minnesota Press, 1994.
Sontag, Susan. *On Photography*. New York: Farrar, Straus and Giroux, 1977.
———. *Regarding the Pain of Others*. New York: Picador, 2003.
———. "Regarding the Torture of Others." *New York Times Magazine,* May 23, 2004.
Stallabrass, Julian. "Sebastião Salgado and Fine Art Journalism." *New Left Review* 1, no. 223 (May–June 1997): 131–60.
Stange, Maren. *Symbols of Ideal Life: Social Documentary Photography in America, 1890–1950*. Cambridge: Cambridge University Press, 1989.
Stein, Sally. "Making Connections with the Camera: Photography and Social Mobility in the Career of Jacob Riis." *Afterimage* 10, no. 10 (May 1983): 9–16.
Stettner, Louis. *American Photographer*. Paris: Suermondt-Ludwig-Museum, 1997.
———. *Early Joys: Photographs from 1947–1972*. New York: J. Iffland, 1987.
———. *Louis Stettner's New York, 1950s–1990s*. New York: Rizzoli International Publications, 1996.
Stiegler, Bernd. "Photography as the Medium of Reflection." In *The Meaning of Photography,* edited by Robin Kelsey and Blake Stimson, 194–97. Williamstown, MA: Clark Studies in the Visual Arts, 2005.
Stoekl, Allan. "Cartier-Bresson: Between Autobiography and Image." *Modern Fiction Studies* 40, no. 3 (1994): 631–41.
Stott, William. *Documentary Expression and Thirties America*. Oxford: Oxford University Press, 1973.
Strasser, Steven. *The Abu Ghraib Investigations: The Official Reports of the Independent Panel and the Pentagon on the Shocking Prisoner Abuse in Iraq*. New York: Public Affairs, 2004.
Tagg, John. *The Burden of Representation*. Amherst: University of Massachusetts Press, 1986.
Tejeda, Isabel, and Marco Pierini, eds. *Francesca Woodman*. Rome: Silvana, 2009.
Tello, Veronica. "The Aesthetics and Politics of Aftermath Photography." *Third Text* 28, no. 6 (2014): 555–62.
Thurston, Meaghan. "At Home in the Dust." *Forum* 11 (2010). http://www.forumjournal.org/site/issue/11.
Time-Life Books. *Photography Year: 1980 Edition*. New York: Time-Life Books, 1980.
Tonelli, Edith, Louis Faurer, and John Gossage. *Louis Faurer: Photographs from Philadelphia and New York, 1937–1973*. College Park: University of Maryland Art Gallery, 1981.
Townsend, Chris. *Francesca Woodman*. Edited by Chris Townsend and George Woodman. London: Phaidon Press, 2006.
Tucker, Anne Wilkes, Louis Faurer, Lisa Hostetler, and Kathleen V. Jameson. *Louis Faurer*. London: Merrell Publishers/Houston: Museum of Fine Arts, 2002.
Valéry, Paul. "The Nude." In *The Collected Works of Paul Valéry,* vol. 12, edited by Jackson Matthews, 47–51. Princeton, NJ: Princeton University Press, 1960.
Vance, Carole. "The War on Culture." in *Culture Wars: Documents from Recent Controversies in the Arts,* edited by Richard Bolton, 220–27. New York: New Press, 1992.

van der Meulen, Sjoukje. "Between Benjamin and McLuhan: Vilém Flusser's Media Theory." *New German Critique* 37, no. 2 (summer 2010): 180–207.
Weski, Thomas. *Click Doubleclick: The Documentary Factor.* Munich: Walther Konig, 2006. See "The Documentary Factor."
Westerbeck, Colin, and Joel Meyerowitz. *Bystander: A History of Street Photography.* Westport, CT: F. F. Sherman, 1994.
White, Edmund. "Génération Mapplethorpe." In *Robert Mapplethorpe,* edited by Jean-Pierre Aubin, 139–61. Exhibition catalogue. Paris: Editions de la Réunion des Musées Nationaux–Grand Palais, 2014.
White, Harrison C., and Cynthia A. White. *Canvases and Careers: Institutional Change in the French Painting World.* New York: John Wiley and Sons, 1965.
Whitfield, Stephen. *The Culture of the Cold War.* Baltimore, MD: Johns Hopkins Press, 1991.
Whyte, William Hollingsworth. *The Organization Man.* New York: Simon and Schuster, 1956.
Willemen, Paul. "Letter to John." In *The Sexual Subject: A Screen Reader in Sexuality,* 171–83. London: Routledge, 1992.
———. "Reflections on Eisenstein and Digital Imagery: Of Mice and Men." *Critical Studies* 19 (2003): 171–89.
Williams, Linda. "Film Body: An Implantation of the Perversions." In *Narrative, Apparatus, Ideology,* edited by Philip Rosen, 507–34. New York: Columbia University Press, 1986.
Williams, Raymond. *The Country and the City.* London: Oxford University Press, 1973.
Wolf, Erika. "The Author as Photographer: Early Soviet Writers and the Camera." *Aperture* 193 (winter 2008): 32–37.
Wollen, Peter. "Introduction." In *Visual Display: Culture beyond Appearances,* edited by Lynne Cooke and Peter Wollen, 9–13. New York: New Press, 1995.
Wylie, Phillip. *A Generation of Vipers.* Toronto: Clarke, Irwin & Company, 1942.
Zeronda, Nancy Danforth. "Street Shootings: Covert Photography and Public Privacy." *Vanderbilt Law Review* 63, no. 4 (2010): 1131–59.

# INDEX

*Page numbers in italics refer to figures.*

www.ingramcontent.com/pod-product-compliance
Lightning Source LLC
LaVergne TN
LVHW010606100826
845148LV00014B/2874